Bae

D1099412

NEW ZEALAND
Cook-Island

Hints for using the Guide

Following the tradition established by Karl Baedeker in 1844, buildings and works of art, places of natural beauty and sights of particular interest, as well as hotels and restaurants of especially high quality, are distinguished by one ★ or two ★★.

To make it easier to locate the various places listed in the "A to Z" section of the Guide, their co-ordinates are shown in red at the head of each entry: e.g., Rotorua L 5.

Coloured lines down the right-hand side of the page are an aid to finding the main heading in the Guide: blue stands for the Introduction (Nature, Culture, History, etc.), red for the "A to Z" section, and yellow indicates Practical Information.

Only a selection of hotels and restaurants can be given; no reflection is implied therefore on establishments not included.

In a time of rapid change it is difficult to ensure that all the information given is entirely accurate and up-to-date, and the possibility of error can never be entirely eliminated.

Although the publishers can accept no responsibility for inaccuracies and omissions, they are constantly endeavouring to improve the quality of their Guides and are therefore always grateful for criticisms, corrections and suggestions for improvement.

Preface

This guide to New Zealand is one of the new generation of Baedeker guides.

These guides, illustrated throughout in colour, are designed to meet the needs of the modern traveller. They are quick and easy to consult, with the principal places of interest described in alphabetical order, and the information is presented in a format that is both attractive and easy to follow.

This guide describes the attractions of New Zealand, with its magnificent scenery, its many striking natural phenomena, its interesting manifestations of Maori culture and much else besides to appeal to visitors. It covers New Zealand's North and South Islands, as well as the associated Cook Islands with their idyllic South Sea beaches.

A quiet cove in the Marlborough Sounds, which offer some of New Zealand's finest sailing waters

The guide is in three main parts. The first part gives a general account of New Zealand, its topography, climate, flora and fauna, population, government and administration, economy, history, famous people, art and culture. A number of suggested routes for visitors provide a lead-in to the second part, in which the principal sights are described; and the third part contains a variety of practical information designed to help visitors to find their way about the country and make the most of their stay. Both the sights and the practical information are listed in alphabetical order.

The new Baedeker guides are noted for their concentration on essentials and their convenience of use. They contain numerous specially drawn plans and colour illustrations; and at the end of the book is a large map making it easy to locate the various places described in the "A to Z" section of the guide with the help of the co-ordinates given at the head of each entry.

Contents

4

Baedeker Specials

Kia

New Zealand, known to the Maoris as Aotearoa, the "land of the long white cloud", is a paradise of overwhelming beauty: scarcely anywhere else in the world is there such variety of scenic beauty within a relatively small area as on these two islands in the South Pacific. Here, in this area of encounter between two continental plates, a landscape can be seen developing. Earth tremors are frequent here, geysers spout high into the air, hot mud bubbles in crater-like depressions and every now and then volcanoes spew out fire. Not far from these "hot spots" soar up the majestic snow-capped summits of the Southern Alps. Imposing fjords and river valleys carved out by glaciers are a reminder that the southern hemisphere, like the northern, had its ice ages. Expanses of evergreen primeval forest with tall ferns and giant kauri trees, areas of desolate wasteland, gleaming white glaciers, rugged peaks and crystal-clear rivers, beaches of white and golden sand bordering the turquoise-blue sea, open parkland and lush green pasture, dense forests of timber, carefully tended vineyards and orchards: only in New Zealand can such sharply contrasting landscapes be found in a relatively small area.

This country at the other end of the world has long been a magnet to people who want to get away from the stresses of everyday

Native heritage
The Maoris still preserve their ancient traditions

Colonial heritage
Mission church, Hokianga Harbour

Ora!

life in the densely populated countries of Europe and to those who seek the delights of nature and the great outdoors – walkers, climbers, bungy jumpers, mountain bikers, off-road enthusiasts, white-water canoers, yachtsmen and anglers.

As they go about the country, too – perhaps in the beautiful Rotorua area – visitors will see something of the life of the Maoris who came to New Zealand from Polynesia many generations ago. In contrast to the peoples of the West, the Maoris attach importance not to the individual but to the tribal community. Reverence for their ancestors also plays a major part in their life. Their everyday life is dominated by traditions and myths, even though externally they have adapted to the way of life of the European immigrants who have settled in the country. Fascinating, too, are their arts and crafts, as displayed for example in the superb carving of their meeting-houses.

But visitors will also enjoy meeting the friendly "Kiwis", as the New Zealanders of European (mostly British) origin call themselves. In their attitudes and activities visitors will sometimes recognise features characteristic of an island people whose nearest neighbours are 1200 miles away to the west, in Australia. Splendid isolation indeed!

Restless earth

Rotorua's geysers, fumaroles and sinter terraces are the outward signs of continuing volcanic activity in the earth's crust

Mountain grandeur

Majestic Mount Taranaki, an extinct volcano

Sheep everywhere

New Zealand has more than 60 million sheep

Kiwi fruit

The vitamin-rich fruit that has conquered world markets

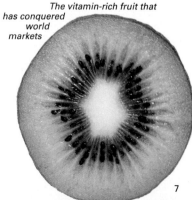

7

Nature, Culture History

Facts and Figures

General

Situation, area and extent

New Zealand occupies an isolated position in the South Pacific, roughly halfway between the Equator and the South Pole. It is about as far away from Europe as it is possible to get – some 25 hours' flying time – and even its nearest neighbour, Australia, is a three-hour flight away to the north-west.

With a total land mass of around 270,500sq.km/104,440sq. miles (the two main islands and a number of smaller ones), New Zealand's land area is rather greater than that of the United Kingdom. The North Island (114,500sq.km/44,210sq. miles) and South Island (150,700sq.km/58,185sq. miles) extend between 34° and 47° latitude south, with a total distance of 1770km/1100 miles between the most southerly point and the most northerly. The southernmost settlement in New Zealand is on Stewart Island. From west to east New Zealand extends between 166° and 179° longitude east. No point on the two main islands is farther than 110km/68 miles from the sea.

The islands

Main islands

In addition to the two main islands (North Island and South Island) New Zealand's territory includes a number of smaller islands and island groups at varying distances from the main islands. The largest is Stewart Island to the south, with an area of some 1700sq.km/656sq. miles. Among the farthest away of the islands are the Kermadec Islands to the north, Chatham and Bounty Islands to the east and Campbell and Auckland Islands to the south.

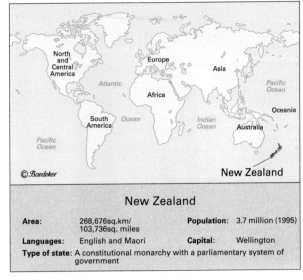

New Zealand

Area:	268,676sq.km/ 103,736sq. miles	Population:	3.7 million (1995)
Languages:	English and Maori	Capital:	Wellington
Type of state:	A constitutional monarchy with a parliamentary system of government		

◀ A traditional Maori ceremony in front of a richly carved meeting-house

Other New Zealand island groups are the Tokelau Islands in Polynesia, the Cook Islands and Niue. The Cook Islands and Niue are associated with New Zealand as self-governing territories.

Tokelau, Cook Islands, Niue

Also belonging to New Zealand is the Ross Dependency in the Antarctic (area 4.75 million sq.km/1.8 million sq. miles), an unpopulated territory consisting of the Ross Sea, the Ross Ice Shelf and Eastern and North-Eastern Victorialand.

Ross Dependency

Visitors to New Zealand will soon realise that life in the southern hemisphere differs from life in Europe or North America. When it is winter in the northern hemisphere it is summer in New Zealand; when the days grow longer in Europe and the trees come into leaf it is autumn in New Zealand; and when the leaves begin to fall in the northern countries there is a feeling of spring in New Zealand. During the day the sun reaches its highest point in the north, not in the south, and accordingly the warmer slopes of a hill are on the north side, not the south.

Down under – the world turned upside down

Topography

Although New Zealand is not a continent but consists mainly of two large islands separated by the 30km/19 mile wide Cook Strait, it offers a remarkable variety of landscape. The two main islands have basically different structures. The North Island is a region of volcanic features and low mountain ranges, with some volcanoes reaching heights of over 2500m/8200ft. In the South Island features of volcanic origin are much less common: here the landscape is patterned by folded mountains of Alpine type, much altered in the ice ages. This difference in topography is matched by differences in climate: lying closer to the Antarctic, the South Island has a markedly rawer climate than the North Island.

Variety of landscape

Both the main islands have very varied coastal landscapes, alternating rapidly between different coastal forms. The coasts of the Northland region are lined by mile-long sandy beaches and dunes. Common to both islands are alluvial plains, deltas and at some points imposing stretches of cliffs. Notable features are the rias (drowned river mouths) in the north-east of the South Island and the fjord-like valleys carved out by glaciers in the south-west of the South Island.

Coastal landscapes

Volcanic activity is very evident in the central region of the North Island. Here the landscape, shaped in the past by volcanic action, is dominated by the volcanoes, still in some degree active, of Mount Ruapehu (2796m/9174ft; the highest peak on the North Island), Mount Ngauruhoe (2290m/7513ft) and Mount Tongariro (1968m/6457ft). Lake Taupo is a huge crater lake, evidence of a gigantic volcanic explosion. Just to the north of this is the Rotorua thermal region, where the whole range of volcanic and post-volcanic phenomena can be observed. In addition to many smaller crater lakes, numerous geysers and hot mud pools there are sinter terraces and hot springs, whose characteristic odours are likely to remain in visitors' memory.

North Island (Te Ika a Maui)

Volcanoes

The North Island's central volcanic region is surrounded by hills rising to over 1700ft/5580ft, giving the island its characteristic hilly character. From the southern tip of the North Island to its East Cape can be seen the continuation of New Zealand's youngest range of folded mountains, which begins at the southern tip of the South Island and reaches its highest points in the Southern Alps. In the east of the North Island is Taranaki (Mount Egmont, 2520m/8268ft) with its beautifully regular cone (frequently hidden in cloud).

The hilly Coromandel Peninsula at the north end of the North Island is of radically different structure from the other hills of the North Island. It

Coromandel Peninsula

11

Topography

New Zealand Mountains, Lakes and Rivers

is built up from volcanic material, in contrast to the other hills, mainly formed from sandstones, clays and limestones.

Northland

To the north of Auckland extends the Northland region, an area of rolling hills with a subtropical climate. The highest peaks are just under

12

800m/2625ft. This region, favoured both climatically and scenically, offers ideal conditions for the development of agriculture and also of tourism.

The predominant feature of the South Island is the Southern Alps, a range of folded mountains which in geological terms are relatively young. In the centre is New Zealand's highest peak, Mount Cook (3744m/12,284ft). In its immediate neighbourhood are other mountains over 3000m/9850ft) – Mount Tasman (3497ft/11,474ft), Mount Sefton (3157m/10,358ft) and a number of other snow-capped peaks. The charm of these mountains is enhanced by numerous imposing glaciers, the most spectacular of which are the 26km/16 mile long Tasman Glacier, the Hooker Glacier and the Mueller Glacier. This mountainous region is now under special protection as Mount Cook National Park. To the west the Southern Alps fall down to sea level in a strip of land only 50km/30 miles wide. This steep gradient over a relatively short distance has produced the long tongues of the Fox Glacier and Franz Josef, reaching down to only 300m/985ft above sea level.

South Island (Te Wahi Ponamu)

Southern Alps

The coastal plain on the west side of the island is separated from the Southern Alps by the Alpine Fault.

Western coastal plain

On the east side the mountains fall away more gradually. In this area there are numerous lakes, which give the eastern slopes of the Southern Highlands their particular charm.

Eastern slopes

In the northern part of the South Island there are two ranges of low mountains. To the north-west are the Tasman Mountains, while to the north-east is the hilly Marlborough region, the continuation of the Southern Alps (see above). The coastal region, known as the Marlborough Sounds, is an extensive system of rias (river valleys drowned by the sea).

Tasman Mountains, Marlborough Sounds

At the other end of the South Island, to the south-west, is the beautiful Fiordland region, which came into being in much the same way as the rias to the north. The fjords are river valleys carved out by the mighty glaciers which flowed down to the sea during the ice ages. The walls of these glaciated valleys, which are frequently U-shaped, are very steep. There are numerous lakes, such as Lake Te Anau, formed by the melting of the ice masses. The mountains, built of granites, gneisses and slates, are dissected by numerous valleys and reach heights of over 1700m/5580ft.

Fiordland

In the southern part of the Central Otago region is another mountainous area, with hills rising to 2000m/6560ft. This is a landscape of continental aspect with wide river valleys and a gentler pattern of relief.

Central Otago

To the south and east of the South Island, most of which is mountainous, there are extensive plains. From the Canterbury Plain on the south side of the island the Banks Peninsula reaches out into the sea. It is formed by an extinct volcano, whose crater lake is linked with the sea and serves as a natural harbour.

Plains in south and east, Banks Peninsula

The Making of New Zealand

The restless geological history of New Zealand resulted from its situation on the boundary between two tectonic plates, the Indian/ Australian plate and the Pacific plate. When the primeval supercontinent of Pangaia began to split up, some 200 million years ago,

Collision between two continental plates

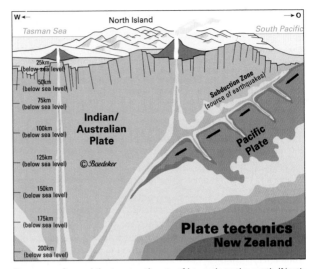

W ← North Island → O

Tasman Sea   South Pacific

25km (below sea level)
50km (below sea level)
75km (below sea level)
100km (below sea level)
125km (below sea level)
150km (below sea level)
175km (below sea level)
200km (below sea level)

Indian/ Australian Plate

© *Baedeker*

Subduction Zone (source of earthquakes)

Pacific Plate

Plate tectonics
New Zealand

there were formed the two continents of Laurasia to the north (North America, Europe, Asia) and Gondwana to the south (South America, Africa, the Indian sub-continent, Antarctica, Australia). The further split-up of these continents began about 150 million years ago. About that time Gondwana was divided into the present continents of South America, Africa and India; Australia, Antarctica and New Zealand still formed a single land mass. Then about 80 million years ago New Zealand was separated from Australia and Antarctica by the formation of the Tasman Sea. New Zealand was thus already isolated when Australia and Antarctica began to separate about 50 million years ago. A look at the globe shows how the regions bordering the Pacific Ocean are caught between ranges of mountains and deep marine trenches. These are part of what is known as the unstable circum-Pacific mobile belt, the border region marked by the collision of continental and oceanic plates. Typical features of this unsettled zone are earthquakes, volcanic activity and the formation of mountain ranges and marine trenches. With its frequent earthquakes and active volcanism this region is well known as the "Ring of Fire".

North Island

The frequent earthquakes, numerous faults, volcanic activity and young folded mountains are the consequence of forces generated by the collision of the Indian/Australian plate with the Pacific plate. The two plates move both on to one another and past one another, and as a result the Pacific plate is forced under the Indian/Australian one in the region of the North Island. This gives rise to enormous pressures and temperature differences in the earth's crust which are vented on the surface in volcanoes, geysers, thermal springs, mud pools, fumaroles (emissions of volcanic gases) and solfataras (emissions of sulphurous gases and water vapour).

South Island

In the region of the South Island, on the other hand, the Pacific plate is thrust over the Indian/Australian plate, leading to the folding of the Southern Alps. The lateral displacement of the two plates along the Alpine Fault now extends for a distance of over 450km/275 miles. It is clearly visible in rocks of the same age in the north-west and south of the South Island.

*A landscape in course of formation:
sinter terraces at Whakarewarewa (Rotorua)*

The liberation of enormous energies on the boundary between the two tectonic plates has created the landscape patterns of New Zealand. In general the formation of mountains is accompanied by volcanic activity, the extrusion of basalts and frequent violent earthquakes. The continuing volcanic activity and recurrent earthquakes are evidence that the movements under the earth's surface are still going on. The movements of the two plates do not proceed steadily and harmoniously but give rise to tensions which are spontaneously discharged. Hence the earthquakes, at least one of which each year in New Zealand reaches a strength of 6 on the Richter scale. During the last 150 years severe earthquakes – for example in the Napier area in 1931 – have repeatedly resulted in heavy loss of life. New Zealand's capital, Wellington, is built on unstable ground: like San Francisco in California, it lies close to a major fault line. It was devastated by a severe earthquake in 1855. Volcanic eruptions are less of a threat; but the eruption of Mount Tarawera at the end of the 19th century and of Mount Ruapehu in the early 1950s caused some loss of life. In the central volcanic zone round Mount Tongariri on the North Island the volcanoes are still active. Along fault lines magma comes to the surface. This can be observed in a flight over White Island in the Bay of Plenty. On this small volcanic island, lying on the northern continuation of the fault lines in the central volcanic zone of the North Island there are always whitish-yellow swathes of sulphurous vapour.

Earthquakes and volcanism

The most ancient rocks on the South Island, some 600 million years old, show that parts of the New Zealand land mass have been in existence since the Pre-Cambrian (beginning about 4.5 billion years ago), when they formed part of the continent of Gondwana. During the Cambrian, Ordovician, Silurian and Early Devonian (570–380 million years ago) sediments were deposited in a zone of subsidence in the

Mountain formation

earth's crust near the continent of Gondwana. The subsequent process of mountain formation, which lasted until about 300 million years ago, is known as the Tahua orogenesis. A consequence of this orogenesis was the formation of a further subsidence zone known as the New Zealand geosyncline. The oldest, though untypical, rock in this sedimentation zone is the Upper Carboniferous marble (320–280 million years ago) which outcrops at Kakahu in South Canterbury, pointing to earlier deposits of limestone. The characteristic rocks of this subsidence zone, however, are slates, sandstones, limestones and volcanic tuffs, which can be dated to the Permian (280–230 million years ago). In the Triassic (230–200 million years ago) greywackes (sandstones containing a high proportion of rock detritus) were formed. They form the backbone of New Zealand and have been subject to folding in the region of the Southern Alps. This phase of mountain formation took place from the end of the Jurassic (150 million years ago) to the Middle Cretaceous (100 million years ago). In the Upper Cretaceous (100–60 million years ago) the mountains were worn down by erosion. New Zealand owes its present form to a continuing process of mountain formation which began 25 million years ago and reached its climax in the Late Tertiary (10–2 million years ago).

All three periods of upthrust were accompanied by volcanic activity, with the deposition of lava and ash. At the same time there were repeated intrusions of plutonite (magma which had hardened under the surface) into the deeper strata. During the Tertiary era sandstones, limestones and clays were formed according to changing conditions.

The Pleistocene period which followed lasted until 10,000 years ago. Developments on the earth's surface were shaped by the ice ages, interrupted by warmer periods.

In the most recent period of the earth's history, the Holocene, the existing land forms have undergone practically no change. Only the most recent sediments in alluvial plains and river valleys are evidence of erosional processes. Earthquakes and local displacements of soil masses, like the most recent landslide on Mount Cook (1991), can take on catastrophic dimensions.

Ice ages
(Pleistocene)

The beginning of the first cold period, the Hautawan, with the Ross glaciation, marks the end of the Tertiary and the beginning of the Neozoic, with the Pleistocene, 2 million years ago. Moraines and banded clays are evidence of the first glaciation. The first cold period was followed, about 1.5 million years ago, by the first warm period (interglacial), the Nukumaruan. The Okehuan cold period, beginning 1.2 million years ago, was less marked than the Hautawan. The following warm period, the Putikan, lasted from 700,000 to 300,000 years ago. The period from 300,000 to 10,000 years ago was marked by the frequent alternation of cold and warm periods. The earliest ice age in this period was the Porikan, which was followed by the Waiwheran warm period. This in turn was followed by the Waimaungan ice age and the Terangian warm period. The second-last ice age, the Waimean, lasted until 120,000 years ago, and the last interglacial, the Oturian, was followed 80,000 years ago by the last ice age, which ended with the beginning of the post-glacial period some 14,000 years ago. U-shaped valleys, fjords, hanging valleys, terminal, lateral and ground moraines, glacier lakes and deposits of fluvial detritus are among the most obvious evidences of these periods, demonstrating the landscape-shaping force of the ice. The still surviving glaciers – for example the Franz Josef Glacier, the Fox Glacier and the Tasman Glacier, which flow down from the high mountain regions round Mount Cook in the Southern Alps – are relics of the ice ages.

Climate

New Zealand's diversity of landscape is reflected in the climatic conditions of the different parts of the country. Thus in the west of the
South Island, in the build-up to the Southern Alps, there are rainy areas
with annual precipitations well over 2500mm/98in. Farther east, in the
rain shadow of the Southern Alps, it is much drier, with annual precipitations of under 700mm/28in. Temperatures show lesser variations,
with annual averages ranging between 9°C/48°F at the south end of the
South Island and 14°C/57°F to the north of Auckland; and even in the
height of summer offshoots of Antarctic cold fronts can briefly bring
day temperatures in the Southern Alps and Central Otago on the South
Island below 10°C/50°F and the snow-line down to 1000m/3280ft, while
on the North Island it is high summer.

The climate of New Zealand is determined mainly by three factors –
its geographical position in the zone of west winds, the mountains at
right angles to the direction of the wind the country's insular situation,
far from any continental land mass and surrounded by great masses of
water (the Pacific Ocean).

Lying between 35° and 47° south, New Zealand is situated in the middle   West wind zone
latitudes of the southern hemisphere. Only the most northerly part of
the North Island, the Northland region, lies in the boundary area of the
subtropical and marginally tropical high pressure zone, with a milder
climate. Like the "higher" latitudes of the northern hemisphere (e.g.
Europe), the "lower" latitudes of the southern hemisphere have the
four seasons of spring, summer, autumn and winter. Here too the
position of the sun changes over the year; but when the sun reaches its
highest position in the northern hemisphere it is at its lowest in New
Zealand; that is, when it is summer in Europe it is winter in New
Zealand, and vice versa.

The west winds which prevail throughout the year are a further
characteristic of the middle latitudes and are mainly responsible for the
distribution of rainfall. Also typical of the middle latitudes is the alternation of passing low pressure areas (cyclones) and high pressure
areas (anticyclones). The former are normally coupled with cold fronts
and are characterised by high rainfall and high wind speeds. In the
Cook Strait between the two main islands stormy winds prevail practically all year. Thus Wellington, New Zealand's "windy city", has wind
speeds of over 50km/30 miles an hour on more than 170 days in the
year. Stable weather conditions with light winds are usually the result
of anticyclones. In the coastal regions regional landward and seaward
winds prevent sultry weather from developing.

Rainfall

The Southern Alps on the South Island, lying almost at right angles to   Weather side
the direction of the prevailing west winds, and the lower mountains of
the North Island have decisive effects on the frequency and intensity of
rainfall in New Zealand. There are marked differences between the
weather side of the hills, which is exposed to the winds, and the lee
side. The air masses coming from the west gain increased humidity
during their passage over the Tasman Sea, but then come up against
the mountains and are compelled to rise up their weather side, leading
to intensive cloud formation and higher rainfall, which is most abundant at the point where the winds first reach the hills, on their west side.
This is particularly with the mountains of the Southern Alps, which in
some areas have an annual rainfall on the weather side of over
7000mm/275in.

On the lee side, as a result of the föhn effect (descending air masses,   Lee side
which become steadily warmer and drier), rainfall is markedly lower.

Climate

The low rainfall of the valleys, intramontane basins and plains lying in the wind shadow is the result of this phenomenon.

Apart from extreme weather side and lee side situations New Zealand's rainfall ranges between 1000mm/40in. and 1500mm/60in.

Seasons

During the winter (June, July, August) the North Island comes under the influence of the west wind zone and has most of its rainfall during these months. The summer months (December, January, February) are under the influence of subtropical and marginally tropical high pressure areas. The consequence is stable weather with low rainfall. This stability can be disturbed by high pressure areas of tropical origin or offshoots of tropical whirlwinds, producing heavy rain and strong winds in the north and east of the island. This occurs only during the summer months. On the South Island, on the other hand, there are no precisely defined dry and rainy seasons: the months of maximum and minimum rainfall vary from region to region. In the south the highest rainfall is during the summer; in the east and north-east the wettest months are May and June (late autumn in the southern hemisphere); while in the west and north the highest rainfall is in spring (September/October).

Temperatures

Relief and latitude

Differing patterns of relief also produce considerable differences in temperature. Temperatures fall, for example, by around half a degree Celsius (nine-tenths of a degree Fahrenheit) for every additional 100m/330ft of altitude; and at night temperatures in the hills are much lower than at sea level. Visitors to the Southern Alps must be prepared for temperatures below 10°C/50°F.

Thanks to the moderating influence of the surrounding water masses, the differences of temperature between the north and the south of New Zealand are smaller than the distance of 1500km/930 miles might suggest. In New Zealand's oceanic climate there are seldom differences of temperature over the year or over the day of more than 10°C/18°F. The main exception to this is Central Otago, a region of almost continental character, where there are greater divergences of temperature.

The highest annual average temperatures, between 13° and 14°C (55° and 57°F), are found in the north of the North Island. For the South Island and other parts of the North Island the annual average lies around 12°C/54°F. Farther south the figure falls to 9°C/48°F.

Seasons

The highest temperatures, over 22°C/72°F, occur in the summer months (December, January, February) on the North Island and the north and east of the South Island. Temperatures seldom fall below 0°C/32°F, even in the New Zealand winter (June, July, August). Only in the Southern Alps, Central Otago and the North Island's central volcanic zone does the thermometer fall below freezing point. In the coastal regions maritime influences prevents this from happening.

Duration of Sunshine

In spite of its heavy rainfall New Zealand has long hours of sunshine, with the annual average ranging between around 2500 hours at Nelson and Blenheim in the north of the South Island and 1500 hours in the Southern Alps and Fiordland. These are extreme figures: for the South Island there are normally between 1600 and 2000 hours of sunshine over the year, falling from north to south. In the wind shadow of the Southern Alps the figure is around 2200, in the coastal regions of the North Island between 2000 and 2200; only in the central volcanic zone

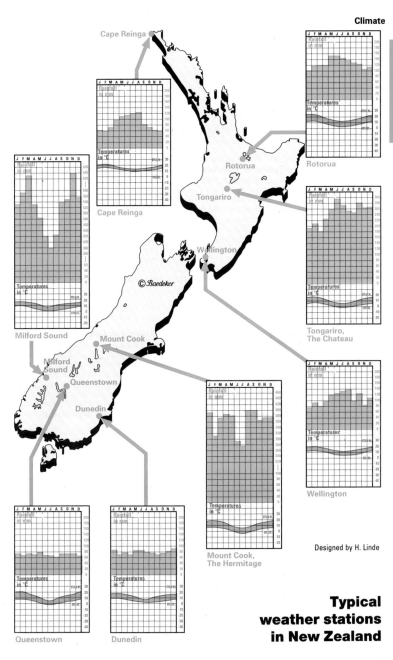

Cape Reinga

Rotorua

Rotorua

Tongariro

Tongariro,
The Chateau

Wellington

Milford Sound

Mount Cook

Wellington

Milford
Sound

Queenstown

Dunedin

Mount Cook,
The Hermitage

© Baedeker

Designed by H. Linde

Queenstown

Dunedin

Typical
weather stations
in New Zealand

of the North Island does the number of hours of sunshine fall below 1800. An annual average of 2000 hours of sunshine is equivalent to 5½ hours a day.

Problem of the ozone layer

See Practical Information from A to Z, Health

When to go to New Zealand

See Practical Information from A to Z, When to Go

Flora and Fauna

Some 80 million years of isolation from other land masses allowed New Zealand's flora and fauna to develop independently. It is not surprising, therefore, that more than 70% of the flora is endemic; that is, it is found only in New Zealand. The development of endemic fauna was confined mainly to birds and insects, though there are also a few species of reptiles and freshwater fish native to New Zealand. For many millions of years plants and animals were left on their own. The development of the flora and fauna was affected by volcanic eruptions and a series of ice ages, but has suffered much more serious inroads since the arrival of Europeans. In a period of two hundred years – in geological terms no more than a moment in the earth's history – numerous species of plants and animals have been driven out of their natural habitat or totally exterminated; and even today many species are still in danger of extinction.

Flora

Native flora

Forests

Originally New Zealand was covered with great expanses of forest. Only small areas of territory – mainly in the high mountain regions and in the wind shadow of the Southern Alps – were unsuitable for trees, either because they were too cold or too dry. Vegetation adapted to the falling temperature gradient from north to south: thus the forests in different parts of the country tend to be of different species. Typical of New Zealand's primeval forests are evergreen deciduous trees and conifers, which have been able to adapt to cold winter temperatures so that they do not, like many European species, shed their leaves.

Kauri

In areas of subtropical climate in New Zealand – mainly the Coromandel Peninsula and the Northland region, but also the area round Auckland – were originally covered with forests of kauris, a species of spruce notable for its gigantic size.

Undergrowth, silver fern

In the undergrowth of New Zealand's forests there are ferns, mosses, lianas, climbing plants and epiphytes, giving visitors something of the impression of a primeval forest. A particularly typical representative of New Zealand's flora is the silver fern, which has been adopted as the country's national plant.

Southern beech

The commonest forest tree is the evergreen southern beech (*Nothofagus*). On the North Island it is found associated with other species of tree, such as the tall totara (*Podocarpus totara*), but on the South Island, for example in Fiordland and Westland, it forms large forests, with light undergrowth composed of relatively few species. In other forests the undergrowth consists of plants growing to different heights, including tree ferns, shrubs and shade-tolerant trees. At higher altitudes the beech forests give place to forests of conifers.

Rimu

The rimu (*Dacrydium cupressinum*) is found throughout New Zealand, growing in mixed forests with other trees. Its sturdy growth makes it a popular decorative tree. It grows very slowly, and some trees may be

A gigantic tree fern

as much as 1000 years old. Its hard, tough wood is a much used building timber.

Its magnificent crimson flowers appear in December: hence its popular name of Christmas tree. It is found mainly on the beaches of the North Island.

Pohutukawa
(Christmas tree)

The rata, a tree with beautiful deep red flowers, is most at home on the South Island. It has an unusual method of reproduction: its seeds are carried by the wind and deposited on other trees, where it forms aerial roots and gradually kills the host plant.

Rata

The kowhai with its yellow blossoms provides another touch of colour in New Zealand's forests.

Kowhai

Tall tussock or tuft grasses are characteristic features of the plains. Expanses of dry grassland are found in the wind shadow of the Southern Alps. Also common is toetoe grass, a species related to the pampas grass of South America.

Grasses

In summer the Alpine meadows of mountainous areas are covered with a magnificent show of flowers. In addition to the daisy-like celmisias there are gentians, various species of orchid and numerous other alpine flowers, including the Mount Cook lily (*Ranunculus lyalii*) and the white buttercup, the largest species in its genus.

Alpine meadows

The most widely distributed New Zealand shrub is the manuka, which flourishes nearly everywhere and is valued as providing good protection against erosion. It is one of the first species to establish themselves on land cleared of forest. Its dried leaves were once used to make a kind of tea: hence its name of tea tree.

Manuka
(tea tree)

Flora and Fauna

Flax

The New Zealand flax (*Phormium tenax*), which has adapted well to conditions in the rainy plains, was formerly of great economic importance to the Maoris. The fibres of this plant are used to make baskets, textiles, etc.

Plants introduced by man

The Maoris brought with them from their Polynesian homeland various useful plants, including the kumara or sweet potato. With the coming of white settlers plants previously unknown in New Zealand began to be brought in on an enormous scale. More than 2000 species came to New Zealand in this way, often unintentionally. The fast-growing Californian pine (*Pinus radiata*) is now common in New Zealand. It is grown for its timber, frequently in monoculture. The Californian giant redwood (*Sequoia sempervirens*) has also been successfully established in New Zealand. Also imported from many different parts of the world are other species of tree (including the oak), fruit trees (among them the Chinese gooseberry or kiwi fruit), garden plants, decorative flowers, clover and broom. Several species of eucalyptus and acacia have also found their way from Australia to New Zealand. In many areas the "new" plants have upset the delicate ecological balance.

Fauna

Native fauna

Birds

New Zealand's native fauna is represented in the first place by more than 250 species of birds. Among them are some very rare species, including the kiwi (see Baedeker Special, p. 24), a nocturnally active flightless bird. Before the coming of man birds had no natural enemies except other members of their own species; and as a result a number of other flightless species were able to develop.

A giant moa

Moa

Other well-known New Zealand birds are the weka, the kakapo, the takahe and above all the moa, now extinct. There were more than two dozen species of the moa, a flightless bird similar to the ostrich. The largest of them could reach a height of no less than 4.5m/15ft. The early settlers in New Zealand, particularly the Maoris, hunted these birds as a welcome addition to their diet and wiped them out before the arrival of the Europeans.

Parrots; kea

Of the four New Zealand species of parrot the mountain parrot known as the kea has the worst reputation. It is said that it attacks and kills sheep. It has become accustomed to man, and tents, sleeping-bags and other human possessions are not safe from its attentions. It is particularly fond of rubber items such as windscreen-wipers and tyres. Untypically for a parrot, it has adapted to conditions in the high mountain regions of the Southern Alps.

Other common species of parrot in New Zealand are kakas and parakeets. Now very rare, and therefore strictly protected, is the kakapo, a flightless nocturnal parrot.

Various species of honeyeaters, including the bellbird and the stitch-bird, are relatively common in New Zealand's natural forests. They live mainly on nectar but also on fruit and insects. Perhaps the best-known New Zealand songbird is the black-plumaged tui, which also belongs to the honeyeater genus.

Rails are not uncommon in New Zealand. One of the largest representatives of the species is the takahe, a flightless bird which was believed to be extinct until a takahe colony of some size was discovered in Northland after the Second World War.

Another flightless bird is the weka, which also belongs to the rail family. This duck-like and very inquisitive bird is often to be seen on camping and picnic sites, where, like the magpie, it looks out for shiny and glistening objects.

The coasts of New Zealand are home to numerous species of seabird. The most striking is the royal albatross, which has a wing-span of up to 3.5m/11½ft. Other denizens of the coastal regions are various species of gull, cormorants, petrels, terns and muttonbirds.

The yellow-eyed penguin is found only in New Zealand. Its habitat is the south coast of the South Island.

New Zealand has innumerable species of insect, which are the main source of food for the country's birds. One of the most interesting insects is a tiny fly related to the gnat whose larvae are found mainly on the roofs of dark caves. They have a fascinating method of obtaining their food. They produce long sticky threads like spiders' webs, and during their digestive process generate a faint light: hence their name. The light attracts insects, which are then caught on the sticky threads, which become the fly's larder. These glowworms – which are not related to the European glowworm – can be observed in the Waitoma Caves (North Island).

Towards evening the masses of mosquitoes and sandflies which then emerge can be a nuisance.

New Zealand also has a number of species of spider. The most dangerous is the katipo, which is closely related to the American black widow spider and the Australian redback. A bite from a fully grown female is painful, and can be fatal.

The family of reptiles is represented in New Zealand by several species of gecko and small lizards. There are practically no snakes.

The tuatara is a lizard-like reptile which is a living representative of a long-past period in the earth's history: a species which in all the other parts of the world died out before the dinosaurs. It is found only in caverns on the offshore islands to the east of New Zealand.

The waters round New Zealand are well stocked with fish and appeal particularly to deep sea anglers. In addition to many smaller fish there are tiger and hammerhead sharks, marlin, swordfish and tuna.

As a result of New Zealand's early isolation it has no native land mammals apart from two species of bat. Off the Kaikoura coast in the north-east of the South Island whole schools of whales and dolphins, including sperm whales and even killer whales, can be observed.

Rats and dogs came to New Zealand with the first incomers in the early historical period, and great numbers of animals new to New Zealand were brought in by European immigrants – useful and domestic animals such as cattle, sheep, horses, goats, turkeys and peacocks, but

Honeyeaters

Rails; takahe

Weka

Seabirds; albatrosses

Yellow-eyed penguin

Insects

Glowworm

Spiders; katipo

Reptiles

Tuatara

Fish

Mammals

Animals introduced by man

23

"Kiwii Kiwii" and "Quaak Quaak"

Walking through a New Zealand forest at night, you will sometimes hear a shrill cry of "kiwii, kiwii" and a muffled "quaak, quaak". This is likely to be your only contact with New Zealand's most famous native animal, for it is a shy creature which is mainly active at night.

This is the kiwi, a non-gregarious flightless bird belonging to the Apterygidae family. About the size of a domestic hen, it has a long curved and pointed beak and straggly greyish-brown plumage. Its wings have shrunk to barely recognisable rudiments, so that it is quite unable to fly. In compensation it has an excellent organ of smell, located at the end of its beak.

The kiwi, of which there are three species, gets its name from the cry of the male bird. The cry of the female is more like the croaking of a frog. It can live for up to 25 years. It goes in quest of its food after dark, following carefully contrived and well trodden paths through New Zealand's forests. It searches for grubs and worms in the foliage with its long pointed beak or digs them out with its strong claws. During the rainy season and when the woodland berries are ripening the kiwi covers great distances in its nightly foraging.

It is only during the mating season that kiwis, which are normally loners, become more sociable. After mating a pair of kiwis will spend the day asleep in their hole and go out together at night in search of food. After the female produces one or two eggs, relatively large in proportion to her own size, it is the male who sits on them. The young birds very quickly become independent, for their parents pay little attention to them, but it may be five or six years before they are sexually mature.

The native inhabitants of New Zealand, the Maoris, regarded – and still regard – kiwis as particularly desirable game birds. Kiwi's feathers were woven into the mats of their chiefs.

The kiwis have been much decimated by man, particularly since the arrival of Europeans in New Zealand, and are now in danger of extinction. Since they cannot fly and are not particularly swift on their feet they are an easy prey for human beings and animals, particularly the animals brought in by the Europeans – rats, dogs, cats, martens and hedgehogs. The kiwi, as New Zealand's national animal, is now strictly protected.

also game animals (including red deer) and various species of fresh-water fish. These were brought in to provide food for the immigrants; but there were also other animals which presented a serious threat to the native fauna, particularly opossums, martens, cats and dogs.

Red deer, opossums, rats, cats and dogs are the species that have had the most devastating effects on the delicately balanced ecosystem of New Zealand. The country's flightless birds were easy prey for dogs and cats which had gone back to the wild, and the nesting-places of many birds were defenceless against the depredations of nest-robbers such as martens and cats. The red deer, without any real natural enemies, multiplied enormously and became a plague, and by biting off young shoots hindered the natural rejuvenation of the forests. The opossums, which for many years have been been increasing in num-bers, have devastated great expanses of forest. The authorities con-cerned with the protection of nature have launched expensive campaigns for dealing with the population explosion in certain spe-cies, including the use of helicopters to hunt them down.

Disturbance of ecological equilibrium

State and Administration

The New Zealand flag has the Union flag in the upper left corner, and in the right half, on a blue ground, the constellation of the Southern Cross. The national coat of arms, adopted in 1956, also features the Southern Cross, symbolising the state, as well as a sheaf of corn, a sheep's fleece and miners' tools, symbolising agriculture, stock farm-ing and mining. In the centre are three sailing ships, reminders of the importance to New Zealand of maritime trade and the settling of the islands from the sea. The supporters are a white woman, representing the European immigrants, on the left and a tattooed Maori in tradi-tional costume, holding a spear, symbolising the original inhabitants, on the right; both figures are standing on silver ferns, New Zealand's national plant. Above the shield is the British crown.

National emblems

New Zealand's national animal is the kiwi: hence the name Kiwi applied to New Zealanders.

New Zealand is a parliamentary democracy on the British model and a constitutional monarchy within the Commonwealth of Nations. The head of state is Queen Elizabeth II, who is represented by the Governor-General. The British political tradition is reflected in the absence of a written constitution, the basis of constitutional law being provided by decisions of the British and New Zealand courts. New Zealand consti-tutional law, however, was brought together and clarified in the Consti-tution Act of 1986. Politically, New Zealand is completely independent of Britain.

Parliamentary democracy and constitutional monarchy

The Governor-General is appointed by the Queen on the nomination of the New Zealand government for a five-year term. He opens and closes the parliamentary session, reads the "speech from the throne" setting out the government's plans for the session, makes various appoint-ments and grants honours. He is head of the executive but can act only in agreement with the Executive Council, which consists of the Cabinet and himself. He may, however, refuse his consent to laws which he believes to be contrary to the constitution. His most important function is to ensure continuity during a change of government. After a general election he is obliged to invite the leader of the victorious party to form a government.

Governor-General

The New Zealand Parliament in Wellington has since 1952 consisted of a single chamber, the House of Representatives. It has 120 members, who are elected for a three-year term by universal, secret and direct

Parliament

25

New Zealand

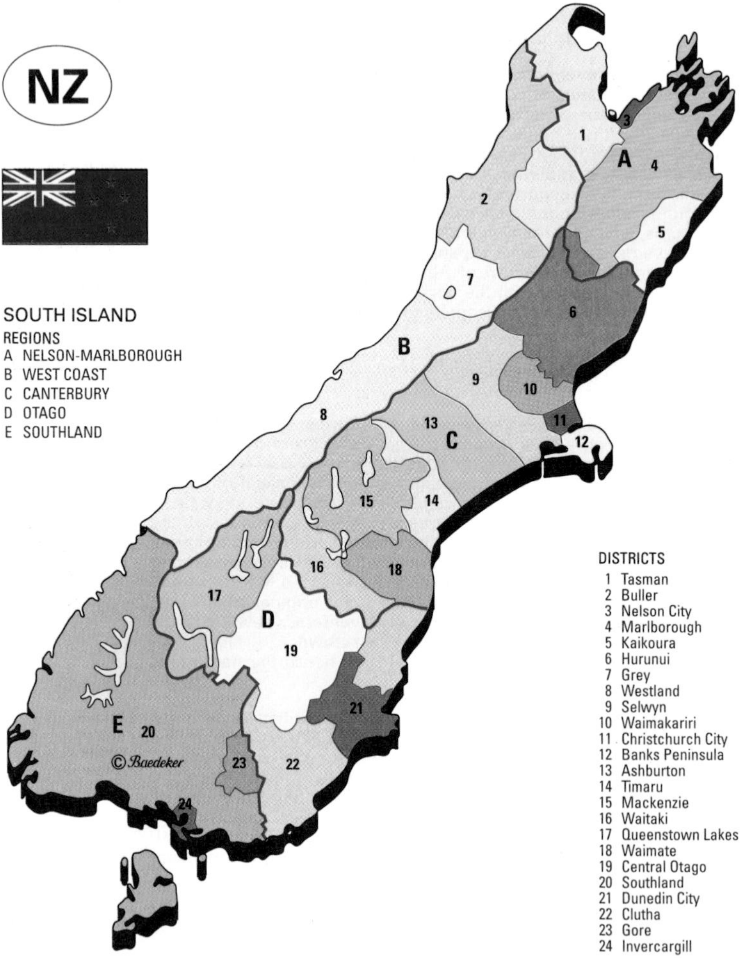

NZ

SOUTH ISLAND

REGIONS
A NELSON-MARLBOROUGH
B WEST COAST
C CANTERBURY
D OTAGO
E SOUTHLAND

DISTRICTS
1 Tasman
2 Buller
3 Nelson City
4 Marlborough
5 Kaikoura
6 Hurunui
7 Grey
8 Westland
9 Selwyn
10 Waimakariri
11 Christchurch City
12 Banks Peninsula
13 Ashburton
14 Timaru
15 Mackenzie
16 Waitaki
17 Queenstown Lakes
18 Waimate
19 Central Otago
20 Southland
21 Dunedin City
22 Clutha
23 Gore
24 Invercargill

© Baedeker

suffrage. The electorate consists of all New Zealanders over the age of 18 and also foreigners with a long-term residence permit who have lived in the country for more than twelve months. Under a recently introduced system of "mixed member proportional representation" electors have two votes, a constituency vote and a party vote. Of the 120 parliamentary seats, 60 are filled by members elected for constituencies. A further five seats are reserved for Maoris, who are elected in five constituencies with separate Maori electoral rolls. The remaining 55 seats are allocated according to the percentage of the party vote from lists of candidates nominated by the parties. This system seems likely to favour the larger minority parties.

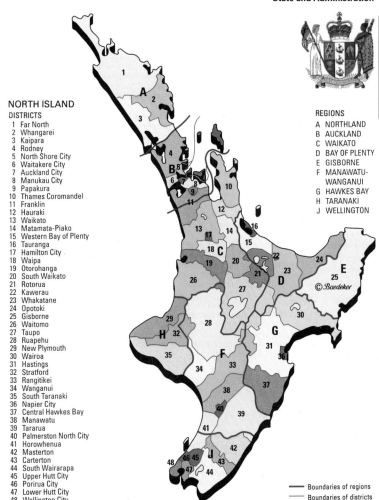

NORTH ISLAND

DISTRICTS

1 Far North
2 Whangarei
3 Kaipara
4 Rodney
5 North Shore City
6 Waitakere City
7 Auckland City
8 Manukau City
9 Papakura
10 Thames Coromandel
11 Franklin
12 Hauraki
13 Waikato
14 Matamata-Piako
15 Western Bay of Plenty
16 Tauranga
17 Hamilton City
18 Waipa
19 Otorohanga
20 South Waikato
21 Rotorua
22 Kawerau
23 Whakatane
24 Opotoki
25 Gisborne
26 Waitomo
27 Taupo
28 Ruapehu
29 New Plymouth
30 Wairoa
31 Hastings
32 Stratford
33 Rangitikei
34 Wanganui
35 South Taranaki
36 Napier City
37 Central Hawkes Bay
38 Manawatu
39 Tararua
40 Palmerston North City
41 Horowhenua
42 Masterton
43 Carterton
44 South Wairarapa
45 Upper Hutt City
46 Porirua City
47 Lower Hutt City
48 Wellington City

REGIONS

A NORTHLAND
B AUCKLAND
C WAIKATO
D BAY OF PLENTY
E GISBORNE
F MANAWATU-
   WANGANUI
G HAWKES BAY
H TARANAKI
J WELLINGTON

© *Baedeker*

—— Boundaries of regions
—— Boundaries of districts

As in Britain, the leader of the opposition and his deputy have official salaried posts.

The government consists of the prime minister and his Cabinet. All members of the cabinet must be members of Parliament. Executive powers are in the hands of the Governor-General and the Cabinet, who together form the Executive Council.

Government

The judicial system is largely based on English common law, supplemented by parliamentary legislation. The supreme court of appeal is the Privy Council in London. Since 1962 New Zealand has had an

Judicial system

ombudsman to consider complaints of maladministration by government departments.

Local government
Under a reorganised system of local government introduced in 1989 New Zealand is divided into 14 regions, nine on the North Island and five on the South Island, which in turn are divided into territorial authorities (towns and districts). In addition there are numerous local authorities for particular purposes. Education, social services and police are central government responsibilities.

Parties
Under the majority voting system the political scene in New Zealand was dominated by two parties, the conservative National Party and the social democratic Labour Party. The new voting system is likely to favour the larger minority parties, such as the Mana Motuhake, a Maori party, the Alliance Party and the New Zealand First Party.

Trade unions
The New Zealand trade union movement was encouraged and promoted by the state from the turn of the 19th century, so that numerous small unions were established. Until 1984 membership of a trade union was compulsory. More recently the influence of the unions has been reduced. In 1992 collective wage agreements were discontinued and replaced by individual or factory agreements.

Foreign policy
New Zealand was a founding member of the United Nations and is also a member of the OECD and the Antarctic Treaty. Co-operation with the United States has continued since the Second World War to be a central feature of New Zealand's security policy, but its increased concern with the Pacific area is shown by its participation in the Colombo Plan of 1950, under which the richer countries of Asia and the Pacific area promised development help, particularly in the technical field, to the less developed countries in the region, its membership (since 1989) of APEC, which seeks to co-ordinate the economic policies of the countries bordering the Pacific, and its military alliance with Britain, Australia, Singapore and Malaysia under the Five Power Defence Agreement.

Population

Density of population
An official Census has been held in New Zealand every five years since 1851. In 1996 the country had a population of 3.6 million inhabitants, or just under 300,000 more than ten years before. During the 1970s and 1980s the rate of population growth was just under 20%.

New Zealand has a land area, excluding its Antarctic territories, of around 270,000sq.km/104,250sq. miles. It has thus a rather larger area than the United Kingdom but is much more thinly populated: 13 to the sq.km (34 to the sq. mile), compared with 234 to the sq.km (606 to the sq. mile) in Britain. This average figure, however, gives a misleading picture of the distribution of population in New Zealand. The North Island – favoured by climate, economy and communications – has an area of 114,758sq.km/44,308sq. miles and a population density of just under 23 to the sq.km (60 to the sq. mile), while the rather larger South Island, with an area of 149,887sq.km/57,871sq. miles, has a density of only 6 to the sq.km (15½ to the sq. mile).

Distribution of population
The low average figures of population density also obscure the fact that five-sixths of the population live in towns with a population of over 30,000. These urban areas also show particularly high growth rates. The process of urbanisation, which has been in progress for decades, is the result mainly of economic development. Extensive rationalisation of agriculture has reduced the number of workers required,

while the processing industries and the growing services sector in the towns have provided new jobs.

This development is particularly marked on the North Island. In 1991 26% of New Zealand's population lived in Auckland, the country's largest city with more than 855,000 inhabitants. The regions established in 1989 – nine on the North Island, five on the South Island – show very different developments in their populations between the Censuses of 1986 and 1991:

Region	Population 1991	Change since 1986 in %
NORTH ISLAND		
Northland	131,620	+3.1
Auckland	953,580	+8.3
Waikato	338,959	+4.2
Bay of Plenty	208,163	+7.0
Gisborne	44,387	−3.4
Hawke's Bay	139,479	−1.0
Taranaki	107,222	−0.3
Manawatu-Wanganui	228,616	+1.6
Wellington	402,892	+1.8
SOUTH ISLAND		
Nelson-Marlborough	113,487	+6.3
West Coast	35,380	−2.7
Canterbury	442,392	+2.2
Otago	186,067	+1.7
Southland	103,442	−2.0

This demonstrates clearly the movement northward and into the large towns, on the North Island mainly to Auckland, Wellington and Hamilton, on the South Island to Christchurch (Canterbury), Dunedin (Otago) and the climatically favoured and scenically attractive region round Nelson. The more remote parts of the country in the east and west of the North Island and the west and south of the South Island were less attractive in terms of climate and availability of jobs, and the northward movement of population began at the end of the 1870s. The South Island, which had largely been spared by the Maori wars and had prospered thanks to the discovery of gold in Otago and on the west coast, declined in economic importance with the run-down of the gold boom. In 1951 68% of the population of New Zealand lived on the North Island; in 1991 the proportion had increased still further to 74%.

The settlement of New Zealand by Europeans (mainly Britons) in the 19th century was held up by continuing conflict with the Maoris. It was only after the end of the Maori Wars and the discovery of gold that a considerable growth in the white population began. Thereafter immigration was promoted by the government, and by 1880 the country had a population of 500,000. The million mark was passed in 1908, after the end of the economic depression of the late 19th century following the collapse of the price of agricultural produce on the world market. After the Second World War the population increased rapidly as a result of immigration and the "baby boom", reaching its second million in 1952 and its third twenty years later. Since the late 1970s population growth has slowed down markedly. This was not solely the result of a stricter immigration policy which does not allow entry to everyone who wants to make a fresh start in New Zealand. The country's economic difficulties, particularly after Britain joined the European Community (January 1st 1973), and the necessary reorientation of the economy led many skilled workers to leave New Zealand.

Population development; immigration

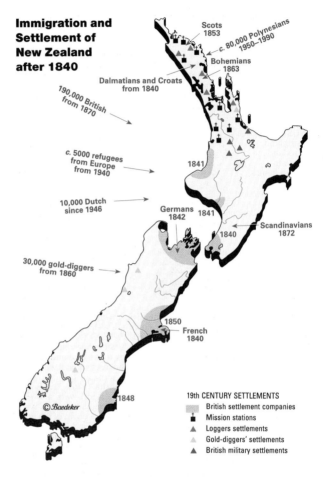

Immigration and Settlement of New Zealand after 1840

Scots 1853

c. 80,000 Polynesians 1950–1990

Bohemians 1863

Dalmatians and Croats from 1840

190,000 British from 1870

c. 5000 refugees from Europe from 1940

10,000 Dutch since 1946

Germans 1842   1841

1841

Scandinavians 1872

1840

30,000 gold-diggers from 1860

1850
French 1840

1848

19th CENTURY SETTLEMENTS

British settlement companies

▮ Mission stations

▲ Loggers settlements

△ Gold-diggers' settlements

▲ British military settlements

© Baedeker

Age pyramid

Some 16% of the country's inhabitants were not born in New Zealand, and the large numbers of young immigrants who have come to New Zealand in recent decades have had a marked effect on the population structure. The age pyramid is more regular than in some European countries, though the base of the pyramid (children and young people up to the age of 15) is shrinking in New Zealand too. In 1981 the average age of the population was 28, in 1986 it was 30 and in 1991 31. In 1991 senior citizens (men and women over 60) made up just under 16% of the population.

Immigration

The immigration system has recently changed. The former selective procedure favouring certain trades and professions ("occupational priority") has given place to a complicated points system divided into various categories, in which age, education and training, work experience, capital and readiness to invest are all taken into account.

Just under four-fifths of New Zealand's inhabitants are of European origin. They or their ancestors are mostly British. An eighth of the population claims either pure or mixed Maori blood: that is, they are descendants of the indigenous inhabitants of New Zealand who moved into the country from the islands of the East Pacific centuries before the discovery of New Zealand by Europeans (see pp. 44 ff.). Some 4% of the total population are so-called Pacific Island Polynesians, who came to New Zealand mainly from the tropical Cook Islands and from the islands of Niue, Samoa, Tokelau and Tonga. Most of them live in the Auckland region.

Europeans and Maoris

The population of European origin differ in age structure from the Maoris and Polynesian islanders. Up to the age of 25 the Maoris and Polynesians feature more prominently; in the age group; from 25 to 34 they are about level with the Europeans; but above 34 the proportion of Europeans increases sharply. In the 1991 Census 10.5% of the working population described themselves as unemployed; among Europeans the overall unemployment rate was 8.5% and for young people up to 19 was 23.6%, but for Maoris and Polynesian islanders the rates were respectively over 20% and no less than 42%.

Around the mid 19th century, after the Maoris had been decimated by tribal wars, wars with the British settlers and European diseases and were reduced to a rootless and aimless existence, it was believed that they faced extinction. A German traveller who published a detailed description of New Zealand in 1863, Ferdinand von Hofstetter, expressed great concern about the decline of the Maori population (by around 20% within 15 years). In 1858 there were no more than 56,000 Maoris. Von Hofstetter was convinced that by about 2000 they would have died out altogether. He also estimated that the European population of New Zealand, which was about 84,000 in 1860, would be half a million in the year 2000. In both cases he was far out. As a result of government measures to protect and integrate the Maoris, combined with the influence of leading Maori figures, the Maoris began to grow in numbers and to become conscious of their cultural independence.

There are small minorities of Indians and Chinese, whose ancestors came to New Zealand at the time of the gold rush. In the 19th century numbers of Dalmatians came to Northland to dig for kauri gum; their descendants specialised in growing wine and citrus fruits. In the 19th century, too, a large group of German immigrants settled in Christchurch, and Ferdinand von Hofstetter reported encountering fair-haired German children and their parents in the Nelson area.

Ethnic minorities

In the last Census just under a quarter of the population declared themselves as of no religion; 22% were Anglicans, 16% Presbyterians, 15% Catholics, 4% Methodists and 2% Baptists; while the remaining 17% of the population belonged to a great variety of other religious groups.

Religion

The Maoris

The Maoris, New Zealand's indigenous Polynesian population, are much smaller in number than the white Europeans. Only an eighth of the population describe themselves as Maoris, and the percentage of Maoris of pure blood is much smaller still. In spite of their adaptation to the way of life of the European immigrants the Maoris have preserved many of their traditions.

General

The word *maori* means "usual" or "common" and was originally an adjective which the early white settlers used to distinguish the native

The Maoris

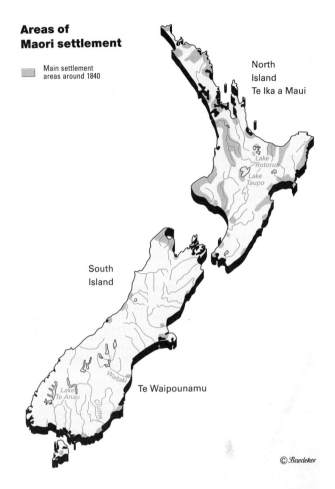

Areas of Maori settlement

Main settlement areas around 1840

North Island
Te Ika a Maui

Lake Rotorua

Lake Taupo

South Island

Te Waipounamu

Lake Te Anau

Waitaki

Clutha

© *Baedeker*

population, who then took over the term to refer to themselves. Before the coming of the Europeans the Maoris had no general name for their race: the largest unit they recognised was the tribe (*iwi*).

Social organisation

At the time of the European settlement of New Zealand there were between 100,000 and 120,000 Maoris, most of them on the North Island, which they called Aotearoa, the "land of the long white cloud". Only about 5% of them were on the South Island, with its less attractive climate.

The largest social unit, the tribe (*iwi*), was divided into a number of *hapus*, clans consisting of some 500 people belonging to various related families. The *hapu* was headed by a chief known as the *ariki*, who derived his legitimacy from the *mana* (see below) of his ancestors – though he could lose his right to rule if he fell short in some way. Important decisions were taken not by the chief alone but by a meeting held on the *marae*, the central square of the village, in front of the

32

meeting-house. The head of each family had the right to speak, but the first and the last word were with the chief, who summed up at the end of the meeting the opinions that had been expressed.

There were trading connections between the various tribes; the goods exchanged were mainly foodstuffs, but also craft products and the semi-precious greenstones. From time to time there were armed conflicts between the tribes about rights to land or about *mana*. Usually, however, these conflicts involved only a few hundred men, and casualties were few in number. This changed with the arrival of the first Europeans, from whom the Maoris obtained arms and ammunition which made the tribal wars fiercer and bloodier (see History).

Settlements

The early inhabitants of New Zealand had originally lived in unfortified settlements known as *kaingas*. It was only in the 14th century that they began to build fortified villages (*pas*). These consisted of a group of houses set round an open space (*marae*). Here too stood the richly decorated meeting-house (see Art and Culture, p. 66), a building or underground rooms for storing food, cooking huts (since meals might not be eaten in the dwelling houses) and men's houses in which unmarried men lived and in which tools and implements were made and restored.

Religion

The Maori religion was animist: that is, various natural phenomena were personified and regarded as gods or spirits. The principal Maori god was Tane, who had separated his parents, the sky and the earth (see Baedeker Special, p. 34). He created the first woman from red earth. He was god of the forest, of the great trees which were of such importance for the construction of canoes and houses, and also of craftsmen, particularly boat-builders and house-builders. When a tree was felled an offering had to be made to Tane to avoid incurring his

A Maori couple face the photographer.
The favourite Maori colours are black, white, red and green

In the Beginning was Darkness

The myths of the Maoris, passed on from generation to generation by word of mouth, tell of the creation of the world, of the gods and of their distant ancestors in Hawaiki, their legendary original homeland. Other sagas speak of the Maoris' ancestors and their voyage in the great tribal canoes over the ocean to Aotearoa (the Maori name for the North Island of New Zealand).

Similar myths are found throughout the Polynesian cultural area. They are related in Tahiti in very much the same terms as in New Zealand.

In the beginning, for an inconceivably long time, there was darkness. "Mother" Earth and "Father" Sky lay so closely together that their children, the gods who inhabited nature, never saw light. Discontented, they resolved to separate their parents. After unsuccessful attempts by his brothers this was achieved by Tane, god of the forests. He thrust himself with all his strength between his father and mother and heaved up the sky with his feet. Then the light of the sun and moon, the half-light of daybreak and the light of full day, now shone down on the earth; but blood from the wounds of the parents who were thus torn apart tinged the sunset and the earth with red (a sacred colour to the Maoris).

Tawhiri, the god of storms, the only member of the family who had been against the plan to separate their parents, sent down hurricanes to the earth which was now flooded with light, devastating Tane's forests and creating such a tumult in the sea that even the sea god Tangaroa sought refuge from his raging brother in the depths of the ocean.

The love between Mother Earth and Father Sky survived their separation, and the sky poured down such floods of tears in the form of rain that they covered what had previously been dry land with water. Unable to bear the sight of their parents' grief, the gods turned their mother Earth gently round, whereupon her sorrow was relieved and her tears turned to dewdrops. The clouds which rose from the valleys into the sky were the answering sighs of Earth. When she was turned round Mother Earth had her youngest son Ruaumoko a suckling at her breast. Now covered by earth, he became the god of earthquakes and was given the fire of volcanoes to keep him warm.

The best known mythic figure of the Maoris is the demigod Maui, a prematurely born member of the family: a sly and tricky character who wheedled out of his blind ancestress a magic jawbone with which he could perform his tricks. Since the days were very short because the sun sank below the horizon immediately after rising, Maui conceived a plan to keep the sun above the horizon longer. With his brothers he made strong ropes from flax with a noose to catch the sun; then one night they set out with the rope and came to the steep abyss where the earth ended and the sun rose in the morning from its deep cave. When the sun rose slowly up the sky the brothers captured it with the noose, and Maui struck it with his magic jawbone until it became weak and covered with wounds, so that when it was released again it followed its course over the sky only very slowly and daylight over the earth lasted longer.

divine wrath. The offerings to the god were usually foodstuffs. Human sacrifices, common in Polynesian culture, were demanded only by the war god Tu, who was also entitled to the first enemy killed.

Communication with the gods was through a priest, known as *tohunga* (the master, or the elect) – a title which was also given to experienced craftsmen such as woodcarvers or tattooers. The priest was required to be of high descent, with a long series of ancestors. Certain religious functions were also performed by chiefs.

Karakias (sacred chants and magic formulae, whose exact performance was essential) played a part at sacrificial offerings, as prayers and invocations in various ritual acts.

Two central elements in the life of the Maoris were *mana* and *tapu*. *Mana*, which can best be translated as "prestige" or "honour", was a power and distinction which was granted to men by the gods and was transmitted to their descendants.

Mana

A man's *mana* could be increased by victories in battle, but could be lost by errors in celebrating ritual formulae or by offending against *tapu*. When enemy chiefs were defeated and enslaved they lost their *mana*.

To the Maoris *tapu* (in its English form "taboo") is a positive force which may not be interfered with in any way. The sacred utensils used by a priest were *tapu*, as were the persons of the priest himself and of the chief. *Tapu* could also apply at certain times to natural and environmental phenomena. There were "protected" times for newly cultivated kumara fields, for hunting fish and birds, for the harvest. Everyday objects, on the other hand, were *noa*, "profane" or "ordinary"; the terms could be applied, for example, to meals – or to women.

Tapu

If anyone offended against a *tapu*, this inevitably brought misfortune or even death.

The wooden sculptures and carved figures on and in the Maoris' meeting-houses and on the high prow and stern of their large war canoes represented not gods but the venerable ancestors, who as the founding fathers of the tribe or family had the power to transmit their *mana* to the tribe (*iwi*) or clan (*hapu*). The fame of their great deeds was kept alive in ceremonial speeches and songs. The meeting-house was the personification of the revered ancestors (see Art and Culture, p. 66).

Cult of ancestors

The first Maoris who came to New Zealand about A.D. 750, brought with them various useful plants, including the kumara (a kind of sweet potato), taro and yam, which formed their staple foods. They also ate fish and birds, as well as the flesh of the rare Maori rat. The protein content of their diet was low, and this may have been one of the causes of cannibalism; but, particularly in later times, enemies killed in war were also eaten in the hope of acquiring some of their qualities.

Food

The personal possessions of the Maoris included stores of food, spears and fruit-trees. Enemies captured and enslaved in war belonged to the chiefs. Within the tribe the *hapus* possessed areas of land, which they distributed between individual families.

Rights of property

In the 19th century the Maoris felt themselves to be strangers in their own country, but in the course of the 20th century they increasingly gained in self-confidence and demanded their rights, and since the 1970s there has been a regular renaissance of Maori culture. Many Maoris now regard their own traditions and culture with pride. Signs of this new feeling are, for example, the establishment of new assembly areas (*maraes*), the inculcation of Maori culture in kindergartens and

Renaissance of Maori culture

primary schools, and the greater use of the Maori language. Although most Maoris also have English as their mother tongue, the Maori language, which is closely related to other Polynesian tongues, is now taught in numbers of schools and educational establishments for adults, and there are also television and radio programmes in Maori.

Maori King Movement

The traditional values of Maori culture are incarnated in Te Arikinui Dame Te Atairangikaahu, who was crowned Maori queen in 1966 and has her residence in Ngaruawahia. She is the sixth supreme chief (the first female one) of the Waikato tribes, in direct descent from Potatau, the first Maori king. The Maori King Movement of 1858 was an attempt to unite the many Maori tribes in a single unit which could counter the superiority of the white men. The Maori queen's principal functions are representational.

Maoris in modern New Zealand society

Although the Maoris are much outnumbered by the white immigrants and there is a considerable gulf between the two cultures, the Maoris are by no means an oppressed minority in present-day New Zealand society. They are, however, markedly disadvantaged as compared with the white population. They have disproportionately large numbers of unemployed, and a high proportion of them depend on social assistance. One consequence of this is a high crime rate, the main cause of which is inadequacy of educational facilities. Descent and social values are still more important to many Maoris than success or possessions, and their culture has no interest in competitiveness.

Although the extended family and family relationships still play an important part in the life of the Maoris, the great majority of them now live in nuclear families. Externally their way of life is little different from that of New Zealand's white population of European descent.

Maori mythology and artistic skills now attract wide interest from New Zealanders as well as from visitors (see Art and Culture, p. 66).

Economy

General

When Britain joined the Common Market in 1973 New Zealand lost its traditionally important British market. Combined with the dependence of New Zealand's exports on world markets and the continuing rationalisation of the economy, this brought the country into deep crisis. The economy was also held back by strong state controls. In 1984 the government set about establishing a free market economy. State control of interest and exchange rates was ended, a value-added tax was introduced, state subsidies were much reduced and restrictions on imports were lifted. Many state-run enterprises were privatised, including postal services and telecommunications, the railways, banking and insurance, house-building and electricity corporations. As a result of these privatisations, cuts in social services and higher taxes inflation was brought down from over 15% to 1.4% (1993) and new state debt from 9% to 2%. Over the same period, however, unemployment rose from 3.4% to over 11%, for the privatised state enterprises shed many workers and many industrial and property companies went bankrupt. In the last few years, after a long period of recession, the economy has begun to grow again, but there seems little prospect of bringing down the high unemployment rate in the immediate future. The economic reforms were accompanied by sharp changes in structure. Industry accounted for an ever greater proportion of the gross domestic product, while the proportion contributed by agriculture fell steeply.

In addition to the loss of the British market, the lack of a strong domestic market and the high transport costs resulting from the country's geographical situation created considerable problems for the

Succulent kiwi fruits, now exported all over the world

country's economy. Nevertheless New Zealand has managed to develop its trade with the states bordering the Pacific (particularly Australia and Japan) and with the countries of the European Union. Since the mid seventies it has co-operated with Australia in the New Zealand–Australia Free Trade Agreement (NAFTA), and since 1990 there has been a common free trade zone, as a result of which trade with Australia has more than doubled. New Zealand's exports to the countries of Asia, too, have tripled. Against this, the proportion of exports to Europe fell from 49% in 1970 to 18% in 1991. New Zealand therefore welcomed the successful conclusion in December 1993 of the Uruguay round of the General Agreement on Tariffs and Trade (GATT) with its long overdue reduction of restrictions on trade.

Agriculture, Forestry, Fisheries

In 1991 9.5% of the working population were employed in agriculture, forestry and fisheries, which contributed 9% of the gross domestic product. 82,000 farm holdings, including 7500 large farms of over 400 hectares/1000 acres, worked a total of 17.8 million hectares (44 million acres) of land, only 3.6% of which consisted of arable land and permanent crops. More than half of the arable land (487,000 hectares/1,203,000 acres) was irrigated. In recent years low world prices for agricultural produce and import barriers have badly affected New Zealand agriculture, and sharp cuts in government subsidies and the cost to farmers of interest on loans have led to loss of income, reduced investment and the abandonment of some farms.

Current situation

Villages are rare in the New Zealand countryside: the typical pattern of occupation of the land is one of scattered farmsteads, mostly consisting only of the farmhouse and sheds for equipment and stores.

A good sheep-shearer can shear up to 300 sheep in a day. The breeds most commonly reared for their wool are Romney (about 40%), Coopworth (about 20%), Petendale (about 10%), Corriedale (about 5%) and Merino (about 5%)

Stalls for the stock are not necessary, since thanks to the mild climate, with only rare night frosts, the animals can stay outdoors throughout the year.

Sheep-farming

The old belief that New Zealand has twenty times more sheep than people is no longer true. As a result of a catastrophic drought in 1988 and, more seriously still, the fall in wool prices since 1991, the number of sheep has fallen sharply. Between 1988 and 1990 it fell from 64.6 million to 57.8 million, and it is now only 52.6 million. New Zealand is the world's second largest exporter of wool (after Australia). In 1988 wool exports brought in almost 1.8 billion NZ dollars; in 1990, with almost the same level of production, the figure fell to only 963 million dollars.

The main sheep-farming areas are in the uplands of the North Island and the south and east of the South Island. The average size of flock is about 1800, the sheep being shorn three times in a period of two years. The predominant breed in the moist New Zealand climate is the Romney sheep, which has relatively coarse wool but yields meat of excellent quality. New Zealand produces 390,000 tons of lamb and 150,000 tons of mutton annually.

Cattle-rearing, dairying

In 1990 New Zealand had 8 million beef cattle and dairy cows and produced some 524,000 tons of beef and 13,000 tons of veal. The predominant breed is Aberdeen Angus, which has been reared in New Zealand for more than a hundred years and is prized for its robustness and the quality of its meat.

Cattle were originally reared in New Zealand alongside sheep to firm up the newly cleared pastureland and crop the remaining shrubs and bushes. They are now found all over New Zealand, frequently still along with sheep. For beef cattle steep slopes in the less good situations are preferred. In such areas the hillsides are patterned with the paths trodden out by the cattle, running parallel along the contours. Dairy cows are found only in good situations where the pasture can be intensively grazed. Dairy farming involves high investments in money and time (for milking) and requires good accessibility for refrigerated transport. New Zealand's climate, high rainfall and long hours of sunshine give its dairy farmers an advantage over their European competitors.

Travelling about New Zealand, visitors will be struck by the number of enclosures with herds of grazing deer. The red deer which were brought to New Zealand for sporting purposes soon became an ecologically disturbing element in the country's forests. Accordingly, particularly in nature reserves, the large herds of deer were hunted down, captured alive and transferred to game farms for rearing. The first licences for game farms were issued in 1970, and there are now more than 4000 throughout the country, rearing mainly red deer, fallow deer and wapiti. More than 3000 tons of meat from these farms are now exported annually.

Game farms

In recent years there has been been a substantial development of goat-rearing as a result of the high demand for goats' wool (mohair, cashmere), milk and meat. Goats are also prized for their grazing habits, since they eat wild herbs and bushes which sheep and cattle disdain.

Goats

High quality pastureland is particularly suitable for the rearing of horses, and there are a number of stud farms in New Zealand, notably to the south of Auckland. Racehorses are much esteemed in New Zealand, where almost every town has a racecourse, but horses are also very profitably exported to Australia and the United States.

Horse-breeding

Compared with New Zealand's endless expanses of pastureland its areas of arable land are very modest; but its intensively cultivated special crops (fruit, particularly kiwi fruits, grapes and hops) in relatively small, climatically favoured areas are of great economic importance.

Arable farming, fruit-growing, horticulture

The kiwi fruit (see Sights from A to Z, Bay of Plenty), now grown throughout the world, was developed in New Zealand in the early 20th century from the Chinese gooseberry. It is a climbing plant which is grown on a trellis and requires protection from the wind, to which it is highly sensitive. It flourishes particularly in the Bay of Plenty on the east side of the North Island, where plantations of kiwi fruit pattern the landscape.

Kiwi fruit

New Zealand apples and pears are widely exported. The main growing areas are in the Bay of Plenty round Tauranga and Hawke's Bay, round Napier and Hastings on the east side of the North Island and the sunny country round Nelson in the north of the South Island. It is planned to double apple production within the next few years to 35–40 million cases. Apart from the export trade in New Zealand fruit, fresh fruit is used in high-tech processing factories to produce juices, preserves and jam. This applies particularly to European types of berry grown in New Zealand, in particular the new boysenberry. Stone fruits (particularly apricots) are grown in the south of the South Island (Otago region) and mainly exported to Australia. Citrus fruits have traditionally been grown in the subtropical Northland round Kerikeri.

Other kinds of fruit

New Zealand is now in process of conquering the Asian market (including Singapore and Japan) with new exotic fruits and crosses. The United States and Australia also offer good markets for new types of fruit such as persimmons, avocados, nashis, passion fruit and tamarillos.

Wine

Wine-growing began in New Zealand in 1819 at Kerikeri, where the early settlers from Europe brought vines with them. Pests and restrictive laws on alcohol at first hindered any extension of the wine-growing area, but New Zealand now has over 5800 hectares/14,300 acres of vineyards. The main wine-producing areas are round Blenheim on the South Island and on the east side of the North Island, particularly round Gisborne/Poverty Bay, Hastings/Hawke's Bay and Henderson (Northland).

Cereals

Cereals (mainly barley and wheat) are grown mainly on the great plains round Canterbury on the South Island.

Forestry

Fully a quarter of New Zealand's area is still covered by forest. The old kauri forests in Northland were stripped by the early European loggers, leaving only a few surviving stands of majestic kauri trees, which are now strictly protected (see Sights from A to Z, Waipoua Kauri Forest). The modern forestry industry depends on non-native species of tree brought in by European settlers. Imported conifers, such as the Californian pine (*Pinus radiata*), which are ready for felling in 25–30 years, do very well in New Zealand. Reafforestation has proceeded without difficulty.

Of the total forested area (about 7.3 million hectares/18 million acres) roughly three-quarters is worked for timber, and two-thirds of this is state-owned, with the rest in private ownership. 1.6 million hectares/4 million acres are in forest reserves in which timber may not be worked and 0.4 million hectares/1 million acres are in inaccessible areas where timber-working would be uneconomic. Half the timber felled is exported, mainly to Australia and Japan, in the form of logs, sawn timber, shavings and wood pulp for papermaking. Timber is New Zealand's third most important export, after meat and dairy products but ahead even of wool.

Fisheries

In 1978 New Zealand introduced a protected fishing and economic zone extending for 200 miles round the islands. Its coastal waters have largely been fished to exhaustion, and the future expectations of the fishing and fish-processing industries are mainly directed towards deep sea fishing. Oyster and mussel farms have been successfully developed. There are valuable catches to be made of orange roughy, squid, snapper, tuna and crayfish. Fish exports worth around 500 million NZ dollars go to Japan, Australia and the United States.

Industry, Mining and Energy

The secondary sector of the economy, which includes energy and water supply and the processing and construction industries, employs 22% of the working population and contributes 27% of the gross domestic product. By far the major employers of labour are the processing industries.

Industry

New Zealand's industry covers a wide spectrum, from heavy industry and mechanical engineering, structural and civil engineering, by way of woodworking, papermaking, textiles and leather goods, to the foodstuff industries. Altogether there are almost 20,000 firms in the

Energy from the earth: the hot underground water of the Wairakei thermal field is harnessed to provide electric power

processing industries, most of them small firms with no more than five employees. Over the last twenty years the number of workers employed in the processing industries has fallen by 40,000 to 260,000, mainly as a result of increasing automation.

The lifting of restrictions on imports threatens the existence of smaller firms in particular.

The objective of New Zealand's energy policy is to reduce the country's dependence on imported sources of energy, mainly oil. Natural gas produced in New Zealand is now making a considerable contribution to its energy needs. Liquid gas and compressed gas are widely available as fuel.

Electricity, energy

The country's hydro-electric and geothermal power potential is being exploited with the aid of elaborate and advanced technical installations; but the changes to the unspoiled natural landscape resulting from the construction of large reservoirs and water channels have attracted opposition from the very active organisations concerned with the protection of nature and the environment. The North Island, which consumes more electricity than the thinly populated South Island, is dependent for its energy supply on thermal and hydro-electric power stations (including a number on the Waikato River) and on geothermal stations (in the volcanic zone, between Taupo and Rotorua). The geothermal power stations work on superheated steam from boreholes in the volcanic region. There are large geothermal stations at Wairakei (1958) on the Waikato River and Ohaaki (1987). There are no nuclear power stations in New Zealand. The use of local coal supplies in the production of energy and the manufacture of steel is to be intensified.

In order to meet the higher energy needs of the North Island a 30km/18½ mile long deep sea cable runs across the Cook Strait, so that surplus power produced by hydro-electric stations on the South Island can be conveyed to the power-hungry north.

Mining

New Zealand was long regarded as a country lacking in raw materials. Nowadays, however, it produces substantial quantities of coal, oil, natural gas, iron, gold, sands and earths. Its coal reserves are estimated at 8.5 billion tons, mainly on the South Island. Oil is extracted in the McKee Field off the North Island and at Ngaere/Taranaki, natural gas at Kupuni/Taranaki and in the Maui Field (50km/30 miles offshore at Taranaki). It is used for the production of energy, in the petro-chemical industry and in the manufacture of synthetic fuel. Iron ore is found in the form of black iron sand in extensive areas on the west coast of both islands, with existing reserves amounting to 550 million tons. It is processed and smelted at Glenbrook, to the south of Auckland.

Gold

Gold played an important part in the opening up and development of New Zealand. It was found in Otago in 1861 and in Westland three years later, when tens of thousands of prospectors flocked to New Zealand. Current output is about 2.4 metric tons a year; it comes mainly from the Coromandel Peninsula on the North Island and Otago and Westland on the South Island.

Pounamu

Pounamu (the Maori name for greenstone, nephrite or jade) occurs in river beds in Westland (South Island). In the traditional Maori culture, which knew no metals, it was an important substance for trade or for the manufacture of weapons (e.g. axe blades) and jewellery. It is now mainly used, particularly at Hokitika, in the manufacture of ornaments and jewellery decorated with old Maori motifs.

Construction industry

A very common type of house in New Zealand, even in the suburbs of towns, is the detached family house with its own garden. Most houses are timber-built and two-storied. Some 20,000 dwellings a year are built, in addition to offices and industrial buildings with a total floor area of several hundred thousand sq. metres (several million sq. feet). In view of the high earthquake risk in New Zealand appropriate types of structure are mandatory.

Commerce and Services

Services sector

The services sector accounts for 65% of the gross domestic product and provides employment for just under 60% of the working population. 28% of workers in the services sector are employed in communal, social and private service industries, 21% in commerce and the hotel industry, 10% in banking, insurance and real estate and 6% in transport and communications.

Foreign trade

The total value of New Zealand's foreign trade in 1990 was just under 19 billion US dollars, an increase of 7.3% over the previous year (imports +8%, exports +6.5%), with an import surplus of 54 million US dollars.

The terms of trade (the change in export prices in relation to the change in import prices) in 1990 was up 14 points on the base year, 1980. This means that for the yield from a constant mass of exports more goods could be imported and paid for.

Tourism

New Zealand is becoming an increasingly popular holiday destination, with the total number of visitors rising from 487,000 in the tourist year 1983/1984 to 1,213,000 in 1993/1994. In 1995/1996 there were around 1 million visitors, bringing in an income of over £1 billion. There is now an ambitious plan to raise the income from tourism to treble that amount by the end of the millennium. The number employed in the tourist industry, at present 120,000, is to be doubled.

Income from tourism makes a very welcome contribution to the gross domestic product of over 5%. This is more than half the proportion contributed by agriculture.

Increasing numbers of New Zealanders are concerned about this invasion of the country by a flood of holidaymakers. The apprehensions that have been expressed about damage to New Zealand's largely unspoiled natural environment are not without foundation. Demands are already being put forward that severe restrictions should be imposed on access to particularly precious nature reserves or that visitor quotas should be laid down. But thought is also being given to the possibility of reconciling the needs of tourism with the protection of the environment. An exemplary attempt has been made in Milford Sound, one of New Zealand's tourist high spots, to channel the streams of visitors in such a way as to safeguard the environment. Careful planning and good management are essential if chaos and devastation are to be avoided.

Criticisms of the tourist trade

Transport

New Zealand has a total of some 93,000km/57,800 miles of roads, of which around 52,000km/32,300 miles are surfaced. 11,500km/7150 miles are classified as national highways, highways and main roads; there are short stretches of motorway round the cities.

Roads

New Zealand Rail runs a network of 4266km/2650 miles (1067km/663 miles of which are narrow gauge) linking all the country's major centres. Only 250km/155 miles are electrified. In their early days the railways made a major contribution to the opening up of New Zealand and to the development of its export trade. Imposing old station buildings bear witness to the former importance of New Zealand's railways. The railway system is not remarkable for its speed: express trains average about 70km/43 miles an hour.

Railways

New Zealand Rail is responsible also for the ferry service between the North and South Islands. Three large ferries carry trains, cars and passengers over the Cook Strait from Wellington to Picton and vice versa.

Shipping

Before the arrival of the Europeans New Zealand's numerous rivers provided means of communication with the roadless interior, and the canoes of the Maoris were soon followed by the river steamers of the Europeans, for example on the Whanganui River.

Because of its situation in the middle of the Pacific, its dependence on overseas commerce and the great distances to its export markets, New Zealand depends largely on sea transport. The growth of container traffic gave an impetus to the development of the ports of Auckland, Wellington, Lyttleton (Christchurch) and Port Chalmers (Dunedin). There are also special installations in regional ports for the loading of cement or the shipping of petro-chemical products (Port Taranaki). Coastal ships ply between the various New Zealand ports, carrying mainly cement, oil and natural gas.

In 1990 New Zealand's merchant fleet consisted of 127 ships with a total of 253,900 GRT, including five tankers. In 1990 the New Zealand ports handled 21.2 million tons of freight.

Transport

Air services

In relation to its population New Zealand has an unusually high passenger air traffic. The two most important international airports are Auckland and Christchurch, which are served by 24 international airlines. The airport at Wellington, the national capital, is the hub for domestic flights and services to and from Australia.

History

The Coming of the Maoris

In contrast to the settlement of Australia by the aborigines, who moved into the country 40,000 or 50,000 years ago over the then existing land bridges, the discovery and settlement of New Zealand are of much more recent date. The aborigines of Australia and the Maoris of New Zealand, two races of very different racial and geographical origins, probably never came into contact with one another. Maori means "usual" or "ordinary" and was originally a term applied by the early white settlers to the natives of the country, who then took it over and applied it to themselves. The Maoris called the white settlers Pakeha, which means "stranger". They had no name for themselves as a whole: there were only the names of the various tribes.

New Zealand was settled by the Maoris in the course of the Polynesian migration movements which began some 4000 years ago in the western Pacific area, travelled by way of Samoa, Fiji, Tonga, the Society Islands, the Marquesas and the Cook Islands and finally reached the remote islands of New Zealand at a date estimated by the latest research at around 2000 years ago. The Polynesian islanders were skilled seamen. Their long voyages in outrigger boats and catamarans were not merely involuntary extensions of fishing trips but planned colonisation enterprises.

For the former inhabitants of tropical islands the climate of New Zealand was unaccustomedly harsh. They lived as hunters and gatherers of berries, fern roots and birds, fishermen and hunters of seals. On the South Island they hunted the moa, a flightless bird resembling an ostrich standing up to 3m/10ft high, which soon died out as a result of changes in climate and vegetation and constant hunting. The inhabitants of Northland learned to cultivate the kumara or sweet potato, an import from South America, though it is not known how or when this reached New Zealand. The cultivation of this vegetable and the storage of the crop made possible the transition from the archaic culture of nomadic moa hunters and gatherers to the classic Maori culture of sedentary tribal groups living in unfortified or fortified villages. Modern critical research, reinforced by archaeological investigations, has established that there was only one early immigration movement, unaffected by later arrivals. From this archaic way of life there later developed the classic Maori culture, whose principal centre was in the warmer Northland region. From there tribal groups in fleets of canoes travelled along the coast or on rivers into the regions farther south, where they subjugated or exterminated the more "primitive" natives they encountered. The classic Maori culture is believed to have established itself throughout the main islands of New Zealand by about A.D. 1500. The older culture survived only in the Chatham Islands, far away to the east.

Archaic and classic Maori periods

Maori mythology presents a different picture of the settlement of New Zealand. It relates that around A.D. 925 a seafarer named Kupe, setting out from the legendary island of Hawaiki near Tahiti, became the first man to discover New Zealand, which he named Aotearoa, the "land of the long white cloud". There he had to fight a gigantic cuttlefish, after which he returned to Hawaiki. 225 years later a chief named Toi sailed from Hawaiki to New Zealand and established the first Maori settlement there. The full occupation of the country is ascribed to a large wave of immigrants from Hawaiki at a later date. From there the

Mythology

islanders set out about 1350 in seven great tribal canoes – the origin of the various Maori tribes.

Discovery and Occupation by Europeans

1642:
Abel Tasman
sights the coast
of New Zealand

In December 1642 the Dutch seafarer Abel Tasman, sailing from Batavia (Indonesia), became the first European to sight the coast of New Zealand. The Maoris suddenly attacked the dinghy of his ships the "Zeehan" and the "Heemskerck", killing a number of his men, and the Europeans responded with their cannon, after which Tasman left the scene of this encounter – which he named Murderers' Bay, now known as Golden Bay, at the northern tip of the South Island – without setting foot on New Zealand soil and sailed back to Batavia, skirting the west coast of the North Island. He named the new land Staten Land after the Dutch States General, taking it to be the west coast of a large unknown southern continent. Dutch scholars later gave the newly discovered South Pacific island world the name of Nieuw Zeeland after the Dutch province of Zeeland (Zealand).

Captain Cook

Following the radical changes in Europe after the Thirty Years' War, the Dutch provinces' conflict with Spain and the war with Britain, the Dutch withdrew from the South Pacific and the initiative passed to Britain and France. Decisive events in clearing up the mystery of the legendary southern continent were the three voyages of Captain Cook (see Famous People) in 1768–71, 1771–73 and 1776–79, on each of which he called in at New Zealand.

The official purpose of Cook's first voyage in the "Endeavour" was to observe and plot the transit of Venus from Tahiti; but he also had a secret commission to sail on from Tahiti to look for the southern continent. Following Abel Tasman's record of his trip, he followed a south-westerly course from Tahiti and on October 6th 1769 sighted the

October 8th 1769

east coast of the North Island of New Zealand. On October 8th he landed on the island near the site of present-day Gisborne. Soon afterwards he hoisted the British flag in Mercury Bay on the Coromandel Peninsula and took possession of the land in the name of King George III. He then spent several months sailing round the coasts of New Zealand, establishing that there were two main islands and giving

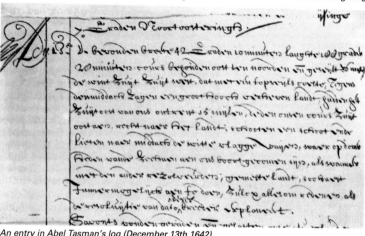

An entry in Abel Tasman's log (December 13th 1642)

Captain Cook frequently put into Ship Cove (Queen Charlotte Sound)

names to many bays and promontories. In 1770 he anchored in Queen Charlotte Sound. On his second voyage, with the "Resolution" and the "Adventure", Cook returned to New Zealand, accompanied this time by two German scientists, Johann Reinhold Forster and his son Georg. After spending some time in Dusky Sound in the Fiordland area (South Island) he put into Ship Cove in Charlotte Sound to refit.

On his first landing in New Zealand in 1769 Cook found the Maoris' way of life in its original unspoiled state. They were eager to acquire the objects offered by the Europeans by way of gift or exchange, principally iron nails, axes and tobacco. Alcohol they disliked. On Cook's second voyage (1772–73) he found the natives very ready to barter. They supplied his ships with fish, sweet potatoes and water in return for the much sought-after European goods.

Encounter with the Maoris

The French now followed in Cook's footsteps. In 1769–70 Jean-François de Surville landed at the north end of Doubtless Bay; then in 1772 Marion du Fresne landed in the Bay of Islands on the North Island and took possession of the territory, which he called France Australe, in the name of King Louis XV. He was unaware of the earlier visits by Cook and his countryman Surville. Relations with the natives were at first friendly but soon degenerated into conflict. The Maoris killed du Fresne and two dozen of his men; whereupon the remaining members of the crew burned down three villages and shot many of the inhabitants.

The French are less successful

The British government saw Australia, also discovered by Cook, as the ideal place for a penal colony, and in 1788 the First Fleet, under the command of Captain Arthur Phillip, arrived in Botany Bay with a consignment of convicts and their guards. Soon afterwards the town of Sydney and Britain's first colony in Australia, New South Wales, were

Changes in Maori life

47

founded. From there ships soon sailed to New Zealand: in 1791 the first whaler arrived, and in the following year seals were hunted for the first time in Dusky Sound. Other Europeans came to barter with the natives for flax and to plunder the abundance of timber in the forests.

Contact with the white men brought changes and problems for the Maoris. They acquired wheat and potatoes, pigs and horses, but also steel axes and above all firearms. The Maoris were particularly anxious to get guns: the tribes living in Northland near the trading post in the Bay of Islands were prepared to sell anything the Europeans wanted – even the dried heads of their enemies, elaborately decorated with tattoos – to get their hands on muskets. The possession of firearms gave the Northland tribes an enormous advantage in the endemic tribal wars over other tribes who had no direct contact with the white men and their weapons. Hordes of warriors equipped with firearms led by power-hungry chiefs like Te Rauparaha in 1819 were thus able to defeat, kill, eat or drive away other tribal groups without firearms on the North Island, and later also on the South Island. Particularly ruthless was Hongi Hika, who visited Britain in 1820 and was received by George IV. On his way home he stopped over in Australia and exchanged the gifts he had received in Britain for weapons, with which he began his predatory expeditions in 1821.

Europeans
and Maoris

In the early 19th century there were still relatively few Pakehas (whites), who established close relations with the Maori tribes, to their mutual advantage. In the course of a few decades, however, the port settlement of Kororareka in the Bay of Islands developed into an infamous haunt of whalers and traders which became known to seamen as the "hell-hole of the Pacific". Maoris were employed by the settlers to do the heavy work; and misunderstandings, maltreatment of Maoris and disregard of Maori customs and usages and the laws of *tapu* led on occasion to serious disturbances and riots.

Missionary Work and Colonisation

1814:
Samuel Marsden
founds the first
mission station

Missionary activity in New Zealand began with the establishment of a mission station in the Bay of Islands by Samuel Marsden (1758–1838) at Christmas 1814. In 1816 Thomas Kendall (see Famous People) founded the first school for Maori children. These Anglicans were soon followed by the Methodists, who built a mission in Whangaroa Harbour in 1823, and French Catholics. It was long, however, before the first conversions were achieved, since the Maoris were put off by competition and conflict between the different Christian denominations. It was only the increasing impotence of the tribal priests in the face of the diseases brought in by the whites and the apparent ability of the whites to disregard the rules of *tapu* without bringing down punishment by the gods that led to a slow increase in conversions. By the middle of the 19th century most Maoris had accepted Christianity in one form or another. Cannibalism had disappeared at an early stage.

British rule

In 1823, when the number of white men in the Bay of Islands had increased, the British government decreed that British subjects in New Zealand were under the jurisdiction of Sydney. But Sydney was more than 2000km/1240 miles away, and in Kororareka the law of the jungle, arbitrary justice and chaos continued to prevail. In 1827 Hongi Hika and his warriors attacked the Whangaroa mission station and destroyed it. Finally in 1833 James Busby arrived in the Bay of Islands, where there was now a white population of over 2000, as the official representative of British interests.

The increasing numbers of settlers were now demanding land to cultivate, and the Maoris sold them land which did not belong to them
personally but to the tribe in return for weapons and tobacco. The
inevitable consequence was bloody conflict when the settlers began to
cultivate the land which they had acquired in good faith. The white men
also disregarded either unknowingly or intentionally the laws of *tapu*
and took possession of Maori land illegally, provoking retaliation by
the Maoris. In 1834, during the occupation of Waimate Pa (Taranaki),
there were the first encounters between British troops and Maori
warriors. The conflict over land escalated after the establishment of the
New Zealand Colonisation Company in 1838. Its initiator, Edward Gibbon Wakefield, had already made a name for himself by his plans for
the colonisation of southern Australia. The company bought up land
on a large scale, mostly from individual Maoris without the consent of
the tribe as a whole. The settlers, to whom this land was sold on at high
prices, were then exposed to attack by the tribe. In order to bring order
into this chaos, and also to forestall possible French plans for annexa-
tion of the territory, Captain William Hobson (see Famous People) was
sent to New Zealand in July 1839 as representative of the Governor of
New South Wales. His mission was to protect both the Maoris and the
white settlers and, in agreement with the Maoris, to proclaim British
sovereignty in New Zealand.

Treaty of Waitangi; New Zealand a Crown Colony

On February 6th 1840 Hobson and some 50 Maori chiefs from Northland assembled in Waitangi signed the Treaty of Waitangi, a document
which marks the birth of the state of New Zealand. The chiefs acknow-
ledged the sovereignty of the British Crown and in return received
confirmation of all existing rights to property, both private and collective, an assurance that Maori land could be acquired only by the
Crown, and all the privileges of British citizenship.

Messengers carried the treaty to all Maori tribes, so that it finally
bore more than 500 signatures. Some chiefs, however, foresaw the
loss of the Maoris' political power and independence and would not
sign. There are still large numbers of Maoris who reject the treaty, and
on the adversary of the signing of the treaty there are still demonstrations calling for the return of their traditional rights at the historic
Treaty House in Waitangi where the treaty – the "Cheaty of Waitangi",
as it has been called – was signed. In 1975 the government established
a special agency, the Waitangi Tribunal, to consider Maori complaints
about breaches of the treaty.

In May 1840, on the basis of the treaty, Britain annexed the North Island
and assumed the right to explore the South Island and thus gain
possession of it too. In May 1841 New Zealand was declared a Crown
Colony, with Hobson as its first Governor. He moved the chief town of
the colony from the still troubled Bay of Islands to Auckland (founded
1840).

War with the Maoris

With the signing of the treaty of Waitangi it seemed, in spite of the
dissent of some chiefs, that all problems between Pakehas and Maoris
had been solved. The government established commissions to exam-
ine all disputed sales of land, and some land was returned to the tribes.
In practice, however, the government sold on – at considerable profit –
the land they had acquired to white settlers, who from 1840 onwards
were flocking to New Zealand in thousands, usually under arrangements made by the New Zealand Company.

"A New Zealand Expedition"

This drawing by Henry Williams, published in the Quarterly Papers of the Church Missionary Society in 1835, shows a fleet of Maori war canoes on one of the North Island's many rivers

Wellington, Wanganui and New Plymouth were now founded on the North Island, while French immigrants established a settlement at Akaroa on the Banks Peninsula, near present-day Christchurch. Although the Company's utopian settlement plans often turned out to be empty words, nevertheless they brought in more than 10,000 new settlers in 57 ships between 1839 and 1843.

In 1844 the Company was forced by shortage of funds to suspend its activities. The more land was acquired by the settlers, however, the clearer it became to the Maoris that they would soon be left with nothing. The colony's electoral law also put the Maoris at a disadvantage, since only personal owners of land had the vote; and as the Maoris' land had from time immemorial belonged to the tribe and not the individual they had no right to vote. Conflict was inevitable.

1843–47: Maori risings

In 1843 what came to be known as the "Wairau affray" took place in the Wairau Valley, to the south of Nelson. A party of white settlers led by Captain Arthur Wakefield, defying previous warnings, were passing through the Wairau valley on their way to survey a piece of land whose ownership was disputed when they encountered a force of Maori warriors of the Ngati Toa tribe. A bloody conflict developed – the only such encounter over land rights on the South Island – in which 21 settlers, including Wakefield, were killed.

There were also troubles in the north. In 1844 Chief Hone Heke several times cut down the British flagstaff in Kororareka/Russell, and in 1845 burnt down the whole settlement. In the following year George Grey, who had been appointed Governor in 1845, ordered British troops to bombard and capture Hone Heke's stronghold of Ruapeka-peka. In 1846 there were also attacks by Maori tribes in Hutt Valley, near Wellington in the south of the North Island; and in 1847 there were further Maori attacks, also repressed, at Wanganui in the south-west of the North Island. Thereafter the country remained peaceful until 1860.

Constitution Act

During this decade the beginnings of a government answerable to Parliament and a system of responsible regional administration began to emerge. The Constitution Act of 1852 reduced the powers of the Governor, as the settlers wished, and established six provinces (Auckland, New Plymouth, Wellington, Nelson, Canterbury and Otago) with their own governments.

The Maori King Movement and New Wars

The Maoris reacted to the increased scale of European settlement by withdrawing farther into the inaccessible interior of the country. In the area round the Waikato River in the centre of the North Island there came into being in the late 1850s a movement for the union of as many tribes as possible in order to counter the land hunger of the settlers. In 1857 this Maori-Kingitanga or Maori King Movement chose Chief Te Wherowhero to be King Potatau I. Although he was not recognised by all the Maori tribes, his Waikato tribes put up fierce resistance to government troops for many years.

The Maoris draw together

There were further risings in other parts of the country. In New Plymouth, on the northern slopes of Mount Taranaki, where the shortage of land was particularly acute, an under-chief sold land at Waitara against the will of the tribe in 1860: whereupon the Maoris, led by Chief Wiremu Kingi, attacked the settlers who set about working this new land. The government sent troops to the area, and the fighting at Waitara marked the start of what became known as the Land Wars. Although an armistice was signed in Taranaki in 1861 there was recurring guerrilla activity over the next twenty years.

War in Taranaki and Waikato

From Taranaki the conflict spread into the very centre of the North Island as far as the Waikato River. Government troops moved into the Waikato area and there were skirmishes at Bombay, Pukekohe and Pokeno. The supporters of the Maori King Movement were driven south. Attacks were launched from gunboats on Maori positions at Meremere and Rangiriri and the Maori king's capital at Ngaruawahia was taken. Finally, after holding out for three days at Orakau, 300 Maoris were defeated and put to flight by 2000 British troops. The troops pursued the fleeing Maoris only as far as the Punui River, to the south of Orakau. South of the river lay the King Country, as it is still called, which the government left in the hands of the surviving supporters of the Maori king – an area into which no white man dared venture until the conclusion of peace. The tribal lands of the rebels were confiscated. After the repression of the Waikato risings the rebellion flared up on the east coast. In a battle for the Maori stronghold of Gate Pa at Tauranga in 1864 government troops had heavy losses. A few weeks later, however, the Maoris suffered an annihilating defeat at Pa Te Ranga and their tribal territories were taken over by the state.

In the mid 1860s the character of Maori resistance changed: it was now motivated by religion. The Hauhau movement (or Pai Marire) – so called after its battle-cry – was a Maori revivalist movement based on the Old Testament. Like the Israelites in Egypt, the Maoris felt themselves oppressed and enslaved by the white men, whom they wanted to drive out of their country. The founder of the movement, Te Ua Haumene, claimed in 1862 to have had a vision at Taranaki of the Archangel Gabriel, who had enjoined him to propagate the new religion. Members of the Hauhau movement believed that their steadfast faith would protect them from enemy bullets and accordingly ran into battle with their right arm raised, screaming their war cry. By 1865 the sect had spread across the whole of the North Island from Taranaki to the east coast. The Hauhau prophet Kereopa and his followers recruited new believers among the east coast tribes which were loyal to the government and fought government troops at Ruatoria and Gisborne before being finally defeated.

Resistance on religious grounds

History

Ringatu

Another religious leader who came from the east coast was Te Kooti. Although he could claim a long line of ancestors he was not a chief and had no tattooing. He co-operated with the government in repressing the Hauhau movement, but in 1866 he fell under suspicion of collaborating with the enemy and was banished, along with 300 Hauhau supporters, without trial, to the remote Chatham Islands, where he founded the Ringatu sect. He saw himself as the Moses of the Maoris, with a mission to give them back their Promised Land. In 1868, after escaping from his place of exile, he and his followers killed 70 white men and Maoris loyal to the government in Poverty Bay. The troops who were sent after him never managed to catch him, and in 1872 he settled in King Country, where he lived under the protection of the Maori King Tawhiao until he was pardoned by the government in 1883.

Civil
disobedience

The Land Wars ended with a campaign of passive resistance centred on the village of Parihaka on Mount Taranaki (Mount Egmont), where from 1866 onwards two Maori prophets, Te Whiti and Tohu, called on their followers to resort to civil disobedience in their opposition to the whites and the government. Te Whiti became one of the leading figures in the Maori revival.

Defeat of
the Maoris

The white settlers and the government emerged from the Land Wars as victors, with the much desired land at their disposal, and the Maoris had been unable to unite. They had at any rate been granted four seats in Parliament; but it was only in the 20th century that they received partial monetary compensation for the injustices they had suffered during the Land Wars. In 1881 peace was officially concluded between the Maori king and the government; the rebels were amnestied and were allowed to leave the King Country.

The Gold Rush on the South Island

War on the
North Island,
prosperity on the
South Island

While war was raging on the North Island, cattle and sheep were able to spread ever farther over the great expanses of grazing land on the South Island. In 1847 the first cargoes of butter and cheese were shipped from the South Island to Sydney. But a means of gaining wealth much more rapidly than by the gradual development of agriculture was provided by the discovery of gold. After small finds at Milton in 1855 and in the Buller River in 1859 the real gold rush began in 1861, when Gabriel Read, a prospector from Tasmania who had gained experience in California and Australia, discovered rich deposits of gold in what became known as Gabriel's Gully at Lawrence, south-west of Dunedin, and announced the fact in the local newspaper. By this time the goldfields of California and Victoria (Australia) had been worked out, so that prospectors flocked from there, along with many newcomers, to Central Otago and had soon opened up gold workings at Clyde, Queenstown and Arrowtown. As a result Dunedin gained in wealth and importance; and in 1869 the University of Otago, New Zealand's first, was established in the town. After the gold in this area was exhausted prospectors and adventurers moved to the remote west coast. Hokitika now grew in size and became an important supply port; passages through the high Southern Alps were explored and provided with roads; and in 1866 a mail coach service began to operate between Christchurch and Hokitika.

With the end of the gold rush in the late 1860s the population moved northward — not to the newly established capital, Wellington, but to Auckland, which, encouraged by the peace with the Maoris, took over the role of the country's economic metropolis, a position held by Dunedin during the gold boom.

Separatist
movement

The wealth brought to the South Island by gold awoke a desire for political independence from the North Island, still involved in its wars

with the Maoris. As a concession to this feeling the capital was transferred in 1865 from Wellington to Auckland, at the south end of the
North Island. The General Assembly of the colony was firmly against
separation, and in 1876 the "Centralists" overrode the opposition of
the "Provincialists" and secured the abolition of the provincial governments. The central government had thus recovered the initiative in the
development of the country.

Reform; the Maoris' Existential Crisis

The final decades of the 19th century saw new developments in agriculture. The New Zealand economy gained a fresh source of revenue in
the export of frozen meat: in 1882 the refrigerator ship "Dunedin"
sailed from Port Chalmers (Dunedin) with the first cargo of frozen meat
for Britain. But New Zealand's export trade, concerned mainly with
agricultural produce, was badly hit by the collapse of prices on the
world market; and in addition the country was heavily in debt, having
taken out large loans in London to finance the development of its
infrastructure by public works in the 1870s. In the recession which set
in after the loss in value of agricultural exports the number of unemployed rose sharply. The government, which from 1891 was in the
hands of the Liberal Party, developed an exemplary social policy under
prime ministers Ballance and Seddon which made New Zealand a
model for the rest of the world. New land laws put limits on the
ownership of large estates, which were particularly common on the
South Island, and made it possible for agricultural workers to have land
of their own. Other social and economic measures provided for restrictions on hours of work (eight-hour day introduced in 1899), protection for children in employment, factory inspection, accident
insurance, health care and state pensions – though these provisions
applied only to members of trade unions.

1891–1912: the Liberal era

Electoral law had already been reformed in 1889; the "one man, one
vote" system was introduced in 1890; and in 1893, after repeated
petitions and demonstrations by feminists, women were given the
vote.

While the population as a whole rose steadily – reaching 815,853 in the
1901 Census – the number of Maoris fell alarmingly to around 40,000.
Feeling like strangers in their own country, the Maoris withdrew into
themselves or sought to eke out a living, in competition with white
workers, on the fringes of white society. The extent to which the Maoris
had given up was exemplified by the gift made to the government in
1887 by Chief Te Heuheu Tukino IV. Faced with the continuing occupation of land by Europeans, he handed over to the government the three
volcanic peaks of Tongariro, Ngauruhoe and Ruapehu, which were
sacred to the Maoris, asking that a reserve should be established for
their protection. This was the origin of Tongariro National Park, New
Zealand's first National Park.

The Maoris – strangers in their own country

A number of Maori revival movements sought to counter this trend.
Many of them had religious foundations and Messianic elements, such
as Hauhau, Ringatu, Wiremu Ratana's Ratana Church and the prophets
of non-violent resistance, Te Whiti and Tohu. The most influential was
the charismatic Wiremu Ratana, who had gained an enormous following with his spiritual healings and also carried considerable political
weight through the Ratana movement; for many years the four parliamentary seats assigned to the Maoris were held by followers of his.

Maori revival movements

A movement for Maori unification with a long tradition is Kingitanga,
the Maori King Movement, founded in 1858; it was, however, confined

Kingitanga

to tribes in the Waikato area. The king or queen has no constitutional, administrative or political functions. The importance of their role is in the social and cultural field and in preserving the ancient traditions of the Maoris. The present queen, like her predecessors before the Land Wars, has her residence in Ngaruawahia, at the confluence of the Waikato and Waipa Rivers. She is informally recognised by the government.

Kotahitanga

In the 1890s Kingitanga faced a competitor in Kotahitanga, the Maori Parliament Movement, which originated at Papawai, near Masterton in the south of the North Island. Its demand was for an independent parliament for the Maoris. Its objectives were given political expression by the Young Maori Party, which was founded in the early 1890s, mainly by students of Te Aute College, near Hastings, among them Apirana Ngati (1874–1850), Maui Wiremu Pomare (1876–1930) and Peter Buck (Te Rangi Horoa, c. 1877–1951). Apirana Ngati, the first Maori to take a university degree, became secretary of the Young Maori Party and for many years represented Maori interests in Parliament. Maui Pomare and the famous anthropologist Peter Buck, who ended his career as director of the Honolulu Museum, were also members of Parliament. James Carroll (1853–1926), the son of a chief's daughter and a white farmer in Wairoa, a member of Parliament who became a minister and then prime minister, sought to promote Mauritanga, the sense of Maori cultural identity. For all these representatives of Maoritanga the only chance of Maori survival lay in assimilation. Thanks to the government's measures for promoting Maori identity the Maoris were in process of recovering lost ground when the influenza epidemic of 1918 hit them disproportionately hard – an event interpreted by some Maoris as the vengeance of the gods they had once worshipped.

New Zealand in the 20th Century

1907:
New Zealand
becomes
a Dominion

New Zealand did not join with the British colonies in Australia which formed the independent Commonwealth of Australia, but remained a Crown Colony until 1907, when it was given the status of a Dominion. In 1911 the population passed the million mark. The Liberal era ended in 1912, when William Ferguson Massey's Reform Party, whose main support was among the farmers, assumed power. His victory was an expression of the farmers' fears of the nationalisation of their land and the increasing strength of the workers' movement, which had demonstrated its power in the strikes of 1912 and 1913 and finally led to the foundation of the Labour Party in 1916. Caught between these two poles, the Liberal Party declined, and in the 1920s re-formed itself as the United Party.

First World War;
inter-war period

In the First World War New Zealand supported the British motherland, forming along with Australia the Australian and New Zealand Army Corps (ANZAC), which fought in Egypt and at the Dardanelles against the Turks and in France and Belgium. At Gallipoli thousands of Australians and New Zealanders fell on April 25th 1915 – now commemorated annually as Anzac Day. New Zealand was represented at the Versailles peace conference and subsequently became a member of the League of Nations. In 1920 it became the mandatory power for the former German possession of Western Samoa.

The inter-war period saw a succession of economic crises and a major political change when the Labour Party came to power for the first time in 1935. Labour sought to overcome the depression by various job creation schemes, measures for the protection of agriculture and improvements in the state health service.

All this was thrown into the background by the Second World War. New Zealand again sent troops, who fought in Greece and Crete, North Africa and later in Italy. And this time the country was also exposed to a direct threat: after the fall of Singapore there was the possible danger of attack by Japan. Only the intervention of American forces in the South Pacific averted this danger. American help for New Zealand also signalled a shift in the country's foreign policy towards the South Pacific area and the United States: a change given expression in the conclusion of the ANZAC Pact between Australia and New Zealand in 1944 and above all in the ANZUS Pact of 1951, under which Australia, New Zealand and the United States formed a defence community.

Second World War; post-war period

In 1947 New Zealand achieved full independence, when Parliament adopted the Statute of Westminster of 1931 and New Zealand became a member of the British Commonwealth of Nations. In the 20th century Britain was still "home" for most British immigrants and their descendants, and those who could afford to do so sent their children to school in Britain. Only in recent decades has Britain moved nearer the margin of New Zealand's world. New Zealand now began to look more towards its South-East Asian, Australian and Pacific neighbours, at first politically in mutual assistance pacts such as SEATO and then economically. Thus New Zealand troops took part in both the Korean and Vietnam wars. After Britain joined the European Community in 1973 New Zealand was compelled to seek new markets for its products, which consisted mainly of agricultural produce. Successes in this field were the lifting of restrictions on trade with Australia in 1982 and the creation of a free trade zone which was destined to serve as a model for the South-East Asian region.

A sovereign New Zealand

In the 1980s New Zealand's attitude to the United States changed. The anti-nuclear policy of Lange's Labour government finally led to the termination of New Zealand's obligations to the United States under the ANZUS Pact, though the pact itself continues in force. New Zealand also sent troops to the Gulf War. The government remained consistent in its policy when France recently carried out tests of atomic weapons on the Mururoa atoll, recalling its ambassador from Paris.

The Maori revival movement achieved some successes in the course of the 20th century. A Royal Commission decided in 1918 that the confiscation of land after the Land Wars had been wrong; but only Crown land was returned to the tribes, land which had passed into private hands being excluded. Various compensation payments were also negotiated in the 1920s. The Waitangi Tribunal established in 1975 investigates Maori claims against the government based on the non-observance of rights and privileges guaranteed under the treaty of Waitangi. The Tribunal is also a point of contact on the present situation and prospects of the Maori tradition. A great step forward was the Maori Language Act of 1987, which established the equality of the Maori and English languages in the public life of New Zealand. The earlier phase of assimilation now gave place to a multicultural approach which gives stronger emphasis to the specific features of the different cultures and also does something to help with the difficult situation of the Pacific islanders in New Zealand.

Maoritanga in the 20th century

A good indication of the revival of Maori culture is the large number of new assembly-places (*maraes*) being laid out, even in towns, where Maoris can meet one another and also white neighbours and guests. Other signs of the revival are the flowering of the traditional arts of woodcarving and weaving and the great interest now shown in Maori mythology and dances. At least since the late sixties young people have also been involving themselves in the Maori movement. There have been demonstrations protesting against Europe-oriented teaching in schools and occupations of land and marches to Waitangi on the anniversary of the signing of the treaty of Waitangi. The Maoris do not want to be dependent on the welfare state and seek to achieve cultural and economic emancipation. This is bound to be difficult in view of the economic situation and the high unemployment rate, which is much higher for young Maoris than for young whites – a consequence of the poorer education and training of the Maoris.

In May 1995 the New Zealand prime minister, in the presence of the Maori Queen Aiairangikaahu, signed a document in which the government apologised for the expropriation of land by British troops in the 19th century. At the same time the union of Tainui Maoris was awarded 110 million US dollars and 170sq.km/66sq. miles of land by way of compensation. This agreement was confirmed by Queen Elizabeth II during a visit to Rotorua in November 1995.

Natural Catastrophes

Earthquakes

As a result of New Zealand's situation on the circum-Pacific "Ring of Fire" it suffers from time to time from severe earthquakes. In February 1931, for example, an earthquake in the town of Napier (North Island) cost 256 lives.

Hell explodes

The volcano of Ruapehu (in Maori "exploding hell") on the North Island becomes active from time to time. In September 1995 and June 1996 there were several violent eruptions which caused alarm and terror, mainly to skiers but also to the population of a wide area.

Ruapehu becomes active at irregular intervals. In 1945, for example, there were rumblings throughout the year; then on Christmas Eve in 1953 a violent eruption killed 151 people and a mighty avalanche of mud destroyed a railway bridge, and soon afterwards a train from Auckland to Wellington crashed.

Famous People

This section contains brief biographies of notable people who were
born, lived or worked in New Zealand or died there.

Peter Buck was born Te Rangi Hiroa in Urenui, to the north of New
Plymouth. After studying medicine at the University of Otago he
served in the First World War as a medical officer. After the war he was
able to devote himself to his real passion, ethnology, and became one
of the leading experts on the Polynesian island world. Later he became
director of the Honolulu Museum in Hawaii and professor of ethnology
at Yale University. One of the founders of the Young Maori Party, he
represented Maori interests in Parliament for many years. He died in
1951 in Honolulu; his ashes are buried near his birthplace at Okoki Pa
under a gravestone in the form of the prow of a canoe.

Sir Peter Buck
(c. 1877–1951)
New Zealand
ethnologist

James Cook, born in Marton, near
Middlesbrough, is famed for his three
circumnavigations of the globe, which
yielded ground-breaking new information about the Pacific and sub-Antarctic
regions. He joined the Royal Navy in
1755, sailed on a number of long voyages, was promoted to lieutenant and
finally was selected by Lord Hawke to
command the research ship "Endeavour". On his first voyage (1768–71), on
which he was accompanied by the as-
tronomer Charles Green, the scientist
Joseph Banks and Daniel Solander, a
Swedish botanist, he was sent to Tahiti
to observe the transit of Venus; but he
also had secret orders to sail on beyond
Tahiti to look for the legendary southern

James Cook
(1728–79)
English seafarer

continent. After discovering the Society Islands he followed Abel Tasman's route to New Zealand and on October 8th 1769 landed near the
site of present-day Gisborne in a bay which he called Poverty Bay
because he found neither water or food there. His first encounter with
the Maoris left several of them dead, but later he was able to approach
the natives in a friendly way and establish good relations with them. He
circumnavigated New Zealand and thus established its insular character, and discovered the strait, now named after him, between the North
and South Islands. He then reconnoitred the east coast of Australia and
in August 1770 passed through the southern part of the Torres Strait,
thus providing definitive proof of the separation between Australia and
New Guinea. On his second expedition (1772–75), on which he was
accompanied by the German scientist Johann Reinhold Forster and his
son Georg, Cook sailed eastwards round the globe and three times
reached south of the Antarctic Circle. He reconnoitred and named the
New Hebrides, Norfolk Island and New Caledonia. From New Zealand,
where he put in at Ship Cove in Queen Charlotte Sound to refit, he
continued eastward to Tierra del Fuego, rounded Cape Horn and at the
beginning of 1775 discovered South Georgia and the Falkland Islands.
After his return to England he was promoted to captain and became a
member of the Royal Society.

The objective of his third voyage (1778–79) was to look for the
North-West Passage between the Atlantic and the Pacific. Again

Famous People

making for Queen Charlotte Sound, he discovered the Sandwich Islands (Hawaii), landed on Alaska and sailed along its north coast as far as latitude 70° 44' north. During his second stay in the Sandwich Islands his relations with the natives were at first friendly, but later he came into conflict with them and was killed on February 14th 1779.

Cook gave names to many places in New Zealand, and a number of places are named after him, including Mount Cook, the highest peak in the Southern Alps, Mount Cook National Park and the Cook River to the south of the Fox Glacier in Westland.

Sir George Grey
(1812–98)
New Zealand
politician

George Edward Grey, born in Lisbon on April 14th 1812, was one of the most influential figures in 19th century New Zealand, holding a number of important government posts: he was governor from 1845 to 1853 and again from 1861 to 1868 and prime minister from 1877 to 1879. After being stationed in Ireland at an early stage in his career he became a political Liberal and was one of the founders of the Liberal Party in New Zealand.

After three years in Australia, where he became governor of South Australia, he succeeded Sir Charles Fitzroy as governor of New Zealand in 1840, at a time when some Maoris had taken up arms against the government. With more troops at his disposal than his predecessors had had, he was able to crush Hone Heke and Kawiti's rising in the Bay of Islands with the help of friendly Maori tribes. In 1853 he was sent to South Africa as governor of Cape Colony, but in 1861, on the outbreak of the land wars in Taranaki, was recalled to his old post and successfully repressed the rebellion.

Grey's great merit, however, was his ability to understand and promote Maori culture. He learned the Maori language, collected Maori mythology and tribal legends, previously handed down orally, and published them in London in 1854. Thanks to his unique knowledge of the Maoritanga and his intuitive understanding of the indigenous inhabitants of New Zealand he was much respected by the chiefs. He died in London on September 19th 1898.

Sir Edmund Hillary
(b. 1919)
New Zealand
climber

Edmund Hillary, born in Auckland on July 20th 1919, is perhaps the most widely known New Zealander. He became world-famous when, along with the Nepalese sherpa Tenzing Norgay (1914–86), he climbed Mount Everest, the world's highest mountain, on May 29th 1953, Queen Elizabeth II's coronation day: a feat for which he was knighted. In 1957, with a British expedition, he made the first journey to the South Pole with a motor vehicle. In 1960–61 and 1963–64 he returned to the Himalayas on research expeditions, and he now spends most of his time there, where he is active in social work with the native population. His books are very popular in New Zealand.

William Hamilton, a sheep-farmer in Mackenzie Country, was fascinated by engines, and actually built racing cars in his own workshop. His particular interest, however, was in the construction of a boat suitable for the wild rivers of the South Island with their numerous rapids. In 1953 he produced the fast and manoeuvrable jetboat, with a turbine propulsion system instead of a propeller, which is now found on rivers all over the world on which traditional types of boat cannot operate. Jetboat trips on the Shotover River, near Queenstown (see Sights from A to Z), are now a very popular attraction.

William Hamilton
(1899–1978)
Sheep-farmer
and constructor

Captain William Hobson was born in the Irish town of Waterford on September 25th 1792. In July 1839 he was sent out to New Zealand as lieutenant-governor on a delicate mission – to persuade the Maori chiefs to accept British sovereignty. His negotiations with them led to the signing of the treaty of Waitangi (February 6th 1840), under which, in return for accepting British sovereignty, they were guaranteed ownership rights to their land. Although his health was poor as a result of an attack of yellow fever while serving in the Caribbean, Hobson then set out on a tour of the whole of New Zealand to persuade other chiefs to sign the treaty. The treaty cleared the way for New Zealand to become a Crown Colony, of which Hobson was appointed the first governor. His decision to buy land on Waitemata Harbour led in 1841 to the transfer of the colony's capital from Russell to Auckland (named after the then First Lord of the Admiralty).

William Hobson
(1792–1842)
British
naval officer

During his period of office Hobson was caught between a variety of interests. The New Zealand Company's new settlers in Wellington pressed on him their desire to get land, which the Maoris understandably were unwilling to give up, since it had been guaranteed to them by treaty. Finally some of them took up arms, and Hobson had great difficulty in dealing with the rising, since the young colony had no troops and no money. Hobson therefore, on his own authority, issued Treasury bills. The Maori chiefs had little respect for a sick man without military support, and Hobson had no success in his dealings with them. The decision had already been taken in London to recall him when he died in Auckland on September 10th 1842.

Hone Heke Pokai, a nephew of the notorious Hongi Hika (see below), came from Pakaraka, near the Bay of Islands. He was one of the signatories of the treaty of Waitangi. Until 1841 his tribe, the Ngapuhi, had profited from the dues that all ships entering the port of Kororareka (Russell) had to pay; but this source of income was taken away when the government introduced customs duties in 1841. As a result the whalers, already hit by the falling price of whale oil, ceased to use the port. This loss of income, combined with mistrust of the government, led Hone Heke to cut down the flagstaff on the harbour, the symbol of British sovereignty, on four occasions in 1844 and 1845. On the last occasion he also attacked the white settlers, who fled to Auckland. All the buildings in the settlement except the churches and the mission station were burned down. This was the beginning of "Heke's War", which ended only in 1846 when he was defeated by a strong British force at Ruapekapeka. Hone Heke died in Kaikohe on August 6th 1850.

Hone Heke Pokai
(c. 1810–50)
Maori chief

Hongi Hika, chief of the Ngapuhi tribe, was born in Kaikohe about 1772. He had good contacts with the white settlers and was regarded as a model of the educability of the Maoris. As a result he was able to travel to Britain in 1820 along with the missionary Thomas Kendall and a Waikato chief. There he helped to compile a Maori dictionary and grammar. He was presented to George IV and was loaded with presents, which he sold in exchange for weapons on his way home. He had realised that the firearms of the whites were far superior to traditional Maori weapons and that with their help he would be able to make himself sole ruler over all Maoris. From his base at Kerikeri he and his heavily armed warriors carried out a series of raids, travelling in

Hongi Hika
(c. 1772–1828)
Maori chief

Hone Heke with his wife and some of his followers

canoes, which brought devastation and death to the Waikato area, round Rotorua, the Bay of Plenty, the East Cape and as far south as Wellington. He was severely wounded in battle in 1827 and died in Whangaroa on March 3rd 1828.

Friedensreich
Hundertwasser
(b. 1928)
Austrian/New
Zealand
artist

The Viennese artist Friedensreich Hundertwasser (real name Friedrich Stowasser) was born on December 15th 1928. He first achieved fame with his paintings and drawings, which were notable for their decorative curving lines and bold use of colour; then in the 1950s he turned to architecture, designing the famous Hundertwasser House in Vienna (1983–85).

Hundertwasser visited New Zealand for the first time in 1973, and in 1986 he became a New Zealand citizen. He settled at Kawakawa on the Bay of Islands and practises, here and elsewhere, an environment-friendly way of life, given expression also in his "green" guest house with its humus toilet.

Famous also is the new flag he designed for New Zealand, though it has not yet been officially recognised. It shows a green spiral on a white ground, representing an opening fern-leaf, which also resembles a favourite Maori type of ornament.

Thomas Kendall
(1778–1832)
British trader
and missionary

Thomas Kendall, a native of Lincolnshire, was originally a trader but, seized with religious zeal, entered the service of the (Anglican) Church Missionary Society. In 1813 he went to Australia, and in the following year, along with other missionaries, he explored the Bay of Islands in

New Zealand. Later he made a second visit along with Samuel Marsden. He is mainly remembered for the fact that he established the first school for Maoris in 1816. He believed that to carry out successful missionary work in New Zealand it was essential to know the language, the customs and the beliefs of the Maoris. With all his piety, Kendall was an unusual character for a missionary: he quarrelled with other missionaries, drank heavily with the whalers and traded in weapons. In 1820 he accompanied the powerful Maori chief Hongi Hika to London, where with Hongi Hika's help he compiled the first Maori grammar and a Maori dictionary; but he was probably also involved in helping Hongi Hika to obtain large quantities of firearms so that he could attack other tribes. In 1823 his way of life led to his dismissal by the Missionary Society. Thereafter he lived peaceably among the natives and then embarked on a new career as a timber merchant. He died in a shipwreck in August 1832.

Kendall was much criticised and disparaged, but it must be said that without his interest and activity many Maori traditions would have been lost.

Te Kooti, or Arikirangi Te Turuki, was born in Poverty Bay. Although not a chief, he was of noble lineage. He fought on the government side against the Hauhau movement, but was imprisoned on suspicion of collaboration with the enemy and was condemned, without trial, to be deported, along with 300 Hauhau supporters, to the Chatham Islands. It is supposed that jealously and resentment were the causes of his arrest. While in exile he founded the Ringatu sect – known as the "raised hand" because he made his raised arm glow in the dark by the application of phosphorus – which still has a few thousand adherents. Te Kooti saw himself as the Moses of the Maoris, whose mission it was to lead them into the Promised Land. In November 1868, after seizing a ship and escaping from the Chatham Islands, he and his followers attacked the settlement of Matawhero, near Gisborne, and killed 33 whites and 37 Maoris loyal to the government. In the fighting that followed he always contrived to escape capture, but many of his supporters were taken and executed. Te Kooti sought refuge in the inaccessible Urewera area and from there launched repeated guerrilla attacks. In 1872, after years of unsuccessful pursuit by government forces, he withdrew to King Country, where he lived under the protection of the Maori king until the official conclusion of peace. He was then pardoned, and in 1891 was granted land at Ohiwa in the Bay of Plenty by the government. He died at Te Karaka on April 17th 1893.

Te Kooti
(c. 1830–93)
Maori leader

Count von Lückner, famed as the "Sea Devil", was born in Dresden on June 9th 1881. During the First World War, in 1916–17, he broke through the British blockade with his auxiliary cruiser "Seeadler" and sank or captured many Allied ships in the Pacific until his own ship was wrecked in a tidal wave. He then sailed in a lifeboat to the Cook Islands and on to the Fiji Islands, where he was taken prisoner and interned on Motuihe Island, near Auckland. His daring flight in the camp commandant's yacht during a Christmas concert caused a sensation throughout New Zealand. He then seized a coastal ship and fled to the Kermadec Islands, where he was again arrested and then held under close guard on an island in Lyttleton Harbour, near Christchurch. He was again planning escape when the war ended and he was released. When von Lückner returned to New Zealand twenty years later he received a surprisingly friendly reception: it became known that during his exploits with the "Seeadler" he had shown great consideration for the safety of the crews of the ships he sank.

Count von Lückner died on April 13th 1966 in the Swedish town of Malmö.

Count Felix
von Lückner
(1881–1966)
German
naval officer

Famous People

Katherine
Mansfield
(1888–1923)
New Zealand
writer

Katherine Mansfield (real name Kathleen Mansfield Beauchamp), born in Wellington on October 14th 1888, the daughter of a banker, is the best known figure in New Zealand literature. As a girl she attended Queen's College in London but returned to New Zealand in 1907. In 1908 she persuaded her father to let her go back to London, where she led a liberated life in the literary and bohemian world. In 1909 she married one George Bowden, but left him a day after the wedding. In 1911 she entered on a liaison with the socialist literary critic John Middleton Murray, whom she finally married in 1918. In her wild life she took no thought for her health and finally fell ill with tuberculosis. She travelled to
France, Switzerland and Germany for treatment, and died while under treatment at Fontainebleau in France on January 9th 1923.

Katherine Mansfield's literary fame rests on her short stories, in which she showed herself a master of the form. Her first published work, "In a German Pension" (1911), was based on her experiences while taking the cure at Bad Wörishofen in Germany, but after 1915, when her much loved younger brother Leslie visited her in London and soon afterwards fell on the western front, she turned to her earlier days in New Zealand for her subjects. Among the best known of her later works are "Prelude", "At the Bay" and "The Garden Party".

Sir Apirana
Turupa Ngata
(c. 1874–1950)
Maori
parliamentarian

Apirana Turupa Ngata was born about 1874 at Te Araroa on the East Cape. In 1906 he took a degree in law – the first Maori to gain a university degree. One of the founders of the Young Maori Party and its Secretary-General, he became an influential member of Parliament, active in promoting the education and training of Maoris, their ownership of land and the better use of land. In 1928 he was appointed the first minister for Maori affairs. His lasting achievement was the revival of Maori traditional arts and crafts, and he was responsible for the establishment of a school of arts and crafts in Rotorua. He died in 1950.

Wiremu (Bill)
Ratana
(1870–1939)
Maori leader and
church founder

The Maori revival movement of Wiremu Ratana was one of the most successful in the history of the Maoris. For many years Ratana lived quietly as a farmer on the family land at Wanganui, but after a vision in 1918 he believed that he had been chosen as God's mouthpiece and enjoined to gather the Maori people and lead them to God. A series of healings, whether real or imagined, brought him an immense following, and not only of Maoris. He met opposition from the Maori King Movement and from the Anglican church, from which he broke away in 1925. The Ratana church was now established in close co-operation with the Methodists. Wiremu Ratana did not, however, confine himself to religion, but associated his movement with the political objectives of the Labour Party. For many years the four parliamentary seats reserved for Maoris were held by supporters of his. His death in 1939 attracted wide sympathy, and his funeral was attended by the prime minister, many members of Parliament and 3000 of his supporters. In 1991 his church still had 47,200 members.

Ernest Rutherford
(1871–1937)
New Zealand
physicist

Ernest Rutherford, born on August 30th 1871 at Spring Grove, near Nelson, was recognised as the leading experimental physicist of his day and the father of atomic physics. After taking his first degree at Canterbury College he worked with J. J. Thomson at Cambridge University; thereafter he taught in Montreal and later returned to Cambridge as director of the Cavendish Laboratory. His ground-breaking scientific achievements were the discovery of alpha and beta radiation in 1898 and gamma radiation in 1900 and the recognition of radioactivity as the result of the disintegration of elements. He formulated the disintegration theory and the Rutherford model of the atom. In 1919 he published evidence for the first artificial transmutation of matter. He had already received a Nobel Prize in 1908, but for chemistry, not for physics. In 1931 he was created Baron Rutherford of Nelson. He died in Cambridge on October 19th 1937 and was buried in Westminster Abbey.

Te Rauparaha, who bore the honorific name of Great Snake, was chief of the Ngati Toa tribe. In the 1820s, from his base on Kapiti Island, off the west coast of the North Island, he started a series of campaigns of annihilation directed against other Maori tribes, particularly in the south. One of the last great chiefs before the coming of the Europeans, he was described as shrewd, valiant, cruel, wily and incalculable. He soon came into bitter conflict with the New Zealand Company over their land purchases at Nelson and Wellington. In 1846 he was captured at Porirua, to the north of Wellington, and held in prison without trial for a year and a half. He died at Otaki on November 27th 1849.

Te Rauparaha
(c. 1768–1849)
Maori chief

Born in Hampstead on April 5th 1809, George Augustus Selwyn was the first Anglican bishop of New Zealand. He was educated at Eton and Cambridge, ordained as a priest in the Church of England in 1834 and appointed a missionary bishop in 1841. A year later he arrived in New Zealand to take up his duties as bishop. He had the advantage of having been a sportsman – he had rowed for Cambridge – and a good walker, for his flock were widely scattered on the two islands of New Zealand. In his travels he covered over 7,000 miles, usually in small ships or boats but often on foot. He also took an interest in politics; he was an adviser to the government and tried to act as a mediator in political conflicts. In 1867 he returned to England as bishop of Lichfield, and died there on April 11th 1878.

In New Zealand he is commemorated by the "Selwyn churches", built to the design of his architect in neo-Gothic style, usually of wood.

George Augustus
Selwyn
(1809–78)
Anglican bishop

Charles de Thierry, who is believed to have been born in the Netherlands in April 1793, the son of French émigrés, is one of the most colourful figures in New Zealand history. After serving in a British cavalry regiment he became a student at Cambridge, where he met the Missionary Thomas Kendall and the Maori chief Hongi Hika. He helped them to purchase weapons and was allegedly granted the whole Northland region by Kendall. After he had unsuccessfully tried to sell his supposed property to the Dutch government he set out for New Zealand to claim his land for himself. He travelled by way of the United States, where he stayed for eight years. He finally arrived in Hokianga, accompanied by a group of adventurers whom he had enlisted, and proclaimed himself "sovereign chief of New Zealand". He was unable to make good his claim, having quarrelled both with the Maoris and with the white settlers. His hopes that France would intervene on his behalf were frustrated when the treaty of Waitangi was signed in 1840. In 1845 the "monarch of Maoriland" went to Auckland, where he became a music teacher; then prospected unsuccessfully for gold in California; and finally set up as a businessman. He died in poverty in Auckland on July 8th 1864.

Baron Charles
de Thierry
(1793–1864)
French traveller
and businessman

Famous People

Alexander Turnbull
(1868–1918)
New Zealand businessman and collector

Alexander Turnbull was born in Wellington in 1868 but went to Britain to be educated. Thereafter he lived in London and later returned to Wellington as a businessman. His passion was books, and from the age of 17 he collected books systematically, spending lavishly. His particular interests were the Pacific area, the Antarctic and New Zealand, Captain Cook and his voyages, and English literature, particularly Milton. He also collected coins and Maori works of art, which he presented in 1916 to the Dominion Museum (now the National Museum in Wellington). He bequeathed his huge collection of books – 55,000 volumes, valuable manuscripts, pictures and maps – to the state. The Alexander Turnbull Library was opened to the public in 1820 and has since then been systematically added to, making it one of the most important research libraries in New Zealand.

The Wakefield brothers
(18th–19th c.)
British settlers

The Wakefield brothers all left their mark, in different ways, on the history of New Zealand.

The best known of them, and the one with the most lasting influence, was Edward Gibbon Wakefield (1796–1862). He drew up a plan for the settlement of the colony of South Australia, but it was only with the settlement of New Zealand that his theories and plans were put into effect. As one of the founders of the New Zealand Association, which later developed into the New Zealand Company, he was largely responsible for the influx of settlers into the new colony. Uncontrolled immigration led to conflicts with the Maoris, and many of the settlers were taken in by Wakefield's promises, which were not always reliable – for the Company was of profit mainly to its founders. Wakefield himself remained in London, pulling the strings of his plans, and it was only at a later stage that he went out to Wellington. He died there and is buried in the Bolton Street Memorial Park.

William Wakefield (1803–48) brought the first settlers to Wellington in 1839–40. He was the driving force in the foundation of the settlement, and is justly called the "father of Wellington".

Arthur Wakefield (1799–1843) also worked for the New Zealand Company. In the course of a journey of exploration in the north of the South Island he came into conflict with Te Rauparaha and his warriors over a disputed land deal and was killed, along with a party of settlers from Nelson, in the "Wairau affray". This encounter led to the Maori wars of the 1840s.

Daniel Wakefield (1798–1858) was a judge in Wellington.

Felix Wakefield (1807–75), the youngest of the brothers, became an engineer and a horticultural expert on the South Island.

Te Whiti o Rongomai
(c. 1830–1907)
Maori leader

Te Whiti o Rongomai was the leader of a passive resistance movement aimed at preventing further losses of Maori land. He established a model village in Parihaka, at the foot of Mount Taranaki, with new methods of agriculture. The Maoris sought to prevent further acquisitions of land by the settlers by setting up fences across roads, removing boundary posts and destroying crops by ploughing them in. In 1881, when Governor Gordon, who was well disposed to the Maoris, was out of the country, Te Whiti and his associate Tohu were arrested and imprisoned on the South Island, without trial, for almost two years and the village was destroyed.

Te Whiti was a gifted orator and one of the first modern Maori leaders, who gave his people courage and hope. He showed that new forms of resistance – civil disobedience, passive confrontation and solidarity – were effective, rather than resort to arms.

Art and Culture

Maori Culture

Maoritanga
(Maori culture)

Visitors can get some impression of the ancient traditions and art forms of the Maoris in the museums of New Zealand, which almost all have examples of fine war canoes and meeting-houses with carved decoration. But Maori culture does not consist solely of museum exhibits: visitors can have direct experience of the artistic skills, customs and traditions of the Maoris in special presentations of songs and dances; for the object of the Maoritanga movement initiated by a number of Maori leaders is to revive and to cherish the culture and history of the Maori people.

Maoris still make up a relatively high proportion of the population on the volcanic plateau in the centre of the North Island, round Rotorua and Taupo, and also in the Waikato area, Northland, East Cape, Taranaki and Wanganui; and in these areas too the evidence of traditional Maori culture – the place of assembly (*marae*), with its community house or meeting-house – is at its most visible. The oldest meeting-houses date from the 19th century, but in recent decades, with the increased self-awareness of the Maoritanga movement, many new houses in traditional style have been built all over the country. The places of assembly are still "special" places, which visitors too must respect. As in the past, they are the scene of welcoming ceremonies

Maori woodcarving is one of the supreme achievements of South Pacific art. The carvers were held in high regard and usually belonged to the upper social stratum

A famous Maori work of art:
the richly decorated store-room in the Rotowhio Pa

and dances; here traditional speeches and songs are recited, weddings, christenings and birthdays are celebrated and solemn ceremonies of mourning (*tangihanga*) are held.

The rock drawings which are among the oldest evidences of Maori culture are mainly to be found in South Canterbury and North Otago, on the South Island. Their exact dating has not been established, but they certainly go at least as far back as the period before the arrival of Europeans. Their meaning is also unknown. Usually drawn with charcoal or ochre, they show a variety of themes, including human figures and animals.

Rock drawings

The woodcarvings of the Maoris rank among the finest artistic achievements of the South Seas. The preferred material was the durable and yet easily workable wood of the totara tree. Most of the richly decorated meeting-houses and storehouses so much admired today are no more than 150 years old, and all the carving is done with modern iron tools. Before the coming of the white men the only implements available to the Maoris were stone and obsidian.

Woodcarving

Since the cult of ancestors played such an important part in Maori life, human figures are among the most important of the carvings. The proportions of the figures are distorted, particular emphasis being given to the head, the most *tapu* and therefore the most important part of the body. The feet were regarded as the least sacred parts, and accordingly are disproportionately small. The hands had usually only three fingers, like birds' claws, and the slanting eyes, inlaid with mother-of-pearl from paua shells, are also like birds' eyes. The figures are depicted in a warlike attitude, with a stone club in one hand, wide-open eyes and stuck-out tongue. The same attitudes are adopted

Figures

67

in the haka war dance: they are deliberately provocative gestures, designed to show contempt for the enemy and ward off evil spirits.

The carvings, whether in relief or in the round, were often painted red – a colour which had high symbolic value throughout Polynesia as the colour of the gods. The paint, which was made from red ochre and fish oil, brought out the grain of the wood and the delicacy of the carving. Unfortunately many old carvings, even those displayed in museums, have been covered with a thick coat of oil paint.

Canoes, paddles, musical instruments, everyday objects and the entrance gates of villages were all richly ornamented with carving. The decoration of the bone caskets in which the skeletons of great chiefs were preserved was particularly elaborate.

Objects made from semi-precious stones

Maori artists also showed great artistic skill in making jewellery and weapons of greenstone. Greenstone, jade or nephrite (*pounamu*) occurred only in rivers on the west coast of the South Island and was a valuable object of exchange and trade. Many hours of patient work were required to transform this very hard material into axes and clubs for chiefs or the amulets in human form (*hei-tiki*) which both men and women wore round their neck. After the Maoris gained access to iron tools and weapons the old greenstone axes were reworked to make *hei-tiki*, which were much sought after by the whites. Jewellery and ornaments with traditional motifs are still made at Hokitika and Greymouth.

The missionaries who from 1814 onwards sought to convert the Maoris disapproved of these naked figures and particularly of the sexual motifs. By the end of the 19th century, with the decline in numbers of the Maoris, the art of woodcarving had been almost entirely forgotten. With the development of the Maoritanga and the help of new teachers of the art like Pine Taiapa, however, Maori woodcarving took on a fresh lease of life.

Carvings as objects of trade

A number of European collections have examples of Maori woodcarving, which became much sought after as objects of trade in the early 19th century.

Meeting-houses

The Maori meeting-house (*whare runanga*) represents a personification of the revered ancestors of the tribe. The roof ridge is crowned by a standing figure (*tekoteko*) of the ancestor, the mask (*koruru*) below this is his face and the barge-boards fronting the roof are his outstretched arms (*maihi*), with his fingers (*raparapa*) at the ends. The interior of the house is his thorax, the beam forming the roof ridge his spinal column, the side posts of the walls his ribs. The rich carving in the interior also has symbolic meaning, with figures of other ancestors, mythical figures and sometimes gods. The carvings were thus a kind of picture-book which illustrated the story of the ancestors' exploits in songs and tales – for written accounts were unknown. The motifs, which have descriptive names, are painted in red, but also in black and white.

Tattooing

The long abandoned art of tattooing was not used for purely decorative purposes but to indicate status. In men the whole face, the buttocks and the upper thighs were tattooed, in women only the chin and lips. Tattooing was an extremely painful process, since it involved piercing the skin.

Music and oratory

The importance of traditional Maori music and oratory was that they replaced written records, which the Maoris lacked, in handing on traditions, mythology and history. The music consists almost exclusively of songs (*waiata*), with little variation in pitch but highly complex rhythms. The songs were accompanied by flutes, and the performers marked the rhythm by stamping their feet and striking their thighs and breast with their fists.

Oratory and singing were closely bound up on ceremonial occasions on the place of assembly (*marae*) and in the meeting-house: both were part of Maori formal rhetoric. Both took their themes mainly from mythology. There were a great variety of songs, but the commonest, apart from the *karakias*, the sacred songs sung only by priests in the course of ritual acts, were mourning songs, sung at solemn funeral ceremonies, and love songs.

Modern songs are based in greater or lesser degree on the Christian choral traditions of the European immigrants; but some modern music groups are also giving fresh life to the old Maori music.

Art

The larger New Zealand museums and art collections contain fine old paintings by European masters and valuable old books.

The first white "discoverers" were accompanied by cartographers and draughtsmen, who made accurate records of their landing, and drawings were made in the early days of the native inhabitants, the flora and fauna and the landscape. On his travels in New Zealand in 1844 George F. Angas (1822–86) painted many pictures of scenery and of Maoris. Many museums also have drawings, often charmingly naïve, by early settlers. The explorer and surveyor Charles Heaphy (1820–81) drew very attractive landscapes in his travels about the country. Gottfried Lindauer (1839–1926), a German immigrant, painted many lifelike portraits of Maoris and scenes from their life. Charles Frederick Goldie (1870–1947), a native of Auckland, became one of the best known and most highly paid artists in New Zealand, mainly because of his naturalistic portraits of Maoris.

Art of the immigrants

Until the 20th century New Zealand art still followed European models, and New Zealand artists trained, worked and exhibited mainly in London. The painter Frances Hodgkins (1869–1947), who came from Dunedin, became well known and successful only in Britain. Her still lifes and landscapes showed strong European influence, particularly Expressionism. After the death of her mother in 1913 she never returned to New Zealand.

20th century

Important 20th century New Zealand artists are Rita Angus (1908–70), the landscapist Mountford T. Woollaston (b. 1910), Ralph Hotere (b. 1931) and the outstanding and very original Colin McCahon (1919–87), who is notable for his large-scale oil paintings on religious, mythological and social themes.

Len Lye (1901–80) became famous for his vigorous sculpture, particularly in America, where he spent most of his time. He was also a painter and film-director. Other notable sculptors and designers were Guy Ngan (b. 1926) and Molly McAlister (1920–79).

Many artists have settled in the sunny regions of Nelson (South Island) and Northland, particularly in the Bay of Islands. Among them is the Austrian painter Friedensreich Hundertwasser, who has spent much of his time since 1973 in the Bay of Islands.

The decorative arts have a long tradition in New Zealand in the woodcarving and weaving of the Maoris. In recent decades numbers of potters have established themselves throughout the country. Avantgarde craft shops and galleries do good business.

Decorative art

Architecture

At the time of the discovery of New Zealand by Europeans the Maoris lived in huts either in open villages (*kainga*) or in fortified settlements

Maori architecture

Colonial architecture: the Post Office, Christchurch

surrounded by palisades (*pa*). An interesting reconstruction of a Maori village, Rewa's Village, can be seen at Kerikeri. A striking feature of Maori houses is the rich carved decoration, including figures and masks with protruding tongues.

19th century houses

The first white whalers and seal-hunters erected tents or reed huts (*raupo*). The better-off settlers brought prefabricated wooden houses with them. With the wider establishment of sawmills wooden houses became the normal type of dwelling, while public buildings were usually of stone. The first European houses were built when missionary activity began in the Bay of Islands, for example at the Kerikeri and Waimate North mission stations.

Settlers' houses dating from the mid 19th century, usually surrounded by verandas, have survived in Parnell/Auckland, New Plymouth and the Christchurch area. In the goldfields houses were mainly built of corrugated iron, which stood up to earthquakes better than stone buildings.

The standard dwelling of the settlers was a cottage. Examples of houses of higher pretensions can be seen in Larnach Castle (Dunedin), Holly Lea (Christchurch) and Alberton (Auckland).

Public buildings

For public buildings the preferred style was neo-Gothic, whose repertoire of forms was taken from English and Norman Gothic. Most buildings were of wood. In the time of the first Anglican bishop, George Selwyn (1809–78), and his architect Frederick Thatcher (1814–90) a number of churches were built in this style – for example, St Mary's in New Plymouth (1845–46) and All Saints in Howick (1847) – as well as secular buildings such as St John's College in Auckland (chapel 1847, College Hall 1849). Another architect who made a name for himself for imposing neo-Gothic public buildings was Benjamin W. Montfort (1825–98). Montfort, who came to New Zealand as an immigrant in

1850, designed the Canterbury Museum and Canterbury College in Christchurch and St Mary's Procathedral (1888) in Parnell/Auckland.

The other style which predominated in 19th century New Zealand architecture was neo-classicism. Government House in Auckland (1856; now part of the University) was the work of William Mason. William H. Clayton designed Government Building – the largest wooden building in the southern hemisphere – for New Zealand's new capital, Wellington, in 1876.

William Armson (1834–83), who came to New Zealand from Melbourne in 1862, contributed to the neo-classical townscape of Christchurch, Dunedin, Oamaru and Hokitika. R. A. Lawson (1833–1903) also built a number of neo-classical buildings in Dunedin and Oamaru.

In the early 20th century British and European architecture still provided the models for New Zealand. John Campbell chose neo-Baroque as a suitable style for the Public Trust Building in Wellington and the Chief Post Office in Auckland. His design (1911) for Parliament House in Wellington, which had been burned down in 1907, was carried out only in part; the left wing – a controversial building which has become known as the "Beehive" – was built in 1964–82 to the design of the British architect Basil Spence. Other textbook examples of the neo-Baroque style in New Zealand are the Railway Station in Dunedin (1904–07) and the Town Hall of Invercargill (1906).

20th century

Functionalism came to New Zealand after the First World War. The first steel-framed high-rise buildings, showing the influence of the Bauhaus, were erected in the 1920s. In 1931 Napier and Hastings were largely destroyed by a severe earthquake in Hawke's Bay and in spite of the economic depression were rebuilt in uniform Art Deco style, giving Napier in particular a very distinctive townscape.

More recently two buildings in particular have given rise to controversy: the "Beehive" in Wellington (see above) and the Aotea Centre in Auckland, a concert hall built in 1974–89 on the model of Aalto's Finlandia Building in Helsinki (1971). The city centres of Auckland, Wellington and Christchurch are now dominated by high-rise buildings with reflective glass façades, with the historic aspect of these cities surviving in the older façades which have been preserved on the lower storeys of modern buildings. In the new housing estates of New Zealand the single-storey detached family house predominates. Because of the danger of earthquakes they are built of wood, and many old buildings have been pulled down as being unsafe in an earthquake.

Literature

In 1854 Governor George Grey published the first collection of the oral traditions of the Maoris. The first New Zealand writer of any note was Frederick Manning (1811–83), an adventurer, sawmill owner and timber merchant with a Maori wife who lived on Hokianga Harbour, in western Northland, at the time of the timber boom. After 1860 he wrote two books under the pseudonym "A Pakeha Maori": "Old New Zealand, a Tale of Good Old Times" and "War in the North", the story of Hone Heke's fight against the British colonial authorities in the 1830s, seen from the viewpoint of a Maori.

Early publications

Samuel Butler (1835–1902) left Britain at the age of 25 and settled on a large farm on the east side of New Zealand's Southern Alps, remote from civilisation. After long journeys of exploration on the South Island he returned to Britain and devoted himself entirely to writing. His first account of his experiences in letters, "A First Year in Canterbury Settlement" (1863) and his utopian novel "Erewhon" (1873) reflect his wide travels in the inaccessible hinterland of Canterbury.

Samuel Butler

Literature

20th century
Katherine
Mansfield

The outstanding figure in early 20th century New Zealand literature was Katherine Mansfield (see Famous People). The daughter of a Wellington banker, her real name was Kathleen Mansfield Beauchamp. At the age of 19 she persuaded her father to let her go to London, where she lived in literary and bohemian circles. In 1909, on health grounds (she had tuberculosis), she moved to Germany and lived for some months in the spa of Bad Wörishofen. This period of her life is reflected in her first book of short stories, "In a German Pension" (1911). After her much loved younger brother Leslie died on the western front she looked back to her earlier days in New Zealand for her subjects ("The Dolls' House", "Prelude" and "At the Bay").

John A. A. Lee

The slum quarters and schools of Dunedin, then a flourishing economic metropolis, marked the early years of John A. A. Lee (1891–1982). His books, particularly his autobiographical novel "Children of the Poor", tell of his experiences as an outsider and of the life of the poor and the social outcasts.

Ngaio Marsh

The writer Ngaio Marsh (1899–1982), a native of Christchurch, worked in the theatre before moving to London to start a new career as a writer of detective novels. Among her best known works are "A Man Lay Dead", "Vintage Murder", "Surfeit of Lampreys", "Died in the Wool" and "Final Curtain". During the Second World War she went back to New Zealand, where she again turned to the theatre and put on some remarkable productions of Shakespeare. In 1950 she returned to London, where, with her financial position secured by the success of her novels, she was able to devote herself to her great love, the theatre.

Maurice F. R.
Shadbolt

Maurice F. R. Shadbolt (b. 1932) belongs to the older generation of contemporary New Zealand writers. In his novel "Among the Cinders" he gives a vivid picture of the old world of gold prospectors, loggers and early settlers. He describes not only the life of the white men but also the very different way of life of the Maoris and the relations between the two.

Hone Tuwhare

These themes, seen from the Maori point of view, also feature in the poems and plays of Hone Tuwhare (b. 1922).

James Baxter

James Baxter (1926–72) is New Zealand's most celebrated lyric poet. Born in Dunedin, he was associated with the pacifist movement, under the influence of his father. He became a convert to Catholicism and in 1969 founded an "alternative" commune for alcoholics, drug addicts and the homeless in the remote village of Hiruharama ("Jerusalem") on the Whanganui River. The commune broke up after his early death.

Allen Thomas
Curnow

The poet Allen Thomas Curnow (b. 1911) taught English literature in Auckland for many years and started writing poems in 1940.

Witi Itimaera,
Patricia Grace

The short stories of two women writers, Patricia Grace (b. 1937) and Witi Itimaera (b. 1944), have attracted international interest. Patricia Grace's book "Potiki" pictures the Maoris' struggle against the destruction of their national habitat.

Keri Hulme

Keri Hulme (b. 1947) is one of the few New Zealand women writers who are known and read in Europe. She has some Maori blood in her veins, and her books are concerned with problems which have their origin in the bicultural past of New Zealand. Her novel "The Bone People", which won the prestigious Booker Prize, depicts the forlornness of the individual when deprived of his traditional bonds. Other successful books are her collection of poetry and prose, "The Silence Between Moeraki Conversations", and her short stories "The Wind Eater".

For Janet Frame (b. 1924 in Dunedin) writing was of existential importance. She spent many years in psychiatric institutions, until her great
talent as a writer was discovered and led to her release. Her first
volume of short stories, "The Lagoon", was published when she was
27. The film version of her biography, "An Angel at My Table" (director
Jane Campion), made her work known in Europe.

Janet Frame

Theatre

The New Zealand theatre followed British and European models
longer than other cultural activities, and it was only after the political
reorientation in the Pacific area that the country began to turn away
from Europe in the cultural field as well. The first professional theatre
company was established in the Downstage Theatre in Wellington in
1964: previously there had only been performances by visiting foreign
companies and amateur groups. In the seventies there were professional community theatres in the larger towns such as Auckland,
Christchurch, Dunedin and Palmerston North.

Fresh impulses were brought to the New Zealand theatre by Bruce
Mason (1921–83). His first play, in 1953, was a critical judgment of
white society, while his later plays dealt with the change in the world of
the Maoris. The first of his five plays on Maori themes, "The Pohutukawa Tree" (1957), is now almost a classic. Mason's view of Maori
culture as a whole is pessimistic. In 1965 he wrote "Awatea" for the
Maori opera singer Inia Te Wiata, and this led to the formation in 1966
of the first Maori professional theatre company. The Maori theatre is
now an established feature of the New Zealand drama scene.

Bruce Mason

A Maori dance group in a richly decorated meeting-house

Maori theatre

In the late seventies there came into being a new Maori theatre movement, differing from earlier movements in its consciousness of a political mission. Performances of song, dance and oratory, frequently with passages in the Maori language, were presented on assembly areas (*marae*), in universities, public halls and theatres.

A drama by the Maori poet and playwright Hone Tuwhare, "In the Wilderness without a Hat", though written in 1977, was staged only in 1985. The starting-point of the action is a funeral ceremony (*tangi*). In the course of argument over the performance of the ceremony a carved ancestor figure (*tapu*) comes to life and intervenes in the discussion. The representation of a *tapu* on the stage was no doubt the explanation of the eight-year delay in the production of the play.

A characteristic of the Maori theatre is that the distance between spectators and actors has been abolished. The theatre thus becomes a community experience, similar to the traditional ceremonies on the *marae*.

Film

Beginnings

The first films produced in New Zealand around the turn of the century were documentaries, newsreel features and films in which the Maoris and the unspoiled natural landscape of New Zealand served as the backdrop for banal love stories. Rudall Hayward, the well-known New Zealand director of the twenties and thirties, invented a special camera and a sound system which enabled him to produce talking films.

After 1945

After the Second World War all the films shown in New Zealand came from Hollywood. It was only in the 1970s that the New Zealand film industry came to life. In 1977 Roger Donaldson produced his film "Sleeping Dogs", and in the same year a Film Commission was established whose function was to support the young New Zealand film industry in the production and marketing of New Zealand films through subsidies paid from tax revenue or the proceeds of the state lottery. While only three films were produced in New Zealand between 1940 and 1970, more than 40 were produced between 1977 and 1985. The Film Commission proved a powerful protector of the New Zealand film industry with its small domestic market. Most of the films produced with help from the Commission were concerned with the history of New Zealand, with the central event of the Land Wars and with the problems of a bicultural society.

Among the best known New Zealand directors are Vincent Ward ("In Spring One Plants Alone"; "State of Siege", after Janet Frame), Geoff Murphy ("Goodbye Pork Pie"), Michael Firth ("Off the Edge") and Mereta Mita ("Patu"). Yvonne Mackay received the first prize at the Frankfurt Children's Film Festival of 1994 for her film "The Silent One".

The greatest success of the New Zealand cinema, which won eight prizes at the Venice Film Festival in 1990, has been "An Angel at My Table", Jane Campion's film version of the autobiography of the writer Janet Frame (see Literature, above). Jane Campion's next film, "The Piano", won several Oscars in Hollywood in 1994. In the same year the film "Once Were Warriors", based on a book by the Maori author Alan Duff, set new box office records; and since "Jurassic Park" the New Zealand actor Sam Neill has become known to wider audiences.

Music

Serious music

The problem of a relatively small domestic market affects the musical scene in New Zealand no less than the artistic scene. Internationally renowned artistes like the opera singers Kiri Te Kanawa and Donald

McIntyre appear much more frequently on European and American stages than in New Zealand; and the New Zealand Symphony Orchestra plays in many other countries as well as New Zealand.

Many pop music groups, too, do not stay in New Zealand, since with a small potential audience they cannot make ends meet and are reduced to relying on cheap equipment and voluntary help. The New Zealand music scene, centred mainly in Dunedin and Auckland, is subject to constant change. Bands are formed today and break up tomorrow. Successful bands usually start by going to Australia and then move on to London or the United States. This was the case, for example, with Split Enz, New Zealand's best known group.

Pop music

Flying Nun, New Zealand's most successful recording company, started in 1981 with performances by music groups on the South Island (Pin Group, Christchurch; The Clean, Dunedin). Their group The Chills soon became popular, set out on a foreign tour in 1985 and had a successful time in Britain. In the eighties recordings of The Straitjackets Fit, The Bats and Headless Chickens were issued, and their export possibilities and image abroad were improved by co-operation with an Australian record firm.

Suggested Routes

While on the North Island the attractions for visitors are the spectacular volcanic areas, the almost tropical vegetation, the idyllically beautiful beaches and the evidences of Maori culture, the appeal of the South Island lies in the majestic snow-capped peaks and mighty glaciers of the Southern Alps, the deeply indented fjords, the wild coastal scenery with its bizarre rock formations, the almost endless expanses of pastureland and the old settlements and mansions of colonial times.

In this section we describe a grand tour of New Zealand, with a number of side trips and alternative routes, and some shorter routes in particular parts of the country. The routes cover all the main sights of New Zealand and open up prospects of the natural and human landscapes of this country "at the most beautiful end of the world". The rubrics in the margin indicate the course of each route. The names of places which are the subject of a separate entry in the A to Z part of this guide are given in **bold** type and places mentioned in the marginal rubrics in *italics*. Most of the towns and other places, regions and individual sights, whether they have a separate entry in the guide or appear in the "Surroundings" section of an entry, are included in the Index at the end of the volume, wiith the help of which they can be rapidly located. The adjoining map gives a general view of the routes, which can be followed in detail in the large map attached to the guide.

Grand Tour (North and South Islands; c. 4600km/2860 miles; 3–4 weeks)

The route

The route starts from New Zealand's multicultural metropolis, Auckland.

The tour begins with a side trip to the Bay of Islands and Cape Reinga, the most northerly point on the North Island. We then return to Auckland and head south-east for the Bay of Plenty.

From there the route turns south and runs inland through the volcanic heart of the North Island. The main attractions are the Rotorua area, Lake Taupo and Tongariro National Park. Then down the North Island to its southern tip, with the national capital, Wellington – the "windy city", but one with many attractions for the visitor.

From there we take the ferry to the South Island and from Picton turn west. The route runs via Nelson and the valley of the Buller River to the fairly wild west coast with its numerous tourist sights, including the Franz Josef Glacier and the Fox Glacier. The coast road ends at Haast.

From Haast we cut through the Southern Alps and come into the lake district on the eastern slopes of the mountains. Skirting Lake Wanaka and Lake Hawea, we reach Cromwell, a road junction where we take the road west to Queenstown. From there the route runs south to Lumsden, from which a side trip to Milford Sound and Lake Manapouri is a must. We then continue to Invercargill, at the southern tip of the island, and follow Highway 1 to the Pacific coast and along the coast to Dunedin. We then continue northward up the coast to Christchurch, Blenheim and Picton, completing the circuit of the South Island.

Auckland–Paihia
(c. 240km–
150 miles)

The starting-point of the tour is ★★**Auckland**, New Zealand's metropolis, a city of international standing which is known as the "city of sails". From here Highway 1 runs north along the Hauraki Gulf into the **Northland** region, passing close to the little town of ★**Puhoi**, founded in the 19th century by immigrants from Bohemia. The road then continues to the industrial town of ★**Whangarei** with its large oil refinery and beautiful surroundings. Beyond this is the ★★**Bay of Islands**, the

Suggested Routes

Grand Tour
NORTH ISLAND
Taranak Route
East Cape Route
Napier-Taupo Route
Urewera Route
SOUTH ISLAND
South Island alternative route
Tasman-Heaphy Route
Arthur's Pass Road

* Cape Reinga

** Bay of Islands

* Ninety Mile Beach

* Waimate North
* Kerikeri ** Waitangi
** Russell
Paihia *
* Hokianga Harbour
** Waipoua Kauri Forest
Whangarei

Hauraki **
Gulf

Great Barrier Island

* Puhoi

* Kaipara Harbour

* Coromandel Peninsula

* Waiwera
** Auckland
* Mayor Island
** Waikato River
Pukekohe
* Bay of Plenty **
East Cape *

Te Aroha

North Island

* Hamilton
* Kawhia
Tauranga

Waitomo Caves ** Rotorua
** Wairakei
Urewera Nat. Park
* Gisborne

* New Plymouth
Tongariro Nat. Park
Lake Waikaremoana

* Egmont Nat. Park
Wanganui River
Lake Taupo

Stratford

* Napier
Hawke Bay

Wanganui

* Cape Farewell
* Marlborough Sounds
Foxton
Palmerston North
* Cape Kidnappers

** Abel Tasman Nat. Park
* Kapiti Island
* Otaki
Masterton
Castle-point

Nelson
Picton
Greytown

Nelson Lakes Nat. Park
Lake Grassmere **
Wellington

* Westport
Buller River

** Pancake Rocks
* Hanmer Springs

** Shantytown
* Arthur's Pass Nat. Park
* Kaikoura

Tasman Sea

** Franz Josef Glacier
Mt. Cook Nat. Park

** Fox Glacier
** Westland Nat. Park
* Christchurch

* Haast Pass Road
Lake Ohau
L. Tekapo
* Banks Peninsula

Pukaki
Ashburton

** Mt Aspiring Nat. Park
Timaru
Peel Forest Park

South Pacific Ocean

** Milford Sound
* Wanaka
Lindis Pass
* Waitaki Valley

** Fiordland Nat. Park
Queens-town
Arrowtown
* Clyde
South Island

Lake Te Anau
* Alexandra
** Moeraki Boulders

Lake Manapouri
Lawrence
Port Chalmers

Lake Hauroko
* Gore
** Dunedin

** Invercargill

* Nugget Point

* Stewart Island
* Bluff

© Baedeker

* major sights

** outstanding sights

starting-point of modern New Zealand. Features of interest are the old
Maori settlement sites, whaling stations and mission stations such as
★Paihia, ★Kerikeri and ★Russell. At ★Waitangi was signed the

Suggested Routes

important treaty of 1840 between the white immigrants and the Maoris.

Paihia–Cape Reinga–Kaitaia
(*c.* 330km/205 miles)

From Paihia the road continues north-west to end at **Kaitaia**, from which a side trip can be made along ★ *Ninety Mile Beach* to ★ *Cape Reinga*.

Kaitaia–Auckland
(*c.* 330km/205 miles)

After returning from Cape Reinga to Kaitaia we take Highway 1, which runs south-east and at ★**Hokianga Harbour** bears west for Taheka, where we take Highway 12. This runs west to the point where Hokianga Harbour opens into the Tasman Sea and then continues south, running parallel to the coast and through ★★**Waipou Kauri National Forest**, one of the last surviving remnants of primeval forest, with its giant kauri trees. Farther south is beautiful *Bayly's Beach*. Here too the little settlement of *Dargaville*, just off the road, is worth a visit. Beyond this Highway 12 comes to the drowned valley system of ★**Kaipara Harbour** and soon afterwards runs into Highway 1. This runs south to Wellsford, from which Highway 16 provides an alternative route westward back to ★★**Auckland**.

Auckland–Tauranga
(*c.* 310km/195 miles)

From Auckland we set out on our journey through the "hot heart" of New Zealand. Highway 1 runs south to Pokeho, where we turn east and follow Highway 2 to the ★★**Coromandel Peninsula**, which can be explored in a round trip on Highway 25. The route then continues to the ★**Bay of Plenty** and the port of ★**Tauranga**, inland from which are extensive fruit plantations (particularly kiwi fruit) and forests.

Tauranga–Rotorua
(*c.* 90km/55 miles)

Beyond Te Puke Highway 33 turns off and runs south into the geo-thermal region of ★★**Rotorua**, where it runs into Highway 5. Here you must allow plenty of time for seeing the profusion of post-volcanic phenomena of all kinds – geysers, pools of boiling mud, hot springs. Also in the area are a number of interesting and well preserved Maori villages.

Rotorua–Taupo
(*c.* 90km/55 miles)

South of Rotorua on Highway 5 is the geothermal area of ★★**Taupo–Wairakei** with its large lake and a very interesting geothermal power station. To the north the ★**Waikato River**, now tamed, flows through wild and romantic gorges.

Taupo–Tongariro National Park
(*c.* 100km/60 miles)

A few kilometres south of Taupo Highway 1 runs past ★★**Tongariro National Park**, which has been listed by UNESCO as a world heritage site. In this mountainous region, marked by continuing volcanic activity, are the two volcanoes of Ruapehu and Ngauruhoe, which are regarded by the Maoris as sacred. This is now a popular climbing and skiing area.

Tongariro NP–Wellington
(*c.* 350km/220 miles)

From Tongariro National Park Highway 1 continues south via Foxton (near which is beautiful Foxton Beach) and **Levin** to ★★**Wellington**, the "windy city" which is New Zealand's capital, with numerous features of interest.

Wellington–Picton (ferry)

From Wellington a ferry crosses the Cook Strait into the very beautiful ★★**Marlborough Sounds**, at the north-eastern tip of the South Island, and puts in at the port of **Picton**.

Picton–Nelson
(*c.* 120km/75 miles)

From Picton the route runs west to the pleasant port town of ★**Nelson**.

Nelson–Greymouth
(*c.* 300km/185 miles)

From Nelson there is a rewarding side trip on the **Tasman–Heaphy Route** to the ★ **Abel Tasman National Park**. The main route continues on Highway 6 through the valley of the ★**Buller River**, with its old gold-mining settlements, to its mouth at ★**Westport**. Highway 6 then runs south along the rugged west coast, shaped by the fierce surf of the Tasman Sea. The first highlight is ★ **Pararoa National Park**, with the ★★ *Pancake Rocks*.

A few kilometres south of ★ **Greymouth** is the old gold-diggers' settlement of ★ *Shantytown* (restored), which preserves something of the atmosphere of the 19th century gold rush.

Via ★ **Hokitika**, where the Maoris quarried the much sought-after greenstones, and Ross, where gold was also found, the road comes to ★ **Westland National Park**, with its two principal sights, the ★★ **Fox Glacier** and the ★★ **Franz Josef Glacier**. These two great rivers of ice, many kilometres long, flow down from the névé fields of the Southern Alps to the evergreen rain forests on the coast.

Greymouth–
Franz Josef
(c. 190km/
120 miles)

The coastal section of Highway 6 ends at Haast, where it turns south-east, follows the Haast River upstream and cuts through the Southern Alps at the ★ **Haast Pass** and winds its way southward between two glacier lakes, ★ **Lake Wanaka** and ★ *Lake Hawea*, towards Wanaka.

Franz Josef–
Wanaka
(c. 280km/
175 miles)

From Wanaka it is possible, with a small vehicle suitable for cross-country work, to take the direct route to ★ **Arrowtown** and ★ **Queenstown** on Highway 89. With a larger car or mobile caravan the easiest route is on Highway 6, which takes the long way round via ★ *Cromwell*.

Wanaka–
Queenstown
(c. 70–100km/
45–60 miles)

Among the many sights round Queenstown are ★ *Shotover Canyon*, ★ *Lake Wakatipu* and the *Remarkables*.

From Queenstown we follow Highway 6, which runs south to Lumsden. From here Highway 94 branches off and runs west to the very beautiful and almost uninhabited ★★ **Fiordland National Park**, with ★★ **Lake Manapouri** and ★ **Lake Te Anau**.

Queenstown–
Te Anau
(c. 180km/
110 miles)

From Te Anau the road continues to ★★ **Milford Sound**, which is sometimes claimed to be the very epitome of New Zealand.

Sights not to be missed here are the Glowworm Cave on Lake Te Anau and the very impressive underground power station on Lake Manapouri.

Side trip to
Milford Sound
(c. 240km/
150 miles)

Returning to Te Anau, we continue to ★ **Invercargill**, from which a side trip can be made to the ★ *Bluff aluminium smelting plant* and the very beautiful ★ **Stewart Island**, lying offshore to the south.

Te Anau–
Invercargill
(c. 160km/
100 miles)

From Invercargill Highway 92 runs through beautiful scenery along the south coast through the ★ **Catlins** region, passing a number of very interesting sites (Cathedral Cave, Nugget Point). At ★ **Balclutha** it runs into Highway 1, which runs north-east to ★★ **Dunedin**, with its many features of interest. From here a side trip can be made to the Otago Peninsula (colonies of seals and seabirds), with ★ *Larnach Castle*.

Invercargill–
Dunedin
(c. 260km/
160 miles)

From Dunedin Highway 1 runs north along the Pacific coast to ★ **Oamaru**, passing the imposing ★★ *Moeraki Boulders* and the old fishing port of ★ *Moeraki*. It then continues by way of *Waitaki* to ★ **Timaru**, from which excursions can be made to ★ *Peel Forest Park* at *Geraldine* and to the rock paintings in the *Cave* area.

Dunedin–Timaru
(c. 200km/
125 miles)

The road then runs over the Canterbury Plains, with the little town of ★ **Ashburton**, and finally comes to ★★ **Christchurch**, capital of the South Island, with its many tourist sights. From here an excursion can be made to the ★ **Banks Peninsula**, with the two natural harbours of ★ *Lyttleton* and ★ *Akaroa*.

Timaru–
Christchurch
(c. 170km/
105 miles)

Suggested Routes

Christchurch–
Kaikoura
(*c.* 300km/
185 miles)

From Christchurch Highway 1 runs north-east to Culverden, from which a side trip can be made to ★ **Hanmer Springs**. The route then continues to ★ **Kaikoura**, situated at the foot of the Kaikoura Range. From here a whale-watching trip is a must.

Kaikoura–Picton
(*c.* 200km/
125 miles)

From Kaikoura the road runs north-east to ★ *Lake Grassmere*, where salt is produced from the waters of the lagoon, and the famous wine-growing region round the attractive little town of ★ **Blenheim**.

The tour of the South Island can be concluded with a trip round the Marlborough Sounds (see above).

Taranaki Route (North Island) (*c.* 1000km/625 miles)

This alternative to the main route on the North Island runs from Auckland to Wellington, via the Waikato River area, Hamilton and the western tip of the island, with the old volcano of Taranaki.

The route

From Auckland the road runs south, passing through the river landscape created by the **Waikato River**, to ★ **Hamilton**. It then comes into the **Northland** region, the highlight of which is the karstic ★★ **Te Kuiti/Waitomo Caves** area, with the world-famed Glowworm Cave. Farther south-west is the port of **New Plymouth**, under the north side of the old volcano of ★★ **Taranaki** (Mount Taranaki or Egmont), the central feature of Mount Egmont National Park. A scenic road runs round the volcano.

From **Hawera**, under the south side of Taranaki, the road runs along the coast to ★ **Wanganui**, from which a rewarding excursion can be made northwards to ★★ **Whanganui National Park**. Then via *Foxton* and **Levin** to ★★ **Wellington**.

East Cape Route (North Island) (*c.* 1300km/810 miles)

This alternative to the main route on the east side of the North Island runs from Auckland to the Bay of Plenty, circles the East Cape and continues via Gisborne to Hawke's Bay, with the Art Deco town of Napier. It then turns inland via Hastings, Dannevirke and Masterton to Wellington. In the course of the tour there are two possible side routes into the volcanic heart of the North Island, the Urewera Route and the Napier–Taupo Route.

The route

From Auckland the route runs south-east to the ★ **Bay of Plenty**, with the towns of ★ **Tauranga** and ★ *Whakatane* and the old Maori settlement of *Opotiki*. If time permits, there is a rewarding excursion to two offshore islands with good bathing, ★ *Mayor Island* and the volcanic ★ *White Island*.

The route then continues to the ★ **East Cape**, the most easterly point on the North Island, where it turns south for ★ **Gisborne/Poverty Bay**. An excursion can be made from Gisborne to the *Mahia Peninsula,* to the south. In ★ **Hawke's Bay** is the little town of *Wairoa,* from which the **Urewera Route** (180km/110 miles) runs north-west through the ★ **Urewera National Park** to the volcanic ★★ **Rotorua** area.

At the south end of Hawke's Bay is the Art Deco town of ★★ **Napier**, from which the **Napier–Taupo Route** (150km/95 miles) runs north-west to the thermal area of ★★ **Taupo/Wairakei**.

From Napier the route turns inland through a region of kiwi fruit plantations and vineyards, via ★ **Hastings** and **Dannevirke**, to **Masterton**, at the foot of the ★ *Tararua Range*. Then via *Greytown, Upper Hutt* and *Lower Hutt* to ★★ **Wellington**.

Alternative route on South Island

(*c.* 700km/435 miles)

This alternative route from Invercargill to Christchurch through the interior of the southern half of the South Island takes in the Otago region and the Mackenzie Country as well as the grand mountain world of the Mount Cook National Park and the Canterbury region.

From Invercargill the route runs north via *Gore* into the uplands of **Otago** and on to **Alexandra**, from which there are two possibilities: a round trip in the footsteps of the gold prospectors or a visit to the *Clutha Hydro-electric Scheme*. The route then continues north via ★ *Cromwell* and over the ★ *Lindis Pass* into the ★ **Mackenzie Country**. From ★ *Twizel* an excursion to ★ **Lake Pukaki** and ★★ **Mount Cook National Park** is a must.

    From Twizel Highway 8 runs north-east past ★ **Lake Takepo** and over *Burke's Pass* to *Fairlie* and *Geraldine*. From there the route follows Highway 72 to ★ **Peel Forest Park**, then to *Erewhon* and *Mesopotamia* and on to ★★ **Christchurch**.

The route

Arthur's Pass Road (South Island)

(*c.* 260km/160 miles)

This route cuts through the South Island from east to west between Christchurch and Greymouth, through magnificent scenery. The trip can also be done by rail (TraNZAlpine Express).

From Christchurch Highway 73 runs north-west and at Springfield reaches the eastern foothills of the Southern Alps. It then climbs steadily to the watershed at ★ **Arthur's Pass**, in the centre of ★★ *Arthur's Pass National Park*. Beyond the pass the road runs down into the wild and romantic ★ *Otira Canyon*. It then follows the Otira River to its mouth, at the reconstructed gold-diggers' settlement of ★ *Shantytown,* and finally comes to the end-point of the trip at ★ **Greymouth**.

The route

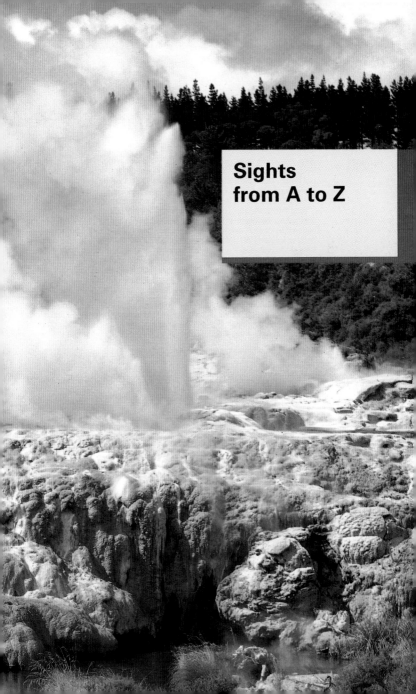

**Sights
from A to Z**

Sights from A to Z
North Island

Region: Auckland
Population: 890,000 (conurbation over 1 million)

Situation and
characteristics

New Zealand's metropolis, Auckland, lies on a narrow isthmus, occupied by numerous volcanic cones, between Manukau Harbour and Waitemata Harbour. The 260m/853ft high volcanic island of Rangitoto separates Waitemata Harbour from the wide expanse of the Hauraki Gulf with its scatter of islands. To the south-west are the Waitakere Ranges.

Since its foundation over 150 years ago the city has extended far to north and south between the two natural harbours. In 1891 Rudyard Kipling called Auckland "last, loneliest, loveliest, exquisite, apart"; but today it is hard to see any boundary between the city and the surrounding country. Villages which were once a long way from the town have long become suburbs and outlying districts of the city with their own shopping and administrative centres. Outside the city centre, the central business district (CBD) of Auckland, the residential areas follow the usual New Zealand pattern of detached family houses with small gardens.

Population

On this narrow land bridge on the North Island live around a third of the whole population of New Zealand. As the principal gateway into New Zealand, it is often called the "capital of Polynesia" because 140,000 of its population are of Polynesian origin.

Auckland, the "City of Sails" and metropolis of the South Pacific, lies in a sheltered situation on Waitemata Harbour

This heavy concentration of population in a relatively small area has given rise in recent years to serious problems. There are great difficulties, for example, in providing an adequate water supply.

Auckland is known as the "City of Sails" because of its inhabitants' passion for boats. On fine summer days the Hauraki Gulf is covered with

"City of Sails"

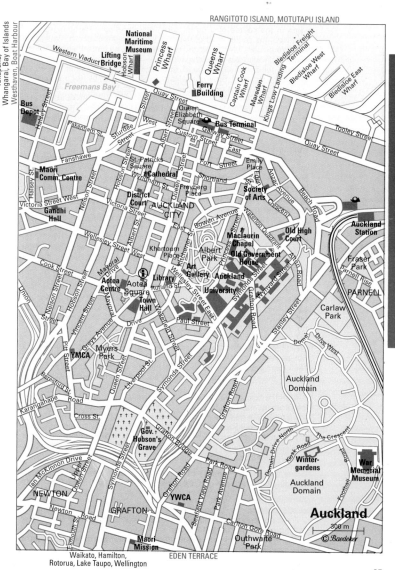

RANGITOTO ISLAND, MOTUTAPU ISLAND

Takapuna, Whangarei; Bay of Islands
Westhaven, Boat Harbour

National Maritime Museum
Western Viaduct
Lifting Bridge
Princess Wharf
Queens Wharf
Captain Cook Wharf
Marsden Wharf
Kings Low Landing
Bledisloe Freight Terminal
Bledisloe West Wharf
Bledisloe East Wharf
Freemans Bay
Ferry Building
Bus Depot
Quay Street
Queen Elizabeth Square
Bus Terminal
Galway Street
Pakenham St.
Sturdee Street
West Street
Custom Street
Quay Street East
Tooley Street
Quay Street
Fanshawe
St. Patricks Square
Albert Street
Fort Street
Emily Place
Maori Comm. Centre
Hobson Street
Nelson Street
Wyndham St.
Cathedral
Shortland
Freyberg Place
Society of Arts
Beach Road
District Court
Victoria Street West
Victoria Street
AUCKLAND CITY
Bowen Avenue
Waterloo Quadrant
Anzac Avenue
Emily Crescent
Gandhi Hall
Wellesley Street West
Albert Street
East St.
Khartoum Place
Albert Park
Maclaurin Chapel
Old Government House
Old High Court
Auckland Station
Cook Street
Mayoral Drive
Art Gallery
Auckland University
Symonds Street
Alten Road
Parnell Rise
Fraser Park
PARNELL
Hobson Street
Nelson Street
Aotea Centre
Aotea Square
Library
Rutland St.
Wellesley Street East
Wynyard Street
Stanley Street
Carlaw Park
Union Street
Vincent Street
Town Hall
Waterloo Drive
Paul Street
Grafton Road
Demel Drive West
Greys Avenue
Myers Park
Queen Street
Liverpool St.
Symonds Street
Grafton Road
Auckland Domain
YMCA
Pitt Street
Beresford Street
Karangahape Road
Cross St.
Gov. Hobson's Grave
Grafton Bridge
Park Road
Demel Drive North
Kinder Road
The Crescent
Winter gardens
War Memorial Museum
Ian McKinnon Drive
Upper Queen Street
Symonds Street
Park Avenue
Auckland Domain
NEWTON
Newton Road
Seafield View Road
Football
GRAFTON
YWCA
Carlton Gore Road
Auckland
300 m
© Baedeker
Maori Mission
Outhwaite Park

Waikato, Hamilton,
Rotorua, Lake Taupo, Wellington
EDEN TERRACE

innumerable sailing boats. Statistics show that one household in four owns a boat.

History

In Maori tradition the neck of land between the Tasman Sea and the South Pacific was originally settled by descendants of the Marama-Kikihura tribe. After numerous inter-tribal feuds over the possession of this area of fertile volcanic soil the Kiwi Tamaki tribe won the day in the early 18th century and established a fortified settlement (pa) on One Tree Hill. There were similar settlements on almost all the other volcanic cones on the isthmus. But when in the course of a burial ceremony in Kaipara Harbour (north of Auckland) the senior chief of the tribe killed a number of other guests he was overthrown, his stronghold was destroyed, he himself was killed and many of his warriors were enslaved.

When the first European and American whalers landed in the Bay of Islands the Ngapuhi tribes of the Northland region, led by Hongi Hika, were quick to equip themselves with weapons and moved south on campaigns of conquest, killing and driving out the local tribes, until the Auckland area was almost completely depopulated. Diseases brought in by the white men also took a heavy toll among the native population. In 1840, when British sovereignty was recognised in the treaty of Waitangi, Governor Hobson, seeking a central site as the seat of administration of the colony, chose the isthmus because of its good communications and safe harbour.

In what is now Albert Park, between the city centre and the University, the Albert Barracks were built to house a garrison of 1000 men. Unlike the other three large New Zealand cities (Wellington, Christchurch and Dunedin), Auckland was not founded as a planned new town, with whole shiploads of immigrants. It was originally occupied by government officials, traders and craftsmen, and the first Scottish immigrants began arriving only in 1842.

William Hobson, the first independent governor of the new colony, was a sick man, and the Colonial Office in London failed to supply him with either the troops or the financial resources he needed. He was attacked by the New Zealand Company because he had chosen Auckland as his capital and because he did not give them all the help they wanted in purchasing land for their new settlements. He died in 1842.

The real "father" of Auckland was John Logan Campbell (1817–1912), one of the first European settlers in the Auckland area. Coming to New Zealand from Edinburgh at the age of 21, he and his partner William Brown established a large farm on One Tree Hill. He was involved also in setting up banks, insurance companies and shipping lines, and gave powerful impetus to the development of the town as its mayor.

To protect the town against Maori raids the government built a chain of "fencible settlements" occupied by troops, for example at Howick, Onehunga, Panmure and Otahuhu. When the land wars broke out in Taranaki in 1860 there was some apprehension that the conflict might spread to the capital; but in fact the fighting took place farther south and Auckland was left in peace.

After the discovery of gold on the South Island Auckland became of less importance, and in 1865 the capital was transferred to Wellington. The town took on a fresh lease of life, however, when gold was found on the nearby Coriander Peninsula and agriculture flourished in the country south of Auckland. Later industrial development and the towns uniquely favourable situation from the point of view of trade and communications gave its economy a further boost.

Name

Governor Hobson, founder of the town, named it after his former commander, then governor-general of India, the Earl of Auckland (1784–1849).

Transport

Auckland's international airport is 23km/14 miles south-west of the city centre on Manukau Harbour.

From Auckland there are express trains to Wellington (the Overlander; 10½ hours) and Rotorua (4 hours).

The road system in and around Auckland is excellent. Roads of motorway standard run through the city in all directions.

The Anniversary Day Regatta on the Monday closest to January 29th commemorates the foundation of the city. At this time of year there are open-air concerts in Domain Park. The great Harbour Festival is held in February. At the end of March the Round the Bays Fun Run attracts tens of thousands of runners.

Important events

The very attractive Waterfront Walk (7km/4½ miles) runs eastward through the city from the Chief Post Office to Mission Bay.

Sightseeing

For good walkers there is the Coast to Coast Walkway (13km/8 miles), which runs from the Ferry Building at the end of Queen Street to Domain Park and on by way of Mount Eden to One Tree Hill, ending at Manukau Harbour. A good way of seeing the main sights is to take the Explorer Bus, which departs from the Ferry Building hourly from 10am to 4pm. It runs round the city in a clockwise direction, stopping at Mission Bay Beach, Kelly Tarlton's Underwater World, Rose Park Gardens (Parnell), Auckland War Memorial Museum (Domain Park; connection to Zoo), Parnell Village, Custom Street (central business district), Victoria Park Market and Hobson Wharf. Passengers can get off and on again at any of the stops.

Sights in the City Centre

Round the wide sweep of Waitemata Harbour extends the central business district of Auckland with its skyline of high-rise blocks. The scene in the harbour is enlivened by the movements of passenger ships and freighters and by innumerable white sailing boats.

Waitemata Harbour

The harbour is spanned by a bridge more than 1km/¾ mile long and some 43m/141ft high; the steel central arch is 243m/797ft long. The bridge was completed in 1959 and widened ten years later. The northern districts of the city and the beautiful bathing beaches and bays on the north side of the harbour are easily reached on Highway 1.

Harbour Bridge

Auckland's Town Hall . . .

. . . and Ferry Building

Auckland

Quay Street	Along the harbour runs busy Quay Street, on which, and on the adjoining Princess Wharf, are the very popular Dockside Markets and China Oriental Markets. The markets are held daily in summer and from Friday to Sunday at other times of year.
Microworld	At 23 Quay Street (open: daily 9am–6pm) is Microworld, where visitors can see the "little things of life" – e.g. the surface forms of rocks and minerals, tiny insects and other creatures, etc. – through microscopes.
★New Zealand Maritime Museum	On Hobson Wharf, at the north-west end of Quay Street, is the richly stocked New Zealand Maritime Museum (open: daily 10am–6pm, weekends in summer until 7pm), which offers a comprehensive survey of the history of seafaring in New Zealand. The exhibits include Maori canoes and outrigger boats, whaling equipment and a variety of old instruments and implements. There is an interesting section devoted to New Zealand sailing yachts which have distinguished themselves in regattas all over the world.
★Ferry Building	The imposing old Ferry Building at the junction of Queen Street with Quay Street, with its fine restaurant, has recently been restored and forms a striking landmark on the harbour front. Built in English Baroque style of brick and sandstone on a base of Coriander granite, it was completed in 1912 to the design of Alexander Wiseman.
Chief Post Office	Adjoining the Ferry Building is the Chief Post Office (CPO), an imposing building of 1911 designed by John Campbell.
Downtown Shopping Centre	Beyond the Chief Post Office is the largest shopping centre in the central area, with an extraordinary range of wares.
Customs House	To the south-west of the Chief Post Office is the richly decorated Customs House (by Thomas Mahoney, 1889). Originally occupied by officers of the armed forces and later by the customs authorities, it now houses various cultural institutions and shops.
★Queen Street (Mall)	The city's busy main artery and show street is Queen Street, along which in recent years numerous high-rise office blocks occupied by banks, insurance companies and commercial firms have mushroomed. Between the Ferry Building and K' Road (see below) are large numbers of department stores, shops and restaurants. For those interested in architecture there is plenty of variety, with imposing colonial-era buildings rubbing shoulders with Art Nouveau, Art Deco and modern glass palaces.
Vulcan Lane	Off Queen Street, on the left, is Vulcan Lane, a little street with many cafés which is particularly busy at lunch-time and in the evening.
St Patrick's Cathedral	To the west of lower Queen Street, at the corner of Hobson Street and Wyndham Street, is St Patrick's Cathedral (R.C.). Built in 1848, it is one of the oldest churches in New Zealand. It has a very beautiful tabernacle presented by the Maoris to Bishop Pompallier, who held the first Roman Catholic service in New Zealand in 1838.
St Matthew's Church	In Wellesley Street, also to the west of Queen Street, is St Matthew's Church (Anglican), built in 1902 in Old English style. From the tower there are good views over the city.
★Town Hall	Farther south along Queen Street, at the intersection with Grey's Avenue, is Auckland Town Hall (by the Clark brothers, 1911), with an imposing tower. The façade is of Oamaru marble, the base of Melbourne bluestone.
Aotea Centre	To the right of the Town Hall is the Aotea Centre, New Zealand's largest concert hall. It is a low building designed by the leading architect E. Wainscott, apparently under the influence of Aalto's Finlandia Hall in Helsinki. The construction of the building was subject to much delay and controversy, and it was finally completed only in 1990. In Aotea Place is a statue of the Earl of Auckland, after whom the city is named.

Close by is Auckland's Visitor Centre, where information material of all kinds is available.

On the southern fringe of the city centre Karangahape Road, familiarly known as K' Road, cuts across Queen Street. It is particularly busy on Friday evenings, when the shops stay open until 10pm and a colourful touch is added by the many South Sea islanders who congregate here.

Karangahape Road

East of the middle section of Queen Street is Albert Park, with its fine old trees. This was the site of the first barracks built in Auckland.

Albert Park

In the eastern half of the park are various institutes belonging to Auckland's renowned University. The University church, St Andrew's, was built in 1849.

Auckland University

The Auckland City Art Gallery, at the south-east corner of Albert Park (Wellesley Street and Kitchener Street), is a must for every visitor. This very impressive building, with towers and high pitched roofs in French Renaissance style, was designed by the Melbourne firm of Grainger and D'Ebro and built in 1889. It houses the famous Grey Gallery, a surprisingly rich collection older European and contemporary New Zealand art, including works by McCahon and Woollaston. The earliest New Zealand works date from the time of Captain Cook, some of whose companions painted remarkable views of different parts of New Zealand.

★★Auckland City Art Gallery (see plan p. 90)

The gallery also has numerous oil paintings by the German artist Gottfried Lindauer (1839–1926), noted for his marvellous portraits of Maoris.

From time to time the gallery puts on spectacular special exhibitions. Recent very successful exhibitions have been devoted to Henry Moore, Manet and Picasso.

Entrance: corner of Kitchener Street and Wellesley Street East. Open: daily 10am–4.30pm; conducted tours Wed.–Sun. from 2pm.

Old Government House, timber building in Neo-Classical style, was built in 1856 (architect William Mason). After the transfer of the capital of the colony to Wellington in 1865 it served as a summer residence for the governor and a guest house for important visitors. It now belongs to Auckland University.

Old Government House

Opposite Old Government House is the Old Synagogue (by Edward Bartley, 1884), now used for small-scale cultural events (concerts, drama).

Old Synagogue

The High Court of 1868 on Waterloo Quadrant, a richly decorated brick building, complete with turrets and gargoyles, was modelled on Warwick Castle. A modern annexe housing the district appeal court spoils the effect of the older building.

High Court

West Side of City Centre

On the west side of the city centre, occupying the site of a power station of 1908, is the extensive Victoria Park Market, which sells fresh fruit and vegetables as well as a variety of odds and ends. It also offers pleasant restaurants and pubs and a variety of entertainments. Nearby is Victoria Park, laid out in 1905.

Victoria Park Market

The Ponsonby district to the west of the city centre has preserved, particularly in Renall Street, numbers of small 19th century houses, once occupied by workers in the nearby harbour, which are now much sought after as town houses. The Post Office (by John Campbell, 1912) is a striking building in English Baroque style.

Ponsonby

Auckland Domain

To the south-east of the city centre is the Auckland Domain, an extensive recreation area with various leisure facilities and sports grounds.

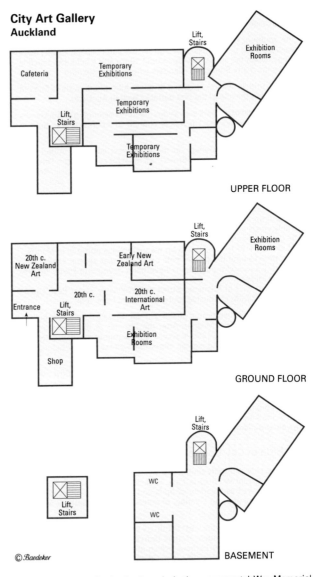

City Art Gallery
Auckland

Cafeteria

Temporary Exhibitions

Lift, Stairs

Exhibition Rooms

Temporary Exhibitions

Lift, Stairs

Temporary Exhibitions

UPPER FLOOR

20th c. New Zealand Art

Early New Zealand Art

Lift, Stairs

Exhibition Rooms

20th c.

20th c. International Art

Entrance

Lift, Stairs

Exhibition Rooms

Shop

GROUND FLOOR

Lift, Stairs

WC

Lift, Stairs

WC

© Baedeker

BASEMENT

★★ Auckland Institute and Museum (War Memorial Museum)

On the highest point in the Domain is the monumental War Memorial Museum. From the steps in front of the museum there are magnificent views over the city centre and Waitemata Harbour.

This Neo-Classical building was erected in 1929 as a memorial to the New Zealand soldiers who fell in the First World War and to house the

Auckland Museum

GROUND FLOOR

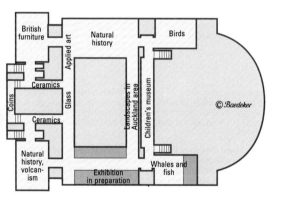

FIRST FLOOR

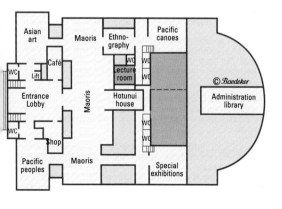

SECOND FLOOR

collections of the Auckland Museum, originally established in 1852. Large extensions were built in the 1960s.

The War Memorial Hall commemorates the dead of all the wars in which New Zealand soldiers fought.

The museum itself contains rich collections of material on the natural and cultural history of the South Pacific area and the history of the city of Auckland.

The Maori Court, a richly decorated meeting-house of 1878, came from the Thames region. The magnificent Maori doorway came from Rotorua. There is also a very fine store-house with carved decoration. Of particular interest is a 25m/80ft long canoe dating from about 1836 in which Maori warriors once sailed in Manukau Harbour. On the walls of the museum are fine portraits of Maori chiefs by C. F. Goldie.

On the first floor are collections of material on the geology, natural and environmental history, flora and fauna (particularly birds and marine mammals) of New Zealand. A notable item is the reconstruction of a giant moa. Also of interest are the collections of craft products (silver, ceramics, glass) old furniture and coins.

Attached to the museum is a planetarium which attracts many visitors.

Open: Mon.–Sat. 10am–5pm (in winter only to 4.15pm), Sun. 11am–5pm; performances of Maori dances daily at 11.15am and 1.30pm, preceded by guided tours of the Maori collection.

Winter Gardens	Close by are the Winter Gardens (glasshouses, both tropical and cold), built for the Auckland Exhibition of 1913. They are now part of Auckland's Botanic Gardens.

Parnell

To the east of the city centre, extending to Hobson Bay, is the old suburb of Parnell. It has preserved many Victorian buildings, which in recent years have been lovingly restored. Swarms of tourists haunt the nostalgic old shops (in particular shops selling craft objects) and restaurants strung along Parnell Road.

★Kinder House	At the end of Ayr Street (corner of Parnell Road; under the east side of the Auckland Domain) is a house built in 1856–57 for John Kinder, a clergyman who came to Auckland in 1855 and also made a name for himself as a painter and photographer. The building was designed by Frederick Thatcher, the architect who did so much work for Bishop Selwyn. It now houses a collection of views of Auckland by Kinder. Open: daily 10.30am–4pm.
Ewelme Cottage	Ewelme Cottage, at 14 Ayr Street (off Parnell Road), was built in 1863–64 for the first clergyman in Howick, one of the "fencible settlements" (see History, above), to his own design. Open: daily 10.30am–noon and 1–4.30pm.
★St Stephen's Chapel	In this little wooden church near Point Resolution, built by Frederick Thatcher in 1856–57, the constitution of the Anglican church in New Zealand was adopted. The chapel looks out on Judges Bay. The old churchyard contains the graves of many townspeople and soldiers of Auckland's early days.
Selwyn Court	Also in the Parnell district (St Stephen's Avenue/Parnell Road) is a church-like building with a tower (by Frederick Thatcher, 1863) built to house Bishop Selwyn's library. Beside this building, now used for meetings, is the bishop's residence.
★St Mary's Pro-Cathedral	Adjoining Selwyn Court, in Parnell Road, is St Mary's (Anglican) Pro-Cathedral (by B. W. Mountfort, 1888), in Neo-Gothic style. This wooden building, one of the largest of its kind in the world, was originally on the other side of the street but was moved in 1982 to its present site beside the new Holy Trinity Cathedral.

From the Rose Garden, which is a sea of blossom from November to March, there is a fine view of Auckland Harbour.

Rose Garden

Outer Districts

This 196m/643ft high volcanic cone (named after the Earl of Auckland's family name) on the south side of the city, from which there are fine views of the surrounding area, was the most southerly point of the site acquired from the Maoris in 1840 for the building of the new capital. There are barely recognisable traces of the Maori fortifications, which are believed to date from the 16th century. Nearby is Eden Garden, with fine old trees.

Mount Eden

Near Mount Eden, in the Epsom district (Gillies Avene), is Highwic House, rebuilt in 1862 in "carpenter's Gothic" style and later further enlarged. It belonged to a large landowner named Alfred Buckland and remained in his family until 1978. It is now a museum (open: daily 10.30am–noon and 1–4.30pm).

Highwic House

Farther south is another volcanic cone, One Tree Hill (183m/600ft), one of the city's finest viewpoints. From the top of the hill can be seen the old ditches and ramparts of the Maori *pa*, dating from the 17th/18th century, which once occupied the site and could accommodate up to 4000 people. On the highest point of the hill there once stood a sacred totara tree, which was ruthlessly felled by the first European settlers.

★ One Tree Hill, Cornwall Park

John Logan Campbell, the real founder of Auckland (see History, above), established a large farm on One Tree Hill in the late 1830s. On the occasion of a royal visit in 1901 he presented much of his land to the nation as Cornwall Park.

In the park is Auckland's oldest surviving building, Acacia Cottage, which was built by Campbell in 1841. When he died at a great age in 1912 he was buried on the summit of One Tree Hill. Beside his grave is an obelisk recording his respect for the Maoris and their achievements.

Acacia Cottage

Also on One Tree Hill is Auckland Observatory (guided visits by appointment).

Auckland Observatory

Under the west side of One Tree Hill, in 12 hectare/30 acres of parkland, is Ellerslie Racecourse, where New Zealand's major horse races are run. There is a small museum on the history of racing.

Ellerslie Racecourse

Aberton House, a two-storey gabled mansion on the slopes of Mount Albert, in the south-west of the city (100 Mount Albert Road; open: daily 10.30am–noon and 1–4.30pm), as built in 1862, and in 1870 Allan Kerr Taylor, a landowner who had become rich during the gold boom, added a ballroom and other apartments. Attractive features are the corner turrets and the verandas running round three sides of the building. It is set in beautiful and well cared for gardens.

Alberton House

On Mount Albert itself there are sparse remains of old Maori fortifications.

Mount Albert

This museum (open: daily 9am–5pm), in the Western Sprigs district (Great North Road), is devoted to the histoy of technology and transport in New Zealand. Its prize exhibits are objects belonging to the aviation pioneer Richard Pearse (1877–1953), who made his first flights about the same time as the Wright brothers. Also of interest are the old coaches, railway rolling stock, trams and vintage cars, as well as the collections of material on printing, photography and calculating machines. Between the museum and the nearby Zoo runs an old-time tram.

★★ Museum of Transport and Technology (MOTAT)

Also in the Western Springs district is Auckland Zoo (Motions Road), housing a wide range of animals in its spacious grounds. A popular attraction is the Nocturnal House, where kiwis can be seen grubbing for

Auckland Zoo

worms – one of the few places in New Zealand where these shy creatures can be seen. Open daily 9.30am–5.30pm, last admission 4.15pm.

★Kelly Tarlton's Underwater World

East of Hobson Bay, in the Orakei district (Tamaki Drive, Orakei Wharf) is Kelly Tarlton's Underwater World (open: daily 9am–9pm), a great tourist attraction. Visitors walk in long acrylic tunnels through huge tanks in which they can observe large numbers of fish of all sizes, including sharks and rays. There is a display devoted to the underwater explorations of Kelly Tarlton (1935–85), in the course of which he studied the marine fauna of the South Pacific and investigated wrecks lying off the coast of New Zealand.

Howick

23km/14½ miles south of Auckland, beautifully situated on the Hauraki Gulf, is Howick (pop. 15,000), an outlying suburb of the city. It was founded in 1847 as one of the chain of "fencible settlements" established by Governor Grey to protect the new town of Auckland on the south.

★Howick Colonial Village

The fencible settlement, with its well-preserved old houses, is now protected as a national monument. Of particular interest is All Saints Church (1847), which, like almost all the churches built in Bishop Selwyn's time, was designed by Frederick Thatcher. The nave was widened in 1862. The old churchyard, with graves of early settlers, is well preserved. Other buildings of interest are the Courthouse (1848) and Bell House (1852), now occupied by a restaurant. The old village is now an open-air museum (open: daily 10am–4pm).

Otara

20km/12½ miles south-east of the city centre is the outlying Otara district, with an interesting Polynesian market where visitors can feel something of the atmosphere of the South Seas. On the main square and in the community house there are colourful displays, particulary on Saturday mornings, of foodstuffs, clothing and art and crafts.

★Devonport

North-east of the city centre, beyond Waitemata Harbour, is the select residential suburb of Devonport with its elegant villas and carefully tended gardens. This is very much a holiday place, with an active beach life, a yacht marina and expensive boutiques.
Devonport also affords the finest view of the Auckland skyline.

Naval Museum

The Naval Museum in Devonport (Spring Street; open: daily 10am–4.30pm) illustrates the history of the Royal New Zealand Navy. Among much else, the collection includes uniforms, medals, ships' bells and ships' boats.

Mount Victoria

This viewpoint on the north side of Waitemata Harbour offers a quite new prospect of the city.

New Zealand Pavilions

The New Zealand pavilions, which attracted great interest at the International Exhibition in Brisbane in 1988, have been re-erected in Montgomerie Road on the south-western outskirts of the city, near the airport. They now house exhibitions on the mythology, history, natural world and environment of New Zealand.

Surroundings

Bathing beaches

Harbours

Thanks to its situation between two much ramified natural harbours Auckland has numbers of beautiful beaches. Particularly popular are the beaches on the north side of Waitemata Harbour between Cheltenham and Long Bay. The best beaches are at Takapuna and Milford.

West coast

There are some very beautiful beaches on the west coast, but with their sheer rocks, heavy surf from the stormy Tasman Sea and treacherous undertow they are dangerous for bathers. The following beaches are recommended for good swimmers: the beach at Piha (40km/25 miles west),

Karekare Beach, White's Beach, Bethell's Beach and the beach at Whatipu, at the entrance to Manukau Harbour.

There are a number of good bathing beaches in Hauraki Gulf. Among the most popular are the beaches on the Whangaparaora Peninsula (40km/25 miles on Highway 1) and at Orewa and Waiwera.

Hauraki Gulf

Tamaki Drive, starting from the Ferry Building, runs for 10km/6 miles past some very beautiful stretches of Waitemata Harbour to Judges Bay, below Parnell Park. It then cuts across Hobson Bay to Ohaku Bay, where many leisure craft and yachts are moored. In Orakei a *marae* constructed jointly by Maoris and whites and a meeting-house can be visited.

Excursions
★Tamaki Drive

On Bastion Point, farther east, there are remains of defensive structures. Some years ago there was a major conflict over land rights between the Maoris and the government when land claimed by the Maoris was due to be sold for building luxury houses. Finally in 1988 the government decided to give the land back and pay compensation.

On the point is the grave of Michael Joseph Savage (1872–1940), a very popular Labour prime minister. The commemorative column stands out against the triple volcanic peak on Rangitoto Island lying offshore from the point.

Then comes Mission Bay, with its beautiful and well equipped bathing beach. The mission station founded by Bishop Selwyn is now a restaurant. A select residential district has grown up round the bay.

Tamaki Drive ends at Achilles Point, at the east end of Heliers Bay, where a tablet commemorates the cruiser "Achilles", which in 1939, along with two other warships, sank the German battleship "Graf Spee".

The Auckland Wine Trail takes in some of the best known wineries in New Zealand at Henderson (c. 20km/12½ miles west) and Kumeu (c. 25km/15½ miles north-west), where visitors are shown round the establishment and can taste the wines. The wine-growers are mainly Dalmatians whose ancestors came to New Zealand to prospect for kauri gum.

★Auckland
Wine Trail

The green hills of the Waitakere Ranges, south-west of Auckland, are a very popular recreation area. A particular attraction is the Auckland Centennial Park (6400 hectares/16,000 acres), to the south of the area. 5km/3 miles west of Titirangi is an information bureau which can provide interesting information about the flora of the region, particularly about the last stands of kauri trees in this area.

Waitakere Ranges

There are some very attractive spots on the rugged west coast, its rocks lashed by the surf of the Tasman Sea, including the beaches at Piha (40km/25 miles west of Auckland). Piha and Karekare are also good start-ing-points for walks in the Waitakere Ranges, here delightfully green with their masses of ferns. Farther north is beautiful Muriwai Beach, where colonies of gannets from the offshore islands have established themselves on the mainland.

West coast

Hauraki Gulf

The Hauraki Gulf, caught between Northland, the city of Auckland and the long northward-reaching finger of the Coromandel Peninsula and scat-tered with numerous islands and islets, is a favourite sailing area and also offers good fishing.

Situation

Much of the gulf and some of the islands are included in Hauraki Gulf Maritime Park, which is home to numerous threatened species of birds, insects and marine creatures. A special permit is usually necessary to visit the islands, and then only on a day trip.

Hauraki Gulf
Maritime Park

There are boat trips to some of the islands near Auckland which are not included in the Maritime Park, particularly Rangitoto, Waikehe and Pakatoa.

The ★★ islands

95

Auckland

A beautiful recreation area within easy reach of Auckland:
the Hauraki Gulf with its many islands

Rangitoto

This volcanic island must still have been active at the time of the Polynesian settlement of New Zealand some 700 years ago, for there are no remains of any fortified Maori settlements. This beautiful island with its rolling hills, lying directly off Waitemata Harbour, was purchased by the government in 1857 and has ever since been a popular destination for excursions from Auckland. From the highest point on the island (260m/853ft) there are marvellous panoramic views. Rangitoto is now a nature reserve and part of Hauraki Gulf Maritime Park. There is a ferry service from Auckland.

Waiheke

Waiheke, a popular holiday island, is densely populated, with over 6000 inhabitants (30,000 in summer), many of whom commute daily to their work in Auckland. In the north of the island there are a number of beautiful beaches (Oneroa, Palm Beach, Onetangi).

Pakatoa

East of Waiheke is the small island of Pakatoa, also popular with holidaymakers.

Motuihe

Motuihe (area 180 hectares/450 acres), lying within easy reach of Auckland, attracts many people from the city on day trips. During the First World War there was a camp for internees and prisoners of war on the island. One of the prisoners interned here was Count Felix Lückner (see Famous People), who made a daring escape from the camp during a Christmas party, seized the camp commandant's yacht and, sailing under the German flag, got as far as the Kermadec Islands before being recaptured.

Kawau

Farther north is Kawau. This island, on which copper had previously been mined, was purchased in 1862 for £3700 by Governor Grey, who converted the mine manager's house into a mansion for his own occupation, surrounding it with a kind of "garden of Eden" containing many exotic plants and animals. The house, restored and furnished in period style, can be visited. There are boat services to Sandspit and Snells Beach.

Great Barrier Island (area 28,000 hectares/70,000 acres; population 600) was so named by Captain Cook because it barred the entrance to the gulf. Once inhabited by loggers felling kauri trees, gold prospectors and copper miners, it is now pasturage for dairy cows and sheep. At the end of the 19th century letters were conveyed from the island to the mainland by carrier pigeon. | Great Barrier Island

Now a strictly controlled nature reserve, Little Barrier Island is a refuge for rare species of birds and plants
    The island can be visited only with special permission from the Department of Conservation. | Little Barrier Island

This tiny islet, with an area of only 9 hectares/22½ acres, lies just off the coast to the north of Cape Rodney. On the island is the Marine Biology Research Institute of Auckland University. | Goat Island

The little island of Tiritiri Matangi (area 207 hectares/511 acres) lies off Whangaparaoa and has a lighthouse. Formerly grazing land, it is now a nature reserve, to which the natural forest is gradually returning. There is a good sandy beach, but apart from this the coast is extremely steep. The island can be visited only during the day. | Tiritiri Matangi

This island, an eroded cone of volcanic lava and scoria, lies immediately off the mouth of the Tamaki River. Here John Logan Campbell and William Brown established their first farm, before moving to One Tree Hill in Auckland. The island is now part of the Hauraki Gulf Maritime Park and can be visited only during the day. A landing should be attempted only at high tide, since at other times there may be dangerous shallows. | Motukorea (Brown Island)

Waiwera

Just under 50km/30 miles north of Auckland on Highway 1 is the pretty little beach settlement of Waiwera, with hot medicinal springs which were already famed in the 19th century. Many people came here to take the cure, and spa establishments and hotels were built to cater for them. The modern spa establishment is open daily from 9am to 10pm. | Situation and importance

To the north of Waiwera is the Wenderholm Reserve, a small nature reserve with attractive picnic areas and fine views of the Hauraki Gulf. | Wenderholm Reserve

Bay of Islands   H/I 2

Region: Northland

The Bay of Islands, so named by Cook in 1769, lies near the north end of the North Island. It has sprinkled with more than 150 small islands, mostly green and wooded. It is a drowned island system, the result of the rise in sea level after the last ice age. Its particular charm lies in its scatter of islands and subtropical climate. It is a popular resort for sailing enthusiasts and anglers. The Austrian artist Friedensreich Hundertwasser settled here and planted thousands of trees on his property, a former farm at Kawakawa. | Situation

The Bay of Islands Maritime and Historic Park extends from Whangaruru in the south to Whangaroa in the north. In addition to numerous islands it takes in areas under protection as nature reserves and places of historical interest on the coast and in its hinterland.
    The park can be explored on a network of hiking trails or by boat. The park offices, with an information centre, are in Russell. There is also a park rangers' station in Kerikeri. | ★★ Bay of Islands Maritime and Historic Park

Maori tradition has it that the legendary Polynesian seafarer Kupe visited the bay in the 10th century. Much later Captain Cook sailed round Cape | History

The Bay of Islands – a paradise for sailing enthusiasts

Brett, which projects far into the Pacific, to enter the bay. The French seafarer Marion du Fresne, following in Cook's footsteps, set up camp on Motorua Island in 1772 and claimed the territory, which he called France Australe, in the name of the French crown. After staying for some weeks and establishing friendly relations with the Maoris du Fresne's two ships were about to continue their voyage when they were attacked by the islanders and du Fresne and some of his men were killed. The reasons for the natives' change of mood are not known: it may be that the Frenchmen unintentionally broke some *tapu*. The surviving French sailors, in retaliation, burned down a number of villages and killed many Maoris before departing.

Missionary activity in the bay began in the early 19th century under the leadership of Samuel Marsden, an Anglican clergyman. Marsden had got to know two chiefs from this area in New South Wales, and they promised him their protection. He landed in the bay in 1814 and preached his first sermon that Christmas. A year later the first mission station was built, soon to be followed by others. At about the same time white settlement also began in the bay. The sheltered harbour of Kororareka attracted whalers, timber fellers and flax traders, and by 1820 a disreputable little port town had grown up, which after the signing of the treaty of Waitangi became the first capital of the British colony of New Zealand.

When war broke out in the north with the destruction of Kororareka/Russell by the Maori chief Hone Heke in 1845 the capital was transferred to Auckland, farther south. The Bay of Islands now attracts swarms of visitors. It preserves numbers of old buildings and other relics of the early days of the colony, for example at Waitangi, Kerikeri, Paihia, Waimate North and Russell.

Sailing and angling

The Bay of Islands was celebrated as an anglers' paradise by the American writer Zane Grey (1875–1939), an ardent big game angler, and it remains a favourite resort of both anglers and sailing enthusiasts.

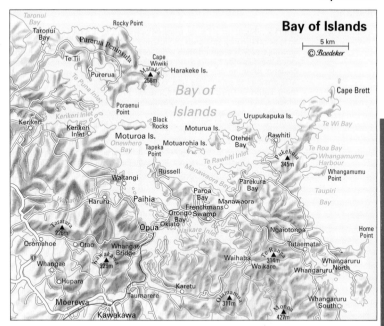

Bay of Islands

|— 5 km —|

© Baedeker

A very pleasant way of exploring the island world of the bay is to take the half-day cruise known as the "cream trip". The term goes back to the days when milk from the various islands was collected by boats which also delivered the mail.

Cream trip

Paihia

In the south-west of the Bay of Islands is the little town of Paihia (pop. 3000), which developed out of a mission station founded in 1823 and is now the chief town in the bay. Among the missionaries who were active in this area were Henry Williams and William Colenso, who were present at the signing of the treaty of Waitangi. Features of interest in the town are St Paul's Church (1926) and the Museum of Shipwrecks (in the barque "Tui"), with treasures recovered from ships wrecked in the area.

From Paihia visitors can take a variety of boat trips, for example the "cream trip" already mentioned and the "Cape Brett trip" to Piercy Island and Cape Brett, at the southern entrance to the bay.

Boat trips

In Otehei Bay (in the outer reaches of the Bay of Islands) can explore the colourful underwater world of the Bay of Islands in a tourist submarine.

Subsea Adventure

There are bus trips from Paihia to Cape Reinga, the most northerly point in New Zealand, with a side trip to Ninety Mile Beach.

Cape Reinga
bus trip

An old-style steam train plies between Opua and Kawakawa, to the south of Paihia.

Steam train

3km/2 miles west of Paihia are the Haruru Falls, which are particularly impressive after heavy rain.

Haruru Falls

Waitangi

Situation and importance

2km/1¼ miles north of Paihia, reached over a bridge, is Waitangi, situated in an inlet off the Bay of Islands, where on February 6th 1840 was signed the famous treaty between British officials and local Maori chiefs which provided the basis for the formal establishment of the British colony of New Zealand. After the War of American Independence Britain was not particularly anxious to establish a new colony in New Zealand, but the government could not prevent the haphazard foundation of settlements by whalers, seal-hunters, traders, speculators, time-expired and escaped convicts and adventurers. Moreover Edward Gibbon Wakefield had formed a company to promote the colonisation of New Zealand, the New Zealand Company, which in spite of the discouraging attitude of the government was determined to press on with large-scale settlement. The missionaries, too, who were now active in New Zealand, had appealed to the government for support in order to prevent the exploitation of the natives by white settlers. And finally there was some apprehension that the French might seek to annex New Zealand. Accordingly in 1832 the government sent out James Busby (1801–71) to the Bay of Island as British Resident, without giving him adequate powers or financial resources. Then in 1840 Captain William Hobson (1793–1842), a man in poor health, was sent to New Zealand as representative of the governor of New South Wales. He was given no troops and no money, but yet was expected to negotiate with the Maori chiefs for the recognition of British sovereignty over their country.

Hobson arrived in New Zealand at the end of January 1840. On February 5th the local chiefs met in front of Busby's house and spent the whole day discussing the terms of the draft treaty which had been prepared by Hobson with the help of Busby and the missionaries. On the following day the treaty was read a second time, discussed and finally signed by the 45 chiefs present. Copies of the treaty were then taken round the whole country by government officials and missionaries and presented to the chiefs who had not been present at the meeting. Much eloquence was applied to persuading them to sign, and advantage was often taken of their ignorance. Even so some chiefs refused to sign the treaty.

The problem with the treaty and its long-winded language was that despite all the explanations offered by the white men the chiefs were unable to understand it, for the idea of sovereignty meant nothing to them. The Maoris recognised no authority higher than the tribe.

On October 2nd 1840 the declaration of British sovereignty was published in London and acquired the force of law. The original copies of the treaty are preserved in the National Archives in Wellington.

The signing of the treaty is commemorated annually on February 6th with ceremonies in Waitangi. In recent years there have been repeated demonstrations by Maoris protesting against the treaty.

Treaty House

The Treaty House was originally built in 1833 by the Sydney architect John Verge as the private residence of James Busby, the British government's representative in the colony. The side wings were added later.

In 1932 it was acquired by the then governor-general and presented to the people of New Zealand. It is now open to the public as a historic monument.

★★ Maori meeting-house

Nearby is a large Maori meeting-house erected in 1940 on the hundredth anniversary of the treaty of Waitangi. The carving was the work of the famous Maori woodcarver Pine Taiapa. It incorporates all the different regional styles and bears witness to the Maoris' new-won national self-awareness. There is also a large canoe decorated with carving, made from the trunks of three kauri trees.

The Waitangi visitor centre supplies a variety of informative material; it is open daily 9am–5pm.

Kerikeri

In a very beautiful setting at the head of the narrow Kerikeri Inlet, which reaches far inland from the Bay of Islands, is the little town of Kerikeri (pop. 3000), a favourite residence of artists and well-to-do pensioners. Citrus fruits and various tropical fruits are grown on the fertile soil in the surrounding area.

Situation and importance

The second mission station in New Zealand was established here in 1819 by John Butler, who twenty years later moved to the new settlement of Wellington (see entry) to continue his missionary activities.

History

Kemp House, also known as the Kerikeri Mission Building, dates from 1822 and is thus the oldest stone building erected by white immigrants in New Zealand. John Butler, for whom it was built, lived in it only for a year before being moved to other work. After some rapid changes of missionaries the house was occupied by James Kemp in 1832 and remained in his family until 1974. After suffering damage from flooding it was thoroughly restored in 1981. The ground floor is in the style of the 1840s, the upper floor in Victorian style.
   Open: in summer daily 10.30am–12.30pm and 1.30–4.30pm, in winter (June–Aug.) closed Thu. and Fri.

★Kemp House

This two-storey stone building was erected in the 1830s to replace a wooden store-house which was burned down. At one time it housed Bishop Selwyn's library, which the bishop felt was safer in a stone building. During the war with Hone Heke it became an ammunition store. It is now occupied by a shop and a small museum of local history, with interesting material on the early days of the mission station.

Stone Store

On the opposite side of the inlet is a reconstruction of a *kainga,* an ordinary unfortified Maori village, as it may have looked before the coming of

★Rewa's Village

In Rewa's Village, a reconstructed Maori settlement near Kerikeri

Europeans. It gives a good impression of the way of life of the Maoris in pre-European days. It is notably lacking in carved decoration: no doubt it was felt that the much esteemed works of art with which meeting-houses and store-houses were decorated were safer in a *pa* (fortified settlement). Rewa, after whom the village is named, was the second most powerful man in the tribe after its chief, Hongi Hika.

Kororipo Pa

On the terraced hill above the inlet is the fortified Maori village of Kororipo Pa; it is reached on a signposted footpath which takes off at the Stone Store. This was the base from which Hongi Hika set out on his raids, thrusting as far afield as Wellington and the East Cape (see entries). In 1814 he met the missionary Samuel Ramsden in Sydney and helped him to establish mission stations at Rangihoua in 1814 and later at Kerikeri.

Russell

Situation

Some 70km/43 miles north-west of Whangarei, idyllically situated on a sheltered site on the Bay of Islands, is the old whaling station of Russell (pop. 1100). The best way to reach it is by ferry from Opua or Paihia; by car it can be reached on a roundabout route via Whakapara.

History

The settlement, originally called Kororareka, was of importance in the early 19th century as a whaling station and a trading post, where honest traders as well as a variety of more doubtful characters did business with the Maoris. There were numerous drinking houses and brothels which gave the place a bad name; but this was also the starting-point of missionary activity in New Zealand. In 1840 the treaty recognising British sovereignty was signed at Waitangi, on the opposite side of the inlet, and Governor Hobson acquired land in nearby Okiato on which to establish the seat of government. But Russell was not long to remain the capital, which was soon transferred to Auckland.

Russell's Christ Church is the oldest church in New Zealand

The name of the place was changed from Kororareka to Russell in honour of Lord John Russell, then British colonial secretary and later prime minister. In 1841 the government buildings in Russell were destroyed by fire. The change of name probably also reflected the inhabitants' desire to throw off the evil reputation of Kororareka. With the transfer of the seat of government to Auckland the Bay of Islands area declined in population and in importance. Customs duties introduced by the government led foreign shipping to avoid the port, and Hone Heke (see Famous People), chief of the Ngapuhi tribe, lost his income from mooring fees. He had signed the treaty of Waitangi, but he now felt himself cheated by the whites, and launched a fight for liberation from British rule. In 1844–45 he four times cut down the flagstaff bearing the British flag, and on the last occasion also, with his warriors, burned down the whole town except the churches and the mission station. The white population fled to Auckland and the war in the north began. After suffering two shameful defeats British forces defeated Hone Heke's men at Ruapekapeka in 1846. Thereafter Russell remained a quiet and remote little town, which still preserves much of the atmosphere of the 19th century.

Christ Church, built in 1836, is New Zealand's oldest surviving church. It was not, like other churches in the Bay of Islands, built as a mission church but as a place of worship for the white settlers. It was renovated and enlarged in 1871.

★ Christ Church

Round the church are many old gravestones, of whalers, seamen, Maoris and early settlers.

Pompallier House, built in 1841–42, was not, as might be supposed, the residence of Bishop Pompallier, who founded the first Roman Catholic mission station here in 1838, but housed the mission's printing press. The house was originally less elegant; it was only after the mission moved to Auckland that the new owners substantially altered it and added the veranda and chimney. Now protected as a national monument, it is furnished in 19th century style and still contains the old printing press. Open: daily 10am–12.30pm and 1.30–4.30pm.

Pompallier House

At the end of the beach, adjoining Pompallier House, is the house known simply as The Bungalow, built in 1853 for a British businessman, James R. Clendon, who was also the US honorary consul. His daughter ran a school here.

The Bungalow

The Captain Cook Memorial Museum in York Street commemorates the great explorer. Notable among the exhibits is a model of his ship, the "Endeavour". Open: daily 10am–4pm.

Captain Cook
Memorial
Museum

On the charming old harbour front there are many relics of the settlement's early days. Among them are the police station, in the old customs house, the Duke of Marlborough Tavern (which claims to have the oldest liquor licence in New Zealand) and an old cannon. Yachts and catamarans of all sizes are moored on the front, and there is great activity there during the holiday season and in the evenings, when the deep sea anglers come in with their catches.

★ Harbour front

From the landing-stage there are pleasant cruises in the Bay of Islands (the "cream trip", the "Cape Brett trip"). Visitors can also take a bus trip to Cape Reinga or cross on the ferry (15 min.) to Paihia.

There are wide views from Flagstaff Hill, on which Hone Heke several times cut down the flagstaff bearing the British flag (monument).

Flagstaff Hill

Kawakawa

16km/10 miles south of the Bay of Islands on Highway 1 is Kawakawa (pop. 2000), now the administrative headquarters of the Bay of Islands district. It

Situation and
importance

was originally a flax-processing centre, and later coal was mined here. Kawakawa is famous for its steam railway, which runs along the main street and connects Kawakawa with the old coal-shipping port of Opua.

★ Waiomio Caves   4km/2½ miles south of Kawakawa, on a side road branching off Highway 1, are the Waiomio Caves (conducted visits daily). This much ramified cave system attracts large numbers of visitors with its bizarre karstic features, variety of stalactitic formations and spectacular glowworm cave. It is owned by descendants of Chief Kawiti, who fought alongside Hone Heke at Ruapekapeka.

★ Ruapekapeka Pa   The old Maori stronghold of Ruapekapeka Pa is of great interest but is not easy of access. To reach it, turn off Highway 1 16km/10 miles south of Kawakawa and follow a poor gravel road (signposted) for 5km/3 miles. This was the scene of the last battle between Hone Heke and British troops. The *pa*, commanded by Hone Heke and his ally Kawiti, could not hold out against the sustained fire of the British forces, and after the storming of the fortress, which was watched by Governor Grey himself, Grey declared peace and allowed the Ngapuhi to return to their tribal territory. The rebels' land was not confiscated, as it was later in the land wars on the Taranaki peninsula, in the Bay of Plenty and at Waikato. The remains of the ramparts of the fort, underground positions and tunnels can still be identified, as well as the British gun positions. (It may be noted in passing that the Maori defences provided a model for the trench systems of the First World War).

From the elevated site of the battle there are fine panoramic views of the mountains of Northland.

Waimate North

Situation and importance   20km/12½ miles west of Paihia (see above) Samuel Marsden established the first Anglican settlement in the interior of the island in 1830. He laid out a farm on the British model so that the natives should not only be converted but should be introduced to useful work. The farm was a great success, and Charles Darwin, emerging from a long journey through primeval forest in 1835, was astonished to find himself in what seemed to him an English village. For a time Bishop Selwyn made the farm his residence and installed a theological seminary here.

★ Mission House   A relic of the early days of the settlement is the mission house, built in 1832 and thus the second oldest surviving building in New Zealand. It is a good example of the early colonial style of architecture. Now restored and furnished in period style, it is open to the public daily in summer.

St John's Church   Beside the mission house is St John's Church (1871), the third church on the site. The churchyard contains 19th century gravestones.

Bay of Plenty   K–M 4

Region: Bay of Plenty

Situation   The Bay of Plenty lies between the Coromandel Peninsula in the west and the East Cape in the east. The main towns are Tauranga (see entry), Whakatane and Opotiki.

Kiwi Coast   The gently curving and very shallow bay is now also known as the Kiwi Coast. Over the last thirty years numerous plantations of kiwi fruit, sheltered by the wind-breaks which are a prominent feature of the landscape, have been laid out here, producing abundant crops thanks to the long hours of sunshine and fertile volcanic soil.

Name   The bay was given its name by Captain Cook (see Famous People), who was able to take in large stores of water and victuals here, after leaving a

Prickly Outside, Succulent Within

It is barely twenty years since a New Zealand product conquered European and American markets and temples of gastronomy: the kiwi fruit, a large gooseberry-like fruit which is esteemed not only for its high content of vitamins C and E but also for its juicy sweet-sour flesh and good keeping quality. It originally came from China, and was long known as the Chinese gooseberry. The plant, which grows to a height of several metres, flourishes particularly on warm sites. It has relatively large hairy leaves and dioecious flowers (i.e. with male and female reproductive organs in separate flowers). The fruit, oval in shape and some 8cm/3in. long, with a thin brown hairy skin, is borne only on the female plants. The juicy greenish flesh contains small black seeds. The fruit reaches its full aroma nine months after flowering. It is harvested in New Zealand in May and June.

After picking the fruit must be stored or processed within two days. With suitable refrigeration it stays fresh for several months. The New Zealand fruit grower Hayward Wright succeeded in producing a particularly large and succulent variety. The plants are cultivated on trellises, in the proportion of one male to seven female plants. An average plant 8m/25ft high can yield up to a thousand fruits.

The kiwi fruit grown in New Zealand has proved an ideal export product. They can easily be preserved, refrigerated or used in the manufacture of fruit juice, wine, liqueurs, jelly and jam.

Exports flourished thanks to large-scale production in plantations and New Zealand technical know-how in the field of refrigeration. By the 1950s they had found markets all over the world. Every kiwi fruit exported bears a small sticker with the legend "The world's finest kiwi fruit". This label was one element in a brilliant marketing strategy. Gooseberries were not particularly popular, and anything Chinese was politically suspect in the international atmosphere of the time: hence the transmutation of the Chinese gooseberry into the kiwi fruit, taking over the name of New Zealand's national bird and the name which New Zealanders apply to themselves.

previous port of call in Poverty Bay (near Gisborne) almost empty-handed. Cook also gave names to the offshore islands such as White Island (after the plumes of steam from its volcano) and Mayor Island.

History

The Maori tribes in the Bay of Plenty were decimated by the raids of the Ngapuhi warriors from Northland, now armed with guns, and these tribal wars hindered missionary activity and white settlement.

After the end of the land wars in the Waikato area there was heavy fighting in the Tauranga area. Many British soldiers were killed during an attack on Gate Pa in 1864; and widespread terror and distress was caused by the Hauhau movement and later by Te Kooti's guerrilla war. After the end of the land wars ex-soldiers were settled in the Bay of Plenty (e.g. at Tauranga, Whakatane and Opotiki) on land confiscated from the Maoris.

Economy

At first the white settlers lived from pastoral farming, but in the 20th century fruit-growing gradually became the main source of income. Citrus fruits brought good profits, but in the 1960s the now fashionable kiwi fruit began to be grown, and it is now an export crop producing record yields.

In the hinterland of the Bay of Plenty and on the volcanic plateau pines are grown as a monoculture. The Californian pine (*Pinus radiata*) flourishes here and has the merit of growing very quickly. The little town of Tauranga has now developed into an important timber-exporting port.

Tourist
attractions

The beaches of the Bay of Plenty are popular with bathers and surfers. There is also good fishing.

Whakatane

Region: Bay of Plenty
Population: 17,000

Situation and
importance

The town of Whakatane, situated in the centre of the Bay of Plenty, at the mouth of the Whakatane River, is the supply centre for an area which depends on agriculture and forestry for a living. In its hinterland there are large plantations of kiwi fruit, and pastoral farming (dairy cattle, sheep, red deer) also makes a substantial contribution to the economy. Farther inland large areas have been planted with pines, and on the outskirts of the town there are large timber-processing plants (including papermaking factories). In summer Whakatane, with its beautiful beach, is a popular holiday resort.

History

Long before the arrival of Europeans this area was densely populated by Maori tribes. Toi, the legendary seafarer from Hawaiki, is said to have landed here and established a *pa* (fortified settlement) at the tip of the Whakatane Heads. An early white settlement was attacked in 1865: whereupon the governor imposed martial law and confiscated large areas of tribal land on the east side of the Bay of Plenty. In 1869 Te Kooti attacked the little military settlement and burned it down, but thereafter he was driven back into the Urewera hills. He was pardoned in 1883 and granted land at Wainui (east of Whakatane), on which he lived for the rest of his life.

In 1987 a severe earthquake caused heavy damage in the area.

Sights

Pohaturoa Rock

On this steep-sided sacred rock in the centre of the town is a *tapu* cave in which the Maoris used to hold their ceremonies. Since 1927 it has been a memorial to the dead of the First World War. Beside the rock is a model of an ancestral canoe of the Mataatua tribe.

From the summit of the rock there is a fine view of the town; and in good weather it is possible to see the white plumes of steam on White Island.

Whakatane
Museum

This little museum in Boon Street has a collection of fine Maori arts and crafts. It is open daily from 1.30 to 4pm.

Some 2km/1¼ miles from the town centre, where Maori tradition has it that the ancestral canoe landed.

Whakatane Heads

3km/2 miles west of the town on the road to Tauranga (see entry) are the Whakatane Board Mills, where timber from the Matahina pine forest, 48km/30 miles away, is processed (wood pulp, etc.). Conducted visits by appointment at 10.30am Mon.–Fri.

Board Mills

Ohope Beach, 6km/4 miles east of Whakatane, is much favoured by surfers and surf anglers. The narrow Ohiwa peninsula separates this beach from a more sheltered one inside the natural harbour.

Ohope Beach

12km/7½ miles south-west, on the road to Rotorua, is the little thermal resort of Awakeri Hot Springs.

Awakeri
Hot Springs

Kawerau

Region: Bay of Plenty. Population: 8000

Some 30km/20 miles inland from Whakatane, to the south-west, and roughly half way between Rotorua (see entry) and the Bay of Plenty, is Kawerau, a planned new town established in 1952 at the foot of Mount Edgecumbe. It lies near the Kaingaroa State Forest with its monocultural plantings of pines.

Situation and
importance

The town is dependent on the Tasman Pulp and Paper Mill, which produces mainly newsprint and cellulose for export. Substantial quantities of sawn timber are also produced and sold mainly to Australia. A decisive factor in siting the mills here was the existence nearby of a geothermal field, and natural hot steam is used to produce power. The mills process an annual 2 million cubic metres (2.6 million cubic yards) of timber from the huge pine forests in the surrounding area. Conducted tours daily at 1.30pm, starting from the main entrance.

Tasman Pulp
and Paper Mill

The 805m/2641ft high extinct volcano is an easy climb. It is possible to bathe in the crater lake on the summit, from which there are breathtaking views in all directions. The hill is sacred to the Ngatiawa tribe as a place of burial, and there have long been protests against afforestation on the hill and demands for its return to the Maoris.

★ Mount
Edgecumbe

22km/13½ miles south-west of Kawerau the Tarawera River, after flowing underground for some distance through a system of karstic caves, plunges down over a 60m/200ft high rock face. A beautiful path runs through the forest to the falls.

Tarawera Falls

Opotiki

Opotiki (pop. 4000), near the east end of the Bay of Plenty, was formerly one of the largest Maori settlements in the bay. On the outskirts of the town is the little St Stephen's church, built in 1864 on the initiative of Carl Volkner (1818–65), a German Lutheran missionary. Volkner, who had worked in Opotiki since 1859, was brutally murdered in the church by supporters of the Hauhau movement in 1865 on returning from a visit to Auckland. The Maoris suspected that he was a government spy and had betrayed them. Because of its nearness to the impenetrable Urewera Ranges Opotiki was frequently attacked by Hauhau groups or Chief Te Kooti's guerrillas.

Situation and
importance

White Island

White Island rises out of the Bay of Plenty to a height of 300m/985ft, some 50km/30 miles north of Whakatane. It is a highly active volcano, the con-

★ Volcanic island

tinuation of a chain of volcanoes on the North Island which runs north from Ruapehu in the Tongariro National Park (see entry). In an eruption in 1914 the eastern flank of the hill was literary blown away and the crater lake was drained. The volcano still shows considerable thermal actiivity: long white plumes of steam rising into the sky – hence the name given to the island by Captain Cook – hissing fumaroles, boiling and bubbling pools of mud, emissions of foul-smelling sulphurous vapours. White Island can be reached by boat from Whakatane and Tauranga (see entries) or on scenic flights by helicopter or light aircraft.

N.B.   Special permission is needed to land on White Island.

Coromandel Peninsula   K 3/4

Region: Waikato

Situation and ★topography

The Coromandel Peninsula, a tongue of land bearing the marks of volcanic activity, extends northward between the Hauraki Gulf and the Firth of Thames in the west and the Bay of Plenty (see entry) in the east. The landscape of the peninsula is full of contrasts, with wild and rugged mountains, mostly forest-covered, and sheer cliffs, but also beautiful sandy beaches. Surfers, divers and deep sea anglers prefer the rocky and much indented east coast; the sheltered west coast, particularly on the Firth of Thames, is a favourite haunt of sailing enthusiasts. In recent years the peninsula, with its still largely unspoiled natural landscape, has attracted many artists and large numbers of holidaymakers. Beautiful semi-precious stones can be found in its rivers and streams and on its beaches. Visitors should beware of dangerous abandoned mine shafts.

The Coromandel Peninsula, a region of rugged cliffs and beaches of fine sand

The peninsula takes its name from a British ship, HMS "Coromandel", which visited the harbour in 1820 to load kauri timber for the Royal Navy. The name was originally given to the port but was later applied to the whole peninsula.

Name

Like Northland (see entry), the Coromandel Peninsula was once covered with kauri trees yielding valuable resin, but by the early 19th century it was ravaged by loggers who flocked to the peninsula from far and wide. They were followed by resin-collectors, who dug over the soil, and then by gold-diggers, who had soon worked out the peninsula's easily accessible seams of gold.

History

The backbone of the peninsula is the Coromandel Range, which extends to the northern tip of the peninsula at Port Jackson.

Coromandel Range

Visitors can explore the varied landscapes of the peninsula on a round trip on Highway 25. A good starting-point is the little town of Thames.

Touring the peninsula

Thames

Region: Waikato. Population: 6500

Thames, the largest place on the Coromandel Peninsula, lies on the west side of the peninsula, at the point where the Waihou River flows into the Firth of Thames. It is made up of the two earlier settlements of Shortland (the port) and Grahamtown (the old gold-diggers' settlement). Captain Cook anchored in the Firth of Thames in November 1769 and surveyed the area at the mouth of the Waihou River. The local Maoris were friendly.

Situation and importance

After the discovery in the Coromandel hills in 1852 of seams of gold-bearing quartz the population of the peninsula increased enormously in the 1860s, for a time passing the 20,000 mark. At that time the town is said to have had more than 80 hotels. The gold rush reached its peak in 1873, but even before the First World War the gold was almost worked out, and the population left Thames altogether or turned to agriculture.

There is an interesting Mineralogical Museum (open: Mon.–Sat. 2–4pm), housed in the former School of Mines. In addition to an extensive collection of minerals it contains models of mines and "stamper batteries" (for crushing the rock) and miners' equipment.

The Thames Museum recalls the days of the early settlers.

The Queen of Beauty pump, behind the power station, once pumped water out of the mine shafts at depths of up to 300m/985ft.

The church to the south of the town occupies the site of the old Maori fortified settlement of Totara Pa, which was destroyed by Hongi Hika.

On a prominent site to the north of the town is a memorial to the dead of the First World War.

On the opposite side of the Firth of Thames, 30km/19 miles from Thames, is the thermal resort of Miranda.

Miranda

To the east of Thames is the Kauaeranga Valley, where in the past large numbers of kauri trees were felled and much resin collected.

Kauaeranga Valley

South of Thames is the little town of Kopu, from which there is a rewarding excursion (32km/20 miles) to Hikuai; the road, winding its way through wild and rugged scenery, was opened only in 1967.

Kopu

North-east and south-east of Thames extends the very beautiful Coromandel Forest Park, which can be explored on a number of walking trails. It has a total area of 63,400 hectares/156,600 acres, of which over 8000 hectares/20,000 acres consist of young planted kauris. Large areas of this rugged highland region are covered with natural rain forest. Information about the forest and its trails can be obtained from the park offices (13km/8 miles east of Thames on the road to Kauaeranga).

★ Coromandel Forest Park

Coromandel

Region: Waikato. Population: 1500

Situation and importance

On the north-west coast of the peninsula is the port of Coromandel, round which gold was worked in the 1860s. There is an interesting museum in the former School of Mines (seen by appointment). Other features are the old Court House (1860) and an old stamper battery for crushing the gold-bearing ore.

Excursions

From Coromandel Highway 25 runs by way of the old gold-digging town of Kuaotunu to Whitianga (48km/30 miles; see below). The road climbs gradually to 347m/1139ft, with fine views of the natural harbours of Coromandel and Whangapoua and of Mercury Bay.

There is a shorter route to Whitianga (33km/20 miles) on a narrow and winding road which runs past the Waiau Falls and through old stands of kauris. On the way it is worth climbing the Castle Rock (525m/1723ft) for the sake of the wide views from the summit.

The road from Tapu to Coroglen, farther south (29km/18 miles), follows a winding course through the Tapu and Waiwawa valleys, with the double peak of the Camel's Back (819m/2687ft) as backdrop. 3km/2 miles before Coroglen there is an unusual, almost square, kauri tree.

The coast road north of Coromandel is narrow and in poor condition, making the trip to Cape Colville, at the northern tip of the peninsula, slow and difficult.

Colville

26km/16 miles north of Coromandel the little township of Colville, an old loggers' camp and the last place for taking in supplies for the journey to the northern part of the peninsula (Port Jackson, Port Charles and Kennedy Bay).

Mount Moehau

At the north end of the peninsula is Mount Moehau (892m/2927ft), which the Maoris regard as a sacred mountain. The commander of the Arawa tribal canoe is believed to be buried on the summit. It is a steep and toilsome ascent – worth it for the sake of the view only in fine weather.

Whitianga

Region: Waikato. Population: 3000.

★ Mercury Bay

Some 70km/43 miles north of Thames, beautifully situated in Mercury Bay, is the very popular holiday resort of Whitianga. The bay is full of fishing boats and pleasure craft belonging to big game anglers and divers. Kupe, the legendary Polynesian seafarer, is said to have fished here. It was here too that Captain Cook hoisted the British flag in 1769 and took possession of New Zealand in the name of George III, while the scientists travelling with him observed the transit of Mercury, giving the bay its name.

Many million cubic metres of kauri timber and thousands of tons of resin from the Coromandel Peninsula were shipped from Whitianga.

Whitianga Rock

On Whitianga there was a fortified Maori settlement (*pa*) which impressed Cook with its defensive strength. It has now largely been demolished.

Shakespeare Cliffs

At Shakespeare Cliffs (easily reached from the Ferry Landing) is a monument to Captain Cook, who lay at anchor here in his "Endeavour".

Buffalo Beach

Near Whitianga is Buffalo Beach, named after a ship which ran aground here in 1840.

Hahei,
★ Cathedral Cave

A few kilometres east of Whitianga is Hahei, with a beautiful beach, at the end of which is the Cathedral Cave, a wide-mouthed sea-cave.

★ Hot Water Beach

To the south of Hahei is Hot Water Beach, where thermal springs gush out of the ground right on the beach.

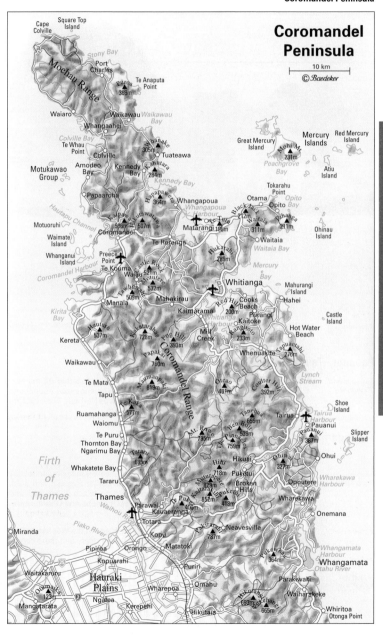

Coromandel Peninsula

10 km

© Baedeker

Cape Colville
Square Top Island
Stony Bay
Port Charles
Te Anaputa Point
Mochau Range
Puru 389m
Waiaro
Waikawau
Waikawau Bay
Whangaahei
Whanake 305m
Colville Bay
Te Whau Point
Colville
Tuateawa
Amodeo Bay
Kennedy Bay
Kahutara 284m
Kennedy Bay
Motukawao Group
Papaaroha
Honapaurere 364m
Whangapoua
Whangapoua Harbour
Great Mercury Island
Mercury Islands
Mohi Mt. 231m
Red Mercury Island
Peachgrove Bay
Atiu Island
Tokarahu Point
Otama
Opito Bay
Opito
Motuoruhi
Papawai 586m
Otautawhao 507m
Coromandel
Matarangi 186m
Black Jack 212m
311m
Mahanga 211m
Ohinau Island
Waimate Island
Te Rerenga
Whanganui Island
Preece Point
Hukarahi 289m
Waitaia
Waitaia Bay
Mercury
Coromandel Harbour
Te Kouma
Waiau
Castle Rock 521m
Moturee
Whitianga
Mahurangi Island
Hahei
Hautapu Channel
Pawhinau 509m
Manaia
Mahakirau
Kaimarama
Red Hill 200m
Cooks Beach
Purangi
Kaitoke
Castle Island
Kirita Bay
Hautura 537m
Matararahie 728m
Fog Hill 393m
Mill Creek
Rangihau
Rangihau 233m
Hot Water Beach
Kereta
Papakai 760m
Coromandel Range
Whenuakite
276m
Papaaotahi
Waikawau
Maumaupaki 819m
Oteao 401m
Counter Hill 392m
Lynch Stream
Te Mata
Tapu
Te Kata 577m
Mt. Raw 795m
Tanehua 659m
Tairua
Shoe Island
Tairua Harbour
Pauanui
Ruamahanga
Waiomu
Te Beck Hill
Te Pinm 339m
759m
Pauanui 387m
Slipper Island
Te Puru
Thornton Bay
Ngarimu Bay
Tararu 695m
Hikuai
Ohio 327m
Ohui
Firth of Thames
Whakatete Bay
Tararu
Hihi 718m
Puketui
Wharekawa Harbour
Moturoa 829m
Broken Hills
Opoutere
Wharekawa
Thames
Te Puke 400m
Te Puke 852m
Puketo 418m
Onemana
Parawai
Kauaeranga
Totara
Waihou
Miranda
Kopu
Pakirarahi 787m
Neavesville
Piako River
Pipiroa
Orongo
Matatoki
Puketoi Range 364m
Whangamata Harbour
Otahu River
Whangamata
Kopuarahi
Puriri
Waitakaruru
Hauraki Plains
Wharepoa
Omahu
Parakiwahi
Waiharakeke
Ohinemuri 123m
Ngatea
Kerepehi
Hikuraki 693m
Otuchange 665m
Whiritoa
Mangatarata
Hikutaia
Otonga Point

Cathedral Cave, on the Coromandel coast

Kuaotunu	North-east of Whitianga is Kuaotunu, once a flourishing gold-mining town but now almost deserted.

Pauanui · Tairua

Situation and importance	These two prettily situated holiday resorts lie close together on the east coast of the Coromandel Peninsula, between Whitianga (see above) and Whangamata (see below), separated only by Tairua Harbour. Their bathing beaches attract large numbers of holidaymakers.

Whangamata

Region: Waikato. Population: 4000

Situation and importance	On the south-east coast of the Coromandel Peninsula is the popular holiday resort of Whangamata, which grew out of an earlier loggers' and gold-diggers' settlement. There is a sheltered bathing beach in the bay, and there are other good beaches farther north at Onemana and Opoutere and to the south at Whirirtoa.
Walks	There is good walking in the Taitua State Forest and in the Wentworth and Parakowhai valleys in the interior of the peninsula. Here and there can be seen the remains of gold workings.

Waihi

Region: Bay of Plenty. Population: 4500

Situation and importance	The once flourishing gold-diggers' settlement of Waihi lies in the southern foothills of the Coromandel Range, near the Bay of Plenty (see entry). Gold

was found here in 1878, and the goldmine on Martha Hill, which was worked until 1952, was the most productive in the whole of New Zealand. Its deepest shaft goes down 550m/1805ft, and there are no fewer than 160km/100 miles of galleries and tunnels. In 1912 there were serious clashes between the mine workers and the mine owners, one consequence of which was the foundation of the New Zealand Labour Party.

When the Martha Mine closed down in 1952 because it was no longer economic to work it there were fears for the future of the town. Since then, however, it has developed into the main commercial centre of a wide surrounding area and some industry has been established in the town. In 1988 gold-mining was resumed.

There are many buildings in the town dating from early gold-mining days, and on Martha Hill are the ruins of the old pumping-house. The new Waihi Gold Mining Company is now working the gold by opencast methods over a large area. A huge hole in the ground, 200m/650ft deep, is to become the central feature of a new recreation area. There are conducted tours of the site by appointment.

★ Martha Hill goldmine

The Arts Centre and Museum recalls the days of the gold rush. All aspects of gold-mining are illustrated by a model of the mine, examples of miners' equipment both old and modern and large numbers of photographs.

Waihi Arts Centre and Museum

This gorge between Waihi and Paeroa is a kind of open-air museum of early gold-mining days. The Karangahake Gorge Historic Walkway (about 1½ hours) runs along the old railway line, passing some of the huge machines in which the ore was crushed.

★ Karangahake Gorge

During the main holiday season an old steam train runs through the gorge from Waihi to Paeroa, a distance of 13km/8 miles.

Old-time railway

11km/7 miles east of the town is a beautiful sandy beach 10km/6 miles long.

★ Waihi Beach

Dannevirke

L 7

Region: Hawke's Bay
Population: 6000

Dannevirke, a town founded by Scandinavian immigrants in 1872, lies on the eastern slopes of the Ruahine Range, 60km/37 miles north-east of Palmerston North (see entry) and 100km/62 miles south-west of Hastings (see entry).

Situation

The Scandinavian settlers were brought in to clear the Totara primeval forest, in an area between Masterton and Takapau known as the Seventy Mile Bush, and to build a road through the area. After clearing the land they lived mainly by pastoral farming; but many left again when the government decided to charge for the passage to New Zealand, which had previously been free.

The construction of sawmills and the coming of the railway in 1884 gave a boost to the economy of the town, and with the arrival of many British settlers it gradually lost its Nordic character.

History

The Domain Park is a very attractive open space with its old trees, enclosures for game and aviaries.

Domain Park

Surroundings

20km/12½ miles north of Dannevirke is the village of Norsewood (pop. 330), which also originated as a loggers' settlement founded by Scandinavian immigrants. In 1888 it was destroyed by fire. Later the Norsewear textile

Norsewood

factory was established here. There is an interesting Pioneer Museum in Upper Norsewood.

Seven Star Abbey West of Norsewood is Seven Star Abbey, a Cistercian house.

Waihi Falls These wild and romantic falls lie in primeval forest 40km/25 miles south-east of Dannevirke on the road to Waipatiki and Horoeka.

East Cape   M/N 4/5

Regions: Bay of Plenty, Gisborne

Suggested tour From Opotiki, on the Bay of Plenty, a road runs north-east along the coast to Hicks Bay and then turns south, bypassing the East Cape, and follows the east (Pacific) coast to Gisborne, on Poverty Bay. The distance between the two places on the coast road is 340km/210 miles. The scenic inland road from Opotiki to Gisborne, running through the Waioeka Gorge and the Waipaoa Valley (Highway 2), is only 150km/95 miles. We recommend a round trip combining both routes. The country is at its most beautiful around Christmas, in the southern summer, when the pohutukawa trees are covered in crimson blossom.

History Somewhere in the East Cape area, on October 8th 1769, Cook and his crew became the first Europeans to tread the soil of New Zealand. Two days before the ship's boy, Nick Young, had sighted, to the south of present-day Gisborne, a promontory which has ever since been known as Young Nick's Head. The first landing in Poverty Bay, however, was a disappointment.

The East Cape, until recently remote and inaccessible, is now an attractive holiday area

Cook sailed on, and after calling in at a number of other points on the east coast finally came to the Bay of Plenty, where he found in abundance all he needed for his ship and his crew.

Thanks to the remoteness of the East Cape from the centres of economic life on the North Island (Auckland and Wellington) and the barriers to communication formed by the wild Raukumara Range and the impenetrable primeval forests of the Urewera Range, this area long remained isolated. European settlement, too, proceeded very slowly. In spite of a massive drift to the towns the proportion of Maoris in the population is still exceptionally high, and around a quarter of the land belongs to Maoris. Much of the land is leased to white farmers. In the early days many European farmers allowed their land to run wild when their lease expired; and in the hilly interior there was severe damage from erosion after the forests were cleared.

Remoteness of East Cape

In the East Cape area magnificent examples of Maori woodcarving have been discovered, such as the meeting-houses and store-houses and the war canoes to be seen in ethnographic museums in Wellington and Auckland. Marvellously carved meeting-houses have been preserved in situ at Hicks Bay, Te Kaha, Tikitiki and Gisborne.

Maori woodcarving

56km/35 miles north-east of Opotiki is the seaside resort of Omaio Beach, which has an excellent tourist infrastructure.

Omaio Beach

70km/43 miles north-east of Opotiki, in a beautiful little bay, is Te Kaha. In the past this was the scene of many inter-tribal feuds, and there was once a fortified Maori village here. Between the 1830s and the 1930s many whalers came from the Bay of Islands (see entry) to the East Cape to hunt the whales passing this way. At Tukaki there is a richly decorated meeting-house erected in 1950. Earlier Maori artefacts from Te Kaha are now in the War Memorial Museum in Auckland (see entry).

Te Kaha

Almost 100km/60 miles north-east of Opotiki is Waihau Bay, with a diminutive township and a guest house established in 1914. From here there are fine views of the coast, extending as far as Cape Runaway.

Waihau Bay

This cape marks the eastern extremity of the Bay of Plenty (see entry). Captain Cook gave it its name while sailing from Poverty Bay to the Bay of Plenty, when a single cannon shot fired into the air dispersed the Maori war canoes which were approaching his ship.

Cape Runaway

120km/75 miles north-east of Opotiki is Whangaparaoa ("Bay of Whales"), which was a favourite whalers' base.

Whangaparaoa

150km/93 miles north-east of Opotiki and 190km/118 miles north of Gisborne is Hicks Bay, named after one of Cook's officers. It has very popular beaches, particularly the one in Horseshoe Bay. Other features of interest are a meeting-house at Tuwhakairiora (1872) and a glowworm cave near the local motel.

Hicks Bay

The East Cape, the most easterly point in New Zealand, can be reached only on a side road from Te Araroa. On the cape is a lighthouse 140m/460ft high from which there are breathtaking panoramic views. Round the cape are numerous wrecks.

East Cape

At Te Araroa is one of the tallest and oldest pohutukawa trees in New Zealand. In 1820 there were savage raids in this area by Ngapuhi tribesmen armed with guns, in the course of which several thousand members of the Ngati Porou tribe are said to have been killed or enslaved.
  Warning: The beach here is highly dangerous for swimmers because of the heavy surf.

Te Araroa

East Cape

Tikitiki

A few kilometres south of Te Araroa, beyond the Raukomara Range, is the little town of Tikitiki, with one of the finest Maori churches, St Mary's. It was built in 1924 as a memorial to the Maori soldiers who fell in the First World War.

Ruatoria

A short distance farther south is Ruatoria (pop. about 800), the chief place of the Ngati Porou, the principal Maori tribe on the east coast. This was the birthplace in 1874 of the Maori politician Apirana Ngata. Features of interest are the Mangahanea Marae estate, with a meeting-house of 1896, the Bungalow, which was the residence of Apirana Ngata, and the Porourangi meeting-house (1888; rebuilt 1934).

N.B.

All meeting-houses in this area are privately owned and can be entered only with special permission.

Mount Hikurangi

To the west of Ruatoria is Mount Hikurangi (1754m/5755ft), the highest peak in the Raukumara Range. A long-drawn-out dispute over the ownership of this mountain was settled only in 1991, when it was assigned to the Maoris.

Waipiro Bay

On the coast below Mount Hikurangi is Waipiro Bay, which at the beginning of the 20th century was one of the largest settlements on the east coast. Its remote situation, however, has been the cause of its decline.

Te Puia

A few kilometres farther south is Te Puia, a little town famed for its medicinal hot springs. From nearby Mount Molly there are magnificent views.

Tokomaru Bay

Farther south, in Tokomaru Bay, the ruins of a frozen meat plant and port installations bear witness to better times. There is a meeting-house of 1934 with fine carving.

Anaura Bay

After his disappointment in Poverty Bay Captain Cook landed on the beautiful sandy beach of Anaura Bay, where the natives were friendly. The strong surf, however, prevented him from taking in supplies of water. He was told that he could get water in Tolaga Bay, a quieter bay to the south.

From the Anaura Bay Walkway (4km/2½ miles long) at the north end of the bay there are fine views.

Tolaga Bay

With its beautiful beach, Tolaga attracts many bathers and anglers. A walking trail runs to Cook's Cove (private property; closed in August and September), where Cook drew water from a spring which has now dried up.

Waihau Beach

40km/25 miles north of Gisborne is the very beautiful Waihau Beach.

Whangara

The little Maori settlement of Whangara lies on the coast 30km/19 miles north of Gisborne. On the gable of the carved meeting-house is a figure of a man riding on a whale. According to a tribal legend the tribe's ancestor arrived here on a whale's back.

Raukumara Forest Park

This hilly and densely wooded nature reserve covers an area of 115,000 hectares/284,000 acres between the East Cape and the Bay of Plenty. It has little in the way of facilities for visitors. The highest peaks are Hikurangi (1754m/5755ft) and Raukumara (1413m/4636ft). The Motu River flows through the park. The best way to reach it is on the old road to Motu, 35km/22 miles east of Opotiki. Information from the Forest Service offices in Gisborne, Opotiki and Ruatoria.

★Route via East Cape

The road from Gisborne to Opotiki by way of the East Cape runs through varied scenery of great beauty which makes the longer journey (twice the length of the direct route on Highway 2) well worth while. But the shorter route too has great scenic attractions, running through the Waioeka Gorge, winding river valleys and an almost unpopulated region of forest-covered hills. Half way along this route, at Matawai, the old coach road via Motu (hard going; only in good weather) can be followed. An attractive trail, the Otoko Walkway, runs along the Waihuka River between Te Karaka and Rakauroa, following an abandoned railway line through the dense forest.

See entry   Gisborne

See Bay of Plenty   Opotiki

Gisborne · Poverty Bay   M/N 5

Region: Gisborne
Population: 32,000

The town of Gisborne lies in Poverty Bay (so named by Captain Cook in 1769), on the southern edge of the East Cape (see entry). Cook landed on Kaiti Beach, where the Turanganui River flows into the sea, but was prevented by the aggressive attitude of the natives from taking in food and water. The country round Poverty Bay is now a fertile fruit-growing area. Situated off the main communication routes and a long way from the most important New Zealand markets, Gisborne was long regarded as the "end of the world", and even today, when communications have been much improved, the population is in sharp decline. Between 1986 and 1991 the number of inhabitants in the Gisborne region fell by 3.4%, the highest reduction in the whole of New Zealand. The population includes a high proportion of Maoris (33%).

Situation and importance

The advance of the Hauhau movement into this region by way of Opotiki in 1865 put an end to a period of peaceful and successful development for

History

Lush grazing for sheep in the Gisborne area

117

Gisborne. Although the Maori tribes on the East Cape were in general well disposed to the government – particularly the Ngati Porou, who had suffered severely during the tribal wars – many Maoris supported the Hauhau movement which had just become active. There was heavy fighting between government troops and rebels at Ruatoria, to the north, and north-west of Gisborne. Then Te Kooti, who had previously supported the government, was arrested on suspicion of treason and deported without trial, along with other Hauhau supporters, to the Chatham Islands. Escaping from there, he returned and wrought a ruthless revenge. In an attack on Matawhero, to the west of Gisborne, 70 whites and Maoris loyal to the government were killed. There was further fighting with government troops, but Te Kooti always eluded capture and in 1872 sought refuge in Te Kuiti (King Country), where he lived until he was officially pardoned in 1883.

Name
The settlement originally bore the Maori name of Turanga, but in 1870 this was changed to Gisborne (after a colonial official of that name) in order to avoid confusion with Tauranga in the Bay of Plenty.

Sights in Gisborne and Surroundings

Kaiti Hill
(Titirangi)
From Kaiti Hill (Titirangi), at the foot of which Cook landed in 1769, there are magnificent views of the town and surrounding area. To the south there is a prospect over Poverty Bay as far as Young Nick's Head. On the summit of the hill is the James Cook Observatory.

Poho-o-Rawiri
At the foot of Kaiti Hill is the Poho-o-Rawiri meeting-house (1925), one of the largest and most modern of its kind, though it departs from the old tradition. The carvings are all by the Rotorua school (see entry). Above the building is a small Maori church.

Gisborne Museum
and Arts Centre
The Museum (open: daily 2–4.30pm), in Stout Street, illustrates the history of east coast culture and displays selected works by contemporary New Zealand artists.

Maritime Museum
The Maritime Museum, on the banks of the river, displays a variety of material, including relics of the "Star of Canada", which ran aground on Kaiti Beach in 1912.

Gray's Hill
Gray's Hill, 10km/6 miles west of Gisborne, also offers fine views of the fertile surrounding plains, the bay and Young Nick's Head.

Manutuke
14km/8½ miles south-west of Gisborne is Manutuke, with two beautifully carved 19th century meeting-houses. The barge-boards on the roof-ridge of the Te Mana-ki-Turanga house (1883) show the god Tane separating the sky from the earth and Maui drawing his great fish out of the sea. The Te Hau-ki-Turanga house (1842) which formerly stood nearby is now in the National Museum in Wellington. The other one still in Manutuke, Te Poho Rukupo, was built in 1887 in honour of the Maori chief Rupuko, who was famed as a woodcarver.

Matawhero
The church at Matawhero, 7km/4½ miles west of Gisborne, is the oldest church in the region. Constructed of kauri wood, it was originally built in 1862 as a store-house for Captain Read, one of the early settlers, and ten years later was converted into an Anglican church. It was the only building spared by Te Kooti when he ravaged the area in 1868.

Rongopai
At Rongopai, 20km/12½ miles north-west of Gisborne, is a meeting-house built in great haste when a visit from the Maori leader Te Kooti, who had been pardoned by the government, was expected – though he did not in fact turn up. The paintings in the interior, with their range of colours, show

a radical break with Maori tradition and strong European influences. When the house was built older Maoris are said to have been appalled by the work of their younger generation of artists.

North of Gisborne, along the coast road to the East Cape (see entry), are a series of beautiful beaches: Wainui Beach (5km/3 miles), Makorori (14km/8½ miles), Whangara (28km/17½ miles), Waihau (45km/28 miles) and Tolaga Bay (55km/34½ miles).

Beaches

The wild and romantic Rere Falls are 50km/30 miles west of Gisborne. The best way of getting there is via Patutahi and Ngatapa.

Rere Falls

At Morere, 60km/37 miles south of Gisborne on Highway 2, are hot springs. The area lies within a nature reserve.

Morere

The Mahia Peninsula, a massive hilly promontory projecting south into the sea, separates Hawke's Bay, to the south, from Poverty Bay. Here, some 80km/50 miles south of Gisborne, are a number of beautiful beaches and quiet holiday places.

Mahia Peninsula

Hamilton   K 4

Region: Waikato
Population: 150,000

Hamilton, New Zealand's fourth largest city, lies in the very fertile plain of the Waikato River. The country's only inland city, it has developed spectacularly since 1950. It has a university and several agricultural and food science research institutes, including the Meat Industry Research Institute of New Zealand.

Situation and importance

The military settlement of Hamilton was established in 1864, after the end of the land war in the Waikato area, on the site of an abandoned Maori village. Instead of being paid the soldiers were given a piece of land to cultivate. The town is named after Captain John Hamilton, who was killed in the Battle of Gate Pa, near Tauranga.

History

Before the coming of Europeans the Maoris had, with much labour, laid out fields of kumara in the fertile but frequently flooded plain. When the white missionaries arrived they adopted European farming methods, and by the 1840s and 1850s there were great fields of wheat in this area, mainly supplying the needs of Auckland. Before the construction of roads the Waikato and Waipa Rivers were the main transport routes in the interior of the country.

In the late 1850s the Waikato tribes sought to unite the Maoris, fragmented and often involved in inter-tribal feuds, against the superior power of the whites. They also felt themselves to be exploited when the bottom fell out of the grain market.

The land war broke out in Taranaki in 1860, but when the fighting ended there the government was ready for action in the Waikato area. Governor Grey had built a military road from Auckland to Waikato – the Great South Road – and fortifications were built south of Auckland to defend the town. General Cameron sent gunboats up the Waikato River, and with their help the Maori strong points, including Meremere, Rangiriri and Ngaruawahia, capital of the Maori king, were quickly taken. There was also fighting at Te Awamutu and Kihikihi. The Punui River to the south of Awamutu was now the frontier with the King Country, where the fleeing Maori king had taken refuge. Maori land up to the river was confiscated and allotted to British soldiers for cultivation; but they had difficulty in draining the swampy terrain, and the land was bought up by firms in Auckland with the necessary capital to drain the swamps. In 1878 the railway came to Hamilton.

Sights in Hamilton

Waikato Museum
of Art and History

The Waikato Museum of Art and History (Victoria and Grantham Streets; open: daily 10am–4.30pm; admission free on Mondays) has a large collection of Maori material, particularly on the Tainui tribe. Its prize exhibit is a carved war canoe of 1845. Also of interest are examples of woodcarving and weaving from Ngaruawahia.

Historic
buildings

The Bank of New Zealand at the corner of Hood Street and Victoria Street dates from 1878; it is due to be converted into a cultural centre. Hockin House (1893), in Selwyn Street, is the headquarters of the Waikato Historical Society. Lake House (1873), in Lake Street, is a masterpiece of Victorian architecture.

Waikato River

The Hamilton Gardens on the banks of the Waikato River are particularly beautiful when the roses are in bloom. An excursion steamer, the "Waipa Delta", plies on the river.

Victoria Street,
Main Street

In Victoria Street, which runs parallel to the river, and Main Street there are a number of private art galleries and sale exhibitions.

Theatres

Hamilton has two theatres: the Founders' Memorial Theatre (London and Tristram Streets), which tends towards the traditional, and the avant garde Left Bank Theatre (Marlborough Place).

Surroundings

Temple View

7km/4½ miles south-west of Hamilton is Temple View, the headquarters of New Zealand's Mormons.

Town centre, Hamilton

A peaceful landscape near Hamilton

50km/31 miles west of Hamilton, on the Tasman Sea, is Raglan, a pleasant seaside resort with a beach of black sand; it is named after Lord Raglan, commander of British forces in the Crimean War. The first white mission station in the Waikato region was established here in the 1830s.

Raglan

20km/12½ miles north-west of Hamilton is Ngaruawahia, once capital of a Maori kingdom of the Waikato tribes, where Chief Te Wherowhero was elected king as Potatau I in 1858. The present queen (since 1966) is the sixth (and first female) ruler of the Waikato tribes. A new king or queen is elected in a solemn ceremonial at the end of the *tangi* mourning ceremonies for the dead ruler in the presence of the body on its bier.

★ Ngaruawahia

During the land wars, which rapidly spread from Taranaki to the Waikato area, it became evident that the situation of the royal residence was a source of danger rather than security. After British gunboats on the Waikato had taken the Maori strongholds at Meremere and Rangiriri in 1863 Ngaruawahia was abandoned without a fight. After the battle of Orakau the king sought refuge with the tribes in King Country.

Maori land was then surveyed by the government and sold. Even after peace was concluded in 1881 it was many years before a new residence of the Maori kings was established here. Finally in 1920 land on the river was bought back from white settlers and the stronghold of Turangawaewae Pa was built. A major part in the rebuilding of the royal residence was played by the Maori princess Te Puea Hernagi (1884–1952). The first building erected was the Arehurewa shrine for relics, followed in 1923 by the Kiwikiwi meeting-house. The first post of the Mahinarangi meeting-house was driven into the ground by the famous Maori politician Apirana Ngati. In 1933 was built Turongo, a residence for King Koroki designed by Princess Te Puea: a six-sided tower-like structure with rich carved decoration. The Kimiora Cultural Complex (1974) contains a large mural painting. The queen's "palace" is not open to the public; it can be entered only on special occasions.

Hamilton

Ngaruawahia Regatta

Since 1896 a canoe regatta has been held annually in March at the Point, the confluence of the Waikato and the Waipa. Its high point is a parade of large war canoes.

A monument at the Point commemorates King Potatau I. Here too is a turret gun from a British gunboat, a relic of the land war of 1863.

Taupiri Mountain

7km/4½ miles north of Ngaruawahia, on the banks of the Waikato, is Taupiri Mountain (288m/945ft). The hill, which to the Maoris is sacred, was returned to them by the government only in 1975. On a site on the slopes of the hill which has been fortified since early times is the *tapu* burial-place of the Maori kings.

Huntly coal mines

On the lower course of the Waikato River, 33km/20 miles north of Hamilton, is the town of Huntly (pop. 7000). Here the river cuts through two huge coalfields which began to be worked in the 1840s. The coal deposits were systematically surveyed by the geologist Ferdinand von Hochstetter in 1859. After a number of serious accidents in the underground workings opencast mining started in 1940. There are now, however, also two new underground mines. Appointments for conducted tours can be made at the Coal Corporation office in Huntly.

Huntly power station

Huntly's coal-fired power station was completed in 1981. Its twin cooling towers, 150m/490ft high, are prominent features of the landscape. When operating at full capacity it produces more electricity than all the hydro-electric power stations on the Waikato River together.

Rangiriri

17km/10½ miles north of Huntly is Rangiriri, which in 1863, during the land wars, was the scene of a bloody encounter between British troops and Maoris. It was only after two unsuccessful assaults on the Maori stronghold here that it finally fell to the British. The main fortifications can still be seen on the west side of Highway 1.

Te Aroha

53km/33 miles north-east of Hamilton on Highway 26 is the old-established spa resort of Te Aroha (Waikato region; pop. 3500), situated at the foot of the hill of the same name on the fringes of the Kaimai Range. It still preserves its turn-of-the century Victorian-style bath-houses and spa establishments. There are three different mineral springs, whose water is used both for drinking and bathing. The old Bath-house No. 1 has now been replaced by a modern establishment. From Mount Te Aroha (952m/3124ft; walking trails, shuttle bus) there are beautiful views. Within easy reach of Te Aroha are the Kaimai Range (walking trails) and the imposing Wairere Falls (150m/490ft high).

Matamata

60km/37 miles east of Hamilton, on Highway 27, is the little town of Matamata (Waikato region; pop. 6000), the commercial centre of an agricultural region (sheep, dairy farming, horse-breeding). The town owes its origin to a 19th century British immigrant named Firth who leased more than 22,000 hectares/55,000 acres of land from the local Maori chief, Wiremu Tamihana. He drained the swamps, built a road to the military settlement of Cambridge and made the Waihou River navigable for cargo vessels. By the end of the century, however, his little empire had collapsed. He is commemorated by the three-storey Firth Tower (3km/2 miles east of Matamata), which he built in 1881 to protect his property against Maori raids. Beside the tower are his house and a number of other old buildings.

Kaimai Range

North-east of Matamata is the Kaimai Range, through which there are a number of walking trails. One particularly attractive trip is to the imposing Wairere Falls, 150m/490ft high. The trail takes off from the Matamata–Okauia–Gordon road.

Cambridge

Half an hour's drive from Hamilton is the very English-looking town of Cambridge (pop. 11,000), on the Waikato River, in the commercial centre of an agricultural area (cattle, sheep, horses; dairy farming). Cambridge was originally a military settlement established during the land wars in the Waikato region on the site of a fortified Maori village. British gunboats could sail up the Waikato River as far as this point. It is disputed whether the town was called Cambridge because the Waikato was thought to resemble the English river Cam or in compliment to the then commander-in-chief of the British army, the Duke of Cambridge. Historically interesting buildings are St Andrew's Church (Anglican; 1881), the Primary School (1879) and the old Court House with its handsome façade, now housing the Municipal Museum.

South-east of Cambridge is Lake Karapiro, a 24km/15 mile long artiificial lake supplying the Karapiro hydro-electric station. It is the highest of a chain of power stations on the Waikato which were brought into operation in 1948.

Lake Karapiro

30km/19 miles south of Hamilton (Highway 3), on the Waipa River, is the old Maori settlement of Te Awamutu (Waikato region; pop. 8500). The name means "end of the river" (that is, the highest point at which it was navigable by canoes). A mission station was established here in 1839. Te Awamutu is now the commercial centre of a dairy farming area. The last battles of the land war in the Waikato region were fought hereabouts in the late summer of 1864. The decisive battle was fought at Orakau, only 8km/5 miles from Te Awamutu, on March 31st 1864. The heroic resistance of Rewi Maniapoto provided material for the early New Zealand film "Rewi's Last Stand".

Te Awamutu

After the end of the land war in the Waikato region British soldiers were settled on land confiscated from the Maoris. The Puniu River marked the boundary between the confiscated land and the King Country, which no white settler dared enter until a peace treaty was signed with King Tawhiao in 1881. The railway reached Te Awamutu in 1880.

St John's Anglican Church (1854) has fine old stained glass and interesting gravestones. Beside it, in sharp contrast, is a modern church built in 1965. In the Civic Centre (Roche Street) is the Te Awamutu and District Museum (open: Tues.–Sat. 10am–4pm, Sun. 2–4pm), which is mainly devoted to the Maoris and the land wars. The Waipa Kokiri Arts Centre (showroom and sales Mon.–Thur. 9am–4pm, Fri. 2–4pm) was established to preserve and maintain the craft skills of the Maoris.

Pirongia Forest Park (15km/9 miles west of Te Awamutu), centred on an extinct volcano 959m/3146ft high, can be explored on a network of trails with mountain huts and fine views.

Pirongia
Forest Park

Hastings

L 6

Region: Hawke's Bay
Population: 58,000

The town of Hastings lies 20km/12½ miles south of Napier (see entry) in the fertile Heretaunga plain with its numerous fruit plantations, vineyards and parks. The town's economy centres on the foodstuffs industries (canning factories, fruit processing, brewing, meat freezing plants).

Situation and
importance

In 1864 a group of twelve settlers, known as the "twelve apostles", bought land in the Heretaunga plain. One of them, Francis Hicks, founded the settlement in 1873. It was originally to be called Hicksville, but this was replaced by its present name, in honour of Warren Hastings, first governor-general of the East India Company. Like its neighbour, Napier (see entry), Hastings was hit by a severe earthquake in 1931, in which several dozen people were killed and many buildings were totally destroyed. The rebuilding of the town was largely in Art Deco style.

History

Sights in Hastings and Surroundings

Exhibition Centre	The Hastings Exhibition Centre (Civic Centre, Eastbourne Street; open: daily 10am–4pm) has a large collection of Maori works of art, and also houses the Ebbett Collection, an art collection assembled by an early 20th century mayor of the town.
Leopard Brewery	There are conducted tours of the Leopard Brewery by appointment.
Havelock North	5km/3 miles south-east of Hastings is the select residential suburb of Havelock North (pop. 9000), named after Major-General Sir Henry Havelock, who distinguished himself in the Indian Mutiny. There are a number of well-known private schools.
Te Mata	From the 400m/1300ft high hill of Te Mata there is a marvellous view of Hawke's Bay. The hill can be climbed on a narrow road or an attractive footpath.
★Te Mata Estate	On the slopes of the hill is the Te Mata Estate, the oldest winery in New Zealand. This relatively small estate produces an excellent wine, Sauvignon Blanc Castle Hill.
Lourdes Chapel	On the road to Te Mata is a the modern Lourdes Chapel (1960) dedicated to the Virgin. Its architect, John Scott, was clearly influenced by Le Corbusier. The timber-built interior is reminiscent of churches built for Bishop Selwyn, such as All Saints in Howick and Old St Paul's in Wellington.
Wineries	Particular attractions in the climatically favoured region round Hastings and Napier are the many wineries, some of them very old-established.
★Hawke's Bay Wine Trail	Some wineries can be visited in the course of a walk on the Hawke's Bay Wine Trail. Information, including brief guides with maps, from tourist offices in Hastings and Napier. Notable wineries include Greenmeadows Mount St Mary's Mission, Vidal's Vineyard (Hastings), Te Mata Estate (Havelock North), Corban's Winery (Napier), Esk Valley Estate (north of Napier) and Brookfields Vineyards (Meeanee, between Napier and Hastings).
Waimarama	30km/19 miles south-east of Hastings by way of Havelock North is Waimarama, with a beautiful sandy beach. From here there are fine views of the high cliffs of Bare Island.
Ocean Beach	Ocean Beach, also reached by way of Havelock North, is another excellent beach.
Pakipaki	In the Maori village of Pakipaki, 6km/4 miles south of Hastings is the Houngara meeting-house (1916), with fine carving.
Te Aute College	30km/19 miles south of Hastings is Te Aute College, a school founded in 1854, mainly for Maori pupils. The school is famed for having taught three future Maori leaders, Maui Pomare, Apirana Ngata and Peter Buck, and is seen by many as the cradle of the influential Young Maori Party. The school has a fine assembly hall, with magnificent carving done by Pine Taiapa in the 1930s.
Waipawa, Waipukurau	43km/27 miles and 50km/31 miles south-west of Hastings are the two little townships of Waipata (pop. 1700) and Waipukurau (pop. 3700), founded in the 1860s by the owners of large sheep farms. 44km/27 miles south of Waipukurau and 5km/3 miles before Porangahau, on a hill just off the road, is a village with the longest place-name in the world – 36 letters in the official spelling and no fewer than 62 in the colloquial version. The name of the hill is a story in itself: "the place where Tamatea, the man with the big knees, who fell down hills, climbed up again and ate them, became known as the land-eater and played a song to his loved one on the flute" (the loved one was his twin brother, who was killed in battle).

Region: Taranaki
Population: 11,000

Under the south side of Mount Taranaki, at the north-west end of Taranaki | Situation and
Bay, is the agricultural market town of Hawera, whose Maori name means | history
"burnt earth". In the face of the threat from the Hauhau movement after the
land wars in the Taranaki region the settlers withdrew southward to Patea.
In 1870 a military post was established at Hawera, and round this a settlement grew up. Angered by the government's tolerance in its dealings with
the Maori leader Te Whiti and the passive resistance and civil disobedience
of his tribe, the local settlers drove out the Maoris and proclaimed the
republic of Hawera; but this separatist movement was quickly put down by
the government.

Sights

Of the fortified Maori settlement of Turuturu-mokai Pa, built long before the | Turuturu-mokai Pa
arrival of Europeans, there remain parts of the ramparts, deep ditches and
storage pits.
  There survive also five outer defences (2.5km/1½ miles north of Hawera;
signposted). In the late 1860 British troops constructed a defensive position
outside the *pa*, which was attacked and overrun in 1868 by Hauhau warriors
and a white defector.

From the 50m/165ft high water-tower at the corner of High Street and | Water-tower
Albion Street there are magnificent views.

The Elvis Presley Memorial Room at 51 Argyle Street has a collection of | Elvis Presley
records and souvenirs of the famous rock star assembled by a local Elvis | Memorial Room
fan.

The Tawhiti Museum, housed in a former dairy, has a rich collection of | Tawhiti Museum
material on the eventful history of the region.

Surroundings

3km/2 miles north-east of Hawera an old railway once used for transporting | Bush railway
logs has been reactivated as a tourist attraction.

7km/4½ miles west of Hawera, at the mouth of the Waigongoro River, is | Ohawe Beach
Ohawe Beach, where the first moa bones were found, making it possible to
reconstruct the skeleton of this long extinct giant flightless bird. It is
believed that there were several species of moa still living in the Taranaki
area in the 14th century.

23km/14 miles north-west of Hawera by way of Okaiawa is the scene of the | Te Ngutu-o-te-
battle of Te Ngutu-o-te-manu (1868), in which government troops suffered | manu
heavy losses in an effort to avenge the taking of their position at Turuturu- | battlefield
mokai Pa.

28km/17 miles south-east of Hawera is the old military settlement of Patea | Patea
(pop. 2000), established in the 1860s, which played an important part in the
land wars. It is now a dairying and sheep-farming region. In good weather
there is a fine view from here of Mount Taranaki (Egmont).
  Here too can be seen a 17m/56ft long concrete model of the Aotea tribal
canoe, erected in 1933 to commemorate the ancestors of the Maori tribes
who once lived in this area.
  The South Taranaki Museum (Egmont Street; open: daily 10am–4pm)
has a collection of Maori artefacts and mementoes of the early days of
white settlement.

Lake Rotorangi   Inland, in a densely forested area, is Lake Rotorangi, a 46km/29 mile long artificial lake on the Patea River. created in 1984 to supply water to a large hydro-electric power station. The lake attracts large numbers of anglers and sailing enthusiasts. It can be reached from Hawera, or via Eltham and Patea.

Hawke's Bay   L/M 6

Region: Hawke's Bay

Situation   This crescent-shaped bay lies on the east side of the North Island, to the north of Hastings (see entry). It was given its name (after Admiral Lord Hawke) by Captain Cook in 1769. It is bounded on the north-east by the Mahia Peninsula and on the south-west by Cape Kidnappers.

Climate   Hawke's Bay has a Mediterranean climate, with little rain and long hours of sunshine, and thus provides ideal conditions for fruit-growing and horticulture, with the main emphasis on vines and various kinds of vegetable. In spite of this the population has been steadily falling in recent years.

Cape Kidnappers, ★gannet colony   Cape Kidnappers, 21km/13 miles east of Hastings at the south end of Hawke's Bay, near Clifton, is noted particularly as a nesting-place for gannets. The birds arrive in the sanctuary here at the end of July. Their eggs are laid between October and November, and the young birds hatch six weeks later. The gannets begin to leave their nesting-place in February, and by April almost all of them have gone.

    The gannet colony can be reached from Clifton only at low tide. It is a 6km/4 mile walk along the sandy beach to an observation platform. There

Cape Kidnappers, south-east of Hastings, is one of the few places where gannets can be seen close up

are conducted tours from Te Awanga and trips in cross-country vehicles to near the site.

In Maori mythology the cape was Maui's magic fish-hook, with which he had hauled the whole of the North Island, like a giant fish, out of the sea. It was given its present name by Captain Cook, who after his first disappointing landing in Poverty Bay had turned back, sailed south and anchored off the cape. On the following morning, when Cook was bargaining with the Maoris who had come out to his ship in canoes, some of them seized a young Tahitian named Taiata, the servant of Cook's interpreter, and carried him off. The young man managed to escape and swim back to the ship: whereupon Cook named the steep rocky promontory Cape Kidnappers. It was another fifty years before the first white men settled here. The first comers were whalers, who set up whaling stations at Mahia, Wairoa and elsewhere. Around 1840 there were still only a few Europeans living in Hawke's Bay; then during the 1840s the missionary William Colenso established a mission station at Clive. He brought the natives the Bible in the Maori language, but he also showed them how to grow grain and fruit. A notable feature of the European settlement of Hawke's Bay and its hinterland is that it was carried out not by poor immigrants but by entrepreneurs well provided with capital who bought huge areas of land from the Maoris and established large sheep farms. They did not work the farms themselves but appointed efficient managers to do it for them.

The hinterland of Hawke's Bay is hilly and sometimes mountainous. The only flat area is the Heretaunga plain near Hastings (see entry), which was drained, divided up into smaller holdings and sold.

In February 1931 the Hawke's Bay area was hit by a severe earthquake which caused heavy damage, particularly in Napier and Hastings, and killed more than 200 people. One consequence of the earthquake was a rise in the level of the sea-bed which created over 3000 hectares/7500 acres of new land in this area.

The little town of Wairoa (pop. 5000), situated on Hawke's Bay between Napier and Gisborne (see entries), is the commercial centre of a large pastoral farming region and a good base from which to explore Urewera National Park, with Lake Waikaremoana. The first Europeans to come here in the 1820s were flax-dealers, later followed by whalers and missionaries. In 1865 there was fighting between the white settlers and supporters of the Hauhau movement, who were finally compelled to withdraw to the roadless fastnesses of the Urewera Range.

The most striking feature on Marine Parade is an old lighthouse of kauri wood which from 1877 to 1958 stood on Portland Island, off the southern tip of the Mahia Peninsula. The Wairoa Museum has mementoes of the early days of settlement and a good collection of Maori material. From the bridge there is a view upstream of the Takitimu meeting-house, with carving by Pine Taiapa.

See Hastings, Gisborne, Napier

Margin notes:
History
Wairoa
Other sights

Hinerau's Track

See Urewera National Park

Hokianga Harbour   H 2

Region: Northland

Hokianga Harbour, a long and much ramified inlet on the west side of the northern tip of the North Island, is a drowned valley system with very

Margin note: Situation and history

different landscapes on each side. On the bare north side are tall sand dunes; on the green south side are the little holiday resorts of Omapere and Opononi, both of which have beautiful beaches. Many ships have come to grief on shallows and sandbanks. Maori legend has it that Kupe, the legendary Polynesian seafarer and discoverer of New Zealand, set out from here on his voyage home to Hawaiki. Much later, probably at about the same time as in the Bay of Islands (see entry), European, Australian and American whalers, timber-dealers and flax-dealers began to put in here. It is believed that the first immigrants settled here in 1827 but from fear of the Maoris moved on to Australia. Until the early 20th century kauri timber and kauri resin formed the bulk of the trade in Hokianga Harbour, which became an important port of call for ships from all over the world. The population was larger than it is today; but the loggers, gum-diggers and sawmill workers gradually gave place to farmers, who pastured their cattle and sheep on the land which had been cleared of trees. Remnants of the original kauri forests have been preserved both north and south of Hokianga Harbour, in the form of Omahuta Forest Sanctuary (north) and Waipoua and Trounson Forests (south).

Baron de Thierry (1793–1864), a French aristocrat living in exile in England, had made the acquaintance of the Maori chiefs Hongi Hika and Waikato in Cambridge during their visit to Britain and had obtained from them, in some dubious fashion, ownership rights over large territories in Northland. In 1837 he turned up in Hokianga with a group of followers, claiming to be "sovereign chief of New Zealand", to carry out his plan for a settlement at Rangiahua. But his plan was impracticable and he was unable to establish his claims; his followers abandoned him, and he lived out his life in poverty in Auckland.

Places in Hokianga Harbour

Horeke

Horeke is a picturesque little port town to the north of Taneke, with its houses built on piles. A shipyard was established here around 1827–28, but by 1830 its Australian owners had run out of money.

Mangungu Mission House

A Wesleyan mission station was established to the west of Horeke around 1838. The Wesleyans had started their missionary work ten years before with the support of Chief Eruera Patuone, who is believed to have had some contact, as a small boy, with members of Captain Cook's crew. One of the missionaries, John Hobbs, had good relations with the natives and spoke Maori, and later he was able to act as Governor Hobson's translator during the negotiation of the treaty of Waitangi. When the population of the area moved south the mission station was transferred to Auckland (1855). The old mission church has disappeared, but the churchyard with its old gravestones is still there. The Mission House, furnished in period style, is now run by the Historic Places Trust; it is open daily noon–4pm during the main holiday season; at other times of year by appointment.

Kohukohu

Kohukohu, on the north side of Hokianga Harbour, was once an important loggers' settlement. The first Roman Catholic mass in New Zealand was celebrated here by Bishop Pompallier in 1838 – an event commemorated by a memorial stone on Totara Point. Kohukohu is now a town much favoured by artists and people who want to get away from city life.

There is a ferry from Kohukohu to the neighbouring settlement of Rawene, to the south.

Omapere

From Omapere travellers coming from the south on Highway 12 have a magnificent view of the spacious natural harbour. There is a pleasant walk along the beach, going west, to the harbour entrance. At high tide spray shoots high into the air from a blowhole.

Onoke

In the little township of Onoke, situated at the point where the Whirinaki River flows into Hokianga Harbour, is a house which belonged to Frederick

Maning (c. 1860), the trader and writer who became widely known under the pseudonym "A Pakeha Maori".

The holiday resort of Opononi, near the Hokianga Heads, has a beautiful beach. A well-known Opononi character was a dolphin called Opo who was particularly friendly with children playing on the beach and is now commemorated in a sculpture by Russell Clark. 2km/1¼ miles farther east, at Pakanae, is a monument to the legendary Polynesian seafarer Kupe. There are fascinating cruises from Opononi on a historic old steamer (restored) round the many arms and inlets of Hokianga Harbour.

Opononi

The old loggers' settlement of Rawene (pop. 350) is prettily situated on a promontory. Some of its houses are still built on piles in the water. This is another little place which has been given a fresh lease of life by artists and dropouts. Notable buildings are the Old Hotel, the former hospital beside the landing-stage and above all Clendon House, built in the 1860s for the successful British businessman James R. Clendon. Clendon had first brought a consignment of convicts to Australia and then became a dealer in kauri wood. In the Bay of Islands he established contacts with American whalers, and finally was appointed US honorary consul in New Zealand. His personal relationships gave him great influence. He built himself a number of houses, three of which have survived – in Russell, in Manawaora (east of Russell) and in Rawene. His house in Okiato (south of Russell), which had served as New Zealand's first Government House, was burned down in 1842. Clendon House, lovingly restored and furnished in the style of its period, stands on the Esplanade in Rawene and is open to the public as a museum (daily 10am–4pm).

Rawene

Kaikohe   H 2

Region: Northland
Population: 4000

Centrally situated in Northland, an hour's drive east of Hokianga Harbour, is the little town of Kaikohe. In this area the Ngapuhi, a tribe famed as being particularly warlike, had many fortified settlements. After earlier tribal wars the "War of the North" was fought out here between Hone Heke and government troops. Two months after Hone Heke's attack on Kororareka (Russell) in May 1845 he fought a battle with British troops at Lake Omapere, which is only 2m/7ft deep and is fed by hot springs near its south-west corner. The British forces suffered heavy losses, but even more Maoris were killed in the successful defence of their pa, 9km/5½ miles north-east of Kaikohe. A few weeks later, in another battle at Ohaeawai (north-east of Kaikohe), British troops again suffered heavy losses. The battlefield is now marked by a simple little Maori church dedicated to St Michael, erected in 1871, within the ramparts of the pa. Six months later Hone Heke was decisively defeated in the battle of Ruapekapeka.

Situation and history

Prominently situated on a hill near Kaikohe is a monument to the widely respected politician Hone Heke (1889–1909), who died young. He was a grand-nephew of the notorious and warlike Maori chief of the same name.

Hone Heke Monument

In Kaikohe's Pioneer Village (open at weekends) visitors can see an old courthouse from Waimate North (1862), a tiny jail, a smithy and other 19th century buildings. There is also an old railway built for the transport of timber.

Pioneer Village

7km/4½ miles east of Kaikohe, reached on a road which branches off Highway 12, are the hot springs of Ngawha. The water, containing mercury and soda, are used in the treatment of skin conditions and rheumatism.

Ngawha hot springs

Kaipara Harbour   I 3

Regions: Auckland and Northland

Topography

It is an hour's drive north from Auckland (see entry) to the southern shore of Kaipara Harbour, a vast natural harbour with numerous indentations and inlets which is a whole system of drowned river valleys. Kaipara Harbour has a total shoreline of over 3000km/1860 miles. Only from a few places is there a general view of its whole area. There are good views from Highway 1 at Bryderwyn and from the road (not asphalted all the way) between Wellsford and Helensville.

History

In the 19th century Kaipara Harbour was an important route for the transport of kauri logs and kauri resin from the great forests of Northland. Nowadays it is much quieter. Most of the peaceful little townships and villages – Helensville, Port Albert, Whakapirau, Pahi, Timopai, Pouto, etc. – can be reached only on secondary and minor roads.

Matakohe

The most notable feature of Matakohe, situated on Highway 12 at the north end of Kaipara Harbour, is the Coates Memorial Church, a non-denominational church built in honour of Prime Minister Joseph Gordon Coates (1878–1943), who is depicted as a knight in armour in a round stained glass window.

★ Otamatea Kauri and Pioneer Museum

Adjoining the church is the famous Otamatea Kauri and Pioneer Museum (open: daily 9am–5pm), which has interesting displays vividly illustrating the days of the early white settlers and the history of kauri felling and resin gathering.

Kaitaia   H 2

Region: Northland
Population: 5200

Situation

Near the northern tip of the North Island is Kaitaia, an important commercial centre for the surrounding area. It is a good base for excursions northward via Waipapakauri and along Ninety Mile Beach to Cape Reinga (see below) or westward to the Maori settlement of Ahipara, at the south end of Ninety Mile Beach. The road to Cape Reinga is good all the way; but most car hire firms ban driving along the beach itself.

Population

The population of Kaitaia includes a strikingly high proportion of Maoris, as well as many descendants of 19th century immigrants from Dalmatia who made a living as gum-diggers.

Aupouri Forest

In Aupouri Forest, to the north of Kaitaia, efforts are being made to halt the drifting of sand and consolidate the dunes by planting pines along the beach.

Surf fishing competition

The Ninety Mile Beach Surfcasting Contest, held annually in January, attracts thousands of angling enthusiasts.

History

Kaitaia was founded in 1834 as a mission station, and grew rapidly when kauri prospectors arrived in Northland. After the First World War tourist development began under the slogan of the "winterless North".

Far North Regional Museum

The Far North Regional Museum (open daily) has interesting displays on kauri resin. It also has an anchor which the French navigator J.-F.-M. de Surville lost during a storm in Doubtless Bay in 1769.

Kaitaia Track

This hiking trail (just under 10km/6 miles long), 3km/2 miles south of Kaitaia, runs through magnificent scenery.

This 11km/7 mile long trail, 26km/16 miles south-west of Kaitaia, runs from the Takahue valley to the wild Mangamuka Gorge.

40km/25 miles south-east of Kaitaia is the Omahuta Forest Sanctuary, with magnificent old kauri trees. Here the original forest vegetation has largely been preserved. There are also many species of birds.

★Omahuta Forest
Sanctuary

A road turns off Highway 1 to the south of Mangamuka Bridge and runs for 13km/8 miles to a parking area from which a footpath goes off into the forest.

Doubtless Bay

Doubtless Bay, 35km/22 miles north-east of Kaitaia, extends from Cape Karikari in the north-west to Berghan Point in the north-east, and is easily accessible on Highway 10. Its main attraction to visitors lies in its beautiful beaches. Offshore there are good fishing grounds for deep sea anglers. Matai Bay and Cape Karikari are favourite haunts of scuba divers.

★Situation

According to Maori mythology Kupe, the legendary seafarer from Hawaiki, made his first landing in New Zealand here, at Taipa. The name Doubtless Bay was given by Captain Cook, who, sailing along this coast in 1769, decided that "doubtless" it was a bay and not an island.

History

Soon after Cook passed this way the French navigator J.-F.-M. de Surville, heading for Peru, arrived in the bay and landed at Whatuwhiwhi. The natives were at first friendly, but turned hostile when a dispute arose over a ship's boat which had been carried away in a storm. Surville burned down the Maoris' huts and took their chief on board as a prisoner. The chief died soon afterwards of scurvy, and Surville himself died in an accident in a boat in heavy surf. Surville lost three anchors in a storm off Doubtless Bay. They were recovered in 1974 and 1982, and one of them can be seen in Kaitaia Museum.

The little township of Cooper's Beach, between two old fortified Maori settlements, has a beautiful bathing beach.

Cooper's Beach

Mangonui, once a centre of the kauri trade, with sawmills and port installations for handling timber, lies in a beautiful setting. It has a number of old buildings as reminders of earlier days. At the landing stage is the Sealab, with an aquarium (open: daily 9.30am–4pm).

Mangonui

Ninety Mile Beach

This seemingly endless and empty sandy beach on the west coast of New Zealand's northernmost tip does not quite live up to its name: it is in fact only 64 miles (103km) long. The gleaming white sand tempts motorists to drive along the beach itself; but this can be highly dangerous. It should be attempted only by drivers with local knowledge and a cross-country vehicle; and visitors should note that all New Zealand car hire firms ban driving on beaches.

★Topography

In January 1932 an Australian, Norman Smith, set a world speed record of 264km/164 miles an hour on a ten mile stretch at Hukatere.

Surfcasting competitions are held annually in January at Ahipara.

Surf angling
competitions

The travelling dunes at Aupouri, which formerly tended to move inland, have been stabilised by sowing grass and lupin seeds and planting conifers.

Travelling dunes,
Aupouri

Cape Reinga

Cape Reinga – the Maori name means "underworld" – is the most north-westerly point on the North Island. It is reached from Kaitaia on a road

Situation

which runs along the narrow tongue of land fringed by Ninety Mile Beach, passing through Aupouri Forest (planted to consolidate the dunes) and an extensive area dug over by kauri gum-diggers in earlier days. At some points it is like driving over a desert.

History

In 1769 Captain Cook almost met the French navigator Surville in this area. During a violent storm their ships were only a short distance apart but they sailed past without seeing one another.

★Lighthouse

From the lighthouse on Cape Reinga there are tremendous views – westward along the coast to Cape Maria van Diemen (so named by Tasman), eastward as far as the North Cape. If visibility is good the Three Kings Islands – so called by Tasman because he sailed past them on Epiphany in 1643 – can be seen in the distance.

The lighthouse, 165m/540ft above sea level, was built in 1941. Below it an ancient pohutukawa tree hangs over the sheer cliff that falls down to the sea. To the Maoris it is sacred, for from here, they believe, souls plunge at sunset into the sea and down into the underworld to return to Hawaiki.

★Cape Reinga Walkway

From Cape Reinga there are very rewarding trails eastward to Spirits Bay (about 10 hours) and southward by way of Cape Maria van Diemen to Ninety Mile Beach and then inland to Te Paki (about 7 hours).

There is no overnight accommodation at Cape Reinga. Information about walks and accommodation in the area can be obtained from the information centre in Kaitaia.

Houhora Heads

Roughly half way between Kaitaia and Cape Reinga, in a beautiful inlet, are the Houhora Heads, with a camping site and a picnic area.

Mount Carmel

Opposite is Mount Carmel (245m/804ft), so named by Captain Cook.

Subritzky House

Subritzky House was built by a 19th century Polish immigrant, and has been lovingly maintained by his descendants.

Lighthouse, Cape Reinga

Near Subritzky House is the Wagener Museum (open: daily 9am–5pm), with a varied collection which includes Maori art, whaling equipment, firearms, everyday objects of the 19th century and kauri resin.

Wagener Museum

Kawhia Harbour · King Country   I/K 4/5

Region: Waikato

Some 100km/62 miles south-west of Hamilton (see entry), on the west coast, is the natural harbour of Kawhia. The area was formerly of great importance to the Maoris as the resting-place of the Tainui ancestral canoe.

Situation and importance

The Maori tribes which lived here, under their chief Te Rauparaha, were driven out of Kawhia in 1821 by other Waikato tribes and moved south to Kapiti Island, where they in their turn killed or drove out the local tribes.

Now a small settlement of 300 people, in the 19th century Kawhia was an important trading centre (timber, flax, grain), which shipped cargoes to Sydney and even as far afield as California. After the land wars and the peace of 1881 it sank into insignificance.

Kawhia

On Te Puia beach, 4km/2½ miles west of Kawhia, hot springs gush out of the sand at low tide, so that visitors can have their own little thermal bath.

Te Puia
Hot Springs

South of the entrance to Kawhia Harbour, reached on a side road, is the Maori settlement of Taharoa, round which are considerable deposits of dark-coloured ferruginous sand. It is processed in modern plants and exported, mainly to Japan.

Taharoa

King Country

Inland from the North Taranaki Bight (west coast), between Mokau and Kawhia, extends the rugged and infertile area known as the King Country. It is a region of karstic limestone, with deep canyon-like gorges, intricately ramified karstic cave systems and bizarre rock formations.

Topography and history

The first Europeans in this area, in the early 19th century, landed on the wild west coast at Mokau and Kawhia. There they traded with the Maoris, exchanging guns for flax and dried tattooed heads, which were much sought after in Europe. Missionaries taught the natives European farming methods, and wheat was being exported from Kawhia.

Between Mokau and Kawhia lived the warlike Te Maniapoto tribes, who believed that their ancestors had arrived here in the Tainui ancestral canoe. They were keen partisans of the Maori King Movement and supported the rebels in Taranaki and Waikato against the government.

After the defeat of the rebels at Orakau the Maori king, whose residence had been at Ngaruawahia on the Waikato River, sought refuge in this area. The Ngati-Maniapoto tribes held on to their land, and white men did not dare to venture into the King Country.

In 1881 the mighty Maori chief Rewi Maniapoto made peace with the government. He sold and leased land to the whites, against the will of the Maoris, and permitted the construction of a railway through the King Country.

Until the middle of the 20th century alcohol was prohibited in the King Country. As a result smuggling and illicit distilling flourished.

Levin   K 7

Region: Manawatu-Wanganui
Population: 19,000

Masterton

Situation and importance	Levin, the commercial centre of a farming region in the western foreland of the Taranua Range, lies 93km/58 miles north-east of Wellington (see entry), to which it supplies vegetables, milk and meat. The town was founded in 1889 as a camp for railway workers and was named after a director of the railway company.

Surroundings

Lake Horowhenua	To the west of Levin is Lake Horowhenua, a popular recreation area for the townspeople. In the lake the Maoris constructed artificial islands on which they built fortified villages (*pas*). The area round Lake Papaitonga, to the south, was the scene of bloody battles between supporters of the Maori leader Te Rauparaha and the local tribes.
Waitarere Beach	8km/5 miles north-west of Levin is Waitarere Beach. Offshore can be seen the wreck of HMS "Hyderabad", which ran aground here in 1878.
Hokio Beach	There are beautiful stretches of beach at Hokio, to the south, and at the mouth of the Manawatu River, to the north. Efforts are being made to consolidate the dunes by planting trees, in order to prevent the sand from being blown on to the fertile fields farther inland.
Foxton	20km/12½ miles north of Levin is Foxton, a much older European settlement. It was founded in 1855, and later was given its present name in honour of Sir William Fox, several times prime minister of New Zealand. Most of the trade in the trading post at the mouth of the river was in flax and timber. When the railway was built a long way from Foxton, however, the town's development came to a standstill.
Sights	There are a number of historic old buildings in Foxton's main street. The old courthouse now houses a museum of local history (open: Sun.), and the old tram station, once served by horse-drawn trams, still survives.
Foxton Beach	Foxton Beach is a pretty little settlement with many holiday and retirement houses.
Flood control	Measures are in place for controlling flooding on the Manawatu River between Foxton and Shannon.

Masterton   K 7

Region: Wellington
Population: 20,000

Situation and history	100km/62 miles north-east of Wellington (see entry), on the fairly steep eastern slopes of the Tararua Range, is the town of Masterton, an important communications hub and supply centre. It is named after Joseph Masters (1802–74), leader of the Small Farms Association, which opposed the settlement plans of Edward Wakefield and the New Zealand Company and demanded that poor immigrants should also be able to acquire and work small holdings of land. Masters won the support of Governor Grey, whose name is commemorated in the little township of Greytown, 23km/14½ miles farther south. In 1853 the Association bought land from the Maoris, divided it up and sold it on to small farmers. Great improvements in agricultural yields were achieved, particularly in hilly country, by the use from 1947 onwards of "aerial top-dressing", a method of distributing fertilisers, seed and pesticides from the air.

Sights in Masterton and Surroundings

Wairarapa Arts Centre	The Wairarapa Arts Centre, which incorporates a Methodist church of 1878 in Bruce Street, has an interesting collection of local and regional art.

30km/19 miles north on Highway 2 is the Mount Bruce Wildlife Centre, run by the Department of Conservation. It is famed for its bird breeding station, which is particularly concerned to aid the survival of the takahe, a threatened species. Open to visitors daily 10am–4pm.

Mount Bruce
Wildlife Centre

To the west of Masterton are the wild and rugged hills of the densely wooded Tararua Range, which lies between the Wairarapa area and the west coast. There are a number of considerable peaks, such as the Mitre (1571m/5154ft). Some 100,000 hectares/250,000 acres of the range constitute Tararua Forest Park, within which are a number of walking trails, with overnight accommodation in mountain huts.

★ **Tararua Range,
Tararua
Forest Park**

22km/14 miles west of Masterton, on the eastern fringes of Tararua Forest Park, is Mount Holdsworth (1474m/4836ft), the central feature of an important nature reserve.

Mount Holdsworth
Reserve

50km/31 miles south of Masterton, at Fall Point, is an 8km/5 mile long trail along the Pacific coast, passing curious honeycomb-shaped rocks.

★ **Honeycomb
Rock Walkway**

Castlepoint (70km/43 miles north-east) and Riversdale (60km/37 miles east) are the only bathing resorts on the long stretch of inaccessible cliff-fringed coast in the south-east of the North Island.

Castlepoint,
Riversdale

Featherston

Region: Wellington. Population: 2600

The little township of Featherston lies 40km/25 miles south-west of Masterton at the foot of the Rimutaka Ranges. This area was first surveyed about 1840 for the New Zealand Company, and the town was named after a senior government official who decided that it should be established here.

Situation
and name

The settlement was originally a mailcoach station. Later, when a railway was built through the Rumutaka Ranges, large numbers of railway workers settled here. During the Second World War there was a camp for Japanese prisoners of war in Masterton. In 1955 the 8790m/9615yd long Rimutaka railway tunnel was driven through the hills.

History

A 16km/10 mile stretch of railway line, on a fairly steep gradient, was abandoned after the opening of the new tunnel. It is now the Rimutaka Incline Walkway, one of the principal trails in Rimutaka Forest Park.

Old railway line,
Rimutaka
Forest Park

The Fell Engine Museum displays a steam engine specially built in 1878 for this steep stretch of line.

Fell Engine
Museum

Near here is the very shallow Lake Wairarapa, formerly home to large numbers of ducks and eels, which provided welcome additions to the Maori diet.
    The lake was sold to the New Zealand government in 1896. Recently it has been incorporated in a large scheme for the prevention of flooding.

Lake Wairarapa

There is an attractive excursion to the wild coast at Palliser Bay and Cape Palliser on a road which runs south on the east side of Lake Wairarapa. This was the scene of a tragic incident in 1942, when a revolt by Japanese prisoners of war was crushed and 48 of them were killed.

Palliser Bay,
Cape Palliser

Greytown

Region: Wellington. Population: 1800

2okm/12½ miles south-west of Masterton is Greytown, once the main centre of the fertile Wairarapa area (fruit-growing, vegetables). The town-

Situation

ship was founded by small farmers in 1854 and named after Governor George Grey, who had supported the Small Farm Association in its efforts to help workers on the land to get their own holdings.

The dense primeval forest was cleared for cultivation; but because of the unpredictable character of the Waiohine River the railway was built at some distance from Greytown and its development was brought to a halt.

Papawai Marae
3km/2 miles away is Papawai Marae, the main stronghold in the 1890s of the Kohatitanga movement, which fought vehemently for self-government for the Maoris. Discussions were held here between the government and representatives of the Maoris. Subsequently the movement was absorbed into the Young Maori Party. The carvings round the *marae* face inwards, not outwards as was the usual practice. A small Maori house which is still standing belonged to the tohunga (priest).

Waiohine Gorge
20km/12½ miles north-west of Greytown, on the edge of Tararua Forest Park, is the wild Waiohine Gorge. Here, for the adventurous, there are walking trails up Mount Omega (1182m/3878ft) and Mount Holdsworth (1474m/4836ft).

Napier   L 6

Region: Hawke's Bay
Population: 53,000

Situation and importance
This important port in Hawke's Bay (see entry) is named after the colonial administrator General Sir Charles Napier. The town was largely destroyed by a devastating earthquake in 1931, when the sea-bed round the Ahuriri Lagoon was thrust upwards and the town, built on a promontory reaching out into the sea, received a large addition to its land area. In spite of the prevailing economic depression the town was rapidly rebuilt, and its previous Neo-Classical style of architecture gave place to the simpler geometric forms of Art Deco and the "Spanish mission style". The new buildings were claimed to be earthquake-proof.

Skilled publicity, emphasising the town's climate, its Art Deco architecture and the varied scenic attractions of its hinterland, has now made Napier a much visited tourist centre.

History
When the first white men arrived in Hawke's Bay, many years after Captain Cook, the local Maoris had been decimated by rival tribes armed with guns or driven north on to the Mahia Peninsula. The whalers, traders and missionaries who came here found only small numbers of natives in the area.

In 1844 a clergyman was sent to Hawke's Bay to establish a mission station, and about the same time the hinterland was developed for pastoral farming. The new settlers soon came into conflict with the government in distant Wellington (see entry), which was drawing handsome revenues from the sale of land but was doing little for the opening up and development of the Hawke's Bay area. Accordingly in 1858 the area was declared an independent province with Napier as its chief town.

During the land wars the east coast round Napier was largely spared by the fighting. In 1866 there was a Hauhau campaign against Napier, but the rebels were beaten back at Omarunui and Eskdale by the settlers themselves.

Earthquake, 1931
On the morning of February 3rd 1931 there was a severe earthquake, shocks from which were felt as far away as Europe. Almost every building in Napier and the neighbouring town of Hastings (see entry) was destroyed and 256 people lost their lives. The sea-bed in the Ahuriri Lagoon was thrust upwards and the town thus acquired well over 33sq.km/12½sq. miles of usable land. The new land is now covered by pasture, various industrial installations, an airport and the districts of Marewa, Pirimai and Maraenui.

Pania of the Reef, a figure of Maori legend on Napier's Marine Parade

After the earthquake Napier was rapidly rebuilt, and its now has a modern layout and an assemblage of Art Deco and "Spanish mission style" architecture which is unique in the world.

Sights

Marine Parade, the town's finest promenade, runs along the seafront, lined with Norfolk pines and is at its most beautiful in the morning sun. It is now equipped with all the attractions and entertainments of a popular tourist resort.

★Marine Parade

The busy focal point of Marine Parade is just off the town centre. The Visitor Centre supplies information of all kinds about Napier and the surrounding area. Well cared for gardens, including the impressive Sunken Gardens, minigolf and a roller-blading rink provide entertainment for young and old.

Visitor Centre, Colonnade, Veronica Bell, Sunken Gardens

In the Mediterranean-style colonnade with a roofed concert platform is the ship's bell of HMS "Veronica", which was the first source of help in the 1931 earthquake.

A major attraction for visitors is Marineland of New Zealand, with its displays by performing dolphins, seals and otters, as well as penguins and gannets. Daily 10am–4.30pm.

★Marineland

Here too is the Lilliput Railway, which is particularly popular with children.

Lilliput Railway

The Stables Museum has films and displays on the 1931 earthquake as well as a very popular waxworks show.
    Farther south are the Mardi Gras Area, used for a variety of events, the "Can Am Cars" and a small lake (boats for hire).

Stables Museum and Waxworks

137

Napier

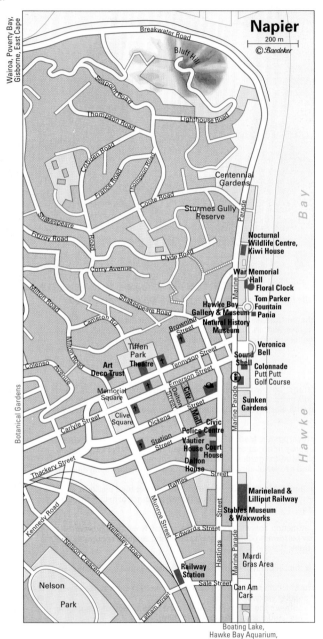

Napier

200 m

© *Baedeker*

Breakwater Road

Bluff Hill

Wairoa, Poverty Bay, Gisborne, East Cape

Seaton Road

Thompson Road

Lighthouse Road

Cobden Road

France Road

Thompson Road

Coote Road

Centennial Gardens

Parade

Sturmes Gully Reserve

Shakespeare

Fitzroy Road

Road

Clyde Road

Nocturnal Wildlife Centre, Kiwi House

Corry Avenue

Milton Road

Shakespeare Road

Cameron Rd

Browning Street

War Memorial Hall
Floral Clock
Tom Parker Fountain
Pania

Hawke Bay Gallery & Museum
Natural History Museum

Marine

Colenso

Avenue

Milton Road

Tiffen Park

Art Deco Trust

Theatre

Tennyson Street

Veronica Bell

Sound Shell

Colonnade
Putt Putt Golf Course

Botanical Gardens

Memorial Square

Emerson Street

Dalton Street

City Mall

Clive Square

Dickens

Street

Sunken Gardens

Carlyle Street

Station Street

Civic
Police Centre
Vautier House Court House
Dalton House

Marine Parade

Thackery Street

Street

Raffles

Munroe Street

Marineland & Lilliput Railway

Stables Museum & Waxworks

Kennedy Road

Wellesley Road

Edwards Street

Hastings

Street

Marine Parade

Mardi Gras Area

Nelson Crescent

Railway Station

Sale Street

Can Am Cars

Nelson Park

Latham Street

Bay

Hawke

138

Boating Lake,
Hawke Bay Aquarium,
Hastings

Art Deco architecture in Napier

A little farther along is Hawke's Bay Aquarium (open: daily 9am–5pm), with an Oceanarium three storeys high in which visitors can see at close quarters a great variety of sea creatures of the Pacific. The sharks' feeding time is a great draw.

Hawke's Bay Aquarium

The Hawke's Bay Cultural Trust and Museum (open: Tues.–Sun. 10am–5pm) has a rich collection of material on the development of culture and art on the east side of the North Island. Much space is also devoted to contemporary art. Particularly interesting is the audiovisual material on the earthquake and the subsequent rebuilding of the town, with many photographs and eyewitnesses' accounts.

★ Hawke's Bay Cultural Trust and Museum

The Natural History Museum has interesting material from the country round Napier and displays on the flora and fauna (particularly the gannets) of the Hawke's Bay area.

Natural History Museum

In the gardens opposite the Museum is a statue of Pania of the Reef, a mermaid-like figure who features in a Maori legend. Pania loved a man and lived with him on land, in spite of her family's appeals to her to return to the reef. One day when she swam out to visit them she was drawn down into the sea and was unable to return to her lover.
   Beside the statue is the Tom Parker Fountain.

★ Statue of Pania, Tom Parker Fountain

Close by, to the north, is the War Memorial Hall, commemorating those who fell in various wars, particularly the First and Second World Wars. In front of the hall is a much photographed floral clock.

War Memorial Hall, floral clock

Farther north still is the Nocturnal Wildlife Centre, with a variety of New Zealand animals which are active at night. In the Kiwi House (open: daily 11am–3pm) visitors can see New Zealand's national bird, which in the wild is an endangered species (see Baedeker Special, p. 24).

★ Nocturnal Wildlife Centre. Kiwi House

New Plymouth

Cathedral	From the Natural History Museum Tennyson Street runs into the town centre, passing the Cathedral of St John the Evangelist, whose roof fell in during a service on the day of the earthquake. It contains a small chapel dedicated to Bishop Bennett, the first Maori bishop, and the Maori politician Apirana Ngata.
★★ Art Deco Walk	After the earthquake the town was rapidly rebuilt, largely in the Art Deco and Spanish mission styles then in fashion in the United States. The result was an assemblage of buildings in these styles (now protected as national monuments) unequalled anywhere in the world and comparable only with the Art Deco quarter of Miami. The Hastings architect Louis Hay, who played a major part in the rebuilding of the town, was strongly influenced by the American architects Henry H. Richardson, Frank Lloyd Wright and Louis Sullivan. Among the first buildings to be erected after the earthquake were the Masonic Hall (by W. J. Prouse of Wellington, 1932) and the Criterion Hotel (by E. A. Williams). There is a brochure giving detailed descriptions of Napier's finest Art Deco buildings to be seen in a walk round the town. There are also guided tours, starting from the Hawke's Bay Museum on Marine Parade (Sunday afternoons, November to May). Information from the Visitor Centre on Marine Parade.
Botanical Gardens	To the west of the town centre, on the slopes of Hospital Hill, are the Botanical Gardens. Close by is Napier's cemetery, with a number of old gravestones.
★Bluff Hill	To the north of the town centre is Bluff Hill, on which are the Centennial Gardens and Bluff Hill Domain. From Bluff Hill Lookout (reached by way of Lighthouse Road) there are magnificent views. In good weather the prospect extends as far as the Mahia Peninsula to the north-east and Cape Kidnappers to the south-east.

Surroundings

Eskdale Park	20km/12½ miles north-west of Napier, on the road to Taupo (see entry; Highway 5), is Eskdale Park, a popular destination for excursions. It lies in a beautiful valley with old-established woodland and vineyards. There was fighting here in 1866 between white settlers and Hauhau rebels.
Tutira	40km/25 miles north of Napier on Highway, situated on a lake (bird sanctuary), is the old sheep-rearing station of Tutira, which was immortalised by the farmer and writer Herbert Guthrie-Smith (1861–1940) in his books. There is an attractive circuit of the area on the Tutira Walkway (9km/5½ miles; steep in places).
Hastings	See entry
Hawke's Bay	See entry

New Plymouth   I 6

	Region: Taranaki Population: 50,000
Situation and importance	Under the north side of the volcano known as Taranaki or Mount Egmont (see Taranaki, Egmont National Park) is the port of New Plymouth, now also an industrial town and the commercial centre of a fertile farming region. The harbour, formed in 1861 by the construction of breakwaters, handled dairy produce (particularly cheese), and now also ships raw materials for the petro-chemical industry. The proximity of rich offshore deposits of

fossil fuels (at Kapuni, Maui and elsewhere) has brought increasing numbers of industrial firms to New Plymouth, creating numerous new jobs.

New Plymouth, so called after its English namesake, was founded in 1841; the first settlers came from Devon and Cornwall. They are said to have found only small numbers of natives in this area – though the presence of many fortified settlements (*pas*) and kumara fields suggests the contrary. Probably the local Taranaki tribes, who had only clubs for use in close combat, were so harried in the early decades of the 19th century by the Waikato tribes, who were already equipped with firearms, that they moved south, where they sought to join up with Chief Te Rauparaha in order to get guns and reoccupy their tribal territory.

Strife soon blew up between the returning Maori tribes and the white settlers, and in 1860 the conflict escalated into fierce country-wide fighting, sparked off by a fraudulent land deal at Waitara, 16km/10 miles east of New Plymouth.

History

Sights

Pukekura Park (Liardet Street) is laid out in Victorian style, with a fountain which is illuminated after dark and a waterfall.

Pukekura Park

Adjoining Pukekura Park is Brooklands Park, another attractive open space.

Brooklands Park

Nearby is the Gables, a wooden house with a pointed gable built in 1848. It was originally a hospital, but later was used as military quarters and an old people's home. It was moved to its present site in the early 20th century. It is now used for art exhibitions and other cultural events.

The Gables

The Taranaki Museum (Ariki Street; open: Tues.–Sun. 10am–5pm) has a large collection of Maori objects from the region, including a stone used as an anchor, a stone axe from an ancestral canoe, a chief's cloak, old sculpture and woodcarving. There is also material on the early days of white settlement.

Taranaki Museum

Beside the Museum is Richmond Cottage, built on another site in 1853 as a schoolhouse and moved to its present position in 1962. It is furnished in the style of its period and illustrates the pattern of life in a well-to-do 19th century household.

Richmond Cottage

Marsland Hill, which commands wide views, can be climbed either from Robe Street or from St Mary's Church. The summit, which was gradually levelled over the centuries, was once occupied by a *pa* (fortified Maori village). During the land wars British troops were stationed on the hill.

Marsland Hill

On Marsland Hill, in the centre of the town, is one of the oldest stone-built churches in New Zealand (built for Bishop Selwyn in 1842), with a notable interior. During the land wars it served as a military post and ammunition depot. In the churchyard are the graves of early white settlers.

St Mary's Church

This gallery in Queen Street collects contemporary New Zealand art. The collection includes some fine works by Len Lye (sculpture, pictures, films). Open: daily 1–5pm.

Govett-Brewster
Art Gallery

New Plymouth's power station, in Breakwater Road, was originally coal-fired, but after the discovery of natural gas nearby it was converted to oil. It has been on stream since 1977. Its 200m/650ft high chimney is a landmark visible far and wide. Conducted tours by appointment.

Power station

Surroundings

A few kilometres south of New Plymouth is the old immigrant settlement of Hurworth, which still preserves a small homestead built in 1855 by Harry

Hurworth

Lava cones, Pungarehu

Atkinson (1831–92), an opponent of Governor Grey who played a prominent part in the Taranaki land war and later became prime minister of New Zealand.

Pukeiti Rhododendron Trust

In the nearby expanse of rain forest between Mounts Patuha (683m/2241ft) and Pouakai (1400m/4600ft) is the Pukeiti Rhododendron Trust, a large nature reserve which is resplendent with blossom in spring.

Pungarehu, Cape Egmont

At Pungarehu, 40km/25 miles south-west of New Plymouth, a road goes off to Cape Egmont, with a lighthouse built in 1881. On the cape are numerous striking conical lava formations.

Waitara

17km/10½ miles north-east of New Plymouth is Waitara (pop. 6000), where the land wars broke out in 1860. It has petro-chemical and foodstuffs industries (frozen meat).

Urenui

15km/9½ miles farther east is Urenui, birthplace of the famous Maori scholar and politician Peter Buck, who is buried under a stone canoe prow near the old Maori fortified settlement of Okoki Pa.

King Country

From New Plymouth a road runs north-east through the gently rolling grassland of Taranaki to the rugged mountainous terrain of the King Country.

Taranaki

See entry

Northland

H/I 2

Situation and importance

Northland is a hilly and sometimes mountainous region at the northernmost tip of the North Island. It lies outside the tectonically active part of

New Zealand: that is, there have been no active volcanoes in Northland for a very long time, and the region is not troubled by earth tremors of any significance.

The present coastline, much indented and eroded by the sea, was formed by a rise in sea level after the last ice age, when many valleys and valley systems were drowned. There thus came into being on the west coast a series of long and intricately ramified inlets. On the east coast, in contrast, there are wide and deep harbour basins and numerous offshore islands.

The mild climate with its rainy winters and dry summers provided ideal conditions for the growing of sweet potatoes (kumara) and their winter storage. It also favoured the growth of giant kauri trees (see Baedeker Special, p. 176). When these died and rotted away they left deposits of kauri resin (gum), a substance resembling amber in appearance, under the ground. Along the coasts and in the tidal reaches of inlets mangroves grow, and pohutukawa bushes cling to even the steepest rock faces.

History

Archaeological research indicates that the Polynesians who settled in New Zealand first established themselves in Northland, which in the Maori classic period was densely populated – as is demonstrated by the fortified settlements on many hills and mountains. Then, when population pressure became too great, some tribal groups moved south into cooler parts of the country.

There is evidence in this region of settlement in both prehistoric and historical times. Just as the ancestors of the Maoris had come from afar and made their home here, so in the early 19th century European whalers, timber-dealers and missionaries came to Northland. Among these new settlers, too, were many time-expired or escaped convicts from Australia. Manners in these immigrant communities were rough-and-ready: Darwin, who arrived in the Bay of Islands (see entry) in the "Beagle" in 1853, was appalled by the "scum of society" whom he found there. Moreover the

Idyll in Northland: a pile dwelling on one of the North Island's numerous natural harbours

143

missionaries who were active in Northland from 1814 onwards were unable to prevent the warlike local tribes from getting possession of guns and ammunition and then attacking the tribes farther south who lacked modern weapons.

The treaty of Waitangi, under which the Maori chiefs recognised British sovereignty in return for a guarantee of their rights, marked the birth of the state of New Zealand. But with the transfer of the seat of government southward to Auckland the importance and the economy of the north declined. In recent years, however, the tourist trade – basing its appeal on the relics of New Zealand's early history and the slogan of the "winterless north" – has given the region a new lease of life.

Sights

See Bay of Islands, Hokianga Harbour, Kaitaia, Waipoua Kauri Forest, Whangarei

Palmerston North   K 7

Region: Manawatu-Wanganui
Population: 71,000

Situation and importance

Palmerston North – named after the 19th century British statesman Lord Palmerston – lies some 150km/95 miles north-east of Wellington (see entry), on the Manawatu River. The "North" distinguishes it from another Palmerston near Christchurch (see entry) on the South Island.

Originally a loggers' settlement, the town is now an important traffic hub and the commercial centre of a region of pastoral farming, with large creameries and frozen meat plants.

Agricultural research

Palmerston North is important also as the seat of Massey University, a national centre of veterinary medicine, nutritional science and biotechnology, and other leading agricultural research and experimental institutions. Among them are the Grassland Research Centre, the New Zealand Dairy Research Institute, the Palmerston North Seed Testing Station and the Awahuri Artificial Breeding Centre.

History

The site of Palmerston North was originally covered with almost impenetrable forests, and the town was founded relatively late, in 1866. At first its only link with the outside world was the Manawatu River, on which timber felled by the loggers was transported to the port of Foxton, on the coast. After the railway from Wellington reached the town in 1886 it developed rapidly. Ever larger areas of forest were cleared to make way for pastoral farming, and creameries, slaughterhouses and meat factories were established.

An agricultural college in the town became in 1928 the Massey University of Manawatu. It is named after a local farmer, William Ferguson Massey (1856–1925), who became leader of the Reform Party and from 1912 to 1925 was prime minister of New Zealand. The new university grew rapidly, and in course of time was joined by other agricultural research institutions.

Sights

The Square

The hub of the town's life is the Square, originally a large open space of almost 7 hectares/17 acres, which in earlier days was traversed by the railway but is now a park, with fountains, and the site of the modern Civic Centre.

Square Edge

The site of the former municipal offices is now occupied by a craft centre (showroom, sales).

Manawatu Museum

The Manawatu Museum in Church Street (open: Tues.–Sun. 2–4pm) is devoted to the history of the region. The collection includes Maori artefacts and reminiscences of the early days of white settlement.

The Manawatu Art Gallery in Main Street WEST (closed Mon.) displays mainly contemporary New Zealand art.

Manawatu
Art Gallery

The Rugby Museum in Cuba Street (open: daily 1.30–4pm) is devoted to New Zealand's national sport.

Rugby Museum

From Monro Hill, named after a British immigrant who settled here in 1870 and founded the country's first rugby club, there is a view of the spacious campus of Massey University (founded 1928).

Monro Hill,
Massey University

From this viewpoint at the end of Cliff Road, on the southern outskirts of the town, there is a fine view of the town. If visibility is good the volcanoes Taranaki and Ruapehu can be seen in the distance.

ANZAC Park
Viewpoint

Surroundings

20km/12½ miles north-west of Palmerston North is Feilding (pop. 13,500), founded in the 1870s as a "special settlement" on land acquired by the Emigrants and Colonists Aid Corporation and divided into small separate holdings for immigrants without the money to buy land. The site was found by William Feilding, after whom the town is named. The first 250 settlers came here in 1874, cleared the forest and established farms, and in due course a meat factory was built. In addition to stock farming (sheep, cattle) fruit and vegetables are now also grown. In spite of its nearness to Palmerston North Feilding has managed to preserve its own character. There are a number of buildings of the late 19th century.

Feilding

North-east of Palmerston North is Ruahine Forest Park (area 936sq.km/361sq. miles), a nature reserve famed for its wildness. Here knowledgable visitors will find many species of flora and fauna which are rare elsewhere in New Zealand. At the end of the few roads running into the forest there are mountain huts and rest areas, from which there are trails leading into the wilderness. The best route to the park from Palmerston North is via Ashhurst and the Pohangina valley. Information from Department of Conservation offices in Palmerston North and Wanganui (see entry).

★Ruahine
Forest Park

16km/10 miles east of Palmerston North on the road to Woodville is the entrance to this wild gorge, carved out by the Manawatu River between the Ruahine Range to the north and the Tararua Range to the south. It is now a Mecca for jetboat enthusiasts and experienced white-water canoeists.

★Manawatu
Gorge

Puhoi

I 3

Region: Auckland
Population: about 200

Just under an hour's drive north of Auckland (see entry), off Highway 1 to the west, is the little township of Puhoi, founded in the 1860s by immigrants from Bohemia.

Situation and
history

Martin Kippner, a sea captain from Bohemia who had visited New Zealand, gave such a good account of the country that a party of villagers from Staab, 100km/60 miles south-west of Prague, were encouraged to make the long and trying voyage and settled in a forested area north-west of the Hauraki Gulf, where they were allotted plots of land and set about clearing the forest for agriculture. In those days the Puhoi River was their only link with the outside world.

Puhoi is now a popular destination for excursions from Auckland. At the entrance to the village is the only wayside cross in New Zealand. The

★Church, cross

church of SS. Peter and Paul, built in 1881, has an altarpiece (1885) reminiscent of the immigrants' Bohemian homeland. In the nearby churchyard are the graves of Bohemian settlers.

Puhoi Hotel
(Puhoi Tavern)

The Puhoi Hotel – previously called the German Hotel – has held a liquor licence since 1879. Photographs on the walls of the pub recall earlier days.

Rotorua

L 5

Region: Bay of Plenty

Information;
excursions

The Tourism Rotorua office in Fenton Street has an abundance of informative material for visitors on the Rotorua area, and also offers sightseeing flights, jetboat trips and excursions to the numerous volcanic, post-volcanic and geothermal features in and around Rotorua.

Situation and
importance

The country round Lakes Rotorua and Tarawera, to the south of the Bay of Plenty (see entry), with its variety of volcanic phenomena, is the oldest-established and most visited tourist area in New Zealand. All over this area are jets of hot steam issuing from clefts in the ground, geysers shooting water high into the air, bubbling pools of mud and glinting deposits of minerals in all the colours of the rainbow on the hot subsoil, and everywhere there is a sulphurous smell of sulphur, of greater or lesser intensity. The white men who came here in the 19th century were filled with a mixture of curiosity, fear and wonderment. The local Maoris had long come to terms with their hot environment. They bathed in the thermal water and used it for heating and cooking. Later they found a role as guides to white visitors. The tourist high spots in the 19th century were the gleaming pink and white sinter terraces at Lake Rotomahana, which were regarded as one of the wonders of the world.

The volcanoes
in Maori
mythology

The legends of the Arawa tribes have their own explanation for the origins of volcanic activity and the thermal phenomena associated with it. Immediately after the ancestral canoe landed, it is said, a tohunga (priest) climbed, with a companion, to the snow-covered summit of Mount Tongariro, where they were in danger of freezing to death: whereupon the priest begged the gods in Hawaiki to send fire to warm them. The fire duly arrived, travelling under the sea, and came to the surface first at White Island and then at various points round Rotorua and Taupo, finally emerging from the summit of Mount Tongariro. The priest was saved, but his companion had already perished from the cold.

Lake Rotorua and the island of Mokoia in its centre also feature in an Arawa legend, the romantic love story of Hinemoa, a girl living on the shores of the lake for whom her parents had chosen a suitable husband, and the young Chief Tutanekai, who lived on the island. He so delighted the girl with his flute-playing that she swam over to the island, supporting herself on empty calabashes, to see him – for to prevent her going her parents had hidden all the canoes.

Rotorua

Birth of a spa

During the land wars the Arawa tribes on the volcanic plateau were loyal allies of the government. They even prevented Maori groups from the Bay of Plenty from travelling through their territory to help the Waikato tribes. In recognition of this Prince Alfred, Duke of Edinburgh, Queen Victoria's son, gave them a bust of his mother, which still stands on the *marae* (place of assembly) in Ohinemutu, the old Maori settlement on the south bank of Lake Rotorua. The Duke was welcomed by the Maoris with a greeting ceremony and traditional dances. He also drank the local medicinal water, giving a boost to the little resort to which people came to drink the waters.

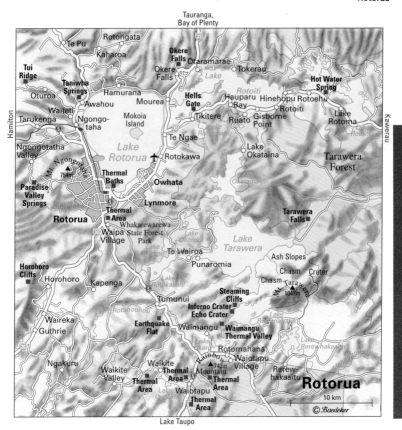

Thereafter Rotorua developed into a very fashionable resort, very much in the style of the great European spas of the period.

The sudden eruption of Mount Tarawera on June 10th 1886 occurred without warning – though an ancient tohunga living in the area had predicted a great misfortune and a party of British visitors accompanied by Maoris had recently reported strange happenings on Lake Tarawera, where they claimed to have seen a ghostly canoe. Then the northern summit of Mount Tarawera burst open, a 19km/12 mile long crack opened up in the ground and lava and ash buried the village of Te Wairoa and other Maori settlements. More than 150 people lost their lives. Even the marvellous sinter terraces had disappeared. The eruption, however, also created new tourist attractions, and the excavation of the buried village of Wairoa drew numbers of curious tourists.

Eruption of Mount Tarawera

The eruption did no harm to the prospects of Rotorua as a health resort: quite the contrary. The construction of a luxurious bath-house in Government Gardens, directly on the shores of the lake, was now planned. A government medical officer had visited a number of fashionable European

Heyday of the spa

147

Tudor Towers, Rotorua

spas and was particularly impressed by the half-timbered bath-house of Bad Nauheim in Germany. Half-timbered construction was very much in line with England's Tudor style, and was much cheaper than a heavily built stone building, which was more subject to damage in an earthquake. The new half-timbered spa establishment was completed in 1908. It had a veranda in front in which visitors could walk about and drink the water.

Thanks to the swarms of visitors coming to take the cure or merely to see the sights Rotorua has now grown into a town of 54,000 inhabitants, with numerous hotels, motels, motor camps and other forms of accommodation. There are pubs and restaurants of all types and souvenir shops to satisfy every taste. For visitors approaching Rotorua from the south on Highway 5 it is like entering some kind of Disneyland.

As a result of the many private boreholes that have been drilled to supply water for baths and for heating, geothermal activity has declined sharply in some places. There are now restrictions on the use of thermal water.

★ Government Gardens

The magnificent Government Gardens, which include both a park and various sports grounds, lie directly on the shores of the lake. They are trim and well cared for, with flowers providing a riot of colour. Visitors can stroll about in the park, or play golf or cricket if they prefer.

★ Tudor Towers

The most eye-catching feature in Government Gardens is Tudor Towers, the old half-timbered bath-house of Rotorua. Since the opening of a new spa establishment in the 1960s the old bath-house has housed the interesting Rotorua Museum (history and natural history of the Rotorua area) and the City Art Gallery (including Maori art). Open: Mon.–Fri. 10am–4pm, Sat. and Sun. 1–4.30pm.

Arawa Memorial

The memorial set up in 1927 to commemorate those who fell in the First World War depicts the varied links between Maoris and whites (the Arawa ancestral canoe, the signing of the treaty of Waitangi, British kings and queens, a missionary preaching).

Behind Tudor Towers is the modern spa establishment, complete with conference facilities and provision for a variety of sports. Its particular attraction is the three Polynesian Pools, which are supplied with water by three different springs. The whole area is pervaded with the scent of orchids.

★Polynesian Pools

North-west of the town is Mount Ngongotaha (757m/2484ft). From its viewing platform there are marvellous views of the town and the lake. The easiest way up is in the Skyline Gondola (lower station in Fairy Spring Road).

★Mount Ngongotaha

From Rotorua there are boat trips to Mokoia Island, in the middle of the lake.

Mokoia Island

Ohinemutu

Immediately adjoining Government Gardens is the Maori village of Ohinemutu, once the most important Maori settlement in the Rotorua area. On the *marae* (place of assembly), beside the meeting-house and the church, is the bust of Queen Victoria presented by the Duke of Edinburgh in 1870, protected by a marvellously carved canopy. Everywhere in the area, between the houses and in the tiny gardens, clouds of steam issue from the ground.

The interior of St Faith's Church (Anglican; 1910) is notable for the fine Maori carving and woven fabrics. One of the stained glass windows shows Christ in the dress of a Maori chief walking on the water of Lake Rotorua.

★St Faith's Church

In the churchyard beside the church the dead are buried in whitewashed stone or concrete coffins resting on the hot ground. Among those buried here are the American missionary S. M. Spencer (1810–98) and Captain Gilbert Mair (1843–1923), who was a great friend of the Arawa and the only white man to be granted the full status of a chief. He had defended Ohinemutu against Hauhau raids and attacks by Te Kooti.

★Churchyard

Opposite the church is a magnificent Maori meeting-house. The interior is richly decorated with old Maori carving; the exterior was renovated in 1941.

★Maori meeting-house

Whakarewarewa

The various geothermal phenomena of the Rotorua area can be most easily observed in the Maori village of Whakarewarewa, 3km/2 miles south of Rotorua, where there are numerous springs and three impressive geysers within a small area.

★Geothermal fields

Whakarewarewa has a Maori Cultural Centre, with a carved gateway, palisades, a meeting-house and a war canoe. There are also performances of Maori music and dances. Within the complex is a Maori arts and crafts centre, with a carving school and a showroom for the sale of craft products (open: daily 8.30am–5.30pm).

★Maori Cultural Centre

Whakarewarewa Forest Park (area 3800 hectares/9500 acres) extends south-east of the Whakarewarewa geothermal field. There are hiking trails to the Blue Lake and the Green Lake.

Whakarewarewa Forest Park

Waimangu Valley · Lake Tarawera

The Waimangu valley was completely reshaped by the eruption of Mount Tarawera in 1886. Old photographs show the splendour of the sinter terraces described by Ferdinand von Hochstetter, which no longer exist. The Maori villages of Te Wairoa, Te Arihi and Moura disappeared under masses of lava and ash, and roads and bridges were destroyed.

★★ Volcanic landscape

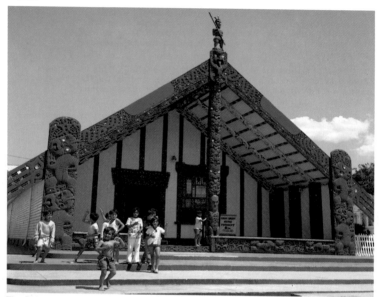

The Ohinemutu meeting-house, a masterpiece of Maori woodcarving

There are now organised excursions to observe the volcanic phenomena in the Waimangu valley. The tour includes a walk along the shores of Lake Rotomahana, passing the Waimangu Geyser, now inactive, which in the past shot water up to a height of 400m/1300ft. Other features are the Waimangu Cauldron, a lake of steaming hot water over 4 hectares/10 acres in extent, the Cathedral Rocks and the Warbrick Terrace. Under Mount Tarawera (1111m/3645ft), which is at present quiescent and unthreatening, is Lake Tarawera, on the shores of which (particularly round Tarawera Landing) there are interesting Maori rock drawings. Finally a boat takes visitors across the lake to the buried village of Te Wairoa, now partly re-excavated. At least half a day must be allowed for the tour.

Te Wairoa

This buried Maori village on the south-western shore of Lake Tarawera can also be visited on your own. 14km/9 miles south-east of Rotorua the road (signposted) runs past Tikitapu (the Blue Lake) and Rotokakahi (the Green Lake) and comes to Te Wairoa. Here there is a small exhibition of old photographs and objects found under the lava which gives some impression of what the village was like before its destruction. Among the houses that have been excavated is the one occupied by the ancient tohunga who predicted some great calamity. There are also the remains of a mill and a tourist hotel, as well as a very old stone-built Maori store-house with archaic figures.

Waiotapu

Situation

30km/19 miles south of Rotorua on the road to Taupo (Highway 5) is the village of Waiotapu, famed for the spectacular post-volcanic features in the surrounding area.

The Lady Knox Geyser, which "performs" with almost unvarying punctuality at 10.15 every morning ▶

Rotorua

★ Lady Knox
Geyser

Waitapu's top attraction is the Lady Knox Geyser, which spouts with almost unvarying punctuality at 10.15 every morning and sends a jet of water high into the air.

This punctuality is achieved, however, with a little artificial help. Soap powder must be thrown into the water, and the sodium carbonate it contains decreases the surface viscosity and sets the geyser off. This was first discovered by convicts who used soap to do their washing in pools of thermal water.

Artist's
Palette

The silicate terraces known as the Artist's Palette shimmer in all the colours of the rainbow, as the pink and white sinter terraces destroyed by the eruption of Mount Tarawera must have done.

★ Champagne
Pool

The effervescent thermal waters of the Champagne Pool, highly charged with minerals, have earned it its name. Like other pools in the area, it sparkles in many colours, predominantly yellow, green and blue.

Tikitere

Hell's Gate

In the north of the Rotorua area is Tikitere, known as Hell's Gate because of its evil-smelling springs of sulphurous water and vigorously bubbling pools of mud. The geothermal field here covers some 10 hectares/25 acres, with seething mud springs, a charming warm waterfall (Kakahi Falls), pools of sulphurous water and clouds of steam hovering over vegetation resembling a primeval forest. There is a small exhibition of displays illustrating the character of the area.

Farther Afield

Rainbow Springs

5km/3 miles north of Rotorua, at Rainbow Springs, are a number of attractive hiking trails running under tall tree ferns. The pools and streams in this area teem with rainbow trout.

Rainbow Farm

At Rainbow Farm visitors can learn about sheep and cattle farming in New Zealand, with demonstrations of milking and sheep-shearing.

Ngongotaha,
Agrodome

7km/4½ miles north of Rotorua, on the western shore of the lake, is Ngongotaha, with the Agrodome, which puts on shows (three times daily) of many different breeds of sheep. Expert sheep-shearers and self-appointed sheepdog trainers demonstrate their skills.

Lake Rotoiti

North-west of Lake Rotorua, some 20km/12½ miles from the town of Rotorua, is Lake Rotoiti, near which are a number of carved Maori meeting-houses. Here too, on a north-western arm of the lake, are the Okere Falls.

Hongi's Track

Through the forested area which extends eastward from Lake Rotoiti to Lake Rotoehu runs Hongi's Track, on which Hongi Hika and his warriors carried their canoes overland from one lake to the other during his expedition of conquest in 1823. On the track is a tree sacred to the Maoris, said to have been planted 400 years ago by Hinehopu, a chief's wife.

Other sights

Other places of interest within easy reach of Rotorua are Paradise Valley Springs (11km/7 miles north-west on Highway 5), Taniwha Springs (14km/9 miles) and Hamurana Springs (17km/11 miles), at the north end of Lake Rotorua.

The lakes in the surrounding area have great attractions in summer for picnickers, trout-fishers and swimmers.

Taranaki

This region on the west side of the North Island takes its name from Taranaki (Mount Egmont, 2518m/8262ft), a volcanic cone which rears up in isolation to the south of New Plymouth. It draws the rain clouds over the Tasman Sea like a magnet, so that it has numerous streams flowing down its slopes. To the Maoris the summit of the mountain was sacred, and they never climbed higher than the snowline. The summit area was declared a nature reserve in the 19th century, when the felling of trees and the use of the land for agriculture was prohibited within a six-mile radius of the summit. Lower down, however, large expanses of primeval forest were cleared, and in place of the forest there is now lush green pastureland grazed by dairy cows. The earlier sawmills have given place to large creameries. Now served by a well planned network of roads, the Taranaki region is one of the most densely populated parts of New Zealand, though in recent years there has been no growth in population.

The commercial centre of the region is New Plymouth (see entry), on the coast to the north of Mount Taranai. In the 19th century there were fierce disputes in this area between the white settlers and the Maoris over the seizure of land by the whites, leading in the 1860s to the Taranaki land wars.

Oil was discovered near New Plymouth in the 19th century, but this was of little economic importance compared with the discovery, more recently, of fields of natural gas off the coast of Taranaki at Maui and at Kapuni, to the south of Mount Taranaki.

Egmont National Park

Egmont National Park (area 33,500 hectares/82,750 acres) is centred on the almost symmetrical volcano of Taranaki, whose highest peak rises up to 2518m/8262ft. With its harmonious conical form, Taranaki has often been compared with Japan's Fujiyama. The Maori name Taranaki has prevailed over the name Mount Egmont (after the Earl of Egmont, First Lord of the Admiralty) given to the mountain by Captain Cook, though that name is borne by the National Park. Within the protected area, which takes in the main summit (2518m/8262ft) and the subsidiary summits to the north, Pouakai (1400m/4600ft) and Patuha (684m/2244ft), the original vegetation cover of primeval forest and scrub has been preserved. In summer whole hosts of walkers and climbers make for the summits (the climb, there and back, can be done in a day from one of the "mountain houses" – see below – in the area), while in winter the slopes of the mountain attract large numbers of skiers.

★★ Taranaki (Mount Egmont)

On Mount Taranaki you should keep a watchful eye on the weather. In these mountain regions it is very changeable, and good weather can suddenly change to mist, rain and cold. The best time of year to climb the mountain is in the summer month of January.

The Maori tradition has it that Tahurangi, the Maoris' great ancestor, was the first man to climb the volcano, demonstrating in this way that he had taken possession of the whole area for the Taranaki tribes. Long ago, according to the legend, Taranaki's place was in the centre of the North Island along with the other volcanoes, where he paid court to the beautiful wife of Tongariro, who was away from home at the time. Then when Tongariro returned and found the faithless pair there was a fierce fight between the two mountain giants and Taranaki was driven away to the farthest point in the west of the island, deepening the bed of the Whanganui River in his flight.

Maori mythology

The first known ascent of Mount Taranaki by Europeans was in 1839, when Ernst Dieffenbach, who was surveying the area for the New Zealand Company, and James Heberley, a whaler, made the climb with Maori guides. The Maoris refused, however, to go beyond the snowline, since to them the

First ascent by Europeans

Taranaki

The symmetrical cone of Mount Taranaki

summit was *tapu* (sacred). The Maoris climbed high peaks only to bury dead chiefs and tohungas in secret caves. In 1885 Frances Fantham became the first woman to reach the summit, giving her name to Fantham's Peak, a subsidiary crater to the south.

Taranaki is returned to the Maoris

In 1978 the government, in a symbolic gesture, gave the summit of the mountain back to the Maori tribes of the Taranaki region, so that it might be included, with their agreement, in the newly established National Park.

Mountain houses

There are a number of "mountain houses" providing overnight accommodation on sites, at altitudes of around 900m/2950ft, which can be reached by car. The climb to the summit from a mountain house takes about 10 hours there and back.

Manganui skiing area

The Manganui skiing area is most easily reached from the Stratford mountain house.

Curtis Falls, Dawson Falls

Waymarked trails lead to two impressive waterfalls, the Curtis Falls and the Dawson Falls. At the Dawson Falls accommodation is available in Dawson Lodge. From here there are trails to Lake Dive and the Stratford mountain house.

North Egmont

25km/15½ miles south of New Plymouth (see entry), at an altitude of 936m/3071ft, is North Egmont, with a visitor centre where full information about the National Park can be obtained. Attractive trails lead to the Holly Hut and Bell's Falls.

Kori Pa

To the south of the little town of Oakura, a short distance inland, is Kori Pa, an old fortified Maori settlement. Standing high above the pass, it was almost impregnable. It was abandoned in 1820, when the local Taranaki tribes fled before the Waikato tribes, who were armed with guns.

At Puniho, 30km/19 miles south-west of New Plymouth (see entry), is a rock which, according to the Maori legend, was brought here by the volcano Taranaki in his flight from the central plateau. To the Maoris the rock was sacred, and on certain ceremonial occasions was clad in a chief's cloak. To touch the rock might be fatal: it is said that 70 enemy warriors who had carried it off all died that day, whereupon the rock returned by itself to its original position. The stone's magical powers suffered from the coming of the white men, and it can now be touched without evil consequences.

Puniho

3km/2 miles higher up (starting from Pungarehu) is the village of Parihaka, established by the Maori leaders Te Whiti and Tohu. In 1866 the villagers began a campaign of passive resistance and civil disobedience against the government; then in 1881 the two leaders were arrested and kept in prison, without trial, for almost two years, and their village was destroyed. The conflict between the Maoris and the whites was not settled until 1926, when the government agreed to pay compensation. The village is now a centre of the Maori renaissance. Here too is Te Whiti's grave. Visitors to the village should respect the feelings of the Maoris.

Parihaka

50km south-west of New Plymouth (see entry) is Oaonui, the supply base for the two offshore production platforms in the Maui natural gas field. The visitor centre has informative material on the extraction of natural gas from the continental shelf.

Oaonui

90km/56 miles south of New Plymouth is Manaia (pop. 1000), the commercial centre of a farming district. It has a large memorial to those who fell in the land wars. On the golf course are two blockhouses built in 1880 to provide protection against attacks by Te Whiti.
  12km/7½ miles north-east of Manaia there was a battle in 1868 between Maori warriors and British troops. The Maori leader Titikowaru enticed the British force into an ambush and annihilated it.

Manaia

North of Manaia, at Kapuni, are fields of natural gas which are now being worked. Evidence of this industrial activity is provided by flares burning off gas, pipelines and a fertiliser factory.

Kapuni

The little market town of Stratford (pop. 6000), on the south-eastern slopes of Mount Taranaki, was founded in 1877 on an old Maori road. In its early days its economy centred on the processing of timber felled during the clearing of the forests. Stratford is now a popular starting-point for walks and climbs on Mount Taranaki (approach route via Pembroke to the Stratford mountain house). Stratford's power station, completed in 1976, is fuelled by natural gas from the nearby Kapuni field.

Stratford

From Stratford the Heritage Trail runs 155km/96 miles north-east to Taumarunui. This winding route takes in some impressive natural features, such as the Mount Dampier Falls and the Tangarakau Gorge.

★Heritage Trail

8km/5 miles north-east of Ringwood, in a densely forested area, is the fortified Maori village of Pukerangiora Pa.

Pukerangiora Pa

16km/10 miles north-east of New Plymouth is Waitara (pop. 6000), where the land wars began in 1860. The main cause of the wars was the land hunger of the white settlers, who, caught between the volcano and the sea, wanted to get the Maoris' farming land. The local tribe, the Te Ati Awa, fled south in the 1820s before the better equipped Waikato tribes. They gave up land in the Wellington area to the whites so that they could return to their tribal territory around 1848. But the whites wanted this land too. Thereupon the Maoris united in opposition to a renegade Maori leader who had gone over to the settlers' side. Government troops then intervened in order to secure the land for the whites.

Waitara

The fortified Maori village of Manukorihi Pa has a meeting-house with magnificent carving, built in 1936 in honour of the influential Maori politician Maui Wiremu Pomare.

Manukorihi Pa

Taupo · Wairakei   K/L 5

Region: Waikato

★Lake Taupo

Lake Taupo, New Zealand's largest inland stretch of water with an area of over 600sq.km/230sq. miles, lies in the very heart of the North Island. Its waters cover several volcanic craters, belying in their remoteness and peace the raging inferno that brought the lake into being. After some 300,000 years of relative calm there was a series of violent eruptions in this area in the 2nd century A.D., when immense masses of volcanic ash and pumice-stone were spewed out and spread over a huge area. Later the empty crater collapsed, giving rise to a caldera, and the accumulated masses of detritus prevented the water which collected in the crater from draining away. Thus Lake Taupo was born.

When this last great eruption in the Lake Taupo area occurred New Zealand had probably not yet been occupied by man, but its effects were felt in distant parts of the world, as records from China and the Roman Empire attest. And in New Zealand itself the massive beds of pumice and ash give impressive evidence of this great natural catastrophe.

A display in the visitor centre of Tongariro National Park (in the village of Whakapapa, to the south of Lake Taupo) illustrates, by a comparison with the devastating eruptions of Mount St Helens in the United States and Krakatoa in Indonesia, the stupendous power of the explosion that gave birth to Lake Taupo.

Rivers

Numerous rivers flow into Lake Taupo from the south, east and west. The largest of them is the Tongariro, which enters the lake in a delta at Turangi (see entry), at the south end. The Waikato, a river with an abundant flow of water, leaves the lake at Taupo.

Settlement

The abundance of fish and birds led Maoris to settle on the shores of the lake at a relatively early stage. But they were greatly in fear of the lake because of the monsters (*taniwha*) which were believed to inhabit its waters.

The first missionaries arrived in the area in 1839, but the white settlers at first showed little interest in the area because they judged the land to be infertile. In 1841 Ernst Dieffenbach, who was surveying the area for the New Zealand Company, was struck with the magnificence of the landscape.

In 1869 a well armed police force was stationed on the lake to take action against Te Kooti's guerrillas. It was then that the healing powers of the thermal waters in the area was recognised and the first bath-houses were built. It was to be many years, however, before any decent roads were constructed.

Lake Taupo, a huge crater lake which came into being after violent volcanic activity in the 2nd century A.D.

Circuit of the lake	A circuit of the lake involves a drive of some 150km/95 miles. On the east and south sides the road runs almost continuously close to the shores of the lake, with magnificent views, passing a series of holiday settlements. Beyond Waihi, because of the hills, it runs at some distance from the lake.
Boat trips	A variety of boat trips on the lake are on offer. Sailing boats, steamers and motorboats take visitors to see the rock carvings by young Maori artists at the north end of the lake and the cliffs at Karangahape, which can be reached only by boat.
★ Trout-fishing	The best fishing grounds on the shores of the lake are at the mouth of the Waitahanui River (15km/9 miles south of Taupo on Highway 1) and at Hatepe (10km/6 miles farther south, also on Highway 1), where fishermen sometimes stand in long rows, almost shoulder to shoulder. Fishing is permitted throughout the year.

Taupo (Town)

Situation and importance	Taupo (pop. 19,000), at the north-east corner of the lake, is still a relatively young town, having grown to its present size only in the 1950s. Its growth was stimulated by the construction of good new roads, the development of the volcanic plateau by reafforestation with pines, the harnessing of geothermal energy and above all by tourism. The lake, in which Californian rainbow trout have flourished since the late 19th century, has now become a popular holiday destination. It also makes a pleasant stopover on the journey from Wellington to Auckland (see entries). Numerous hotels, motels, holiday houses and motor camps cater for visitors; many of them have their own swimming pools of thermal water.
Sights	From the shores of the lake, where the modern, rather characterless, town centre lies, there are superb views. There is a fine Maori gate with delicate carved decoration. In the evening the outlines of a huge artificial trout are picked out by innumerable lights. The early days of the settlement established by the security forces are recalled by a protective wall and the old courthouse of 1881.
★ Thermal baths	The luxurious Brett Thermal Pools, in the style of Japanese bath-houses, are open daily from 8am to 9.30pm. The A.C. Baths in Spa Road (open: daily 8am–9pm) were originally established for the use of the police force, the A(rmed) C(onstabulary). There are also thermal baths at Tokaanu on the south side of the lake, near a small geothermal field.
★ Taupo Walkway	This 3-hour walk, starting from County Avenue in Taupo, follows the Waikato River to the Huka Falls (4km/2½ miles) and on to the Aratiatia Rapids (11km/7 miles). Skirting the forest, it affords a succession of beautiful views.
Taupo Lookout	From the end of the Huka Falls Loop Road it is a short distance to the Taupo Lookout, at the local radio station. In good weather there are fine views over the town and the lake to the distant mountains.
Waikato River Lookout	This viewpoint overlooking the Waikato River, also known as Hell's Gate, is most easily reached from Spa Road.

Wairakei

★ Geothermal field	One particular attraction in the Lake Taupo area is the large geothermal field at Wairakei, which lies just under 10km/6 miles north of the town of Taupo. It is conveniently laid out for visitors travelling by car: the circuit of Wairakei Park covers a distance of 40km/25 miles, but there are so many things to see on the way that a full day should be allowed for the trip.

From Highway 1, going north, the Huka Falls Loop Road goes off on the right just beyond Taupo. At the Huka Falls the mighty Waikato River thunders down over an 11m/36ft high rock face. Huka Valley, a reconstructed pioneering settlement (open: daily 10am–5pm), offers a presentation of "living history".

At Honey Hive New Zealand visitors are given an introduction to New Zealand's highly developed beekeeping industry, and can sample the honey.

The geothermal power station with its visitor centre (open: 9am–noon and 1–4pm) is a must for every visitor to New Zealand. An excellent audio-visual show introduces visitors, with the aid of pictures and models, to the construction and operation of the Wairakei power station and the whole chain of power stations on the Waikato River.

★★ Geothermal
Power Project

The new Taupo Observatory of the New Zealand Institute of Geological and Nuclear Sciences is well worth a visit for the sake of its very informative displays, models and film shows illustrating the volcanic past and present of New Zealand. This is an excellent introduction to geothermal phenomena and the study and monitoring of volcanic activity. Open: daily 10am–4pm.

★★ Taupo
Observatory

Armed with this information, we continue through the "organised chaos" of steaming and hissing pipes and pipelines to the Lookout, from which there is a general view of the area.

The densely wooded Wairakei Thermal Valley offers a variety of post-volcanic phenomena, including a small geyser, a hot waterfall to which it gives rise, bubbling mud pools and multi-coloured mineral deposits.

Lookout,
★ Wairakei
Thermal Valley

5km/3 miles north of Wairakei is the Aratiatia Dam with its associated power station, the first of a series of hydro-electric stations on the Waikato

Aratiatia Dam

Geothermal power installations, Wairakei

River. As a result of the diversion of water to the power station the Aratiatia Rapids are now dry; but following demonstrations of protest against the construction of the power station water is allowed to flow in the old river bed daily from 10 to 11.30am and 2.30 to 4pm.

Wairakei golf course

Wairakei has a golf course on which, for a very reasonable fee, golfers can play a round in this strange steaming and bubbling landscape.

★Craters of the Moon

2km/1¼ miles south of Wairakei are the Craters of the Moon – steaming, hissing and sometimes smelling of rotten eggs. There are paths through the area, and for their own safety visitors must keep to them.

Orakei Korako (the Hidden Valley)

★Geothermal field

The Hidden Valley, 30km/19 miles from Taupo, is reached from a side road linking Highways 1 and 5. To reach the thermal field it is necessary to take a boat over the Waikato River. Part of the area was flooded by the damming of the river in 1961, but this does not interfere with the walkway round the geysers, sinter terraces, mud pools and hot springs. The finest feature is the Great Golden Fleece, a range of sinter terraces 38m/42yd long and over 4m/13ft high. Boat trips daily 8.30am–5pm.

Turangi

At the south end of Lake Taupo is Turangi (pop. 4500), once a quiet little holiday place, which has developed at a furious rate since construction work on the Tongariro hydro-electric power scheme began in 1964. Farmers and forestry workers have settled here as well as construction workers and technicians, and Turangi has also become a centre of the timber industry. Above all, however, the town has gained from the development of tourism: it is a good base not only for exploring the surrounding area but also for excursions to Tongariro Forest Park (see entry).

On the way from Turangi to Tokaanu the pipelines of the Tongariro hydro-electric scheme can be seen on the hillside above the road. Under the scheme the Whanganui, the Tongariro and other rivers are linked by open channels and underground tunnels. Before the water flows into Lake Taupo it drives the turbines of another power station. Since the water level of Lake Taupo can thus be controlled, the output of the eight hydro-electric stations on the Waikato River is, indirectly, increased. During the construction of this complex system care was taken to ensure that the flow of water in the Tongariro River was maintained in order to avoid endangering its stocks of trout.

Tongariro National Trout Centre

4km/2½ miles south of Turangi is the Tongariro National Trout Centre, a state-run hatchery where rainbow trout are bred. In addition to meeting domestic needs the centre also exports roe to other countries. Conducted tours daily 9am–4pm.

Mount Pihanga

Over Turangi looms Mount Pihanga (1325m/4347ft), which in Maori mythology, as the only "female" volcano, is courted by the "male" volcanoes in the surrounding area. From the Pihanga Saddle Road Viewpoint there is a marvellous view of Lake Taupo. Near here is the idyllic Lake Rotopounamu.

Tokaanu

The little township of Tokaanu, 5km/3 miles west of Turangi, is known for its thermal springs (spa establishment open daily). St Paul's Church (Anglican) has an appealing Maori-style interior.

Waihi

8km/5 miles west of Turangi is the village of Waihi, in an idyllic but also a dangerous situation. It has twice suffered severe damage from landslides. In 1846 Chief Tuwharetoa Te Heuheu Tukino and many members of his tribe were killed when a landslide dammed the stream and an avalanche of mud engulfed the village.

The village has a very handsome Roman Catholic church, St Werenfried's (1889), with a beautiful Maori-style interior and fine stained glass depicting the Virgin and Christ in Maori dress. The meeting-house (1959) contains older carved decoration. Notable also is the tomb of Chief Te Heuheu Tukino.

Near the village are the 90m/295ft high Waihi Falls.

South-east of Turangi is Kaimanawa Forest Park (area 76,000 hectares/188,000 acres), with magnificent southern beeches. It lies immediately east of Tongariro National Park (see entry), separated from it by Highway 1 (Desert Road).

Kaimanawa
Forest Park

Tauranga

L 4

Region: Bay of Plenty
Population: 71,000

On the west side of the Bay of Plenty (see entry) is the town of Tauranga, whose Maori name means "calm water" or "sheltered anchorage" – referring to the natural harbour enclosed by the long, narrow island of Matakana. The fertile soil and temperate climate provide ideal conditions for the growing of kiwi fruit, plantations of which, with their tall hedges as windbreaks, pattern the landscape.

Situation and
importance

The settlement of Tauranga was established in the 19th century on confiscated Maori land as a military base and became a market and supply centre for the surrounding area. More recently the beautiful beaches near the town have made it a popular holiday resort and a favourite place for retirement homes.

After the infertile pumice soils in the hinterland of the volcanic plateau had been turned into good grazing land with the aid of cobalt fertilisers and, after thirty years, the huge coniferous forests were ready for felling the population of the Tauranga area increased sharply. And in more recent times Tauranga has lost none of its attraction. Communications have been much improved, for example by the construction of a railway tunnel through the Kaimai Range, providing direct connections with Hamilton and Auckland, and a new harbour bridge. The harbour, at the foot of Mount Maunganui, is now New Zealand's leading port for exports.

Sailing this way in 1769, Captain Cook was struck by the number of fortified Maori settlements (*pas*) in the Tauranga area. He concluded that the inhabitants must have many enemies and be exposed to frequent attack. The first missionaries, in 1828, were horrified by the brutality with which villages were attacked and their inhabitants slaughtered, and their early missionary efforts were frustrated by the tribal wars. Success was finally achieved in 1838, when a missionary bought land from the Maoris and built a mission station. In 1864 the government sent troops to the little settlement to prevent the sending of reinforcements to the Maori forces in the Waikato land war. Two defensive positions were also established. The Maoris retaliated by building a strongly fortified *pa* (Gate Pa) opposite the entrance to the missionary settlement. British troops surrounded it, and there was bitter fighting. The Maoris managed to escape, but were defeated a few weeks later at Te Ranga, and thereafter much of their tribal territory was confiscated. As late as 1928 a government commission approved the confiscation as an appropriate punishment for rebellion, and the Maoris had to wait until 1981 before a law was passed giving them compensation for the confiscated land.

History

Sights

The missionary Alfred N. Brown (1803–84) built a mission station known as The Elms in 1838 on a site he had bought from the Maoris. The house, with a small chapel and a small library in the garden, has survived almost

★The Elms
(Tauranga
Mission House)

Tauranga

Deep-water harbour, Mount Maunganui

unchanged. The garden front is particularly beautiful. The old trees, two Norfolk pines and an English oak, have grown to enormous size. Now protected as a national monument, the house is furnished in the style of its period. Conducted tours daily at 2pm.

Strand, Monmouth Redoubt

The Monmouth Redoubt (1864), with well preserved earthworks and a number of old cannon, can be reached from the north end of the Strand. It is named after the Monmouth Light Infantry, who were stationed here. Beside the entrance is a carved Maori war canoe set up here in 1970.

Otemataha Pa

The site of the old fortified Maori settlement of Otemataha Pa is now occupied by a cemetery containing the graves of many who fell in the fighting at Gate Pa and Te Ranga. It is reached by way of the railway bridge at the end of Cliff Street.

★Tauranga Historic Village

In this open-air museum on Seventeenth Avenue the colonial period is brought to life again, with examples of old workshops, 19th-century-style shops and simple quarters for troops. The scene is particularly lively at weekends, when historic craft markets are held. In keeping with the period, there is also an old steam train.

Mount Maunganui

Only a few kilometres from Tauranga, and now easily reached over the new harbour bridge, is the independent town of Mount Maunganui (pop. 12,000), situated on the other side of the natural harbour, which at this point is equipped with the most modern transport facilities.

In summer the town, lying at the foot of the steep-sided hill (232m/761ft) from which it takes its name, is a popular holiday resort. There are a number of footpaths running up the hill, which was once crowned by a fortified Maori settlement.

Bathing beaches

Mount Maunganui has marvellous beaches (Ocean Beach, Papamoa Beach, etc.).

A number of natural hot water pools give evidence of the volcanic activity found all over this region (see Rotorua). | Hot water pools

In the north-west of the Bay of Plenty, some 35km/22 miles north of Tauranga, is Mayor Island, formed from an extinct volcano 387m/1270ft high, with two craters containing lakes. There are remains of a fortified settlement on the hill. | Mayor Island

Mayor Island is a favourite haunt of deep-sea anglers. Every year in late summer and autumn (December–May) there are great angling competitions in the waters round the island.

There are boat trips to Mayor Island from Tauranga and Whangamata.

Te Kuiti · Waitomo Caves   K 5

Region: Waikato
Population: 5000

The little town of Te Kuiti lies 80km/50 miles south of Hamilton (see entry) at an important road junction. From here it is only a short distance to the famous Waitomo Caves, and from here also Highway 3 runs down to the Taranaki coast. Originally established as a railway workers' camp, Te Kuiti is now the commercial centre of the King Country, a region in which the main occupations are farming, mining (limestone and coal) and timber-working. | Situation and importance

After the battle of Orakau the supporters of the Maori king fled to this area, where he was safe from pursuit – for no white man dared venture into the King Country. In 1872 the Maori leader Te Kooti also sought refuge in the King Country after his rebellion in the east was crushed. In 1887 a camp was established here to house workers employed on the construction of the railway from Wellington to Auckland. | History

The pride of Te Kuiti is a magnificent Maori meeting-house, built in 1878 for Te Kooti. After he was pardoned by the government in 1883 he presented the house to the tribe which had taken him in during his period of exile. | Sights

20km/12½ miles north of Te Kuiti is Otorohanga (pop. 2500), which has a bird park (open: daily 10am–5pm), with a Kiwi House in which the birds can be observed in night-time conditions and a walk-in aviary housing other native species. | Otorohanga

Pureora Forest Park (area 83,000 hectares/205,000 acres), 60km/37 miles south-east of Te Kuiti, is famed for the many different species of birds to be found here. There are a number of trails through the park. The soil was formed from pumice ejected during the last eruption of Mount Taupo some 1850 years ago. | Pureora Forest Park

Waitomo Caves

20km/12½ miles north-west of Te Kuiti are the Waitomo Caves, an intricately ramified karstic cave system famed for its bizarre stalactitic and sinter formations which attracts large numbers of visitors, particularly in the main summer holiday season. | ★Karstic cave system

The principal attraction is the Glowworm Cave, through which an underground stream flows. The cave was first explored in 1887. Glowworms, the larvae of insects which can live only in conditions of fairly high humidity, produce long sticky threads like a spider's web to which other small insects | ★★ Glowworm Cave

163

are attracted by the faint light generated by the glowworms during the digestion process. Visitors are taken through the dark cave in boats and can observe the glowworms hanging from the ceiling of the cave and twinkling like innumerable stars. Conducted tours daily 9am–4.30pm in winter, to 5.30pm in summer.

Aranui Cave

2km/1¼ miles from the Glowworm Cave is the Aranui Cave, which is dry and therefore has no glowworms. Its attractions are the varied stalactitic and sinter formations. Conducted tours daily from 2.30pm.

Ruakuri Cave

This "Dogs' Cave", near the Aranui Cave, is the largest of the Waitomo caves. Like the Glowworm Cave, it has a stream flowing through it, and consequently also has glowworms. Adventurous visitors can join an abseiling and black-water rafting tour or the "Lost World" tour.

Waitomo Caves Museum

In addition to a variety of exhibits on caves and caving, the Museum puts on audio-visual shows on the Waitomo cave system and on glowworms.

★ Ohaki Village and Weaving Centre

The road to the caves runs past the reconstruction of a Maori village as it may have looked before the coming of Europeans. Here visitors can watch skilled Maori craftsmen at work and have the opportunity of buying souvenirs of their visit.

★ Waitomo Walkway

This interesting trail, which takes off from the car park in front of the Glowworm Cave, runs through the forest, passing limestone formations in the steep-sided gorge of the Waitomo River, to the Ruakiri Natural Bridge, an arch left by the collapse of a cave. The complete circuit takes about 4 hours.

Tongariro National Park   K 6

Region: Manawatu-Wanganui
Area: 750sq.km/290sq. miles

Situation

Tongariro National Park, established in 1887 and included in UNESCO's list of world heritage sites in 1991, lies in the heart of the North Island, just to the south of Lake Taupo (see entry). It is about 350km/220 miles south of Auckland and about the same distance north of Wellington.

Getting there

From Lake Taupo Highway 47 runs via Turangi to the National Park; then continue on Highways 4 and 49 to Ohakune and Waiouru, returning to Turangi on Highway 1, the notorious Desert Road. This circuit (without diversions and side trips) is about 180km/120 miles.

There are regular bus services from Turangi to the National Park, Ohakune and Waiouru, and railway stations at Waiouru, Ohakune and the National Park.

Information

Tongariro National Park Headquarters and Visitor Centre, Whakapapa. The visitor centre (open: daily 8am–5pm) supplies general information, maps and descriptions of the various paths and trails.

Exhibitions

There are interesting exhibitions on the National Park and its flora and fauna, with audio-visual presentations daily at 11am and 2 and 4pm.

There are also information offices in Turangi (see Lake Taupo) and on the Mountain Road, Ohakune (open: Mon.–Fri. 8am–4pm).

Season

The National Park is open throughout the year. The skiing season on Mount Ruapehu usually lasts from June to October.

N.B.

Since the weather in the National Park is very changeable, warm clothing and protection against rain should be taken on a walk of any length. Stout

Mount Ngauruhoe, a volcano in Tongariro National Park which is still active

footwear is necessary, particularly above the snowline. Good maps are essential, since the routes are sometimes not adequately waymarked. You should take sufficient food with you; water from streams in the park should be boiled because of the danger of parasites.

Throughout the National Park there are only nine huts equipped with mattresses. The ski huts at Iwikau and Tukino can be used only by members of ski clubs. In addition to the luxury hotel Château Tongariro there are other hotels and more modest types of accommodation at Whakapapa, the National Park railway station, Turangi, Ohakune and Waiouru.

Accommodation

The central features of the National Park are the three volcanoes of Tongariro (1968m/6457ft), Ngauruhoe (2291m/7517ft) and Ruapehu (2797m/9177ft). They are part of a chain of volcanoes which extends north by way of the volcanic White Island to the Kermadec and Tonga Islands. These volcanoes, relatively young in geological terms, have repeatedly erupted in recent centuries, as attested by Maori traditions and observations made since the European settlement, but have rarely caused catastrophic damage. The most serious recent incident was at Christmas in 1953, when the crater lake on Mount Ruapehu overflowed and great masses of water and mud poured down, destroying the railway bridge at Tangiwai, derailing the Wellington–Auckland express and killing 151 people. The last time Ruapehu, which is snow-capped throughout the year, showed any volcanic activity was in September 1995, when it spewed out huge masses of rock and lava and great rivers of mud flowed down its snow-clad slopes.

★★Topography

Mount Ruapehu

Mount Tongariro, the most northerly of the three volcanoes, is also the lowest. Its summit is broken down into a number of craters. On the slopes of the hill, at Ketetahi, there is an active geothermal field, with hots springs, fumaroles and seething pools of mud.

Mount Ngauruhoe is almost continuously active, and there are frequently plumes of smoke and steam over its summit. A series of minor

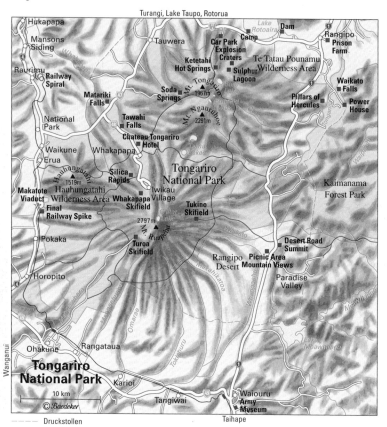

Turangi, Lake Taupo, Rotorua

Hukapapa
Mansons Siding
Lake Rotoaira
Dam
Rangipo Prison Farm
Tauwera
Car Park
Camp
Explosion Craters
Ketetahi Hot Springs
Te Tatau Pounamu Wilderness Area
Sulphur Lagoon
Raurimu
Railway Spiral
Soda Springs
Mt. Tongariro 1967m
Waikato Falls
Matariki Falls
Pillars of Hercules
Power House
National Park
Tawahi Falls
Mt. Ngauruhoe 2291m
Waikune
Chateau Tongariro Hotel
Erua
Whakapapa
Tongariro National Park
Silica Rapids
Hauhungatahi 1519m
Iwikau
Kaimanama Forest Park
Makatote Viaduct
Hauhungatahi Wilderness Area
Whakapapa Village
Whakapapa Skifield
Tukino Skifield
Final Railway Spike
2797m
Mt. Ruapehu
Pokaka
Turoa Skifield
Desert Road Summit
Rangipo Desert
Picnic Area
Mountain Views
Horopito
Paradise Valley
Lake Moawhango
Ohakune
Rangataua
Tongariro National Park
Karioi
Wanganui
Waiouru Army Museum
10 km
© Baedeker
Tangiwai
Taihape

– – – – Druckstollen

eruptions since 1954 have changed the form of the mountain, particularly on the west side.

The three volcanoes are constantly observed and monitored so that in the event of an eruption the local population can be warned in time. But the New Zealanders and their visitors from other countries are not unduly concerned about the dangers of an eruption: there are numerous very popular skiing areas on Mount Ruapehu, and the many very interesting walking trails in Tongariro National Park are well used.

The National Park offers a great variety of scenery. The first impression is of bare lava-covered slopes and expanses of brown tussock grass; but on the rainier west side of the hills the landscape ranges from rain forest by way of montane forest and sub-Alpine scrub vegetation to the Alpine zone. Round the snow-covered craters are bizarre lunar landscapes with greenish-blue crater lakes and steaming crevices in the ground. Finally the dry east side of the mountains, towards the Rangipo Desert (Highway 1, the Desert Road), is barren and inhospitable.

Mythology

The Maoris revered and feared the smoking mountain peaks, which to them were *tapu*, and accordingly the volcanoes were the subject of many traditions. The subterranean fires were said to have been kindled when the children of the gods forcibly separated their parents Papa (Mother Earth) and Rangi (Father Sky). They resolved to turn Mother Earth round in order to put a stop to her floods of tears and her complaints. But the youngest of her children, Ruaumoko, still an infant at her breast, was turned along with his mother and came to lie under her. He was then given the underground fires to keep him warm, and became the god of volcanoes and earthquakes, who can blow away men like flies.

According to another tribal legend all the mountains on the North Island were once gathered together in the centre of the island. All of them were male except one, Pihanga (south of Turangi). All the other mountains paid court to her, but she favoured Tongariro, who defeated all the others and drove them away. Taranaki travelled west and came to a stop on the Tasman Sea, having carved out the bed of the Whanganui River in his passage; Potanaki (Mount Edgecumbe) reached the Bay of Plenty and stopped at Kawerau; but Tauhara, a slow mover, got only as far as Lake Taupo.

In the tradition of the tribes of Taupo and Rotorua their ancestor Ngatoro, commander of the Arawea tribal canoe, landed in the Bay of Plenty and moved inland to take possession of the land. He decided to climb Mount Tongariro along with a slave girl, and asked his followers to fast until he returned. His people disobeyed his command, whereupon the gods were angered and sent a snowstorm which almost killed Ngatoro and his companion. In this extremity he called on the gods in his distant homeland of Hawaiki to send him fire. The fire duly came, creating on its way the geothermal fields of Rotorua and Taupo and then burst out of the volcanoes to warm Ngatoro. He threw the body of the dead slave girl, Auruhoe, into the crater of Ngauruhoe, which since then has borne her name.

The Maoris living on the south side of Lake Taupo had for generations revered the volcanic peaks and buried their dead chiefs and tohungas in caves on the slopes of the mountain. In 1887 Chief Horonuku Te Heuheu Tukino, fearing that white settlers would occupy this sacred area, made over the summit area, within a radius of a mile, to the state on condition that a protected area would be established to safeguard the summit as a holy place. To the original area the government added further land to bring the National Park to its present size. Tongariro National Park was the first National Park in New Zealand and the second in the world (after the Yellowstone National Park in the United States).

Establishment of the National Park

After the completion, in 1908, of the railway between Auckland and Wellington, which skirts the south and west sides of the National Park, the number of visitors increased. In 1919 the government decided to set up a skiing area on the western slopes of Mount Ruapehu, and to provide access a road (Bruce Road) was built up to the village of Iwikau (alt. 1622m/5322ft). In 1929 a luxury hotel, Château Tongariro, was built half way up, 9km/5½ miles from the turn-off of Bruce Road from Highway 47 (Turangi to Tongariro National Park).

Bruce Road, Iwakau

Nearby was established the holiday village of Whakapapa, with a wide range of accommodation for visitors and the National Park's visitor centre.

Whakapapa

The Turoa skiing area, on the south-western slopes of Mount Ruapehu, is a recent development. It can be reached from Ohakune on the Ohakune Mountain Road.

Turoa

The road to this fortified Maori village on the western edge of the National Park is signposted on Highway 47 (Turangi). Here in 1889 Te Kooti was defeated in the last great battle of the land wars. The defences have been partly demolished.

Te Porere Pa

To the west of Rangipo, on Lake Rotoaira, is the Poutu Redoubt, the base for the British attack on Te Kooti's stronghold of Te Porere Pa.

Poutu Redoubt

Volcanic landscape in the Tongariro area

Little mountain lakes shimmering like jewels below Mount Ngauruhoe

The Raurimu Spiral is a remarkable feat of railway engineering which achieves a sharp descent of 200m/220yd in one complete circle, three horseshoe curves and two tunnels.

★Raurimu Spiral

The Makatote Viaduct, crossing a valley between Pokaka and Erua, was constructed in 1908 – the last viaduct on the main line between Auckland and Wellington. Highway 4 runs under the bridge.

Makatote Viaduct

Walks in Tongariro National Park

The National Park is the finest walking country on the North Island. It offers scope both for short walks and for more strenuous hikes taking several days.

The best known trails taking off from the visitor centre in Whakapapa Village are the Alpine Garden Track (1.5km/1 mile), the Taranaki Falls Track (a circuit of 6.5km/4 miles), the Whakapapanui Track (3km/2 miles), the Silica Rapids Track (7km/4½ miles) and the Waihohonu Track (an all-day walk from Highway 1 to Château Tongariro or vice versa: transport problem).

Round Whakapapa

This walk across the country round Mount Tongariro takes a whole day (about 9 hours' actual walking).

Tongariro Crossing

This walk, starting from the end of the Ohakune Mountain Road in the south, circles round Ngauruhoe and Tongariro to join the Desert Road. It takes 4–5 days.

Round the Mountains Track

The little town of Ohakune (pop. 1500) lies on the south-western edge of Tongariro National Park (Highway 49). The clearance of forest in this area made it possible to obtain rich yields of vegetables on the good volcanic soil. The coming of the railway promoted the development of the town, which is now a popular all-year holiday resort, a good centre from which to visit the National Park and Mount Ruapehu.

Ohakune

The very beautiful Ohakune Mountain Road winds its way up through the forests of the National Park to the Mangawhero Falls and the Turoa skiing area on the western slopes of Mount Ruapehu (2797m/9177ft). This involves climbing from 600m/1970ft to 1600m/5250ft. At this height snow lies from June to October.

★Ohakune Mountain Road, ★Mount Ruapehu

From the park ranger station at the near end of the Ohakune Mountain Road there is a 3km/2 mile circuit through the Mangawhero Forest.
It is a two-hour walk to the imposing Waitonga Falls, one of the highest (63m/207ft) in Tongariro National Park.

Walks

11km/7 miles west of Ohakune is Raetihi (pop. 1300), on Highway 4, which once marked the boundary between the Wanganui area and the King Country. In 1918 a devastating forest fire in this area destroyed nine saw-mills and 150 houses. The local timber-working industry took a long time to recover from this severe setback. Prominent features of the town are the twin towers of a church belonging to the Ratana sect.

Raetihi

For a rewarding trip from Raetihi, take the Whanganui River Road, which runs west from Raetihi to Pipiriki and then follows a winding and fairly strenuous route through the wild and romantic valley of the Whanganui River.

Whanganui River Road

20km/12½ miles north of Ohakune an imposing railway bridge 79m/260ft high, built in 1907), spans a valley, crossing Highway 4.

Railway bridge

A few kilometres south of Tongariro National Park, on Highway 1, is Waiouru (pop. 3000). In these inhospitable uplands (alt. about 800m/2625ft)

Waiouru

The "sleeping" volcano Mount Ruapehu

covered with tussock grass is the largest military camp in New Zealand, with an extensive training area. The little town has the highest railway station on the North Island. In good weather there is a fine view from here of the volcanic mountains in the Tongariro area.

Military Museum

Waiouru has an interesting military museum, the Queen Elizabeth II Army Memorial Museum, which displays uniforms and equipment of the New Zealand army and other military equipment. There are also dioramas of world-famous battlefields. Open: daily 9am–4.30pm.

Rangipo Desert

To the north of Waiouru is the Rangipo Desert – not a real desert, but a barren region of poor soil and arid winds.

Urewera National Park   L/M 5

Regions: Bay of Plenty, Hawke's Bay, Gisborne
Area: 2110sq.km/815sq. miles

Information

Urewera National Park Headquarters and Visitor Centre, Aniwaniwa, and ranger stations at Taneatua and Murupara will give advice about walks in the National Park, much of which is difficult of access, and information about the exact position of mountain huts. Walkers undertaking long hikes and requiring accommodation in the huts must inform the park authorities.

Getting there

The principal means of access to the National Park is Highway 38, which cuts through it from north-west (Rotorua) to south-east (Wairoa, Hawke's Bay). The best approach from the north is from Whakatane (see Bay of Plenty) along the Whakatane River.

Highway 38, the only route through the park from Rotorua via Murupapa and through the Urewera Ranges to Wairoa, was completed only in 1930.

220km/137 miles long, it is poorly asphalted if at all and is very hilly, with numerous bends.

There is only limited accommodation at Aniwaniwa and Waikaremoana, on the east side of Lake Waikaremoana.

Accommodation

The first section of the park was established in 1954, and there have been repeated extensions since then, so that it is now New Zealand's third largest National Park. It lies in the Urewera Ranges, the densely wooded hills which are still regarded as the most remote and inhospitable part of the North Island. The endless dark forests, never cleared by European settlers, prevent the soil from being washed away by erosion and reduce the rate at which water drains away.

Situation and
★topography

The Tuhoe tribe which occupied the Urewera area was isolated and had little contact with other tribes even in pre-European times. According to their tradition their ancestor was born of a marriage between a maiden of the mist and a mountain, and accordingly they were known as the "children of the mist". Mist often shrouds the mountains in this rugged region, which is too cool for growing sweet potatoes (kumara). Until recently the Tuhoe tribe lived mainly on roots, berries, birds and fish.

History

Since the tribe had no interesting objects for barter and trade the European immigrants had no interest in the area, and even the missionaries soon gave up.

Te Kooti, who had supported the government against the Hauhau rebels until his arrest and deportation in 1866, found refuge and supporters in the Urewera Ranges. From here, in a skilfully planned campaign of guerrilla warfare, he could launch lightning attacks on military bases and settlements and swiftly withdraw. The Ringatu sect which he had founded also had many adherents here.

The other leading figure in the area was Rua Kenana (1869–1937), founder of a religious sect similar to the Mormons. He saw himself as Jesus's younger brother and a prophet. His Te Wairau Tapu sect was associated with a move for the revival of the Maoris' self-awareness and way of life. The members of the sect, who from 1905 met in a large circular temple at Maungapohatu and revered their leader as Te Kooti's heir, achieved a new – though still modest – prosperity through common ownership of property and modern methods of work.

But Rua Kenana, who was against military service, came into conflict with the New Zealand government. The police, seeking to arrest him in 1916, became involved in a gun fight with his supporters – an event often called the last battle in the struggle between the Maoris and the Pakehas (whites).

Sights

Te Kooti and Rua Kenana are still revered in the Urewera region. They are depicted together in a mural painting by Colin McCahon in the National Park's visitor centre at Aniwaniwa.

Aniwaniwa

The visitor centre is the starting-point of Hinerau's Walk, a very beautiful trail through the striking landscape of the National Park, with the chance of seeing many rare species of birds.

★Hinerau's Track

Other attractive walks are to the Bridal Veil and Aniwaniwa Falls and to the little Lake Waikareiti, higher up in the hills.

In the centre of the National Park, at an altitude of 614m/2015ft, is Lake Waikaremoana, which is 55km/35 miles long and over 250m/820ft deep. It is believed to have come into being some 2000 years ago when a landslide dammed the Waikaretaheke River. At the south end, where the river flows out of the lake, is a hydro-electric station. This quiet lake attracts holiday-makers who appreciate remoteness and peace. A walk round the lake

★Lake
Waikaremoana

Unspoiled natural beauty in Urewera National Park

takes between three and five days; overnight accommodation is available in mountain huts. Fishing is permitted at certain points.

Ruatahuna

The scattered Maori settlement of Ruatahuna, on the western slopes of the Huiarau Range and the upper course of the Whakatane River, can be reached by way of Highway 38. From here it is worth making a side trip (4km/2½ miles) to Mataatua to see (after politely asking permission) a very fine Maori meeting-house with impressive carvings.

Maungapohatu

The lonely settlement of Maungapohatu, where the self-styled prophet Rua Kenana gathered his flock, lies 20km/12½ miles north of Ruatahuna, below Mount Maungapohatu (1366m/4482ft), which is almost always shrouded in clouds and mist. It was formerly a sacred burial-place for tribal chiefs. Nothing remains of Rua Kenana's circular temple, which stood above the present meeting-house.

Waikato River   K/L 4/5

Region: Waikato

New Zealand's
longest river

The Waikato, New Zealand's longest river (425km/264 miles), rises as the Tongariro River on Mount Ruapehu, the 2787m/9144ft high volcano in Tongariro National Park (see entry) which is snow-capped all year round, flows through Lake Taupo and emerges from it as the Waikato River at Taupo (see entry). The Maori name Waikato-taniwha-rau means "the flowing water of the hundred water monsters". Before the river was tamed in the 20th century by the construction of dams, power stations and flood barriers it fully justified its name with its waterfalls, whirlpools, rapids, marshy areas and floods.

At Mercer, north of Huntly, the Waikato suddenly turns abruptly west and flows into the Tasman Sea in a wide estuary, over black ferruginous sand. Until the last great eruption of Mount Taupo some 1850 years ago the Waikato flowed not to the west, as it does now, but east into the Firth of Thames.

Ferdinand von Hochstetter, surveying the coalfields round Huntly for the New Zealand government, compared the Waikato with the Rhine and the Danube and called it the Mississippi of the Maoris. The local Tainui tribes were warlike and self-assured. The Waikato region was densely populated and bloody tribal feuds were endemic, for every insult and every attack called for *utu* (revenge and retaliation) in order to preserve the *mana* on which the tribe's reputation and authority depended. In the early 19th century there was a major conflict between rival tribes in the area north of Te Awamutu which was settled by the traditional hand-to-hand battle. From 1820 onwards many of the local Maoris were killed, and even more were enslaved, in attacks by Ngapuhi tribes from the north, now armed with European weapons. After this visitation the Waikato tribes were keen to trade with the Europeans, exchanging mainly flax for firearms. The missionaries too were successful in their evangelising work. The Maoris were quick to learn the modern farming methods taught by the missionaries, growing wheat on the fertile soils of the region and soon exporting it to Auckland and even to Australia.

The fertile soil also aroused land hunger among the increasingly numerous white settlers. In order to present a united front against the whites the Waikato tribes joined in a tribal union and in 1858 elected an old chief, Te Wherowhero, as king. After his death in 1860 his belligerent son at once joined in the fight over land in Taranaki. The British authorities built a military road to Mercer, on the Waikato, and British gunboats were able to sail up the river to the Maori positions. The Maoris defended their fortified positions with all the means at their disposal. The final battle in the Waikato war was fought at Orakau, and after his defeat the Maori king fled with his surviving followers into the King Country. The old tribal territory on the Waikato was confiscated; the land was cleared of trees, drained and converted into fertile grazing and arable land by British soldiers; and Hamilton became the commercial centre of the Waikato region, as it still is.

The enormous potential of the Waikato as a supplier of electric power was soon realised, and a whole series of dams and hydro-electric stations were built. The Tongariro Hydro-electric Power Scheme was carried out in the area south of Lake Taupo. A chain of eight hydro-electric power stations was built on the river after its emergence from the lake: at Aratiatia (13km/8 miles downstream from Taupo; 1964), Ohakuri (80km/50 miles downstream; area 13sq.km/5sq. miles; 1961), Atiamuri (88km/55 miles downstream; 1958), Wakamura (112km/70 miles downstream; 1956), Maraetai (123km/76 miles downstream; 1952; extension 1970), Waipapa (134km/83 miles downstream; 1961), Arapuni (161km/100 miles downstream; 1929) and Karapiro (188km/117 miles downstream; 1947).

Hydro-electric development

These eight hydro-electric stations are supplemented, north of Taupo, by the geothermal power station at Wairakei and two coal-fired power stations at Huntly and Mercer, which use the water of the Waikato not for the production of energy but for cooling.

Waipoua Kauri Forest   H 2

Region: Northland

From Dargaville take Highway 12, which runs north-west to Hokianga Harbour. Some parts of the 20km/12½ mile stretch through primeval forest are not asphalted and are difficult to negotiate in heavy rain.

Getting there

Waipoua Kauri Forest lies on the south side of Hokianga Harbour (see entry), 65km/40 miles north-west of Dargaville. This 9000 hectare/22,500

Situation and importance

acre expanse of primeval forest has the largest surviving stands of kauri trees in New Zealand.

Waymarked trails lead from Highway 12 to two imposing kauri giants: Tane Mahuta ("god of the forest") and Te Matua Ngahere ("father of the forest"). Tane Mahuta is the largest known kauri, standing 51.5m/170ft high, with a trunk measuring over 9m/30ft across; it is estimated to be 1200 years old. Te Matua Ngahere is only 30m/100ft high but has a still thicker trunk than Tane Mahuta; it is around 2000 years old.

★★ Giant trees

New Zealand's kauri forests were bought up from the 1870s onwards to make room for new settlements. Legislation for the protection of nature was introduced only in 1932. When European settlement began there were vast expanses of kauri forest extending from Northland to south of Auckland, as well as on the Coromandel Peninsula. The straight trunks of the kauris, with no side branches, were much sought after for use as ships' masts and in the early days of settlement were New Zealand's principal export. After the loggers came the gum-diggers, who dug deep down into the ground in search of lumps of resin from long dead kauri trees. The resin was used in the manufacture of paints and lacquers.

History

South-east of the Waipoua Kauri Forest is the Trounson Kauri Park (area 500 hectares/1250 acres), which was established by James Trounson in 1919. Its stands of kauris are younger but equally dense. As in the Waipoua forest, there are walking trails, picnic areas and camping sites.

An excellent introduction to the history of kauri-felling and gum-digging is provided by the Kauri and Pioneer Museum in Matakohe, 50km/30 miles south of Dargaville (see Whangarei).

Trounson Kauri Park

Wanganui

K 6

Region: Manawatu-Wanganui
Population: 42,000

The town of Wanganui lies in the estuary of the Whanganui River, on the south-west coast of the North Island. Before the coming of the Europeans the river was an important transport route for the Maoris' canoes. There were frequent conflicts between the various tribes, as the numerous fortified villages along the river show. There was particularly fierce fighting between the local Maoris and the warriors of Te Rauparaha, who had been driven out of his home area at Kawhia on the west coast and now launched plundering expeditions from his base on Kapiti Island, much farther south.

Situation and history

In 1840 the New Zealand Company, directed by William Wakefield, "bought" (as they saw it) 16,000 hectares/40,000 acres of land from the Maoris in exchange for pipes, mirrors and cloth. The Maoris, however, took a different view of the transaction: they regarded these things as gifts, which they reciprocated with gifts of sweet potatoes, sucking pigs and so on. In the same year the New Zealand Company began settling new immigrants on the land. They were in a difficult situation, for they had far more new arrivals than they could provide for in Wellington, where their purchases of land had gone wrong.

The fertile plains at the mouth of the Whanganui were easy to deforest and cultivate, and the wide river, navigable without difficulty in its lower reaches, was a convenient transport route which obviated the expense of building roads. Inevitably there were conflicts with the local Maoris. In 1847 British troops were sent in to support the white settlers. In the following year a treaty was signed which gave the Maoris £1000 in return for 32,000 hectares/80,000 acres of land. For the moment this resolved the dispute. The local Maori tribes did not take part in the land wars which had now

◀ Te Mahuta, the tallest known kauri tree

175

Two Giants – the Kauri and the Kahikatea

The giant **kauri** tree is found only on the North Island of New Zealand north of latitude 39° south. Remnants of the much larger forests of pre-European New Zealand are to be found in the Auckland area, on the Coromandel Peninsula and in Northland between Hokianga Harbour and Dargaville.

Until well into the 20th century timber from the kauri, a tree resembling a spruce, and the resin which it yielded were New Zealand's principal exports. Its easily worked wood was prized by shipbuilders and furniture manufacturers alike, while its resin (gum) was used in the production of paints and lacquers.

Great numbers of European immigrants found employment felling the giant trees and digging deep into the ground in search of fossil kauri resin, a substance resembling amber.

As a result the kauri – one of the world's tallest trees - has been almost exterminated. Of the great expanses of forest once covering well over a million hectares (2.5 million acres) there survive only a few remnants, barely amounting to 150 hectares/375 acres.

The kauri (*Agathis australis*), a member of the araucaria family with oval leaves about 7cm/2.75in. long and a centimetre (.4 of an inch) wide, can reach a height of over 50m/165ft. The trunk, straight and without branches, can be up to 6m/20ft thick, and bears a magnificent crown.

Kauris are relatively slow growers. The bark of a young tree (50–70 years old) is quite smooth; that of an older tree tends to be scaly. Fully grown kauris are often several hundred years old. Individual trees (e..g. in Waipoua Kauri Forest: see pp. 173–75) are anything up to 2000 years old.

The wood of the kauri, which is rich in resin and highly aromatic, was used by the Maoris in pre-European times to build their long war canoes. Resin was also used – as it was by the Indians of Mesoamerica in pre-Columbian times – in religious ceremonies (e.g. in the preparation of incense). Soot from burnt kauri resin was used in the process of tattooing.

The giant kauri trees were felled by the Maoris, using only the simplest stone tools, only after solemn ceremonies had been performed. There was none of the over-felling later practised by European settlers.

The **kahikatea**, known to the British settlers as white pine, is a member of the evergreen Podocarpaceae family. It grows even higher than the kauri (up to 60m/200ft) but has a relatively slender trunk. It is found mainly in humid areas on both the North and the South Islands. The species has existed since the Mesozoic period.

broken out, and the settlement of Wanganui was able to develop unhindered.

Sights in Wanganui and Surroundings

The Queen's Park, laid out on the site of fortifications built by the early settlers, has now in effect become the cultural centre of the town, for within it, side by side, are the Wanganui Museum, the Serjeant Gallery and the War Memorial Hall.

Queen's Park

The best view of the Queen's Park is from the neighbouring Cook's Gardens, which lie rather higher up, on the site of an old military fortification, and are now a pleasant open space, with various sports grounds. Here in 1962 the middle-distance runner Peter Snell achieved his first world record.
    Farther up the hill are a 19th century wooden fire-watching tower and an observatory.

Cook's Gardens

The Wanganui Museum is richly stocked, with an excellent collection of Maori arts and crafts, including greenstone jewellery and weapons, as well as a 23m/75ft long war canoe of 1810, rowed by 70 men, and a series of portraits of Maori chiefs by the German painter Gottfried Lindauer. There are also mementoes of the days of the first white settlers and the conflicts with the Maoris. Open: Mon.–Fri. 10am–4pm, Sat. and Sun. 1–4.30pm.

★ Wanganui Museum

The Serjeant Gallery (named after a well-to-do local family) occupies a large and imposing building. The collection consists mainly of works by British and New Zealand artists of the 19th and early 20th century, including C. F. Goldie and the local woman artist Frances Hodgkins. The gallery is open daily in the afternoon.

★ Serjeant Gallery

The Moutoa Gardens are a small park of historical interest on the Whanganui River, on the spot where land deals were negotiated in earlier days. It was originally intended to be the site of the town's market-place. There are a number of monuments commemorating historical events, including the battle of Moutoa (1864), in which the local Maoris defeated a party of Hauhau warriors who were bent on destroying the town. There are also a war memorial in honour of Maoris who died in the First World War and a monument to the Putiki chief Te Rangihiwinui Kepa, who fought on the government side in the land war and became known as Major Kemp.

Moutoa Gardens

From Durie, on which there are an outlook tower and a war memorial, there are fine views of the town, the coast and, in the distance, Mounts Ruapehu and Taranaki.

Durie Hill

This Maori church, built in 1937, has magnificent carvings by the great Maori woodcarver Pine Taiapa.

Putiki Church

Putiki Pa, a Maori stronghold on the banks of the river, held out against hostile attacks until the 19th century; but in 1829 Te Rauparaha and his warriors overpowered and massacred the defenders. In 1891 the river overflowed its banks and washed away the meeting-house and many Maori canoes. A new meeting-house and a store-house were then built.

Putiki Pa

The best beaches in the vicinity of Wanganui are west of the town at Castlecliff, on the Whanganui estuary and at Mowhanau and Ototaka.

Beaches

Farther Afield

23km/14½ miles south-east of Wanganui is the Maori village of Ratana (pop. 500), which gave its name to a religious movement. This had great

Ratana

influence on the revival of Maori consciousness and still has many adherents throughout the country. The handsome twin-towered church was built
in 1927. Beside the church is a small museum devoted to Wiremu Ratana
(1870–1939), founder of the Ratana sect, who had a great reputation as a
healer. In the large meeting-house are models of the seven Maori ancestral
canoes, Abel Tasman's "Heemskerck" and Cook's "Endeavour". Ratana's
birthday is celebrated annually on January 25th as a popular festival.

Waverley
50km/31 miles north-west of Wanganui is Waverley (pop. 1600), near which
are ancient rock drawings (difficult of access).

Wellington   I 8

Region: Wellington
Population: 326,000

Getting there
By air: There are services from all the major New Zealand airports, particularly from Auckland and Christchurch, to Wellington International Airport
(8.5km/5½ miles south-east; shuttle bus to Cathedral Square).

By rail: Wellington is the southern terminus of the main line from Auckland, and there are also connections with New Plymouth and Gisborne. The
station is in Bunny Street.

By ferry: There are up to four crossings daily from Picton, on the South
Island (3½ hours) and two crossings daily from Lyttleton/Christchurch (10
hours). Ferry terminal: Aotea Quay.

By road: From Auckland on Highways 1, 3 and 4 via Wanganui
(655km/407 miles), or on Highway 1 via Lake Taupo (670km/416 miles: a
faster road).

★★ Situation and importance
Wellington, New Zealand's capital city, lies at the south-western tip of the
North Island in a supremely beautiful situation, surrounded by water and
steep-sided hills, with its picturesque natural harbour, Port Nicholson.
Another characteristic of the city is the strong and sometimes stormy west
wind which blows in almost constantly from the Cook Strait, giving Wellington its name of the "windy city". One disadvantage that goes with its
magnificent situation, however, is a shortage of level ground, so that the
city has been compelled to spread into widely scattered areas of land
between the hills and inlets of the sea, which are linked by a network of
winding roads, sometimes running high above sea level. Some land was
gained by earth movements during a severe earthquake in 1855, when the
harbour area rose about 1.5m/5ft, and more recently land reclamation
schemes have created more room in the city centre and for the airport; but
it has still been necessary to resort to high-rise building in the central area
to meet the city's requirements. Wellington now has the most modern
skyline in New Zealand, but at the cost of losing much of its Victorian
architectural heritage. Many old shops and offices were demolished on the
ground that they were not earthquake-proof, to be replaced by steel-
framed and glass-fronted tower blocks, which have turned many streets in
the city centre into channels for the wind. The residential areas have now
moved far out into suburbs and satellite towns – north-east to Hutt Valley
(Petone, Lower Hutt, Upper Hutt), north to the Kapiti Coast (Porirua, Paekakariki, Paraparaumu), and so on. Access to the city centre is provided by
urban motorways and suburban rail lines, tunnelling through the hills and
destroying more of the city's older buildings.

Wellington is the seat of New Zealand's Parliament and government, and
thanks to its situation on the north side of the Cook Strait is an important
traffic hub for communications with the South Island. As the metropolis of
New Zealand, however, Wellington has now been overtaken by Auckland
(see entry) – a reversal of past history, when Wellington fought for years to
supersede Auckland as capital.

View of Wellington from Mount Victoria

Wellington is the home of the New Zealand Symphony Orchestra and the New Zealand Ballet Company. The International Festival of the Arts, with some 300 events and exhibitions, is held in March in alternate (even-numbered) years. An event which attracts larger attendances, however, is the rowing race in January by the city's lifeguards across the Cook Strait from the South Island. Other events in Wellington's year are the state opening of Parliament and Tulip Sunday at the beginning of October, when the Botanic Gardens are a glorious show of colour.

Culture; events

On offer are bus trips to the harbour, along the coast and into the hills surrounding the city, usually combined with an ascent by cable car or a cruise round the harbour. Information from the Public Relations office (see Practical Information).

Good value if you want to do your own sightseeing is a Daytripper ticket ($5) for the city's Stagecoach buses.

Sightseeing tours

At weekends Wakefield Market, at the corner of Jervois Quay and Taranaki Street, offers a wide range of cloths, arts and crafts and above all fashion jewellery. There are a variety of shopping centres, large department stores and elegant boutiques on Lambton Quay.

Shopping

History

According to Maori mythology Kupe, the legendary seafarer and discoverer of New Zealand, sailed into the bay and camped on the Miramar peninsula. The first permanent settler, however, is said to have been Tara, son of Whatonga, who like Kupe had come from Hawaiki and had set out from Hawke's Bay to look for new land for settlement. From him the harbour got its Maori name of Te Whanganui-a-Tara ("great harbour of Tara"), and his descendants formed the Ngai-Tara tribe, which built fortified settlements on all the hills round the harbour.

Mythology

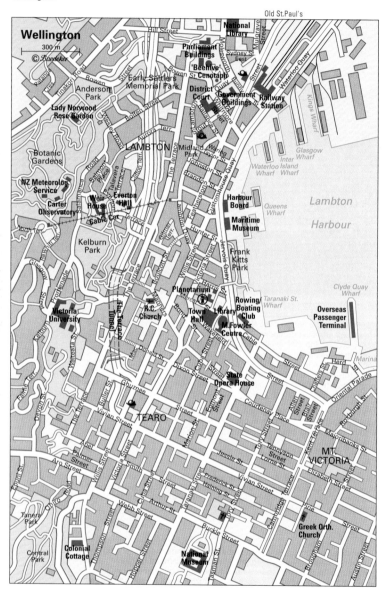

Wellington

300 m

© Baedeker

Map labels:
Old St.Paul's
National Library
Parliament Buildings
'Beehive' Cenotaph
Hill Street
Bowen Street
Sydney St. East
Mulgrave St.
Waterloo Quay
Early Settlers Memorial Park
Anderson Park
District Court
Government Buildings
Railway Station
Kings Wharf
Lady Norwood Rose Garden
Bolton Street
Aurora Terr.
Sign St.
LAMBTON
The Terrace
Midland Park
Waring Taylor St.
Johnston St.
Glasgow Wharf
Botanic Gardens
Salamanca Road
Talavera Terrace
Clifton Terrace
Brandon St.
Inter Island Wharf
Waterloo Wharf
NZ Meteorolog. Service
Carter Observatory
Weir House
Everton Hall
Cable Car
Customhouse Quay
Harbour Board
Maritime Museum
Queens Wharf
Lambton Harbour
North Terr.
Kelburn Park
Lambton Quay
Hunter St.
Jervois Quay
Frank Kitts Park
Clyde Quay Wharf
Glasgow St.
The Terrace
Willis Street
Victoria St.
Harris St.
Planetarium
Rowing/Boating Club
Taranaki St. Wharf
Overseas Passenger Terminal
Victoria University
The Terrace
The Tunnel
Boulcott St.
Manners St.
Bond St.
R.C. Church
Town Hall
Library
M. Fowler Centre
Cable St.
Marina
Herd St.
Dixon Street
McDonald Cres.
Ghuznee Street
State Opera House
Cuba Street
Courtenay Place
Allen St.
Blair St.
Cambridge Terrace
Kent Terrace
Oriental Parade
VIVIAN Street
TE ARO
Marion St.
Taranaki Street
Tennyson St.
Lorne St.
MT. VICTORIA
Majoribanks St.
Roxburgh St.
Abel Smith Street
Aro Street
Willis Street
Victoria Street
Cuba Street
Jessie St.
Vivian Street
Elizabeth Street
Palmer St.
Webb Street
Frederick St.
Haining St.
Brougham St.
Pirie St.
Austin St.
Tasman St.
Arthur St.
Buckle Street
Greek Orth. Church
Tennant Park
Colonial Cottage
National Museum
Central Park

Captain Cook discovers the harbour

On his first voyage, in 1770, Cook saw the entrance to the harbour, but it was only on his second voyage that he noticed the arms of the sea running far inland, forming a good natural harbour. Wind and tides, however, carried the "Resolution" out to sea. Georg Forster, in his record of the voyage, described high, barren, blackish hills and the inquisitive Maoris who came out in canoes to look at the "Resolution".

Half a century after Cook Te Rauparaha and his warriors from Kapiti Island fell upon the harmless tribes of the south. Those who survived the slaughter fled into the hills and the dense forests, and their place was taken by the Te Ati Awa tribe, who had themselves been driven out of their tribal territory in Taranaki. And so when the first white settlers arrived about 1840 the local Maoris, in terror of the other tribes to the north and north-east, saw the white men as the lesser evil and hoped for their protection. The first white visitors – flax traders, whalers, seal-hunters – only stayed briefly in the area, and when the sailing ship "Tory" put into the bay in 1839, carrying agents of the New Zealand Company sent from London to assess the scope for settlement, they found hardly any white men there. The expedition was led by William Wakefield, brother of the founder of the Company, Edward Gibbon Wakefield. No sooner had the ship anchored than Wakefield went ashore and bought from the Maoris who happened to be there, in return for 100 guns, blankets and the usual trinkets. vast stretches of land which did not belong to them – for he either did not know or chose to ignore the fact that the Maoris had no conception of private property. The "Tory" was soon followed by other vessels bringing the first settlers, and by the end of 1840 they numbered more than 2500. The first arrivals settled at Petone, in Hutt Bay, calling their settlement Britannia. But they had great difficulty in making anything of the marshy land and dense scrub, and they also had to contend with flooding and a minor earthquake (which they took for an attack by the Maoris). Accordingly they soon moved farther south-west to the site of present-day Thorndon, where, on what is now Lambton Quay, they erected a prefabricated house which they had brought from Britain. Originally designed as a school, it also served for many years as a courthouse, a ballroom and even the seat of the provincial government. Round this building grew up the New Zealand Company's first and most successful settlement, named after the Duke of Wellington, who had been a great supporter of Wakefield's plans.

The first settlers; foundation of the town

In 1865, after many years of complaints by New Zealanders in the south about the remoteness and inaccessibility of Auckland as capital, the decision was taken to transfer the capital to Wellington, situated conveniently close to the South Island. During the move the steamer "White Swan", carrying officials and official documents, sank off the east coast. Its passengers were rescued but most of the documents were lost. Wellington now succeeded Russell/Okiato and Auckland as New Zealand's third capital, and soon enjoyed a boom, thanks to the transfer to the new capital of diplomatic missions, banks, businesses and shipping agencies and to the foundation of the Victoria University. Residential districts and industrial installations extended over the whole of Hutt Valley as far as the Rimutaka Ranges, and the city also expanded over the hills to the west coast.

Wellington becomes capital

Thorndon

The most imposing building in the Parliamentary and government quarter is the Old Government Building (1876) at the north end of Lambton Quay. Like the other buildings in this area, it stands on the old sea-bed which was thrust upwards in the 1855 earthquake and proved a welcome addition to the narrow strip of level ground fronting the harbour. Although this massive four-storey building in Italian Renaissance style (area 9400sq.m/ 11,240sq.yd) looks as if it were built in stone, it is in fact wholly of wood – the second largest wooden building in the world. The architect, W. H. Clayton, son-in-law of the then prime minister Sir Julius Vogel, used kauri, rimu and matai wood, which turned out to be so expensive that the government dispensed with an official opening ceremony. The building originally

Parliamentary and government quarter

★Old Government Building

had 22 chimneys, but these were removed as an earthquake risk. In front of the building is a statue of the Labour leader and prime minister (1940–49) Peter Fraser.

Parliament Buildings

To the north of the Old Government Building is an even more remarkable building, the ultra-modern circular structure popularly known as the Beehive which houses ministerial and government offices and the Cabinet Room. Built in 1964–81 to the design of the British architect Sir Basil Spence, it is still the subject of controversy. Next it is Parliament House (1922), built of granite and Tabaka marble from the South Island. The chamber in which Parliament sits is modelled on the House of Commons chamber at Westminster. There are conducted tours of the building on weekdays. The chamber of the upper house, which was abolished in 1952, is now used only for the state opening of Parliament.

Here too is the General Assembly Library Building, a two-storey Neo-Gothic building of 1897. In the gardens are statues of Richard Seddon, prime minister of New Zealand 1893–1906, and John Ballance, leader of the Liberal Party and Seddon's predecessor as prime minister.

★National Library

Farther north again, past some other government buildings, is the National Library (Molesworth Street), which was opened in 1987. The nucleus of the national collection was formed by the Alexander Turnbull Library, previously kept in Turnbull's old house in Bowen Street, near the "Beehive". The library now has over 250,000 volumes, including a very valuable and almost complete collection of accounts of travel and discovery in the South Pacific. In the fine Reading Room is a mural by the Maori artist Cliff Whiting depicting the separation of Mother Earth and Father Sky.

Mulgrave Street

Thistle Inn

To the east of the National Library is Mulgrave Street, running north–south. At its south end, on the corner of Sydney Street, is the Thistle Inn, Wellington's oldest hotel. Originally built in the 1840s, it was rebuilt after a fire in 1866.

The "Beehive", Wellington

The cable car running up to the Botanic Gardens, from which there is a magnificent view of Wellington

To the north are the National Archives, which have a display of important documents bearing on the history of New Zealand, including letters written by Captain Cook, the petition which led to women getting the vote and the original of the treaty of Waitangi. The National Portrait Gallery is housed in the same building.

National Archives

Beyond this is Old St Paul's Church (Anglican), perhaps the finest of the "Selwyn churches" built for Bishop Selwyn by Frederick Thatcher. Externally a plain white wooden building in Neo-Gothic (Early English) style, it has a charming interior in which the beauty of the wood is enhanced by the effect of light. Originally Thorndon's parish church, it became Wellington's Cathedral until it was superseded in 1972 by the present Cathedral opposite the National Library.

★Old St Paul's

From the north end of Mulgrave Street Murphy Street continues north-west, passing the Katherine Mansfield Memorial Park (presented to the city by her father), crosses the urban motorway and runs into Tinakori Road, at the far end of which (No. 25) is the plain wooden house, very much in the style of old Thorndon, in which Katherine Mansfield (see Famous People) was born in 1888. The house, which was built by her father in the year in which she was born, has been restored to its original condition and is now a museum (open: Tues.–Sun. 10am–4pm).

Katherine Mansfield Birthplace

From Lambton Quay to Cuba Street

Lambton Quay, which runs south from near the railway station, and its continuation Willis Street form Wellington's busy main artery and commercial street. The name "Quay" is a reminder that the shoreline originally ran here: all the land to the east of this street was thrust up from the sea-bed in the 1885 earthquake.

Shopping and business street

Wellington

Antrim House

There are no spectacular sights along this street and few old buildings apart from the District Courts (1879) and the Public Trust Building (1908). There is, however, another old building in Boulcott Street, which opens off Willis Street. At No. 63 is Antrim House, a handsome mansion of kauri wood (1904), now hemmed in by high-rise buildings. It was built by Thomas Turnbull for the shoe manufacturer Robert Hannah and is open to the public (Mon.–Fri. noon–3pm). Otherwise glass and steel façades predominate in this area – with the Bank of New Zealand, at the south end of Lambton Quay, towering above them all – behind which are luxury shops, department stores and shopping malls.

Civic Centre

This modern and rather cold aspect of the city is continued in the Civic Centre, nearer the harbour, with the old Town Hall, the elegant Wellington City Library (designed by Ian Athfield) and the Michael Fowler Conference Centre. Diagonally opposite the Conference Centre is the Capital Discovery Place (also by Ian Athfield), a hands-on museum designed for children in which science and technology are presented in a vivid and accessible way (open: Wed.–Sun. 10am–5pm). The City Art Gallery (open: daily 11am–5pm, Thur. to 8pm), housed in the former Public Library, has a large collection of modern art and puts on periodic special exhibitions and film shows.

Cuba Street

Adjoining the Michael Fowler Centre is the Cuba Street pedestrian precinct, where the pace of life is quieter than in hectic and expensive Willis Street and Lambton Quay. Visitors may feel tempted to relax in one of the many restaurants.

Other Sights

★ Botanic Gardens

★ Cable car

The Botanic Gardens (area 26 hectares/65 acres) lie in the centre of the city on the Kelburn Hills. The cable car which runs up to the gardens is an experience in itself. This 610m/667yd long funicular railway, opened in 1902, climbs from Lambton Quay, opposite Grey Street, to a height of 122m/400ft. The old wooden cars were replaced in 1979 by modern cars made in Switzerland. From the top there is a magnificent view of Wellington.

The Botanic Gardens were opened in 1869. At the entrance are the Carter Observatory belonging to the Meteorological Institute and a number of other University scientific institutes. The high points of the gardens are the Lady Norwood Rose Garden, with over 500 varieties of roses, the Begonia House, the herb garden, the Maori herb beds and a garden designed to inculcate concern for the environment. The walk through the gardens ends at the north exit in Glenmore Street, which has preserved its Victorian-style wrought-iron gates and porter's lodge.

Bolton Street
Memorial Park

From here it is a short distance to the Bolton Street Old Settlers Memorial Park, with the old Sexton's Cottage (restored) and the graves of noted citizens and politicians, including Edward Gibbon Wakefield (see Famous People) and Richard Seddon.

Victoria University

To the south of the upper station of the cable car is the campus of the Victoria University. In the Hunter Building is a geological museum. More interesting perhaps for most visitors is the old Roman Catholic cemetery in Mount Street, with the oldest graves in Wellington (1840).

★ National
Museum

The National Museum and National Art Gallery occupy a Neo-Classical building (by Gummer and Ford, 1930) in Buckle Road, on the south side of the city centre. In the park surrounding them is the Shrine of Remembrance, commemorating New Zealanders who fell in the two world wars.

The Museum has 15 departments covering the whole range of New Zealand's history and natural history, including its old natural history collections dating from the 1860s, herbaria incorporating material collected by Cook's companions Joseph Banks and Daniel Solander and by William Colenso, relics and documents on early European settlement down to 1900, and the figurehead of the "Resolution", in which Cook made his second and third voyages. The Museum also has a fascinating collection of Maori objects, with particularly fine pieces from Taranaki and the east coast. A notable item is the magnificently carved meeting-house of Te Hau-ki-Turanga (1843) from Manutuke in Poverty Bay, one of the oldest and finest of surviving Maori meeting-houses.

The National Art Gallery displays paintings, drawings, graphic art and sculpture by New Zealand, Australian and European artists of the 19th and 20th centuries, including many early views of New Zealand.
   The Museum and Gallery are open daily 10am–4.45pm.

National
Art Gallery

Mount Victoria (196m/643ft), immediately east of the city centre, is the best known and also the windiest of Wellington's viewpoints. A narrow winding road, signposted "Lookout", runs up from Oriental Bay to the Byrd Memorial below the viewing platform. From the terrace on the summit there is a magnificent panoramic view of the widely spread city, the harbour, Cook Strait, Hutt Valley and Kelburn Park with the University buildings. The Byrd Memorial commemorates the American aviator Richard Byrd, who made the first flight over the South Pole from his base in New Zealand.

★★ Mount
Victoria

There are at least two features to be visited in Wellington Harbour, Frank Pitts Park and the Maritime Museum.
   Frank Pitts Park is a good viewpoint from which to observe activity in the harbour. In the park is a mast from the ferry "Wahine", which sank with 51 passengers in a storm in the harbour in 1968, and a bronze representation of the two ships in which Abel Tasman discovered New Zealand in 1642.

Harbour

The Wellington Harbour Board Maritime Museum (open: daily 1–4.30pm) is primarily devoted to the history of the harbour.

Maritime Museum

Surroundings

The 40km/25 mile long City Marine Drive – suitable for bicycles as well as cars – runs round the Miramar peninsula to the east of the city, keeping close to the coast almost all the way and passing a number of bathing beaches.

★★ **City Marine
Drive**

The circuit begins in Oriental Bay, once a place where whales were beached and cut up and now a select residential suburb with charming wooden houses reaching up from the shore to Mount Victoria. On the hill to the right is a large building (1905) once occupied by St Gerard's monastery, and to the left is the Freyberg Swimming Pool, named after Lord Freyberg, born in London but brought up in New Zealand, much decorated in the First World War, commander-in-chief of New Zealand forces in Europe and North Africa in the Second World War and the seventh governor-general of New Zealand. From here the road continues round Point Jermingham into Evans Bay, from which there is a view of the Miramar peninsula.

Oriental Bay

Continuing past the airport, built on a sandbank reclaimed from the sea which links the Miramar peninsula with the mainland, we come to the west coast of the peninsula, on whose northern tip, Point Halswell, is the Massey Memorial, built on the site of a fortified Maori settlement (*pa*). It commemorates William Ferguson Massey, prime minister of New Zealand 1912–25. The exertion of the ascent is rewarded by a tremendous view of Wellington and Port Nicholson.

★★ View from
Massey Memorial

Then on to Mahanga Bay and Point Gordon, a fort built in the 1880s, when, after the opening of the port of Vladivostok, there was concern in New Zealand about the possibility of an attack by Russia.

Point Gordon

Waikanea, Otaki,
Kapiti Island, Palmerston North

**Wellington
Surroundings**

5 km

© *Baedeker*

Worser Bay, Lyall Bay	The route continues to Scorching Bay and Worser Bay, both of which have beautiful bathing beaches. The harbour pilots' office used to be in Worser Bay. Then on, southward, to Breaker Bay and along the south end of the airport into Lyall Bay, from which there is a view of the mountains of the South Island; the beach here is popular with bathers and surfers.
	The coast road continues past a series of rocky promontories to Houghton Bay, Island Bay (with a good surfing beach) and Owhiro Bay, where the road comes to an end.
★ Walk to Red Rocks and seal colony	From here it is a two-hour walk to the Red Rocks, a volcanic formation between the footpath and the sea. At Sinclair Head, 3km/2 miles farther west, a colony of seals can be observed in winter.
	The return route from Owhiro Bay runs inland on Happy Valley Road, Brooklyn Road and Nairne Street (at No. 68 an old cottage of 1858, now a museum) and so back to Willis Street.
Eastbourne	Eastern Bay Drive runs along the east side of the harbour, passes through Petone and comes to Eastbourne, which also has beautiful bathing beaches. From here there is a pleasant walk on a waymarked track to beautiful Butterfly Creek, where there is an attractive pool for bathers.
Butterfly Creek	
Pencarrow Head	Another trail (16km/10 miles there and back) runs from Eastbourne to Pencarrow Head, on the east side of the entrance to the harbour, where

New Zealand's first lighthouse was built in 1859. From here there is a very fine view of Port Nicholson.

Amateur botanists will enjoy a visit to the Otari Museum of Native Plants, which is not a museum but a very beautiful garden, with specimens of all the plants that grow in New Zealand and the Chatham Islands. The museum (open: daily 9am–5pm) is reached by way of Wilton Road (signposted to Karori), west of the city centre.

Otari Museum of Native Plants

The Dowse Art Museum in Lower Hutt (Laing's Road) has an excellent collection of contemporary New Zealand art (open: Mon.–Fri. 10am–4pm, Sun. 11am–5pm).

Dowse Art Museum

Along the Kapiti Coast, from Paekakariki by way of Raumati to Waikanae, there are a series of very beautiful bathing beaches. There are also three interesting museums.

★ **Kapiti Coast**

The Tramway Museum in Elizabeth Park, Paekakariki (45km/28 miles north of the city centre on Highway 1), is a popular attraction at weekends. Here old tramcars which once ran along Lambton Quay carry passengers on nostalgic trips to the Memorial Gates at McKay's Crossing. The gates commemorate the 2nd US Marine Division, which was stationed here during the Second World War.

Tramway Museum

The Engine Shed in Paekakariki has a fine collection of old steam engines (open: Sun. 8am–5pm).

Engine Shed

Near the Tramway Museum is the Southward Car Museum, with a large collection of veteran and vintage cars, including a Cadillac which belonged to Marlene Dietrich, another which belonged to Al Capone and the first two cars – made by Mercedes-Benz – to run on New Zealand's then dusty tracks in 1898. The museum is some 50km/30 miles north of the city centre, 3km/2 miles south of Waikanae (open: daily 9am–5pm).

Southward Car Museum

A trip by ferry to the South Island will be an unforgettable experience. The crossing takes 3½ hours. From the harbour the ferry cuts across the Cook Strait and then sails for an hour or more through the magnificent scenery of the Marlborough Sounds to the little port of Picton.

★★ **By ferry to the South Island**

15km/9½ miles north-east of Wellington is the outer suburb of Lower Hutt (pop. 95,000), which was named after a director of the New Zealand Company. It lies on the lower course of the Hutt River, which is flanked by steep hills. Near here is Petone, where the first settlers arrived in 1840; but frequent flooding by the Hutt River soon led them to move their settlement farther south. After reaching agreement with the local Maoris on the sale of the necessary land they cleared the forest and laid out gardens. But as the expanding city of Wellington gradually extended its tentacles to the lower course of the Hutt River the settlement of Lower Hutt became a residential suburb, and some of the market gardens gave place to factories. There are now also a number of research institutes and television studios.

Lower Hutt

The Dowse Art Museum (open: daily 10am–4pm) in Laing's Road has a fine collection of New Zealand art. Notable items are the carved Maori storehouse and the collection of glass.

Dowse Art Museum

Christ Church, in Easter Hutt Road, is the oldest Christian church in the Wellington area. Built of wood in 1854, it was well restored in 1989 after a fire.

Christ Church

The Settlers Museum in the suburb of Petone (on the Esplanade; open: Tues.–Sun. in the afternoon) has an interesting collection of material on the white settlement of the area, as well as extensive archives which are of particular interest to genealogists.

Petone

Settlers Museum

Wellington

Markets
The Settlers Market in Jackson Street and the Station Village Market at the corner of Hutt Road and Railway Avenue attract large numbers of visitors on Thursdays and Sundays.

Wainuiomata valley
The road continues south-east through the Wainuiomata valley and in 20km/12½ miles reaches the sea. The rocks exposed here show clearly the various upthrusts caused by earthquakes. The most recent spectacular upthrust of the sea-bed resulted from the 1855 earthquake. The uppermost raised beach was thrust upwards some 6500 years ago.

Rimutaka Forest Park
10km/6 miles south of Wainuiomata, in Catchpool Valley, a road goes off to Rimutaka Forest Park (camping sites, picnic areas). There are a number of walking trails in the park, including particularly the Five Mile Track to the Orongorongo River (4 hours), the Middle Ridge Track (2 hours) and the Butcher Track (tough rock climbing; 1 hour), from which there are beautiful views of Wellington's harbour.

Otaki
75km/47 miles north of Wellington, on the South Taranaki Bight, is Otaki (pop. 6500). The Otaki area formerly had a relatively large Maori population, and was controlled in the early 19th century by Te Rauparaha from his base on nearby Kapiti Island. It is now the commercial centre of a fertile vegetable-growing area.

The first Maori university, the University of Rauwaka, was founded in Otaki as the logical development of earlier Maori pre-school and school education projects.

The British missionary Octavius Hadfield (1814–1904), later bishop of Wellington, worked in Otaki from 1839 onwards and taught the Maoris to cultivate the excellent local soil. He strove to maintain good relations between the white settlers and the Maoris, and was able to restrain Te Rauparaha from attacking Wellington. His uninhibited expression of his views on the Taranaki land war, however, made him unpopular with the government.

Otaki's main sight is the Rangiatea Maori church, the finest Maori church in New Zealand, which lies 3km/2 miles off Highway 1. The building of the church began in 1849 with the felling of huge totara trees. The roof-ridge, borne on three tall pillars, is 26m/85ft long. Opposite the church is the grave of Te Rauparaha; legend has it that his body was transported to Kapiti Island.

1km/¾ mile farther on is a Roman Catholic mission station established in 1844. The church was built in 1857.

Upper Hutt
30km/19 miles north-east of Wellington, in the valley of the Hutt River, is the satellite town of Upper Hutt (pop. 38,000). The population includes many commuters who travel into Wellington to work; but the town also has a number of factories and other institutions, such as the New Zealand Central Institute of Technology.

Tararua Forest Park
Upper Hutt is a good base for walks in the wild and densely wooded Tararua Range. A particularly attractive route is the Puffer Track.

Kapiti Island

Region: Wellington

Situation and importance
This long narrow island (area 1760 hectares/4350 acres) lies off the west coast at Waikanae, 70km/43 miles north of Wellington. It is now a nature reserve, and can be visited only with the permission of the Department of Conservation. There is no overnight accommodation on the island. The east side, facing the mainland, has gentle wooded slopes, but the cliff-fringed west coast falls sharply down to the Tasman Sea.

History
In the early 19th century Chief Te Rauparaha, whose tribe had been driven out of their territory round Kawhia by other Maori tribes, established

himself on the island. Through trade with the white settlers he contrived to acquire so many guns that he was able to mount plundering raids as far south as Christchurch on the South Island. Finally he was arrested and sent to prison for two years. Although he never became a Christian he supported the missionaries in the building of the Rangiata church at Otaki.

Whanganui National Park   I/K 6

Region: Manawatu-Wanganui
Area: 740sq.km/286sq. miles

Whanganui National Park, which extends on both banks of the Whanganui River from its mouth at Wanganui (see entry) to Taumarunui, was established only in 1987. It is planned to develop Pipiriki as the headquarters of the park.

★ National Park

Whanganui River

The Whanganui River, 200km/125 miles long, rises on the western slopes of Mount Tongariro, flows through Taumarunui and then through almost impenetrable forest country, via Pipiriki and Wanganui, into the Tasman Sea. The country through which it flows is for the most part hilly and densely wooded. Below Pipiriki the river is tame enough, but higher up there are rapids, waterfalls and narrow gorges. The Whanganui River Road is narrow but runs through a riverine landscape of great beauty.

The ★★ river

Maori tradition is unanimous that the bed of the Whanganui was carved out by Taranaki (Mount Egmont) when he fled west from the central plateau

Mythology

Luxuriant vegetation in the catchment area of the Whanganui River

189

after being vanquished by Tongariro in the contest for the fair Pihanga. The legendary Polynesian discoverer Kupe is said to have sailed up the river, at least in its lower reaches, in his canoe.

History

In the pre-European period the river was an important canoe route linking the interior of the island with the west coast, with numerous branch routes up its tributaries. The 19th century settlers and travellers also used the river, which was navigable as far up as Taumarunui, on their way to Rotorua. Excursions on the river, usually lasting three days, with accommodation in an elegant hotel in Pipiriki (now burned down), remained popular well into the 20th century.

A whole chain of Anglican mission stations were established along the river from 1843 onwards, and a French nun, Marie Aubert, founded a Catholic mission in 1883 under the name Jerusalem.

Round the turn of the century the river valley began to be turned into farming land. On the lower course of the river, round Wanganui, and on its upper course, round Taumarunui, the transformation went well, but on the river's middle course, above Pipiriki, there were serious difficulties. White settlers, mainly old soldiers, and even Maoris who moved into this area had to contend with luxuriant vegetation, poor soils and rapid erosion, and nothing could persuade them to stay – not even the bridge built over the river at Mangapurua in 1936, which soon became known as the "bridge to nowhere".

★ Boat trips

Although passenger and freight traffic on the Whanganui River was discontinued in 1958 as uneconomic, cruises on the river are now again available to meet the increasing demands of the tourist trade. There is, for example, a five-day cruise from Taumarunui to Wanganui (October–March). From Wanganui, Pipiriki and Taumarunui there are jetboat trips, and in summer visitors can paddle down the river in a canoe from Taumarunui to Wanganui (see entry) at its mouth, a distance of 232km/144 miles.

Up-to-date information about boat trips on the Whanganui can be obtained from the visitor information centre in Wanganui (corner of Guyton Street and Hill Street).

★ Walks

The most beautiful stretches of the river can be reached only on foot. There are a number of walking trails (e.g. the Matamateaonga Track) which take walkers to particularly attractive spots on the river.

Whanganui River Road

The Whanganui River Road, completed in 1934, follows the river upstream from Wanganui to Pipiriki, with many bends. There are also some roads in the Taumarunui area.

There are a number of places of interest on the Whanganui River Road:

Upokongaro

11km/7 miles north of Wanganui is Upokongaro, with St Mary's Church (Anglican; 1877) and the remains of a Maori *pa*.

Atene (Athens)

Atene (35km/22 miles) has a small meeting-house of 1886. There is a rewarding hike on the Atene Skyline Walk (6–8 hours).

Koriniti

The Maori settlement of Koriniti (48km/30 miles), once a place of considerable size, has two carved meeting-houses – although most of the Maoris have now left the area. The road beyond Koriniti is unasphalted and in poor condition.

Operiki Pa

North of Koriniti is Operiki Pa (49km/30½ miles), a well planned fortified Maori settlement with high ramparts.

Kawana

The grain mill at Kawana (56km/35 miles) was built in 1854 and was in operation until 1913. It has now been restored as a monument of technology.

The former Catholic mission station of Ranana (61km/38 miles) lies just downstream from Moutoa Island, once the site of a large Maori *pa*. In 1864 the local Maoris repelled an attack by Hauhau warriors.

Ranana

The village of Hiruharama is idyllically situated in a bend on the river. The French nun Marie Aubert established a Catholic mission here in 1883.
    The village gained a certain notoriety as the home of a commune in which the writer James K. Baxter (1926–72) spent his last years.

Hiruharama
(Jerusalem)

Pipiriki (79km/49 miles) had an elegant hotel which was burned down in 1959. Now it only has an attractive camping site. During the land wars it was a major centre of the Hauhau movement. It is planned to establish the headquarters of Whanganui National Park here.

Pipiriki

Whangarei

Region: Northland
Population: 44,000

Whangarei, the largest and most important town north of Auckland, lies on a much indented natural harbour which runs far inland on the east coast of Northland. The town developed late but at a hectic pace. The nearby deep-water harbour on Marsden Point can take large tankers, and a large oil refinery was built there. The oil-fired station which it supplied with fuel was closed down in 1992. There are also modern factories producing cement, fertilisers and glass.
    An imposing backdrop to this modern port and industrial town is provided by the five peaks of Mount Mania (404m/1444ft).

Situation and
importance

Although European immigrants established a settlement here in 1839, constant disputes with the local Maoris hampered its development, and in 1845, during the war with Hone Heke, most of the settlers fled to Auckland.
    The development of Northland was held back by its poor infrastructure, and an all-weather road from Auckland was built only in the mid 1930s. The breakthrough came in the sixties, when an oil refinery and an oil-fired power station were built, and these were gradually followed by other industrial installations.

History

Sights in Whangarei and Surroundings

The Clapham Clock Museum (open: daily 10am–4pm) in Water Street (Rose Garden) has a collection of some 800 old clocks, the earliest of them dating from the 17th century.

Clapham
Clock Museum

On Mount Parahaki (242m/794ft) is a large war memorial. From the top of the hill there are fine views of the town and harbour. The hill can be climbed either on foot (from Mair Park; about 1 hour) or by car (on Memorial Drive).

Mount Parahaki

This park, 2km/1¼ miles from Whangarei on the Ngunguru road, is notable for its giant kauri trees and a beautiful waterfall.

Reed Memorial
Kauri Park

6km/4 miles from Whangarei on the Ngunguru road are the 24m/80ft high Whangarei Falls.

Whangarei Falls

This open-air museum lies 8km/5 miles west of Whangarei on Highway 14 (the Dargaville road), in the grounds of the Clarke Homestead (established 1885). The nucleus of the museum was the old doctor's house, to which a number of other old houses, a schoolhouse and a chapel were later added.

★ Northland
Regional Museum

24km/15 miles east of Tutukaka are the Poor Knights Islands, a happy hunting-ground for divers. There are cruises and fishing trips to the islands from Whangarei.

Poor Knights
Islands

Other excursions   Other places of interest round Whangarei are Tutukaka, Ngunguru, Mata-pouri, Wolley Bay, Sandy Bay and Hikurangi (round trip about 80km/50 miles), Parua Bay and the beautiful beaches of Pataua (round trip about 90km/56 miles).

Marsden Point: industrial installations

A prominent landmark in the Whangarei area is the striped tower (120m/395ft high) of the oil-fired power station (opened 1967, closed down 1992) on Marsden Point, 30km/19 miles south-east of Whangarei. The adjoining oil refinery was built so that New Zealand could import cheap crude oil rather than expensive end products. Nowadays, however, more than 40% of the refinery's raw material comes from the oil and natural gas fields in the Taranaki region. The deep water harbour on Ramsden Point can handle tankers of up to 130,000 GRT.

In Marsden Point Visitor Centre (open: daily 10am–5pm) visitors can see an audio-visual show illustrating the development of this industrial area and the technology of the refinery.

Dargaville

Region: Northland
Population: 5000

Situation and history

The little town of Dargaville, founded in 1872 by an Irish immigrant, lies 60km/37 miles south-west of Whangarei. Later immigrants from Dalmatia settled in the town, originally as gum-diggers (prospectors for kauri resin). Later they and their descendants took up wine-growing.

Dargaville rapidly developed into an important centre of the trade in kauri timber and kauri resin. Ships sailed into Kaipara Harbour and then up the broad Wairoa River to Dargaville.

Nowadays Dargaville is a popular base for excursions to Trounson Kauri Park (35km/22 miles north) and Waipoua Kauri Forest (52km/32 miles north: see entry).

★Northern Wairoa Museum

This interesting museum is in Harding Park, on a hill above the town from which there is a fine view of the Wairoa River. The museum displays a variety of objects from the pre-European period and the early days of white settlement, including kauri wood and kauri resin.

An item of particular interest is a war canoe dating from the pre-European period, built using only stone tools. The canoe was buried on North Head (70km/43 miles south of Dargaville) in 1809 after inter-tribal fighting and was rediscovered only twenty years ago.

A recent addition to the museum's collection is the masts of the Green-peace ship "Rainbow Warrior", which was sunk by French agents in 1985.

Bayly's Beach   13km/8 miles west of Dargaville is Bayly's Beach, a wild stretch of coast with numerous travelling dunes.

Waipu

40km/25 miles south-east of Whangarei, picturesquely situated at the out-flow of the Waipu River into Bream Bay, is Waipu (pop. 1700), founded in the 1850s by Scottish immigrants who had previously tried their luck in Nova Scotia and at Adelaide (South Australia).

In the centre of the town is a monument commemorating the founders of the town in the form of a tall column bearing the Scottish lion rampant. The Waipu House of Memories displays mementoes of pioneering days, family trees and the collected sermons of the Rev. Norman McLeod, the minister who brought the original settlers here.

Bream Bay   In Bream Bay there are a number of beautiful beaches, including Waipu Cove and Lang's Beach (10km/6 miles south).

Whangaroa Harbour

Region: Northland

Whangaroa Harbour is a picturesque inlet, a natural harbour which is part of a drowned valley system, near the northern tip of the North Island. This wild and sparsely populated area is reached on Highway 10 and a side road which branches off it. It is an hour's drive north from the Bay of Islands (Pahia).

Situation and
★ topography

In 1809 a ship from Sydney, the "Boyd", sailed into Whangaroa Harbour to load kauri wood. Among the ship's crew were a number of Maoris, including a young chief, who was apparently killed by white seamen. In revenge for this crime all the white men who went ashore were massacred, and that night the Maoris boarded the ship in search of plunder and set fire to the powder barrel. The ship was burned out and only four men survived.

Massacre on
the "Boyd"

Thereafter white men avoided the inlets in Northland, and even the missionaries restrained their zeal.

The wreck of the "Boyd" still lies on the sea-bed off Red Island and is regularly visited by excursion boats (daily in summer from Whangaroa and Totara North) and divers.

White men did not return to the area until the 1840s. In the 1870s a shipyard was established at Totara North which in the course of time built several dozen ships.

In a number of small inlets – Matauri Bay, Tauranga Bay, Wainui Bay – there are idyllically beautiful bathing beaches, reached on a road which runs along the coast, affording magnificent views.

★ Bathing beaches

The wreck of the Greenpeace ship "Rainbow Warrior", blown up by French agents in Auckland harbour in 1985, was sunk off Matauri Bay and now attracts numbers of scuba divers.

"Rainbow
Warrior"

SOUTH ISLAND
The majestic bulk of Mount Cook, the highest peak in New Zealand's Southern Alps: magnificent walking country in summer, a popular skiing area in winter

195

Sights from A to Z
South Island

Abel Tasman National Park G/H 7/8

Region: Nelson
Area: 225.3sq.km/87sq. miles

Situation

The Abel Tasman National Park (established 1942) lies at the northern tip of the South Island, on the promontory between Tasman Bay and Golden Bay.

Information

The Department of Conservation maintains visitor centres at Motueka and Takaka and ranger stations at the Totaranui and Marahau camping sites, at any of which you can get information and maps, and also permission to spend the night in the park (in a hut or your own tent).

Season

The Abel Tasman National Park – one of the most visited of New Zealand's National Parks – is open throughout the year. The main season is in December and January, and to be sure of a place on a camping site or a bed in a hut at that time of year you must book months in advance.

History

This National Park, the smallest in the country, was established in 1942 on the 300th anniversary of Abel Tasman's discovery of New Zealand in 1642. Tasman anchored near the Tata Islands in what is now known as Golden Bay, but when the aggressive local Maoris attacked his ship's boat and killed some of his men he decided not to go ashore, and thereafter called the bay Murderers' Bay.

Discovered by Abel Tasman in 1642: beaches of enchanting beauty on the north coast of the South Island

The French seafarer and explorer Dumont d'Urville, who surveyed the north coast of the South Island in 1826–27, was overwhelmed by the beauty of the coastal scenery. In our day holidaymakers, walkers, water sports enthusiasts and scuba divers are drawn to the National Park by its beautiful coves and inlets, bizarrely shaped limestone cliffs, tiny islets and beaches of golden sand, some of which can be reached only by boat or on foot. Since the establishment of the National Park the vegetation has recovered from the effects of earlier over-felling.

★★Topography

In the south-west of the National Park there are a number of cave systems, some of them still not completely explored. The best known cave is Harwood's Hole, which is 300m/1000ft deep.

Caves

Caves in this area can sometimes be dangerous because of the brittle rock.

Warning

The Wainui Falls Walk (about 2 hours there and back) runs from the Takaka–Totaranui road to the Wainui Falls (21m/69ft high).

Walks
Wainui Falls Walk

The Lookout Rock, from which there are fine views of Golden Bay, is also reached from the Takaka–Totaranui road (about 1½ hours there and back).

Lookout Rock

Farther north is Gibbs Hill (400m/1300ft), from which there are even better panoramic views. A half day should be allowed for this walk, which starts from the same road.

Gibbs Hill

This is a half-hour walk from Totaranui along the north side of the bay.

Pukatea Walk

South of Totaranui along the beach are Skinner Point (about 40 minutes there and back), Goat Bay (about 1¼ hours there and back and Waiharakeke Bay (about 3½ hours there and back).

Skinner Point,
Goat Bay,
Waiharakeke Bay

North of Totaranui are Anapai Bay (about 1½ hours there and back), Mutton Cove (3 hours there and back) and Separation Point (about 5 hours there and back), the most northerly point on the promontory.

Anapai Bay,
Mutton Cove,
Separation Point

From Torrent Bay there are popular walking trails to the Cleopatra Pool (about 1½ hours there and back), Falls River Valley (about 1½ hours) and Cascade Falls (about 2 hours).

Cleopatra Pool,
Falls River Valley,
Cascade Falls

There are pleasant walks to a number of beautiful coves and inlets to the north of Marahau.

North of
Marahau

The Coastal Track is a three-day walk offering magnificent coastal scenery. It begins at Marahau, on the boundary of the National Park, and runs north along the coast to Separation Point, at the northern tip of the promontory, and then turns west to reach Wainui Inlet, at the north-west corner of the park. There is overnight accommodation on some of the inlets (advance booking essential). Since some rivers and lagoons can be crossed only at low tide, you should plan your walk according to the tides. The most difficult crossing is likely to be the estuary of the little Awaroa River.
　　Information on vouchers for accommodation in huts, etc., Department of Conservation offices in Takaka, Nelson, Motueka and Karamea Field Centres.

★★ Coastal Track

Abel Tasman National Park Enterprises; tel (03) 528 7801, in Old Cederman House (19th c.), 4km/2½ miles north of Motueka, runs guided walks and boat trips in the National Park.

Organised trips

The walking trails in the interior of the peninsula are for experienced cross-country walkers only.

N.B.

Surroundings

On the north-western edge of the National Park is the little township of Takaka (Nelson-Marlborough region; pop. 1300), which was founded in

Takaka

A shaky footbridge leads to a hidden bathing cove

1842. It lies at the foot of Marble Mountain, which provided the marble used in the Parliament Building in Wellington (see entry) and the Cathedral in Nelson (see entry). Features of interest are the little Takaka Museum and the Golden Bay Work Centre and Artisan Shop.

Golden Bay

There are a series of beautiful beaches in Golden Bay (Pohara, Tata, Paton's Rock, Tukurua).

Pupu Springs

5km/3 miles away are the Pupu (or Waikoropupu) Springs, which have an abundant flow of water – most of it from the Takaka River, which in a dry summer can disappear completely underground. Gold-diggers were active in this area in the 19th century.

Collingwood

30km/19 miles north-west of Takaka, at the mouth of the Aorere River, which here flows into Golden Bay, is the little village of Collingwood (pop. 200), named after Nelson's Admiral Collingwood. The first settlers came here in 1842, and the place enjoyed a boom from 1857 onwards, when gold was discovered in the neighbourhood. The village is a good base for long walking expeditions in the surrounding area.

Te Anaroa Caves

8km/5 miles south-west of Collingwood are the karstic caves of Anaroa. Near the caves are bizarre rock formations.

Cape Farewell

30km/19 miles north of Collingwood is Cape Farewell, the most northerly point on the South Island. From the cape the Farewell Spit, a narrow sandbank 35km/22 miles long (bird sanctuary) reaches out to the east.

Wharaiki Beach, Whanganui Inlet

To the west of the cape are beautiful Wharaiki Beach and Whanganui Inlet (Westhaven).

★★ Heaphy Track

Bainham, 30km/19 miles south of Collingwood, is the starting-point of the famous Heaphy Track, named after the explorer and surveyor Charles

Heaphy. The walk (78km/48 miles; 4–6 days) runs through the dense prime-val forests of the North-West Nelson Forest Park and along the west coast, with magnificent views, particularly on the west coast, and ends at Kara-mea. The track follows an old Maori route to the deposits of greenstone on the coast, later used by gold prospectors. The walk is facilitated by slender suspension bridges spanning gorges overgrown with ferns and huts pro-viding overnight accommodation.

Walkers can return on the Heaphy air taxi. Information, vouchers for accommodation in huts, etc., from Department of Conservation offices in Takaka, Nelson, Motueka and Karamea Field Centres. All-weather clothing and walking boots are essential. The track is not difficult, though it climbs to 900m/2950ft.

The Kaituna Track (about 3 hours) runs from the Aorere valley (15km/9 miles south of Collingwood) to the excavations and spoil-heaps of the 19th century gold-diggers.

Kaituna Track

25km/15½ miles south of the National Park, on Tasman Bay, is the little port of Motueka (pop. 5000). In its fertile hinterland are large plantations of berry fruits, kiwi fruit, apples, hops, tobacco, etc. Before the arrival of white settlers there was a large Maori population in this area. For many years it was accessible only by boat.

Motueka

The Te Ahurewa Maori church was built in 1897 on the initiative of Frederick Bennett, who in 1928 became the first Maori bishop.

14km/8½ miles north of Motueka is the magnificent beach of Kaiteriteri, and 10km/6 miles beyond this is the beautiful beach of Marahau, at the end of the Coastal Track along the coast of the Abel Tasman National Park.

★Kaiteriteri Beach, Marahau Beach

A few kilometres south of Motueka is the fruit-growing area of Upper Moutere, originally settled by German immigrants. The Lutheran church was built in 1905. In the churchyard are gravestones with German inscriptions.

Upper Moutere

Kahurangi National Park

To the west of Motueka extends Kahurangi National Park (area 500,000 hectares/1,000,000 acres), which was established in August 1995. The cen-tral feature of this park in the wild Tasman Mountains (up to 1700m/5600ft) is the largest and deepest cave system in the southern hemisphere, the sandstone, marble and karstic caves of Kahurangi. There are almost 600km/375 miles of walking trails in the National Park; the most popular are the Heaphy Track (see above) and the Wangapeka Track.

★Topography

A favourite excursion from Motueka is to the Riwaka Cave (16km/10 miles west). The Riwaka River flows out of the cave.

Riwaka Cave

Alexandra

D 12

Region: Otago
Population: 5000

Alexandra, the largest town in Central Otago, lies on the Clutha River, 200km/125 miles north-west of Dunedin and 100km/62 miles south-east of Queenstown. It grew up during the gold rush of the 1860s and was origi-nally called Lower Dunstan, but was later renamed in honour of the Danish Princess Alexandra, who married the Prince of Wales in 1863.

Situation and history

The alluvial gold in the surrounding area was soon exhausted, but there was a second gold rush in the 1890s, when the river beds were dredged out in a search for further deposits. There are now few reminders of gold-digging days in Alexandra. The construction of reservoirs and irrigation channels has promoted the development of flourishing fruit plantations (stone fruit, particularly apricots). The expanses of green in the valley are in sharp contrast to the bare arid hillsides.

Sights in Alexandra and Surroundings

Shaky Bridge

The very picturesque Shaky Bridge (now for pedestrians only) was built in 1879.

Sir William Bodkin Museum

The Sir William Bodkin Museum (open: Mon.–Fri. 2–4pm, sometimes 11am–4pm; closed in winter) in Thomson Street illustrates the methods used for working gold in this area. Old photographs show, for example, the dredging of river beds and the large numbers of Chinese who came here to try their luck.

Tucker Hill Lookout

From bare Tucker Hill, north-east of Alexandra, there are good views of the little town in its setting of fruit plantations and of the junction of the Clutha River (dredged out in the quest for gold) and the winding Manuherikia River. The peaks of the Remarkables outside Queenstown (see entry) can sometimes be seen in the distance.

Old gold-digging settlements (round trip 180km/ 110 miles)

Alexandra is a good base for a tour of gold-digging settlements in Central Otago. The tour begins on Highway 85, which runs north to Omakau (pop. 200); then north-west to Matakanui, now almost a ghost town, at the foot of the Dunstan Range. The route then continues to Drybread, the decayed gold-digging town of St Bathans and Hills Creek, and then returns through the Ida valley to the old gold-digging town of Oturehua, now occupied by farmers. The old Golden Progress workings and the Hayes Engineering Works have been partly preserved or restored. Then by way of Lake Idaburn (curling and skating in winter) to Ophir, where the finding of gold in 1863 attracted thousands of hopeful prospectors. The old court house and post office here have been preserved. An old suspension bridge then crosses the Manuherikia River to return to Alexandra.

Clyde

Region: Otago Population: 900

Situation and importance

10km/6 miles north-west of Alexandra on Highway 8, on the River Clutha, is the little township of Clyde, where gold was found in 1862. The settlement, originally called Dunstan, grew up at the south end of Cromwell Gorge and at one time had a population of 4000 gold-diggers, with banks and hotels. It has preserved a few buildings dating from the time of the gold rush.

When the gold was worked out the water of the river, previously used for gold-panning, served for the irrigation of fruit plantations.

Sights

A prominent feature of the little town is the memorial to the gold-diggers. The old courthouse of 1864 in Blythe Street, now houses the Clyde Historical Museum (open: Tues.–Sun. 2–4pm), which vividly illustrates the history of gold-digging in this area, including the spectacular "gold robbery" of 1870, when the gold stored overnight in the supposedly secure local jail disappeared.

Other buildings dating from the days of the gold rush are the Athenaeum (1874), a theatre and concert hall, the former Town Hall of 1869, now a hotel, the old Hartley Arms Hotel (1865), Dunstan House (1900), Naylor's Victoria Store (1874), now a restaurant, the old Post Office, St Michael's Church (1877; Anglican), St Dunstan's Church (1906; R.C.) and St Mungo's Union Church (1894).

Clutha Hydro-Electric Scheme

In spite of strong objections from environmental interests and the possible earthquake hazard the Clutha Hydro-Electric Scheme has been proceeding in stages since 1977. A massive 58m/190ft high dam was completed in 1992 1km/³⁄₄ mile north of Clyde, forming an artificial lake (Lake Dunstan) 26km/16 miles long. It has now filled Cromwell Gorge and drowned the old township of Cromwell (see below). The lake will supply water to a hydro-electric power station with four huge generators (still under construction), and its water is also being used for the irrigation of the local fruit plantations.

Cromwell

Region: Otago
Population: 3000

30km/19 miles north-west of Alexandra, at the junction of the Clutha (coming from Lake Wanaka and Lake Hawea) and the Javarau (coming from Lake Wakatipu), is the new township of Cromwell, built here in substitution for the old one at the north end of Cromwell Gorge, now drowned by the waters of Lake Dunstan.

Situation and importance

 The most important buildings from the old gold-diggers' settlement, founded in the 1860s, have been re-erected as Old Cromwell Historic Village in Melmore Terrace. The Cromwell Museum (open: daily 10am–4pm) has interesting material on the history of the town.

8km/5 miles west of Cromwell on Highway 6 is the Kawerau Gorge Mining Centre (part of the Otago Goldfields Park), where visitors are introduced to the laborious processes of gold-working (presentations daily at noon and 3pm).

★Kawerau Gorge Mining Centre

White-water enthusiasts will find plenty of scope on the Kawerau River, whether in kayaks, rubber dinghies or jetboats.

★Kawerau River

 Other old gold-digging settlements round Cromwell, now all but abandoned ("ghost towns"), are Bendigo and Logantown to the north and Bannockburn and Carricktown to the south.

100km/62 miles north-east of Alexandra, in the barren Maniototo plain, is Naseby. Once an important gold town, with anything up to 5000 prospectors grubbing for gold in the area from 1863 to the 1930s, it now has a population of no more than 150.

Naseby

 To supply the gold-diggers with the water they needed long water channels were constructed, and these are now used for irrigation. Some old buildings still survive to recall the great days of the past, such as the Briton Hotel, a brick building of 1863, St George's Church (Anglican), which dates from 1865, and the Athenaeum, also of 1865. The Manototo Early Settlers Museum is housed in a building of 1878.

 There are pleasant walks to the Welcome Inn, on a hill above the little town, and to Naseby Forest (area 25sq.km/9½sq. miles), planted with imported conifers (Douglas fir, larch, pine).

60km/37 miles north-east of Alexandra, at the foot of the Dunstan Range, is St Bathans, another gold-diggers' town which has lost its one-time importance. Of its once numerous hotels there remains only one, the Vulcan Hotel (1869). Other old buildings are St Alban's Church (Anglican; 1882) and St Patrick's Church (R.C.; 1892). The rather showy Post Office, with the postmaster's house, has been restored.

St Bathans

The Blue Lake occupies a great trench excavated in the search for gold, 800m/880yd long by 50m/55yd across and over 50m/165ft deep. The deep blue colouring of the water is clouded only by the inflow of surface water.

Blue Lake

The Department of Conservation looks after the widely scattered remains of gold-mines and gold-diggers' settlements in Otago. Information from DoC offices in Alexandra, Queenstown and Dunedin.

Otago Goldfields Park

Arrowtown   C 11

Region: Otago
Population: 1000

★ Situation and
importance

20km/12½ miles north-east of Queenstown, in the valley of the Arrow River and at the foot of the Crown Range, is the old gold-diggers' settlement of Arrowtown. Thanks to its charming setting it has now developed into an important tourist centre.

Gold was found here in 1862, but only a year later gold-mining suffered a severe setback when many prospectors were drowned in a devastating flood.

Sights

Many old miners' houses have been restored in recent years. The old Jail in Cardigan Street dates from 1875. The former Bank of New Zealand building (1875) now houses a branch of the Lakes District Centennial Museum, which is devoted to the history of the area round Lake Wakatipu. It has informative displays on gold-mining. Open: daily 9am–5pm.

On the Arrow River, below the town, visitors can hire pans and try their hand at washing for gold.

An unusual feature is the Chinese quarter on the west side of the town. In the late 1860s many East Asians came here to work in the gorges of the Arrow and Shotover Rivers. They were undemanding and hard-working, and this involved them in disputes with the white prospectors. As a result they were required to live outside the town. Their little stone houses and brick cottages have now been restored, as has the Chinese shop in Bush Creek.

Macetown

Macetown, another ghost town, lies on the Arrow River 15km/9½ miles upstream. The town was abandoned because of its remote situation and

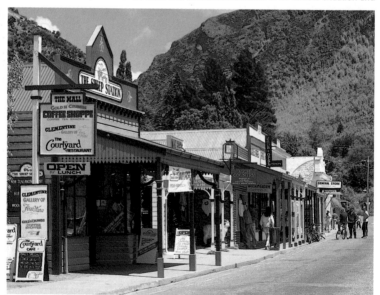

Relics of gold rush days in Arrowtown, with something of the atmosphere of the Wild West

harsh climate, and all that now remains is three buildings and a plant for crushing the gold-bearing ore. The old road through the gorge to Mace-town, built in 1883, is practicable only for cross-country vehicles, on horse-back or on foot, and there are many fords to cross. It is advisable to enquire about the state of the road before setting out. There is no overnight accom-modation in Macetown.

Arthur's Pass   F 9/10

Regions: Canterbury and West Coast
Altitude: 921m/3022ft

In winter, when there may be sudden falls of snow, the Arthur's Pass Road may be negotiable only with chains, or sometimes not at all. Because of the sharp bends and steep gradients in the Otira Gorge vehicles with trailers, caravans and vehicles over 13m/42½ft in length are banned.

Warning

When gold was found on the west coast in 1863 the authorities in Christ-church were concerned to find some way over the barrier of the Southern Alps into Westland. Most prospectors travelled by boat to Hokitika (see entry) on the west coast, and the gold recovered was also shipped from there. But transport overland was safer and more reliable than the voyage on the wild Tasman Sea. There was of course the narrow Harper Pass which had been used by the Maoris to get to the Westland greenstone deposits; but the swarms of prospectors and their heavily laden pack horses soon reduced the track to impassability. In 1864, therefore, two surveyors, Arthur and George Dobson, set out on horseback through the valleys of the Waimakariri and Bealey Rivers, and Arthur found the pass which now bears his name; but the steep descent on the west side to the Otra River, and particularly the Otra Gorge, were difficult to negotiate.

Situation and history

The TraNZAlpine Express skirting the Otira Gorge on its way over Arthur's Pass

In 1865 work began on the building of a road over the pass. An army of almost 1000 workmen armed with picks and shovels hewed the road out of the rock, and within a year a coach was able to drive on it from Christchurch to Hokitika. Beef cattle, too, were driven over the pass to supply the building workers and gold-diggers.

In the 1920s a railway line was laid broadly parallel with the road, bypassing the Otira Gorge in a tunnel 8.6km/5½ miles long.

Arthur's Pass (town)

After the railway line was completed the camp which had accommodated the track-layers and tunnellers became an alpine holiday resort, from which beautiful walking trails lead into the majestic mountain world. Here too is the National Park visitor centre, with informative displays on the natural history of this part of the Southern Alps and on the construction of the road and the railway line.

Arthur's Pass National Park

Information

Information and maps on walking trails in the National Park can be obtained from the visitor centre in Arthur's Pass village.

Season

The National Park is open throughout the year. The main summer season is in December and January. There is skiing in winter.

★★Romantic alpine landscape

The tourist potential of this wild and romantic road was soon realised. The first sightseeing tour was organised in the 19th century, running over the pass to the west coast and continuing south to the Franz Josef and Fox Glaciers. In the course of time the view gained ground that the government must take steps to protect the unique vegetation of this area, and in 1901 70,000 hectares/175,000 acres of land round the pass were declared a nature reserve. After various extensions to the protected area Arthur's Pass National Park was established in 1929. With an area of almost 1000sq.km/390sq. miles, it is New Zealand's fourth largest National Park.

The scenery of the National Park shows great variety, since the park takes in the two very different sides of the Southern Alps. The altitude ranges between 245m/804ft on the Tamarakau River and over 2000m/6560ft on Mounts Rolleston, Murchison and Franklin. Rainfall ranges between an annual 5000m/200in. on the west side and 1700mm/67in. on the drier east side.

Walks

Among the finest and best known walks from Arthur's Pass village are the Devil's Punchbowl Walk (about 2 hours), the Bridal Veil Nature Walk round the 130m/425ft high Bridal Veil waterfall (about 2 hours), the Dobson Nature Walk (about 4 hours) and the Bealey Valley Walk (about 4 hours).

Temple Basin ski area

At the higher levels there is an abundance of snow in winter. The Temple Basin skiing area attracts large numbers of keen skiers.

Ashburton   F 10

Region: Canterbury
Population: 16,000

Situation and importance

The town of Ashburton lies on the Ashburton River in the Canterbury Plains, 90km/56 miles south-west of Christchurch. The town and the river are named after Lord Ashburton, a prominent member of the New Zealand Company founded by Edward Gibbon Wakefield. The wide Canterbury Plains, with the Southern Alps in the distance, are now the granary of New Zealand, reminiscent in aspect of the American Middle West, though only 150 years ago, when Bishop Selwyn was travelling about his immense diocese, the plains were arid, treeless and covered with brown tussock grass.

The remains of hunting camps of early Maori nomads have been dis-   History
covered in this area, and simple rock paintings have been preserved under
rock overhangs. The present town grew up at an important ford on a coach
route, centred on an inn built here in 1858 for the accommodation of coach
drivers. Twenty years later farmers began to irrigate the arid land; trees
were planted and fields brought into cultivation.

The Domain Park demonstrates the success of irrigation in making the land   Sights
fertile: here the steppe vegetation of the 19th century has given place to
grass and trees which afford welcome shade. The town has preserved a
number of 19th century brick buildings and five churches.

Surroundings

43km/27 miles north-west of Ashburton is Mount Somers, a little town with   Mount Somers
numerous limestone quarries which supplied stone for building 19th century Melbourne.

The two little townships of Erewhon (90km/56 miles north-west) and Meso-   Erewhon,
potamia (100km/62 miles north-west) were formerly commercial centres   Mesopotamia
for the huge sheep farms in the area.

50km/30 miles north of Ashburton is Rakaia Gorge, a popular destination   Rakaia Gorge
for excursions, particularly in summer.

In winter the skiing area on Mount Hutt (50km/30 miles north-west) attracts   Mount Hutt
many winter sports enthusiasts.

Balclutha · Clutha River D 13

Region: Otago
Population: 4000

Balclutha, the commercial centre of a prosperous sheep-farming area, lies   Balclutha
80km/50 miles south-west of Dunedin on Highway 1, on the lower course of
the mighty Clutha River, which here divides into two arms enclosing the
fertile island of Inchclutha. The Gaelic name of Balclutha ("town on the
river Clutha or Clyde") points to the Scottish origins of the original settlers.

In the past the Clutha River and many of its tributaries were rich in alluvial   Clutha River
gold. Around the turn of the century almost 200 dredgers gouged out the
bed of the river, leaving the huge spoil heaps still visible today.
   In 1878 Otago had a particularly hard winter, with an abundance of snow,
and when the snow melted there was severe flooding in the Clutha valley.
As a result the southern arm of the river changed its course and Port
Molyneux lost its harbour.

The Clutha Valley Scheme, under which a whole series of dams and associ-   Clutha Valley
ated hydro-electric power stations will be built in the valley, is aimed at   Scheme
taming the sometimes destructive force of the river. It is feared that this will
dramatically change the landscape.

Banks Peninsula G/H 10

Region: Canterbury

The Banks Peninsula reaches out into the South Pacific south-east of   Situation and
Canterbury (see entry), with Highway 75 as its main artery. The peninsula,   topography

with its two deep natural harbours, Lyttelton on the north-west coast and Akaroa on the south-east, consists of two huge extinct volcanic craters. It has a mild climate in which even frost-sensitive sweet potatoes (kumara) grow.

History

In 1770 Cook named the peninsula, which he took for an island, after the botanist Joseph Banks who was accompanying him. In the early 19th century seal-hunters, whalers and flax and timber dealers established temporary settlements here. In 1835 a Prussian whaler called Georg Hempelmann (1799–1880) settled at Peraki, on the south coast of the peninsula, and established its first whaling station. He claimed to have acquired large tracts of land on the peninsula and was involved in a long and unsuccessful struggle with the government for recognition of his rights. His logbook is displayed in the Canterbury Museum in Christchurch. The white settlements on the peninsula were able to expand unhindered because of a conflict between local Maori groups in the late 1820s, when the practice of exacting *utu* (revenge and retaliation) led to the rival tribes massacring one another; and then Te Rauparaha, conqueror of the North Island, and his warriors fell upon the decimated tribes and almost wiped them out. In 1838 the French whaler and sea-captain Jean Langlois bought land from the few remaining Maoris, and two years later, soon after the proclamation of British sovereignty, French immigrants founded the colony of Akaroa (see below).

By 1900 the forests which had previously covered the peninsula had been cleared by grubbing out or burning. Until the building of the road that is now Highway 75 the numerous bays and inlets on the coast of the peninsula could be reached only by boat.

Sights

Lyttelton

13km/8 miles south of Christchurch, on a sheltered natural harbour formed by the crater of an extinct volcano, is the port of Lyttelton (pop. 3000), named after Lord Lyttelton, a leading member of the Canterbury Pilgrims and Settlers Association (see Christchurch, History), which during the 19th century was the gateway of New Zealand for many thousand immigrants. The "pilgrims" of Christchurch landed in 1850 on the north-western shore of Lyttelton Harbour, which is still the city's port. The arrival of the pilgrims is commemorated annually on December 16th by the Bridle Path Walk (8km/5 miles) from the harbour over the steep hills to Christchurch. A railway tunnel was driven through the hills in 1867, followed in 1964 by a road tunnel, which provide fast connections between Lyttelton and Christchurch.

★Lyttelton
Historic Walk

The most interesting features in the town can be seen by following the Lyttelton Historic Walk. Information about them can be obtained in the excellent Lyttelton Historical Museum (open: Tues., Thur., Sat. and Sun. 2–4pm) on Gladstone Quay, which in addition to its material on local history has sections on oceanography and Antarctic exploration.

The Timeball Station of 1875 in Reserve Terrace, which signalled Greenwich Mean Time by dropping down at 1pm each day, operated until 1935. The building, which was erected by convict labour, has been restored and is open to the public daily from 10am. Other notable buildings are Holy Trinity Church (Anglican; 1860), St Joseph's Church (R.C.; 1865) and the Presbyterian Church (1864) in Winchester Street.

Ripapa Island

On the tiny island of Ripapa in Lyttelton Harbour there was once a Maori *pa*. In 1885, when there was apprehension about a possible Russian invasion, a fort was built on the island. For a time the island served as a quarantine station and a prison. Among the prisoners detained here was the "Sea Devil" Count Felix von Lückner (see Famous People).

View of the Banks Peninsula, where British settlers landed in 1850 and founded the town of Christchurch, a few miles away

80km/50 miles south-east of Christchurch is Akaroa (in Maori, "long harbour"), which has a population of some 800. There are a number of interesting old buildings. The Roman Catholic parish church of St Patrick was built in 1864; it was the third church of the mission station established by Bishop Pompallier in 1840. The Maison Langlois-Eteveneaux in Rue Lavaud was built in 1845 by A. Langlois and was occupied from 1858 to 1906 by the Eteveneaux family; it is furnished in the style of its period. Associated with it is a small museum (open: daily 10.30am–4.30pm) with mementoes of the brief French episode. The Neo-Gothic St Peter's Church (Anglican) in Rue Balguerie was built in 1863. Another fine example of carpenter's work is the old Custom House of 1852. On the hill called L'Aube, with a modern lighthouse (1980), is the French settlers' cemetery.

    5km/3 miles south of Akaroa is a little Maori church of 1878.

★**Akaroa**

In Okains Bay is the Maori and Colonial Museum (open: daily 10am–5pm), which displays objects from the surrounding area and the Chatham Islands. Items of particular interest are the carved Maori meeting-house and the old pioneers' houses.

Okains Bay

There are a number of walking trails on which the hilly peninsula can be explored, including the Mount Herbert Walk and the Summit Road Scenic Walk. The Banks Peninsula Track is a four-day walk.

Walks

The best known of the trails is the Bridle Path between Lyttelton and Christchurch, the route followed by the first Christchurch settlers.

Bridle Walk

From Akaroa you can drive back to Christchurch on the winding Summit Road, which runs round the edge of the old volcanic crater, with fine views. At Hilltop it runs into Highway 75.

Summit Road

Blenheim   H/I 8

Region: Nelson-Marlborough
Population: 22,000

Situation and importance

The town of Blenheim lies on Highway 1 near the north end of the South Island, on the Wairau plain near the mouth of the Wairau River. The Blenheim area is one of the sunniest in New Zealand, with no fewer than 2600 hours of sunshine in the year. Not surprisingly, therefore, this is a great wine-growing area, and Blenheim's annual Wine Festival in February is a major event in the year.

Name

The town was originally called Beaver because the first settlers felt like beavers in the mud after the Wairau River overflowed its banks. Then in 1859, when the province of Marlborough was instituted, it was renamed after the Duke of Marlborough's victory over the French at Blenheim in 1704.

History

The Wairau affray, the South Island's only serious confrontation between whites and Maoris over rights to land, took place in 1843 to the north of Blenheim. Settlers in Nelson who had made what they claimed to be a legal purchase of land set out, in spite of warnings, to survey the land. Chiefs Te Rauparaha and Te Rangihaeata then intervened and the conflict escalated. In the affray that ensued some of the whites were able to make their escape, but others were killed or taken prisoner, including Captain Arthur Wakefield, a brother of Edward Gibbon Wakefield and leader of the Nelson settlers. In retaliation for the death of a female relative of his chief had all the prisoners killed. The government in Auckland rejected the people of Nelson's demand for severe punishment because the settlers had been in the wrong; and besides the government had neither the troops or the money for a war against the Maori chiefs. The Maoris, who had withdrawn from the disputed territory, interpreted the governor's leniency as weakness.

In 1855 there was a severe earthquake which caused heavy damage. The level of the plain sank by almost 2 metres (6½ feet), and the Opawa River now became navigable as far upstream as Beaver (Blenheim). When Marlborough became a provincial authority in 1859 Blenheim and Picton were rivals for the honour of becoming the seat of the provincial government. Blenheim won, and remained provincial capital until the provincial governments were abolished in 1876.

Sights

The old government buildings in the High Street are now occupied by the police. At the corner of the High Street and Seymour Street is the cannon in return for which Captain Blenkinsopp claimed to have acquired Te Rauparaha's land in the Wairau area in 1831. In the Brayshaw Museum Park in New Renwick Road are old agricultural implements and a reconstruction of an immigrants' settlement.

Surroundings

Wairau Affray Memorial

At Tuamarina, between Blenheim and Picton on Highway 1, is a monument commemorating the Wairau affray. Those who fell in the battle are buried on the nearby hill.

Riversland Cob Cottage

4km/2½ miles south of Blenheim on Highway 1 is the Riverlands Cob Cottage of 1859 (restored), built of cob (a mixture of clay and chopped straw).

Lake Grassmere

35km/22 miles south on Highway 1 is Lake Grassmere, on which are the only saltpans in New Zealand. Seawater is pumped into the main lake, which has an area of almost 700 hectares/1750 acres, and is then left to evaporate in small ponds. An average of 50,000 tons of sea salt is produced here every year. Gleaming white pyramids of salt are everywhere to be seen. Conducted tours by appointment.

New Zealand's best wines are produced in the Blenheim area. There are regular tours of the wineries. The Marlborough Wine Trail, starting from Blenheim, gives visitors an excellent introduction to New Zealand wine-making, taking in such well known wineries as Montana, Te Whare Ra, Cellier le Brun and Cloudy Bay.

★ Marlborough Wine Trail

Buller River   F/G 8

Regions: Nelson-Marlborough, West Coast

The Buller River – named after a director of the New Zealand Company – is the principal river on the west coast of the South Island. Issuing from Lake Rotoiti, in Nelson Lakes National Park, it flows west through high mountain country, enclosed in steep-sided gorges and flanked by dense forest. Then, after a course of 169km/105 miles, it flows into the Tasman Sea at Westport. In 1929 and 1968 the area was hit by violent earthquakes which led to massive landslides.

Buller valley

Highway 6 follows the winding course of the river to Howard Junction, with picnic areas at particularly attractive spots. The finest scenery is in Upper Buller Gorge and from Lower Buller Gorge to Sinclair Castle.

130km/81 miles south-west of Nelson (see entry), in a bend on the upper course of the Buller River, is the remote little township of Murchison (pop. 700). Above it rears Mount Murchison (1469m/4820ft), named after the Scottish geologist Sir Roderick Murchison.

Murchison

Murchison came into being during the gold rush of the 1860s and there-after developed into the commercial centre for the remote farms in the interior of the country. In 1929 the area was devastated by a severe earth-quake with its epicentre near Murchison, and the whole landscape was altered by landslides. Bridges, roads and buildings were destroyed, but thanks to the sparsity of the population only 17 people lost their lives.

Canterbury (region)   F–H 9–11

The Canterbury region, bounded on the east by the Pacific and on the west by the Southern Alps, extends for some 100km/60 miles from east to west and 300km/185 miles from north to south. Within this area are great expanses of plain, torrential rivers and New Zealand's mightiest mountains.

Situation and topography

The region has a population of around 440,000, most of them living near the coast. The largest town is Christchurch (see entry). The density of population falls rapidly towards the interior of the South Island and the mountains. Between 1986 and 1991 the population of the whole region increased by 2.2%.

Population

In the early days of the Polynesian settlement of New Zealand nomadic Maoris lived on the coast, often hunting moas by lighting fires to direct their movements.

Early settlement

When the first white men came to this area the moas had long since died out. The wide plains of Canterbury, grass-covered and treeless, were ideal grazing land. After Te Rauparaha's raids in the 1820s and 30s, which had decimated the local tribes, the white settlers received an almost friendly reception and found the Maoris ready to let them have land. The first

The first white men

In the Canterbury region: sheep as far as the eye can see

settlers established themselves in the first half of the 19th century on the Banks Peninsula (see entry) and in the Christchurch area.

Edward Gibbon Wakefield and the "gentlemen's colony"

The decisive wave of settlers came later. Edward Gibbon Wakefield, the initiator of the New Zealand Company, formed to promote the settlement of New Zealand, planned to establish an Anglican settlement, and was supported in this by a young Conservative, John R. Godley. After the Company's earlier foundations at New Plymouth, Wellington, Wanganui and Nelson, which had suffered from a chronic shortage of land, Wakefield hoped that this time his ideal of a "gentlemen's colony" would be realised. The new settlers – only wealthy men – would buy land on a large scale and establish large farms on the model of English estates. The land would be worked by selected, reliable workers who would have no claim to own land of their own. They were given free passage to New Zealand, 'tween decks, if their honesty was vouched for by an Anglican clergyman. The first ships arrived in 1850 with a consignment of carefully selected craftsmen, workers and tradesmen. From the outset class-consciousness prevailed.

The wool barons

The well-to-do landowners left the coastal regions to arable farmers, while they themselves acquired vast areas of grazing land on the pattern of the sheep stations of Australia and the large sheep runs in the adjoining region of Marlborough, to the north. Wool was the fastest road to wealth. But Wakefield was once again to be disappointed. He had seen his new colony as similar to conditions in England, consisting of large mixed farms near villages and the village church. The huge New Zealand sheep farms ranging from 15,000 to 60,000 hectares (37,500 to 150,000 acres) in extent soon made their owners wealthy "wool barons". This was felt to be unjust and undemocratic, and later legislation and tax reforms were introduced enabling small farmers with limited resources to acquire land. Many of the larger farms, over-grazed and ravaged by erosion, were abandoned.

James (Jock) Mackenzie, a Scottish shepherd and sheep-stealer, became New Zealand's first folk hero. With the help of his sheepdog Friday he stole thousands of sheep from the huge Levels station and drove them into the then unknown highlands of what is now the Mackenzie Country, in the foreland of the Southern Alps.

James Mackenzie

Closely connected with Canterbury was the English writer Samuel Butler, who lived here for four years as owner of the huge farms of Mesopotamia and Erewhon. He then sold his land at a considerable profit and returned to England. In his utopian novel "Erewhon" he gave literary immortality to the Canterbury region.

Samuel Butler

100km/60 miles west of Christchurch is Lake Coleridge, a typical elongated glacier lake surrounded by mountains and open tussock grassland which is now a Mecca for anglers. It is named after a prominent member of the Canterbury Pilgrims and Settlers Association (see Christchurch, History). The first state-owned hydro-electric station came into operation here in 1911. The water which formerly flowed into the Harper River was diverted through underground pipelines into the Rakaia River. Near here are the winter sports areas of Porter Heights and Mount Olympus.

Lake Coleridge

Catlins   D 13

Region: Otago

This very beautiful but remote and sometimes marshy stretch of upland country, with its many waterfalls and surf-fringed coast, lies in south-eastern Otago. It takes its name from a whaler who acquired large tracts of land from the Maoris around 1840. The government would not recognise the purchase, and his descendants were allowed to keep only 92 hectares/227 acres.

Topography

The great forests on the east coast attracted large numbers of loggers. Sawmills were established, and the timber was shipped from Hinahina. The only settlement surviving from the time of the timber boom is Owaka (pop. 400), at the entrance to Catlins Forest Park.

Forest Timber

Catlins Forest Park

The entrance to Catlins Forest Park can be reached from Highway 94 or, coming from the west, via Wyndham. The park office, with a small exhibition on the Catlins area, is in Owaka.

Access

Catlins Forest Park, 600sq.km/230sq. miles of largely virgin forest, extends along the Catlins River to the almost unpopulated coastal area, lashed by heavy surf. There are a number of attractive walking trails through the forest and along the Catlins River.
  On the coast there are numerous inlets and caves. The name Cannibal Bay recalls the bloody deeds of the 1830s, when the notorious Maori leader Te Rauparaha pressed his raids as far as the south of the South Island.

★Virgin forest

Yellow-eyed penguins now breed elsewhere on New Zealand's coasts and are now very rare in this area. Colonies of seals can be seen at some points in the uninhabited coastal areas.

Yellow-eyed penguins and seal colonies

Chatham Islands

Population: 750

Getting there

There are scheduled flights to Chatham from Christchurch and Wellington.

Situation

The Chatham Islands lie in the South Pacific some 800km/500 miles east of Christchurch. There are three main islands: Chatham, Pitt and South-East Island.

Chatham

The largest of the islands, Chatham, has an area of 900sq.km/350sq. miles and a population consisting mainly of fishermen and farmers. It is relatively flat. Its most striking feature is the large central lagoon, and there are also a number of shallow lakes. The chief place on the island is Waitangi, with a population of around 300.

From Chatham the other islands (mostly bird sanctuaries) can be visited in local fishing boats. There is little in the way of accommodation – a tourist lodge, a modest hotel and a few rooms in private houses. There is no restaurant or baker's shop and only two small general stores.

History

The first inhabitants of the Chatham Islands, described in the literature as the Moriori, came from Polynesia. According to the local tradition the ancestors of the present population came from Hawaiki in two canoes; a third canoe is said to have reached Pitt Island rather later. The Moriori developed in complete isolation from the inhabitants of the main islands of New Zealand. Their great limitation was the lack of any tall trees whose timber could be used for building houses or canoes, and accordingly their dwellings were very primitive. They developed an art of their own in the form of tree carving (cutting figures into the bark of trees).

Their first contact with white men was in 1791, when Lieutenant Broughton, in the course of an expedition led by George Vancouver, saw land that was not shown on any map. The islands were named after Broughton's ship, the "Chatham".

After 1800 whalers and seal-hunters frequently visited the islands. In the 1820s Maoris who had been driven out of their tribal territory in Taranaki learned of the existence of the Chatham Islands and sought a safe refuge there. Under pressure from the many Taranaki Maoris who now flocked to the islands, together with the many white men who visited them, the numbers of Moriori gradually declined, and the last pure-blooded survivor died in 1933.

The New Zealand Company bought the Chatham Islands in 1839, and soon afterwards tried to sell them on at a profit to a German colonising syndicate. The proposal was vetoed by the British government, which then incorporated the islands in the colony of New Zealand.

Te Kooti and the Ringatu sect

The charismatic Maori leader Te Kooti, who had fought on the government side against the Hauhau rebels on the North Island, was suspected of espionage and in 1866, without trial, was interned on Chatham along with 300 Hauhau supporters. While there he founded the Ringatu sect, which was based on the Old Testament. In 1868 Te Kooti and his followers seized a ship, burned down Waitangi, the chief place on the island, and made their escape to the east coast of the North Island, carrying out a brutal massacre at Gisborne. Thereafter Te Kooti and his guerrilla fighters were a thorn in the government's flesh for many years.

Crayfish boom

Until the end of the Second World War the Chatham Islands remained undeveloped. Between 1968 and 1972 a boom in the crayfish fisheries brought prosperity. Since then fishing has remained the islanders' main source of income.

Sights

There is a small museum in Waitangi containing Moriori artefacts and documents on the coming of the white men and the Taranaki Maoris. There is also material on the career of Te Kooti.

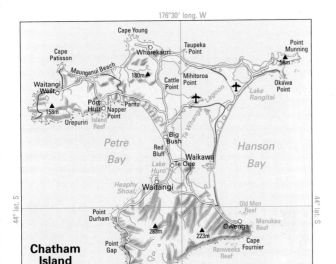

Chatham Island

10 km

© Baedeker

At some places on the main island, particularly on the west side of the central lagoon and on the east coast, there are rock drawings scratched on the limestone cliffs, almost all depicting seal-like figures.

The tree carvings of the Moriori were always of human figures.

Christchurch   G 10

Region: Canterbury. Population: 307,000

By air: The city's international airport, which is served by numerous domestic and foreign airlines, is in the suburb of Harewood, north-west of the city centre. There are several connections daily with Wellington and Auckland on the North Island and Dunedin on the South Island.

By rail: Express trains run daily on the Christchurch–Blenheim–Picton, Christchurch–Dunedin–Invercargill and Christchurch–Greymouth (on the west coast; TraNZAlpine Express) lines.

By boat: Many cruise ships sailing in the South Pacific and cargo vessels carrying some passengers call in at Lyttelton's deep-water harbour.

Getting there

Christchurch, the largest town on the South Island and its economic and cultural centre, lies on the east coast, just north of the Banks Peninsula, in whose natural harbour of Lyttelton the first settlers landed in the 19th century. The city extends over an almost treeless plain which is bounded on the south-east by the hills, rising to some 400m/1300ft, between the city and Lyttelton Harbour. In summer an unpleasant hot, dry wind from the north-west often blows for days at a time.

Situation and importance

With its spacious parks, its numerous sports grounds and well cared for gardens – amounting altogether to more than 3000 hectares/7500 acres of green space – Christchurch has become known as the Garden City. The city's architecture and atmosphere lead many visitors to declare that it is

The Garden City

213

1 Victoria Clock Tower
2 Cranmer Courts
3 Cranmer Centre
4 Christ's College Dining Hall
5 Canterbury Museum
6 Arts Centre Clock Tower Block
7 Antigua Street Boatsheds
8 Nurses' Memorial Chapel
9 Pegasus Arms Building
10 St Michael and all Angels

11 Library Chambers
12 Canterbury Club
13 Original Municipal Chambers
14 Prov. Government Buildings
15 Methodist Church
16 Theatre Royal
17 New Regent Street
18 Regent Theatre
19 Former Chief Post Office
20 Former Government Building

21 Press Building
22 State Trinity Centre
23 Christchurch Club
24 Fishers Building
25 Shands Emporium
26 McKenzie and Willis Building
27 Former Kaiapoi
   Woollen Company
28 Cathedral of the
   Blessed Sacrament

the most "British" of New Zealand's towns. Its situation in an extensive plain has allowed its planners to lay it out on a rectangular grid with broad main streets. Only the winding course of the Avon River and the diagonal line of the High Street and Victoria Street disturb the regularity of its plan.

The city takes its name from Christ Church, Oxford, the college of its founder John Godley.

Name

Every year on December 16th the Canterbury Pilgrims and Settlers Association holds a religious service in the Cathedral to commemorate the arrival of the first "pilgrims" in 1850. On the Sunday nearest the 16th there is a "memorial walk" from Christchurch through the Port Hills to Lyttelton Harbour, where the first British settlers landed.

History

◄ *Christchurch Cathedral*

215

The original deal for the purchase of land to build a settlement on had an epilogue many years afterwards; for the land had been bought from Te Rauparaha, a Maori chief from the North Island, and not from the local Ngai Tahu tribes whom he had killed or driven out. It was only eighty years later, in 1920, that the government agreed to pay compensation to the real owners of the land. Since 1973 payments have been made annually towards the cost of health, education and social services for the Ngai Tahu tribes.

There were uncertainties about the site of the settlement, for the Otago Association which founded Dunedin was also interested in the plains round the Banks Peninsula. The Canterbury Association grew out of the partnership of Edward Gibbon Wakefield with a young Conservative named John Robert Godley, scion of a family of large landowners. Godfrey was in entire agreement with Wakefield's ideas on colonisation – to sell the land at a high price to capitalists, to enlist reliable Anglican farm workers and tradesmen with a certificate of character from a clergyman, offer them free passage and employ them on large farms on the English model. Class distinctions were to be rigidly observed: this was not to be a democratic community of hungry and landless emigrants like the first settlements of the New Zealand Company at Nelson and elsewhere on the North Island, where Wakefield had been unable to realise his idea of a colony of gentlemen. Godley arrived in Lyttelton eight months before the first settlers to prepare for the arrival of his "pilgrims". In the early years of the settlement the original conception was realised. Round the town there came into being a community of arable farmers under the authority of the church, very much on the English model. After the drought years 1850 and 1851 in Australia wealthy sheep-farmers from there came to the Christchurch area and established huge sheep runs from which they expected to draw equally huge profits. By 1855 all the available land was taken up. The Canterbury Association, which had brought no fewer than 3500 settlers – mostly Anglicans from England but also some Scottish Presbyterians, Irish Catholics and German Lutherans – to the Christchurch area, was now dissolved.

The city

The "Englishness" of the original settlement is still evident in the city centre. The settlers planted trees with which they had been familiar at home, mainly oaks and willows, and the architecture of the second half of the 19th century is very much in the English style. And the settlers were not slow to form clubs for "English" games like cricket and tennis.

Visiting the town in its early years, Bishop Selwyn complained that there were not enough churches and schools. In those days the churches, like other buildings, were simple wooden structures, but in 1855 a beginning was made with the construction of more permanent and more dignified churches. The style preferred for Anglican churches was Neo-Gothic: the Neo-Classical style was felt to be too secular.

Benjamin Mountfort

The aspect of the city owes a great deal to the architect Benjamin Mountfort, who was responsible for a series of major public buildings, including the Provincial Council Buildings, the Canterbury Museum and the Great Hall of the University (now the Arts Centre).

Sightseeing

The main sights of Christchurch can be seen in a three-hour walk. The first stage begins in Cathedral Square and leads past the Regent Theatre and over the Avon Bridge, with the Scott Memorial and the visitor centre. Then along Cambridge Terrace, passing the Bridge of Remembrance, to the Botanic Gardens, with the Arts Centre and the Canterbury Museum.

From the Canterbury Museum the second stage leads past Christ's College to Hagley Park and along Armagh Street to Cranmer Square, with two former schools, the Girls' High School and the Normal School. At the end of Chester Street is the city's oldest stone-built church, the Methodist Church of 1864. At the south end of Durham Street, where it reaches the Avon, are the Provincial Government Buildings. On the far side of the bridge are Victoria Square and the modern Town Hall.

From Victoria Square the third stage continues along Oxford Terrace, skirting the Avon, to Madras Street, and south along this to Latimer Square. From there Worcester Street runs back to Cathedral Square.

The Arts Centre houses both ballet and theatre companies (Southern Ballet, Court Theatre, University Theatre). On the University campus in the Ilam district is the Ngaio Marsh Theatre (named after the detective story writer, a native of Christchurch). | Theatres

At the corner of Victoria and Kilmore Streets is Christchurch Casino – New Zealand's first. | Casino

Sights

The city's principal sight is the Cathedral, a prominent landmark with its 65m/213ft high spire. It was designed by the famous London architect Sir George Gilbert Scott. The foundation stone was laid in 1864, but only a year later work came to a stop because of shortage of money and was not resumed until 1873. The direction of the work was entrusted to Benjamin Mountfort, who modified Scott's plan by adding turrets, pinnacles and small balconies; but the building was not completed until 1904, six years after Mountfort's death and 40 years after the start of work – though the first services were held in the nave in 1881. | ★Christchurch Cathedral

In the interior of this monumental church are a series of pictures illustrating the history of the Anglican church and its bishops in New Zealand. There is also fine stained glass.

The spire has three times suffered damage in earthquakes. Visitors can climb to the viewing balconies half way up (open: Mon.–Fri. 8.30am–5pm, Sat. 11.30am–5pm) from which there are magnificent views of the city centre.

Behind the Cathedral is the State Trinity Centre, originally a church (by Benjamin Mountfort, 1874) and now used for lectures and meetings. | Trinity Centre

The large open square in front of the Cathedral is the hub of the city's life and the pride of old-established citizens. There was great indignation when George Bernard Shaw, visiting Christchurch in 1935, admired Petre's Neo-Classical Roman Catholic cathedral and dismissed the Anglican cathedral as "too academic". | ★Cathedral Square

In front of the Cathedral is a statue of John Godley, founder of Christchurch. | Godley Memorial

On the south-west side of the square is the old Chief Post Office (1879), a building in Italian Renaissance style designed by P. F. M. Burrows. | Post Office (photograph, p. 70)

The Edwardian-style Regent Theatre was built in 1905 as the Royal Exchange. It was converted into a cinema in 1930. | Regent Theatre

The Press Building, on the north-east side of Cathedral Square, was built (by Collins and Harman, 1909) to house the offices of "The Press", Christchurch's oldest newspaper (founded 1861). A striking feature of this four-storey building in English Late Gothic style is that the windows are different on each of the floors. | Press Building

To the south of Cathedral Square is the City Mall (pedestrian zone), Christchurch's principal shopping street. | City Mall

In Latimer Square, to the east of the Cathedral, is the Christchurch Club (1861), an imposing wooden building in Italian Renaissance style designed by Benjamin Mountfort. This was the meeting-place of the "wool barons" and owners of the great sheep farms. The writer Samuel Butler was also a member, though he complained that his fellow-members could talk of nothing but money and sheep. | Christchurch Club

Christchurch

Theatre Royal	The Edwardian-style Theatre Royal in nearby Gloucester Street was built in 1908 to the design of the Luttrell brothers. It has a very handsome auditorium.
Canterbury Society of Arts Gallery	Farther along Gloucester Street is the Canterbury Society of Arts Gallery (open: Mon.–Sat. 10am–4.30pm, Sun. 2–4.30pm), which specialises in modern art. There is a showroom with works for sale.
St Michael and All Angels	In Oxford Terrace, to the west of the Cathedral, is the church of St Michael and All Angels (by W. F. Crisp, 1872), the oldest surviving Anglican wooden church. It has a beautiful interior and fine stained glass. The free-standing clock-tower (1861) was designed by Benjamin Mountfort.
★Provincial Council Buildings	The Neo-Gothic Provincial Council Buildings (by Benjamin Mountfort, 1859–65) to the north of the Cathedral, beyond the little river Avon, are among the finest buildings in the city. It was originally a wooden building centred on a courtyard, a stone extension and tower being added later. The showpiece of the building is the ornate Neo-Gothic Council Chamber, with wall mosaics, stained glass windows, massive and richly decorated barrel vaulting and galleries for spectators and the press. In 1924 an annexe was built in Armagh Street. Conducted tours by appointment.
Visitor Information Centre	Along the Avon River to the south is the Visitor Information Centre, housed in the former City Council Chambers (1887), a red-brick building in Queen Anne style. It stands on the site of the Canterbury Association's Land Office of 1851.
Women Memorial	Beyond the Visitor Centre is the Women Memorial, the city's youngest bronze memorial, erected in 1993 on the 100th anniversary of the confirmation of women's right to vote.
Scott Memorial	Opposite the Visitor Centre is a memorial honouring Robert Falcon Scott, who set out from Christchurch in 1912 on the expedition which took him to the South Pole and to his death on the return journey. The memorial, erected in 1917, was the work of his widow Kathleen (Lady Kennett), a sculptor.
★Boating on the Avon	Visitors can see a different aspect of Christchurch from a punt on the sluggish river Avon. Punts (with punter only) can be hired at the Visitor Centre or at the old Antigua Boatyards in Cambridge Terrace.
Bridge of Remembrance	Farther south is the Bridge of Remembrance, built in 1923 as a memorial to the New Zealanders who fell in the First World War.
★Canterbury Museum	On the eastern edge of the Botanic Gardens, in a building of 1870 designed by Benjamin Mountfort, is the Canterbury Museum (open: daily 9am–4.30pm, 6.30pm in summer), which has a fine collection of material on the city's colonial past, as well as magnificent Maori woodcarving and objects carved from greenstone. Displays in the main hall illustrate the history of Antarctic exploration from its beginnings down to the recent past. The first director of the Museum and one of the most important collectors of material was a geologist, Julius von Haast, who had carried out extensive surveys of the South Island. He used his large collection of moa bones in exchanges with other museums to build up the Canterbury Museum.
★Arts Centre	Near the Museum are the Neo-Gothic buildings (also designed by Mountfort and built from 1876 onwards) formerly occupied by Canterbury University, which were converted into the Arts Centre in the 1970s, when the University moved west to the Ilam district. The finest features of the buildings are the Great Hall (1882), the central clock-tower (1877) and the main entrance. At the west corner of the main block is the room in which Rutherford (see Famous People) carried out his early physical experiments.

The old University building, now the Arts Centre

The famous philosopher Karl Popper (1902–94) also taught here from 1937 to 1945. The Arts Centre is home to various dramatic, ballet and musical ensembles, and almost every day there are performances of high artistic quality. Here too there are a great variety of shops, galleries and stalls displaying and selling art and craft objects, as well as cafés and restaurants. It is a busy and bustling scene, particularly at weekends, when there is a big crafts market in the area adjacent (Sat.–Sun. 10am–4pm).

Behind the Museum is the McDougall Art Gallery (open: daily 10am–4.30pm), which displays mainly works (paintings, sculpture, ceramics) by older and contemporary New Zealand and British artists.

★ McDougall Art Gallery

Beyond the Arts Centre and the Museum is Hagley Park, with an area of 180 hectares/450 acres. It is planted with trees brought from Europe. Within the park are various sports grounds, including the Harley Cricket Oval, a golf course and a riding track.

Hagley Park

In the centre of the park, enclosed within a loop of the Avon, are the Botanic Gardens.

Botanic Gardens

North-west of Hagley Park, on the banks of the Avon, is the mansion of Mona Vale (1905), set in a 4 hectare/10 acre park planted with old trees. The mansion (entered from Fenalton Road) is open daily to the public.

Mona Vale

Christ's College, to the north of the Canterbury Museum, was established soon after the foundation of Christchurch as a boys' secondary school in the tradition of the British grammar school. The earliest buildings on the site date from 1857. The Big School of 1863, designed by Superintendent FitzGerald, is the oldest school building still in use in New Zealand. The New Classrooms of 1886 were designed by Benjamin Mountfort, the Dining Hall on the street front, the Hare Library with the clock and Jacob's House (1915–25) by Cecil Wood.

Christ's College

Christchurch

★ Town Hall
North-east of the Provincial Council Buildings, in Victoria Square, is the eye-catching modern Town Hall of 1972. This attractive and imposing building was designed by the Christchurch architects Warren and Mahoney. Within the complex are a conference hall, a large auditorium seating 2000, other conference and banqueting rooms and a restaurant. There are occasional conducted tours.

Park Royal Hotel
The adjoining Park Royal Hotel (1988) is another notable modern building designed by Warren and Mahoney.

Victoria Square
In Victoria Square are a green-patinated bronze statue of Queen Victoria (1903) and another of Captain Cook (1932).

Victoria Clock Tower
North-west of the Town Hall, in Victoria Street, is a clock-tower which was brought from Britain in 1860 for the Provincial Council Buildings but turned out to be too heavy for their light roof structure. In 1897 it was set on a massive stone plinth to celebrate Victoria's Diamond Jubilee. It was moved to its present site in 1930.

★ Cathedral of the Blessed Sacrament
The Roman Catholic Cathedral of the Blessed Sacrament in Barbados Street (south-east of the city centre), the finest Neo-Renaissance church in New Zealand, was built in 1901–05. The Cathedral, with a high dome over the crossing, was designed by F. W. Petre and was much admired by George Bernard Shaw.

Rugby, Cricket and Sport Museum
Farther to the south-east is Lancaster Park, with the Rugby, Cricket and Sport Museum (open: daily 10am–4pm).

New Regent Street
New Regent Street was laid out uniformly in "Spanish mission style" in 1932, after the demolition of the old Coliseum.

Surroundings

South-east
Ferrymead Historic Park
At Mount Pleasant is Ferrymead Historic Park, an open-air museum with a reconstruction of a pioneering settlement, an old tramcar and a stretch of old railway line on which the first train in New Zealand ran in 1863. Open: daily 10am–4.30pm.

★ Mount Cavendish
From the end of Tunnel Road the Mount Cavendish Gondola, an aerial cableway, runs up to the summit of Mount Cavendish, on which there are viewing terraces and a restaurant. There are breathtaking panoramic views of the city, the coast and the wide plain extending to the Southern Alps.

Bridle Path
The steep Bridle Path followed by the early settlers runs over the hills from Lyttelton Harbour to Christchurch.

Summit Road
The beautiful Summit Road runs along the Port Hills, the rim of the crater, with various side paths branching off to viewpoints. The best approach to the Summit Road is from Sumner, in the east, on the Evans Pass Road to Gebbies Pass. The road, with many bends, has a total length of some 70km/43 miles. The return route to Christchurch is over Dyer's Pass or via Lyttelton and the road tunnel.

Red Cliffs
At Red Cliffs, near Monck's Bay, is a cave in which Julius von Haast found large numbers of moa bones in 1872

Banks Peninsula, Lyttelton
See Banks Peninsula

South
Ngaio Marsh House
The house in the Cashmere district once occupied by Ngaio Marsh, the well known author of detective stories, actress and theatre director, was built in 1907; it is now a museum.

Also in the Cashmere district is The Sign of Takahe, a house with the aspect of a small castle which was built for Harry Ell, a local politician who was active in the campaign for the preservation of the Port Hills between Christchurch and Lyttelton. The house, which was half finished when he died in 1934, was completed by the city in 1949 and is now a gourmet restaurant. From the hills there are magnificent views.

Sign of Takahe

Farther south is the Sign of Kiwi, a roadhouse on the Summit Road built on the initiative of Harry Ell.

Sign of Kiwi

Some distance west of Hagley Park is Riccarton House (1856), the former residence of the Dean family, in a park which has been left in its natural state. The family was settled here before the arrival of the Canterbury "pilgrims". The little cottage which they built in 1843 is now open to the public as a museum.

West
Riccarton House
(Deans Cottage)

To the south-west, on the old Wigram airfield (9km/5½ miles west of the city centre), is the Museum of the Royal New Zealand Air Force (open: Mon.– Sat. 10am–4pm, Sun. 1–4pm), with a number of old military aircraft, aeronautical apparatus and flying equipment. There are also showings of war films.

Air Force Museum

12km/7½ miles west of the city centre is the Yaldhurst Transport Museum (open: daily 10am–4pm), with a collection of veteran and vintage cars.

Yaldhurst
Transport
Museum

Near the airport is the Orana Park Wildlife Reserve, Christchurch's Zoo, with open-air enclosures reproducing natural conditions as closely as possible and a much visited nocturnal house for kiwis.

North-west
Orana Park
Wildlife Reserve

On Orchard Drive, a short walk from the airport building, is the International Antarctic Centre, which illustrates the importance of the Antarctic to the world with excellent displays and audio-visual shows.

International
Antarctic Centre

Beyond the airport is Tiptree Cottage (1864), a three-storey building of wood and cob (a mixture of clay and chopped straw) which is open to the public as a museum.

Tiptree Cottage

This magnificently carved Maori meeting-house of 1906 stands on the Rehua *marae* (assembly place) in Springfield Road.

North
Te Whatu Manawa
Orehua

This large park with facilities for sports of all kinds was laid out for the 1974 Commonwealth Games. Particular attractions are the giant water slide and a large maze.

North-east
Queen Elizabeth II
Park

This new *marae* (assembly place) on Pages Road in the eastern suburb of Aranui is not meant only for Maoris.
   Of particular interest are the carved entrance gateway and the meeting-house, in modern style, with carvings in the tradition of various different tribes.

East
★ Christchurch
National Marae
(Nga Hau E Wha)

Dunedin

E 12

Region: Otago. Population: 121,000

By air: There are several flights daily from and to Christchurch, Queenstown, Wellington and Auckland.
   By sea: Cargo boats with cabins for passengers occasionally call in at Dunedin or the neighbouring port of Chalmers, as do some of the large cruise ships sailing in the Pacific or round Australia.
   By rail: There are express trains daily between Dunedin and Christchurch and between Dunedin and Invercargill. There are also occasional tourist trains through the Taieri Gorge to Middlemarch.

Getting there

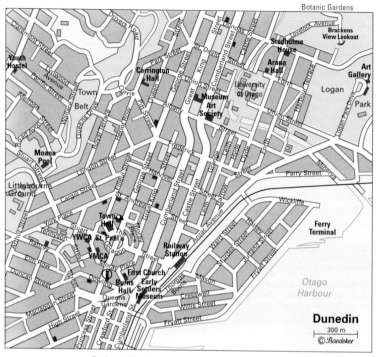

Dunedin

By bus: There are regular bus services several times a day between Dunedin and the larger towns on the South Island.

Situation and importance	Dunedin, the economic and cultural capital of the south, lies in Otago Harbour, a natural harbour reaching far inland, surrounded by hills and mountains.
Name	Dun Edin is the old Gaelic name of Edinburgh. The name is a reminder that the town was founded by Scottish immigrants, who originally thought of calling it New Edinburgh.
History	In February 1770 Captain Cook sailed past the Otago Peninsula. He was struck by the long white beaches to the south but did not notice the mouth of Otago Harbour.

Before the arrival of Europeans the Otago Peninsula had a large Maori population, who worked the much sought after greenstone found on the west coast of the South Island. The tools, weapons and jewellery made from this green jade were also valued on the North Island as objects of trade and exchange. Even before the coming of the Europeans the population had been greatly reduced by inter-family and inter-tribal feuds.

The Maori population was still further reduced by brutal seal-hunters and whalers and by the diseases (influenza, measles) which they brought with them. In 1817 there was bloody fighting between the local Maoris and the crew of a whaling ship, in which 70 Maoris were killed and their village, Otakau, burned down. From the name of the village came the name Otago

Bird's eye view of Dunedin

which was applied to the natural harbour, the peninsula and finally the whole region.

After the foundation of Nelson Edward Gibbon Wakefield, always looking for additional land for new immigrants from Europe, won the support of senior Scottish churchmen for the establishment of a new settlement in the south of the South Island, and the Otago Association was formed.

In 1843, in what was known as the Disruption, more than 400 ministers of the Church of Scotland, led by Dr Thomas Chalmers (after whom Port Chalmers, just north of Dunedin, is named), left the established Church and founded the Free Church of Scotland. Two leading members of the Free Church became the founding fathers of Dunedin: William Cargill, a veteran of the Napoleonic wars who became a businessman, and Thomas Burns, a nephew of the poet and a minister of the church.

In 1844, when a delegation from the Otago Association was about to leave London, news came of the Wairau affray, a bloody confrontation between the white settlers of Nelson and Te Rauparaha's Maoris in which Edward Gibbon Wakefield's brother Arthur was killed. After some hesitation Frederick Tuckett was sent out to find a suitable place for the new settlement, and he decided on a site in the sheltered natural harbour of Otago. William Wakefield, who was charged to establish the settlement, persuaded Governor Fitzroy to waive the Crown's exclusive right to acquire land, laid down in the treaty of Waitangi, and the Otago Association was then able to buy land directly from the Maoris, paying only £2400 for 162,000 hectares/405,000 acres. The first settlers landed in 1848 and established themselves with the support of the local Maoris and an influential whaler named Johnny Jones who had settled nearby.

The finding of gold in Central Otago in 1861 brought a great increase of population, and Dunedin was soon larger than Auckland and the wealthiest settlement in New Zealand. Trade and industry flourished in the town.

A further upswing in the town's economy began in 1882, when the first refrigerator ship sailed for Britain with a cargo of frozen meat. The first frozen meat plant in the world was established in Dunedin. From 1863 the town's streets were lit by gas. In 1879 a cable tramway system on the model of San Francisco's cable cars began to operate, and the first electric trams ran in 1903.

After the turn of the century, when the gold rush petered out, many young people moved north, where the climate and job prospects were better. This trend has been reversed in recent years, and the population is again growing.

The town
As a result of this stagnation in the economy and in population the city centre has been preserved largely unchanged. In the prosperous Dunedin of the 19th century imposing public buildings were built in stone, at a time when the usual building material in the rest of New Zealand was wood. Easily worked limestone was readily available in the Oamaru quarries.

The town's well-to-do citizens built handsome terraced houses with columns, oriel windows and balconies. Particularly fine examples are to be seen in Stuart Street and the High Street.

Theatres
The old Methodist Church at the corner of Moray Place and Stuart Street is the home of the Fortune company. The little Globe Theatre at 104 London Street specialises in avant garde plays. The Regent Theatre, on the Octagon, also offers an excellent repertoire.

Events
The Otago Agricultural and Pastoral Summer Show (popularly, the A and P Show) is held at the end of January, with a full programme of events. In the middle of February there is the week-long Dunedin Festival (exhibitions, concerts, parades, sporting events). The Scottish Week at the end of March maintains Scottish traditions, with bagpipes, highland dancing and sporting events. Important film festivals are held annually in April/May (the Dunedin Film Festival) and at the end of July (the International Film Festival).

Factory visits
Visits to various food and drink factories are very popular – for example to Cadbury Chocolate (Cumberland Street), Speight's Brewery (Rattray Street) or Wilson's Whisky (New Zealand's only whisky distillery). Visits should be booked in advance through the Visitor Information Centre.

Sights

Octagon
The central feature of the city is the Octagon, an eight-sided square with a statue of Robert Burns erected in 1887. A market is held in the square on Friday.

St Paul's Cathedral
On the west side of the square is the Neo-Gothic St Paul's Cathedral (Anglican), built in 1915 to the design of the London architects Sedding and Wheatley. In the early years of the town, founded as it was by Scottish Presbyterians, there were practically no Anglicans, but as their numbers increased they built their first church in 1862. The wooden bell-tower, intended to be only temporary, was built in 1910.

The first woman bishop in the Anglican church, Dr Penny Jamieson, was enthroned in St Paul's in 1990.

★ Municipal Chambers
Adjoining the Cathedral are the imposing Municipal Chambers (Town Hall), with a façade in Italian Renaissance style and a handsome clock-tower. It was built in 1880 to the design of the young Melbourne architect R. A. Lawson.

Civic Centre
To the south is the Civic Centre, with the Public Library and the Visitor Information Centre. The Library has a large collection of books and documents going back to the town's early days. The archives are much consulted by genealogists.

The Law Courts, Dunedin

The oldest Christian church in Dunedin is the former Congregational Church (by David Ross, 1864) at the corner of Moray Place and View Street (to the west of the Octagon). It was about to be demolished when it was acquired by the Seventh Day Adventists.

Seventh Day Adventist Church

Still farther west, in Rattray Street, is St Joseph's Cathedral (R.C.; by F. W. Petre, 1878–86). The architect seems to have taken as his models the Gothic cathedrals of Amiens and Reims.
  Petre, who also designed large churches in Oamaru, Timaru, Invercargill, Wellington and Christchurch, was, along with the Scottish-born R. A. Lawson, who came to New Zealand by way of Australia, the leading architect working in Dunedin; but his plan for the cathedral, with a tower over the crossing, proved to be too expensive. There were delays and cutbacks, and his original design was much modified.

★St Joseph's Cathedral

St Dominic's Priory, built in 1877, is now privately owned.

St Dominic's Priory

From the Octagon Stuart Street runs south-east. At its lower end are two impressive buildings dating from Dunedin's heyday, the Law Courts and the Railway Station.

Stuart Street

The Law Courts, designed by the government architect, were built in 1902. Over the main entrance are the royal arms.

Law Courts

Adjoining the Law Courts is the Police Station, a brick building of 1896 which was originally designed as a prison.

Police Station

Diagonally opposite, in Anzac Avenue, the Railway Station, a massive fortress-like structure, dominates the scene. In Flemish Renaissance style, it was built in 1904–06 to the design of George Troup. Though mocked for

★Railway Station

225

Dunedin

his "gingerbread" architecture, the architect was knighted for his work. The interior is magnificent, with colonnades, balustrades and mosaic paving.

★ Early Settlers' Museum

To the south of the station is the Early Settlers' Museum (open: Mon.–Fri. 9am–4.30pm, Sat. 10.30am–4.30pm, Sun. 1.30–4.30pm), with much interesting material from the town's early days, including many portraits of the Scottish founding families, and exhibits illustrating the town's technological achievements (street lighting, trams, railway, etc.), also period vehicles.

★ First Church

South-east of the Octagon, on Moray Place and Burlington Street, is the First Church (by R. A. Lawson, 1868–73), a Neo-Gothic building with a handsome tower. The foundation-stone was laid by Thomas Burns, co-founder of the town.

★ Princes Street

From the Octagon Princes Street runs south. A street with a fashionable air, it has a number of notable buildings.

Southern Cross Hotel

To the south-west, at the corner of Princes Street and the High Street, is the Southern Cross Hotel, built in 1883 and still preserving its original splendour. Particularly fine are the entrance lobby and the stucco-decorated rooms on the first floor.

Wain's Hotel

Close by is the sumptuous façade of Wain's Hotel, a luxury hotel opened in 1878. Notable features are the grotesques on the ground floor windows.

ANZ Bank

The ANZ Bank occupies a building of 1874 designed by R. A. Lawson which has preserved its Neo-Classical façade.

Bank of New Zealand

The Bank of New Zealand (by William Armson, 1879–83) is in a richly decorated Neo-Renaissance style. The banking hall has a magnificent ceiling.

★ Otago Museum

1km/¾ mile north-east of the Octagon, caught between the two carriageways of Highway 1 (Great King Street and Cumberland Street), is the Otago Museum, in a large and handsome building designed by David Ross (1876). The Museum's rich collections bear witness to the prosperity of Victorian Dunedin and the interest in self-improvement of its citizens, who presented their art treasures to the Museum.

The Museum has five main departments: the culture of the Maoris and the Pacific area, the natural history of New Zealand, archaeology and ancient and classical civilisations, oceanography, and science and technology (with a hands-on science centre for children, Discovery World).

Of particular interest is the Museum's large collection of objects made from greenstone, including axe-like weapons and amulets. Many of these items were made by the local Maoris on the Otago Peninsula. There is also a very fine carved meeting-house of 1872–75 from Whakatane on the Bay of Plenty (North Island).

The Museum is open Mon.–Fri. 10am–5pm, Sat. and Sun. 1–5pm.

Otago Art Society Museum

Close by, in the handsome old post office of Dunedin North, is the Museum of the Otago Art Society (open: daily 2–4.30pm).

★ University of Otago

The University of Otago, New Zealand's first university, was founded in 1869. The imposing Neo-Gothic buildings on the little river Leith, north of the city centre, were designed by Maxwell Bury, who took the University of Glasgow as his model. Particularly impressive features are the handsome clock-tower, the main entrance and the staircase hall. The building in Castle Street is now occupied by the University administration. The first chancellor of the University was Thomas Burns, one of the founding fathers of Dunedin. Round the old buildings are various later buildings occupied by University institutes, including the Dental School, the only one in New Zealand. Here too are the professors' houses, also designed by Maxwell Bury, built of red brick with contrasting white gable arches.

The Hocken Library (Albany Street, Castle Street block; open: Mon.–Fri. 9.30am–5pm, Sat. 9am–noon) was bequeathed to the city by the bibliophile Dr Thomas M. Hocken in 1910 and has been enlarged since then. The collection includes printed works, maps, pictures and manuscripts, mainly concerned with New Zealand and the South Pacific.

Hocken Library

The Dunedin Art Gallery (open: Mon.–Fri. 10am–5pm, Sat. and Sun. 2–5pm), a few hundred yards east of the University in Logan Park, has a rich collection of older and modern New Zealand and European art. Of particular interest are numerous works by Frances Hodgkins, who achieved fame in London only late in life. Her father was one of the founders of the Art Gallery. The work of Colin McCahon is also well represented.

★Dunedin Public Art Gallery

From this viewpoint, north-west of the Art Gallery, there is a good view of the city centre. Thomas Bracken (1843–98) was a poet and politician who wrote the New Zealand national anthem "God defend New Zealand".

★Bracken's Lookout

North-west of Bracken's Lookout are the Botanic Gardens (area 30 hectares/75 acres), established in 1863. Old trees, both native and European, afford shade, and there is a wide range of New Zealand's flora, well cared for and well labelled. The gardens are at their most beautiful when the azaleas and rhododendrons are in flower (August–October).

★★Botanic Gardens

To the west of the Otago Museum, in the city's "town belt" (green belt), is the mansion of Olveston (1906), designed by the English architect Ernest George. Its first owner was David E. Theomin, a businessman and art collector who came from Olveston, near Bristol, and settled in Dunedin in 1879.
   The house was opened to the public in 1966. This sumptuous mansion in turn-of-the-century style gives some impression of the way of life of the prosperous middle classes in those days. The oak staircase and balustrade were made in England. There are numerous pictures illustrating many aspects of life in colonial New Zealand. Conducted tours by appointment.

★Olveston

Surroundings

From Signal Hill (393m/1289ft), reached from the Northern Cemetery on Opoho Road and Signal Hill Road, there are magnificent views to the south over Otago Harbour and the city. On the hill is a monument commemorating the 100th anniversary of the treaty of Waitangi. It incorporates a piece of rock from Edinburgh Castle, an anniversary gift from Scotland. Bronze figures symbolise the past and the future.

Signal Hill

8km/5 miles north of Dunedin is Mount Cargill (676m/2218ft), from which there are fine views of the city, Otago Harbour and the Otago Peninsula.

Mount Cargill

12km/7½ miles north of Dunedin, on the north side of Otago Harbour, is the deep-water harbour of Port Chalmers (pop. 3000). The town is named after Thomas Chalmers, one of the founders of the Free Church of Scotland. From here the colonisation of Otago began; from here the first steamer carrying frozen meat sailed for London; and from here Scott, Shackleton and Byrd set out on their Antarctic expeditions. In the 1970s, when container shipping became established, Port Chalmers took on a new lease of life. The harbour of Dunedin, which had been developed at great expense, proved unsuitable for this traffic.

★Port Chalmers

The Scott Memorial commemorates Captain Scott, who sailed from here on his last tragic expedition in 1910, and near this is a monument commemorating the first shipment of frozen meat to London in 1882. The Port Chalmers Flagstaff on the Aurora Terrace Lookout was once a signal station for keeping watch on shipping traffic in Otago Harbour.

Dunedin

Notable churches in the city are the Iona Church (1883), with a 50m/165ft high tower, the Anglican church of the Holy Trinity (1875) and the Roman Catholic church of St Mary Star of the Sea (1874). The Port Chalmers Museum (open: Sat. and Sun. 10.30am–4.30pm), in the old Post Office (by W. H. Clayton, 1877), displays a variety of material on the history of the port and on New Zealand shipping.

Glenfalloch Woodland Gardens

10km/6 miles east of Dunedin are the Glenfalloch Woodland Gardens, laid out in 1873, with native and exotic trees. The mansion set in the gardens was built of kauri wood two years earlier. The gardens are at their most beautiful in spring, when the azaleas, rhododendrons and fuchsias are in bloom.

Portobello Aquarium

The Trust Bank Aquarium in Portobello (20km/12½ miles east of Dunedin) is run by the University of Otago. Here visitors can see examples of almost all New Zealand's marine fauna. Open daily Dec.–Feb., at other times of year only at weekends and in the holidays daily noon–4.30pm.

Otakou Maori Site

25km/15 miles east of Dunedin, on a site once occupied by a large Maori settlement, a Maori church and meeting-house were inaugurated in 1940 on the 100th anniversary of the treaty of Waitangi. There is a small cemetery containing the graves of three important chiefs.

★Taiaroa Head

Taiaroa Head, the northern tip of the Otago Peninsula, is famed as the nesting-place of royal albatrosses. Nearby are colonies of yellow-eyed penguins, seals and sealions. There are boat trips from Dunedin to the steep and rugged cliffs of Taiaroa.

★Larnach Castle

50km/31 miles from Dunedin on the Otago Peninsula, is Barnacle Castle, also known as the Camp, which was built for a wealthy banker named William Larnach between 1871 and 1887. This extraordinary building is

Larnach Castle

228

said to have been modelled on a Scottish castle; the construction was supervised by the well-known architect R. A. Lawson. The house, which has a ballroom with an area of 250sq.m/2700sq.ft, cost its owner a fortune. William Larnach (1833–98) came to Dunedin in 1867 as manager of the Bank of Otago and had a successful career as a politician. After a series of misfortunes, both financial and personal, he shot himself in the Parliament Building in Wellington. After his death the house suffered many vicissitudes. The surrounding land was broken up into small lots and sold, and the house was bought by the government, with 14 hectares/35 acres of land, and converted into a psychiatric clinic. Later it became a tourist hotel and night club. Then in 1940, badly run down, it was sold for a song. Only in recent years has its value as a relic of Dunedin's early days been recognised. It has now been restored, at great expense, and is open to the public daily 9am–5pm. From the battlements of the tower there are fine views.

There are popular bathing beaches in the suburbs of St Kilda and St Clair, to the south of Dunedin on the sandbank linking the Otago Peninsula with the mainland. From St Kilda, where there are many sports clubs, the John Wilson Ocean Drive runs along the edge of the beach. | Beaches

Half an hour's drive north-west of Dunedin is the wild and romantic gorge of the Taieri River. Visitors can jet through the gorge on a jetboat or rattle through it on the Otago Excursion Train. | ★Taieri Gorge

Fiordland National Park   A–C 11–13

Region: Southland
Area: 12,523sq.km/4835sq. miles

The Fiordland National Park, the largest by far of New Zealand's National Parks, occupies an immense wilderness area in the loneliest part of New Zealand, an expanse of rugged mountain country in the south-west of the South Island, with numerous fjords reaching finger-like far inland. | Situation

Visitor Centre in Te Anau. | Information

This is a region of deep fjords in the west, much ramified lakes in the east and mountains covered with dense forests of evergreen southern beech. At the higher levels and on the summits grow long beard lichens and various mosses. It is also a region of very high rainfall (up to 6000mm/240in. a year), which gives rise to its grandiose waterfalls and locally catastrophic avalanches in winter. | Topography

The National Park is bounded on the north by the Darran Mountains, which rise to 2746m/9010ft in Mount Tutoko. In the east a number of large lakes form a transition to the drier grazing country of Southland. On the west the mountains fall steeply down to the Tasman Sea, which is almost incessantly lashed by the "roaring forties".

The longest fjords are (from south to north), Preservation Inlet, Dusky Sound, Doubtful Sound, George Sound and Milford Sound (see entry), which is the best known and most accessible of the fjords.

These narrow, deep inlets were originally valleys hewn out by ice age glaciers which were later drowned by the sea. On the eastern edge of the ridge of mountains which runs down the whole of the South Island the glaciers carved out a series of elongated lakes, of which Lake Te Anau (see entry) is by far the largest. Others are Lake Manapouri (see entry), Lake Monowai, Lake Hauroko and Lake Poteriteri.

Walks in the Fiordland National Park

The grandiose mountain country of the Fiordland National Park appeals particularly to walkers and climbers who like to "get away from it all" and enjoy the unspoiled beauty of nature. There is plenty of scope in this area for hikes of several days, often very strenuous, exploring lonely mountain forests, lakes and fjords.

Information about walking trails and accommodation and detailed routes can be obtained from Department of Conservation offices in Te Anau and Tuatapere. Walks must be planned well in advance, since accommodation in mountain huts must be booked in plenty of time. Except on organised tours walkers must carry all their gear and food with them. They must be prepared for changeable weather and long-continuing rain: rainproof clothing, stout footwear and sandfly and mosquito repellents are essential requirements.

★★ Milford Track
The world-famed Milford Track runs from Lake Te Anau to Milford Sound (see entries). Four days must be allowed for this grandiose mountain route. Advance booking of accommodation in huts is essential. There are guided walks for groups.

★ Hollyford Track
This route runs along Hollyford Valley, in the north of the National Park, follows Lake McKerow and continues to the coast at Martin's Bay. The walk takes at least four or five days. Guided walks are available. Accommodation in huts must be booked in advance.

★ Routeburn Track
Starting from the road to Milford Sound, this track (a three-day walk) runs over the Harris Saddle (1279m/4196ft) to the north end of Lake Wakatipu at Kinloch. It is often walked as an extension to the Milford Track.

Kepler Track
The Kepler Track (four days) runs from Lake Te Anau to Lake Manapouri (see entries).

Scenic flights
There are scenic flights (in helicopters, seaplanes or conventional light aircraft) from Te Anau and Milford, offering wide views of mountains, forests and fjords.

Fiordland cruises
The Fiordland Travel firm offers six-day cruises in the motor sailing ship "Milford Wanderer". Visitors can thus follow in the footsteps of Captain Cook as they sail into the remote fjords in the south of the National Park.

Boat trips
There is plenty of scope for very rewarding boat trips on Lake Te Anau and Lake Manapouri and in Milford Sound and Doubtful Sound.

★ Dusky Sound
Dusky Sound, New Zealand's longest fjord (44km/27 miles), is also one of the most beautiful, with numerous wooded islands and inlets. It was given its name by Captain Cook, who sailed past the fjord on his first voyage in 1770 as evening was falling. In 1773, on his second voyage, he sailed into the sound and spent over six weeks overhauling his ship, the "Resolution", and taking in supplies. He encountered groups of shy Maoris, who had perhaps withdrawn to this remote area in the face of attacks by more aggressive tribes. Georg Foster gives a vivid account of the meeting with the Maoris and also of a plague of sandflies. Nowadays the area is almost uninhabited, but the sandflies are still there. The seals which were once common in the fjord were almost wiped out by seal-hunters, but since the ban on seal-hunting their numbers have increased.

The fjord can be reached by land only on difficult tracks taking off from the road along Doubtful Sound or, in the south, from Lake Hauroko. The best way of seeing the fjord, with its many islands and inlets, is on a seaplane flight. Cruises in a motor sailing ship, run by Fiordland Travel, start from Deep Cove, in Doubtful Sound. Information from the National Park's Visitor Centre in Te Anau.

100km/62 miles north-west of Invercargill (see entry), in a beautiful setting of steep and densely wooded hills, is Lake Hauroko. Winds and storms blow in from north and south unhindered, sometimes making boating on the lake dangerous. 6km/4 miles east of the lake, on the borders of the National Park, is a camping site.

Lake Hauroko

A number of beautiful walking trails run round Lake Hauroko, among them the Lookout Bluff Track and the Boundary Track. There is a four-day walk from the north end of the lake (Hauroko Burn) to Supper Cove on Dusky Sound.

See Lake Manapouri

Doubtful Sound

See entry

Milford Sound

Fox Glacier · Franz Josef Glacier

E 10

Region: West Coast

The Fox Glacier and the Franz Josef Glacier, 25km/15 miles north, reach down from some of the highest peaks of the Southern Alps, in Westland National Park (see entry), to around the 300m/1000ft contour, amid dense green forests. They were originally named after Queen Victoria and her consort Prince Albert; but in 1865 the German geologist Julius von Haast renamed the more northerly of the two after the Austrian Emperor Francis Joseph, and in 1872, when the then prime minister of New Zealand visited the glaciers, the one to the south was given his name.

Map, pp. 256–57

The glaciers are at their most impressive at sunset. The very high rainfall (up to 5000mm/200in. a year) produces dense rain forests but also means many rainy days. Stable weather conditions prevail in winter, when the snow-capped peaks which form the backdrop to the glaciers can often be clearly seen. In summer, during the main holiday season, the two holiday resorts at the foot of the glacier are overcrowded: it is essential, therefore, to book well in advance.

At both glaciers there are very interesting visitor information centres with detailed information about glaciers and rain forests. Both centres run guided walks and excursions and can arrange for accommodation.

Visitor centres

The 13km/8 mile long Fox Glacier and the 10km/6 mile long Franz Josef Glacier both make a considerable descent over a relatively short distance. It is because of this steep and relatively rapid descent that they reach so far down. Both glaciers have retreated since the coming of European settlers, but in particularly cold and rainy winters they begin to grow again.

The glaciers

A 7km/4½ mile long road and a footpath lead to the mouth of the Fox Glacier. A walk over the glacier is not difficult with suitable footwear. For inexperienced glacier walkers a guided walk (available twice daily) is to be recommended.

★★ Fox Glacier

From the Peak Indicator, a viewpoint 9km/5½ miles farther west, there are magnificent views, in clear weather, of the mountain peaks and the slowly moving glacier. The view is particularly fine at sunrise or sunset.

20km/12½ miles west, below the village of Fox Glacier, Gillespie's Point reaches out into the wild Tasman Sea. Gold was found here in the 19th century.

Gillespie's Point

Over the last 200 years the relatively steep Franz Josef Glacier has frequently advanced and then withdrawn again. On balance, however, it has retreated markedly. Melt-water from the glacier forms the Waiko River.

★★ Franz Josef Glacier

A narrow road (6km/4 miles) runs along the south side of the Waiko valley to the parking area at the mouth of the glacier. On the way there it is worth taking the side roads going off to Peter's Pool, the Sentinel Rock and various lookouts with views of the glacier.

A walk (2 hours there and back) over the wide river bed and rocks polished by the ice leads to a viewpoint at the glacier's mouth. For a walk over the glacier itself it is best to join one of the guided tours which are available twice a day.

There is a breathtaking view of the glacier from the Alex Knob (1295m/4249ft).

Alex Knob

The village called Franz Josef Glacier is a popular tourist resort. The little church of St James was built in 1931. From its chancel window there was until recently a good view of the glacier.

Franz Josef Glacier (village)

8km/5 miles north of the village on Highway 6 is the idyllic little Lake Makourapi, whose waters mirror the majestic alpine peaks and green expanses of forest. The lake is the haunt of many species of birds.

Lake Makourapi

25km/15 miles north of Franz Josef Glacier village is Okarito, a small township founded by gold-diggers in the 1850s. In good weather there are marvellous views of the Southern Alps from here.

Okarito

The Okarito Lagoon is a bird sanctuary, established to protect the white heron. This is its only nesting-place in New Zealand. There are guided bird-watching walks from November to February.

Okarito Lagoon

A sightseeing flight over the glaciers by helicopter is a memorable experience. Some tours include a landing on one of the peaks, with their deep covering of snow. Popular targets for photographers are Lakes Matheson and Gaul, in which, in fine weather, the surrounding snow-capped peaks are mirrored (best seen in the early morning).

Helicopter flights

Greymouth

F 9

Region: West Coast. Populaton: 11,000

Greymouth (named after Governor George Grey) is the main commercial centre on the west coast and an important port. Its economy was originally based on gold-mining, later on coal and timber, and then also on cattle and dairy farming.

Situation and importance

The port, situated at the mouth of the Grey River, is constantly exposed to the threat of flooding, either by the river or by the wild Tasman Sea. Flood protection measures were finally completed in 1991. Rain is frequent and often goes on for a long time, and a bitterly cold wind known as the "Barber" blows down the Grey valley. These climatic factors have contributed to the steady decline in population which has been going on since the end of the 19th century.

There is a rail link between Greymouth and Christchurch over Arthur's Pass (see entry). The five-hour run on the TraNZAlpine Express, passing through the Otira Tunnel and the gorges in Arthur's Pass National Park, is a great tourist attraction. The west coast line to Hokitika (see entry) now carries only goods.

Rail services
★ TraNZAlpine Express

Greymouth grew up on the site of the old Maori settlement of Mawhera. The first white man to explore the wilderness on the west coast was

History

◀ The Franz Josef Glacier

233

A bar of gold rush days in Shantytown

Thomas Brunner in 1846. During the Westland gold rush of the 1860s Greymouth was an important supply centre.

★Shantytown — 3km/8 miles south of Greymouth is the reconstructed golddigging settlement of Shantytown, which attracts swarms of visitors throughout the year. The atmosphere of the 1860s is recalled in this open-air museum of old buildings transferred to this site from other parts of the country and furnished in the style of their period. They include a church, Coronation Hall, a general store, stables, a jail, a hospital, a printing office and the workshops of various craftsmen. A steam railway line of 1897 runs through the dense forest to an old sawmill. There are old gold-miners' claims at which visitors can try their hand at washing for gold, selling any they find to gold-dealers.

Kumara — The old gold-diggers' settlement of Kuara (pop. 300) lies 25km/15 miles south of Greymouth on the road which runs through the Otira Gorge to Arthur's Pass. In its heyday it had a population of anything up to 4000. In the bed of the nearby Taramakau River there was large-scale gold-prospecting in 1982.

Woods Creek Track — 11km/8 miles east of Shantytown is the Woods Creek Track (about 1 hour), running through an area which was turned upside down by gold-diggers in the 1860s.

Point Elizabeth Walkway — 11km/7 miles north of Greymouth, at Raparahoe, is the start of this attractive trail (about 4 hours each way), which runs along the coast through dense primeval forest with tree ferns and nikau palms. It affords fine views of the coast and the highest peaks of the Southern Alps.

Brunner — 12km/7½ miles east of Greymouth on Highway 7 is the Brunner coalfield, with four coal-mines which were formerly of great imporance – Dobson,

Wallsend, Stillwater and Taylorville. The rich deposits of coal on both sides of the Grey River were discovered by Thomas Brunner while surveying the west coast in 1846–48, and the coal began to be mined in 1864. An accident in the Brunner mine in 1896 cost 67 lives.

An old suspension bridge over the Grey River leads to the Brunner Mine, now closed down and scheduled as New Zealand's first protected industrial monument. Industrial heritage trails and dispays illustrate and explain the history of coal-mining on the west coast.

★ Brunner Industrial Site

32km/20 miles south-east of Greymouth, in a setting of great scenic beauty, is Lake Brunner, the largest lake on the west coast, which offers ideal conditions for fishing and boating. It was formed in a basin scooped out by a glacier which was closed off by a terminal moraine.
The lake is known to the Maoris as Moana Kutuku, the "Lake of the White Heron". Herons are still occasionally to be seen on the shores of the lake.

★ Lake Brunner

50km/30 miles east of Greymouth, on a side road off Highway 7, is Lake Hochstetter, named after the German geologist Ferdinand von Hochstetter, which was enlarged by the construction of a dam in 1876. Good fishing; picnic spots.

Lake Hochstetter

Haast Pass

D 11

Regions: Southland and Otago

The Haast Pass (named after the German geologist Julius von Haast), the lowest passage through the Southern Alps (564m/1850ft), provides a link between the Southland region to the west and the area round Lake Wanaka (see entry) in the Otago region. The road follows an ancient Maori track to the deposits of greenstone on the west coast. The road was completed in 1965 after many years' work and is asphalted all the way. It runs through grandiose rugged scenery which is often shrouded in cloud. In winter the road is rarely blocked by snow, since in this area the precipitations mostly fall in the form of rain. There are a number of attractive rest areas.

★ Situation and importance

The old Maori track over the pass was rediscovered by Charles Cameron in 1863 on his way from Dunedin to look for gold on the west coast. Mount Cameron (1763m/5784ft), on the west side of the pass road, is named after him. Cameron was followed soon afterwards by Julius von Haast, first director of Christchurch Museum.

History

Hanmer Springs

G 9

Region: Canterbury
Population: 1200

140km/87 miles north of Christchurch, situated in a sheltered hollow at an altitude of 366m/1200ft, is the spa and holiday resort of Hanmer Springs, noted for its abundantly flowing thermal springs. It is a quiet little place, surrounded by Hanmer Forest, with the hills of the Hanmer Range (skiing in winter) as a backdrop.

★ Situation and importance

The springs, which had long been used by the Maoris for therapeutic purposes, are said to have been discovered in 1859 by the manager of a

History

farm at Culverton. Soon afterwards the government built a sanatorium, a psychiatric clinic and a soldiers' convalescent home. Since 1971 alcoholics have also been treated here.

Spa establishment
The modern spa establishment (with water at a temperature of 38°C/100°F) is open daily from 10am to 8pm.

★Waiau River
For the more adventurous visitors there are jetboat trips and white-water rafting on the nearby Waiau River, as well as bungy jumping from the 31m/102ft high bridge over the river.

★Hanmer Forest
Hanmer Forest covers an area of 17,000 hectares/4250 acres, much of it natural southern beech forest. Various exotic species were planted by convict labour in 1902. Nowadays the new plantings are mainly of Californian pine and Douglas fir, timber from which is sold mainly in Christchurch. There are walks and walking trails, of varying length, through the forest, and the beauties of the scenery can also be seen on a 16km/10 mile long motor road, the Forest Drive; permission to drive on it must be obtained from the local visitor centre.

★Molesworth Station
In summer cross-country vehicles can travel from Hanmer Springs to the remote Molesworth Station, the largest in New Zealand. This former sheep farm with some 180,000 hectares/450,000 acres of grazing land has gradually been acquired by the State. In the past repeated burning of the grass, over-grazing and a plague of rabbits led to severe damage by erosion. Part of the land has now been improved on good ecological principles and provides grazing for cattle rather than sheep.

Hokitika   E/F 9

Region: West Coast
Population: 4000

Situation and importance
The little town of Hokitika lies in a setting of great scenic beauty on the west coast. At the time of the gold rush in the 1860s it had a population of over 10,000, with hotels, theatres, casinos and even an opera house with seating for 1400. Gold is still worked in deep shafts in the Goliath Mine, but the revenue from timber-working is now much greater than from gold-mining.

★Greenstone
Fine jewellery is made from greenstone (jade and nephrite) in specialist workshops. The local deposits of jade were known to the Maoris before the coming of Europeans.

Sights
In the 19th century Hokitika was briefly the seat of the provincial government of Westland, and the old Government Building can still be seen. In front of it is a statue of "King Dick", as Richard Seddon, the local member of Parliament for 27 years and prime minister of New Zealand in the 1890s, is known here. At the town's most important street intersection (Sewell Street/Weld Street) is a clock-tower commemorating the New Zealanders who fell in the Boer War and the coronation of King Edward VII. The West Coast Historical Museum has a collection of Maori weapons and jewellery in greenstone, as well as extensive material on the days of the gold rush. The town's principal landmark is the Neo-Romanesque St Mary's Church (R.C.), built in 1914 in place of an earlier church erected by an Irish immigrant in 1865.

Surroundings

Clock-Tower, Hokitika

20km/12½ miles south of Hokitika are the idyllic Lake Kaniere and the very impressive Dorothy Falls.

Lake Kaniere, Dorothy Falls

25km/15 miles south is the Hokitika River Gorge, with an old suspension bridge, a popular destination for excursions.

Hokitika River Gorge

30km/19 miles south of Hokitika is the village of Ross (pop. 1000), in an area which in the past yielded great quantities of gold. In 1909 a nugget weighing almost 3kg/6½lb was found; it was presented to King George V by the New Zealand government as a coronation gift. When all the gold was worked out the village depended for its survival on its sawmills, limestone quarries and the industrial processing of opossum skins.

Ross

The local visitor centre, housed in a restored gold-digger's cottage, has a small museum of relics of gold-digging days. St Patrick's Church (R.C.) was built by Irish immigrants in 1866.

From Ross the Water Race Walk and the Jones Flat Walk (each 1 hour's walking) lead to the old goldfields.

Invercargill

C 13

Region: Southland
Population: 52,000

Invercargill, New Zealand's southernmost town, lies in an open plain on the banks of the New River estuary. It was laid out from 1856 onwards by the town planner John T. Thomson on a geometric plan, with broad streets and open spaces. It takes its name from William Cargill, one of the Scottish founding fathers of Dunedin; the prefix "inver" refers to its position at the mouth of a river. Many of the streets are named after Scottish rivers.

Situation and history

Originally the New River estuary served as a natural harbour, but its functions as a harbour were later taken over by Bluff, at the southern tip of the South Island. The lush Southland pastures were for many years the town's main source of income; later a number of large slaughterhouses and meat freezing plants were established; and a further boost was given to Invercargill's economy by the construction of an aluminium smelter at Bluff (see below).

Nugget Point, at the southern tip of New Zealand

Sights

★ Southland
Museum and
Art Gallery

Subantarctic
Islands
Interpretive Centre

The town's principal sight is the Southland Museum and Art Gallery. It has fine natural history collections from the Southland region (including petrified wood from nearby Curio Bay) and relics of the wild days of the whalers, but its particular treasures are its examples of Maori arts and crafts. The Art Gallery is housed in a striking pyramid-shaped building at the entrance to Queen's Park. Open: Mon.–Fri. 9am–5pm, Sat.–Sun. 1–5pm.

Tuatara House

The Tuatara House provides near-natural conditions for specimens of this lizard-like reptile dating back to the time of the dinosaurs, which is now very rare.

Queen's Park

Queen's Park, an area of 80 hectares/200 acres with various sports grounds, a duckpond, a game park and a children's playground, is entered from Queen's Drive. The Winter Gardens are open daily.

Town centre

The Town Hall, a symmetrically designed building by E. R. Wilson, was built in 1906; it reflects the prosperity of the town in those days. The Kelvin Chambers of 1864 recall Southland's short-lived independent provincial government: the region broke away from Otago in 1861 but was reincorporated in it in 1870. Lennel House (102 Albert Street), a mansion set in a beautiful garden, was built in 1880 to the design of John T. Thomson; it is still in private ownership.

Churches

The town's principal churches, all built in brick, are close together: St John's (Anglican; 1887), the Neo-Byzantine First Church (Presbyterian; 1915) and St Mary's (R.C.; by F. W. Petre, 1894–1905). St Mary's has a very beautiful interior in white Oamaru limestone.

★ Anderson Park
and Art Gallery

7km/4½ miles north of the town centre is Anderson Park (area 24 hectares/60 acres), with a mansion which belonged to Robert Anderson, a local entrepreneur who presented the whole property to the town. It now houses a large art collection which includes some very fine Maori portraits, early views of Bluff and some good examples of modern New Zealand art. Also in the park is a magnificently carved Maori meeting-house. Open: Tues., Wed., Thur., Sat. and Sun. 2–4.30pm.

Surroundings

10km/6 miles west of Invercargill is beautiful Oreti Beach.

Oreti Beach

30km/19 miles south of Invercargill, at the southern tip of the South Island, is the port of Bluff (pop. 2500), situated on a promontory reaching out into the Foveaux Strait under the Old Man Bluff (265m/869ft), from which there are wide views. The port's main trade is in frozen lamb, and it also has a small fishing fleet. The oysters and crayfish of the Foveaux Strait are much prized. The town's Maritime Museum is devoted to the history of the town and of the oyster fisheries.

There is a ferry service between Bluff and Halfmoon Bay on Stewart Island.

Bluff

On Tiwai Point, on the north-east side of Bluff Harbour, is New Zealand's only aluminium smelter, a joint New Zealand–Japanese enterprise. Since the discovery of large deposits of bauxite at Weipa on the Cape York peninsula in Australia aluminium oxide has been shipped from there to Tiwa Point and smelted in Bluff, the huge quantities of electricity required being provided by the hydro-electric station on Lake Manapouri. The smelter provides employment for some 1200 workers. The aluminium is mainly exported to Japan. Conducted 2-hour tours (no under-12s) by appointment (tel. (03) 218 5494) Mon.–Fri. at 10am.

★Aluminium smelter

Stewart Island (see entry), across the Foveaux Strait from Invercargill, can be visited either by air or by ferry (about 2½ hours from Bluff) to Halfmoon Bay.

Stewart Island

A very attractive alternative to the inland route to Balclutha and Dunedin on Highway 1 is the coast road running through Catlins Forest Park (see entry), with possible side trips to the Cathedral Caves, Tautuku Beach and Nugget Point.

★Coast road to Balclutha

Kaikoura   H 9

Region: Nelson-Marlborough
Population: 2200

The little town of Kaikoura lies on the north-east coast of the South Island at the foot of the Seaward Kaikoura Range, just north of the rocky Kaikoura Peninsula, which is famed for its colony of seals.

The Maori name Kaikoura means "eating crayfish" – a reference to the rich crayfish fishing-grounds which were much prized by the Maoris. In the 19th century whaling also made a major contribution to the economy of the town. There are still a few relics of the old whaling stations in the form of whalebones (e.g. in the Garden of Memories).

Situation and importance

Fyffe House, in Avoca Street, was built around 1860 for a whaler named George Fyffe. It is now protected as a historic monument.

★Fyffe House

The old landing-stage of 1882 recalls the time when the town's only connection with the outer world was by sea. Fishing-boats now moor at the new landing-stage of 1906.

Landing-stage

Some boat-owners offer whale-watching trips.

Whale-watching

Kaikoura

★ Kaikoura
Peninsula

From the northern tip of the peninsula there is a magnificent view of the high hills of the Seaward Kaikoura Range. On the rocks at the end of the peninsula lives a colony of several hundred seals, which can be observed in the course of a short walk from Kaikoura.

Maori
meeting-house

Near the hospital is the Takahara Marae (place of assembly), which has been given a new lease of life by the construction of a modern meeting-house. From the little Maori cemetery there is a good view of the mountains across the bay. The old Maori *pa* was taken in 1828 by Te Rauparaha, the warlike chief from the North Island. From here it is a short distance to the Kaikoura Lookout.

Maori Leap Cave

3km/2 miles south of Kaikoura is the Maori Leap Cave, a karstic sea-cave hollowed out by the surf in which large numbers of bird and seal skeletons were found. Guided visits by arrangement through the local visitor centre.

Karamea   G 8

Region: West Coast
Population: 500

Situation and
importance

Karamea, near the north-western tip of the South Island, is the end-point of the Heaphy Track (see Abel Tasman National Park). It has a dry and sunny climate. In 1874 incomers from Nelson settled in the fertile surrounding area. Until the building of a road from Westport in 1915 Karamea could be reached only by sea or on the Heaphy Track. A severe earthquake in 1929 destroyed the harbour at the mouth of the river.

Wanga Peka Track

South-east of Karamea is the start of the Wanga Peka Track, which runs through the North-West Nelson Forest Park.

★ Fenian Range

To the north of Karamea is the Fenian Range, in which is a whole system of karstic caves. In the Oparara valley are a number of natural bridges formed by the collapse of caves. The Honeycomb Caves, in which the remains of many extinct species of birds were found, can be entered only with special permission from the Department of Conservation.

Lake Manapouri · Manapouri Power Plant   B 12

Region: Southland (Fiordland National Park)

★ Situation

Lake Manapouri, perhaps New Zealand's most beautiful lake, lies 30km/19 miles west of Te Anau. With an area of 142sq.km/55sq. miles, it has not less than three dozen islands and islets. The lake is surrounded on all sides by high hills; only on the east, where the Waiau River flows out of the lake to link it with Lake Te Anau, is the landscape more open. The surface of the lake is 178m/584ft above sea level; at its deepest point (443m/1453ft) the bed of the lake is well below sea level.

In the 1960s plans to raise the level of the lake by 12m/40ft under a proposed hydro-electric scheme to supply power to the aluminium smelter at Bluff aroused fierce controversy and in 1972 led to the fall of the government. Thereafter a compromise was reached under which the water level of the lake was to remain unchanged. The hydro-electric station was installed in a cavern deep under the lake: a technological achievement which draws thousands of visitors every year. (The power plant can be seen only on an organised excursion: see below.)

★★Manapouri power plane

In order to carry out the project it was necessary to construct a new landing-stage for ships carrying equipment and supplies at Deep Cove in Doubtful Sound (see below). These were then carried in trucks up a steep works road and over the Wilmot Pass (671m/2202ft) to the construction site. Nowadays the landing-stage and the road are used mainly for tourist traffic.

Excursion to Doubtful Sound

★★ Organised whole-day excursion

One of the very few fjords in Fiordland National Park easily accessible for tourists is Doubtful Sound. It can only be reached, however, on an organised excursion. Excursions are run throughout the year by Fiordland Travel.

Lake Manapouri

The first stage of the excursion, which starts from Manapouri, is by boat over Lake Manapouri, with its many islands and steep surrounding hills.

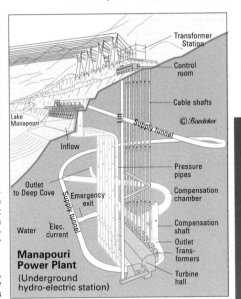

Transformer Station

Control room

Cable shafts

© Baedeker

Lift

Supply tunnel

Lake Manapouri

Inflow

Pressure pipes

Outlet to Deep Cove

Emergency exit

Compensation chamber

Supply tunnel

Water

Elec. current

Compensation shaft

Outlet Trans-formers

Manapouri Power Plant
(Underground hydro-electric station)

Turbine hall

Idyll in Doubtful Sound

Lake Ohau

Underground
power plant

The next stage is by bus to the power plant. A steep spiral tunnel leads up to the underground power plant, where seven giant turbines are installed in a huge cavern 200m/656ft below the surface of the lake.

Deep Cove,
★Doubtful Sound

After a conducted tour of the power plant the bus continues over Wilmot Pass to Deep Cove, at the east end of Doubtful Sound, a fjord running 20km/12½ miles inland between steep rock walls, with many branches and inlets. It was given its name in 1770 by Captain Cook, who did not venture in through the narrow entrance to the fjord, being doubtful whether he would find a harbour there and be able to get out again. After a cruise on a catamaran to the mouth of the fjord on the wild Tasman Sea the bus returns to the power plant; then by boat across Lake Manapouri to Manapouri, with the possibility of continuing by bus to Te Anau.

Lake Ohau   D 11

Region: Canterbury

★Situation and
importance

Lake Ohau, in a beautiful setting 30km/19 miles west of Twizel, forms the boundary between the Canterbury and Otago regions. This glacier lake has an area of 60sq.km/23sq. miles. In good weather the snow-capped peaks of the Southern Alps are mirrored in its waters. It is linked by canal with Lake Pukaki and Lake Tekapo – all three lakes being integrated into the hydro-electric scheme on the upper course of the Waitaki River.

Lake Ohau is a popular holiday resort in summer, attracting large numbers of fishing, boating and camping enthusiasts.

Mount Sutton

Visitors also come here in winter to ski on Mount Sutton, high above the lake.

Lake Pukaki   E 10/11

Region: Canterbury

Situation and
importance

13km/8 miles north of Twizel is Lake Pukaki, the second largest glacier lake in Canterbury region, with an area of 81sq.km/31sq. miles. The mighty Tasman River, fed by melt-water from great glaciers, flows into the north end of the lake, which lies 500m/1640ft above sea level. The lake's high content of "rock flour" (finely ground particles of rock held in the glacial melt-water) gives its water a milky turquoise colour.

Waitaki River
hydro-electric
scheme

With the construction of the Pukaki Dam and Pukaki Canal in the late seventies the lake was incorporated in the hydro-electric scheme on the upper course of the Waitaki River. The dam at the south end of Lake Pukaki, along the top of which Highway 8 runs, was built to control the water level of the lake. The hydro-electric station is near the east side of the lake at the mouth of the Tekapo Canal. Lake Pukaki is also linked with Lake Ohau by a canal.

★To Mount Cook
National Park

The asphalted road to Mount Cook National Park (Highway 80) branches off Highway 8 south-west of Lake Pukaki and runs along the western shore of the lake. In good weather there is a magnificent view of the majestic mountain peaks to the west.

Lake Tekapo   E 10

Region: Canterbury

Lake Tekapo, the largest of the three glacier lakes in Canterbury's Mackenzie Country, with an area of 88sq.km/34sq. miles, lies 50km/31 miles northeast of Twizel in a magnificent setting under the peaks of the Southern Alps, its milky turquoise-coloured waters surrounded by treeless slopes covered with tussock grass.

Situation and
★ topography

At the south end of the lake, near the village of Tekapo, is a dam built in 1954 which enables the level of the lake to be regulated. It is normally between 704m/2310ft and 710m/2330ft above sea level. The first hydro-electric station, Tekapo A, was built in 1951. The second, Tekapo B, was built in 1977 and supplied with water by a 25km/15 mile long canal from Lake Pukaki (see entry) to Lake Tekapo.

Tekapo
power plant

The village of Tekapo (pop. 400) at the south end of Lake Tekapo is famed for the Church of the Good Shepherd, built in 1935 for the herds on the huge sheep farms of the Mackenzie Country. Through the chancel window there is a view of Lake Tekapo and the snow-capped summits of the Southern Alps. Beside the church is a bronze figure of a sheepdog carved by a sheep farmer's wife.

Tekapo
(village)

Sightseeing flights from Tekapo are operated by Air Safaris, taking visitors over the largest glaciers and the highest peaks in the Southern Alps.

★ Sightseeing
flights

16km/10 miles south of Tekapo on Highway 1 is the Irishman Creek farm, where William Hamilton (see Famous People), inventor of the jetboat, once lived. He is commemorated by a small museum.

Irishman Creek

Above Lake Tekapo to the south-east is Burke Pass (671m/2202ft), which carries the road (Highway 8) from the Mackenzie Country to Fairlie. It is named after Michael Burke, who surveyed the area in 1855. His interest in

Burke Pass

The Church of the Good Shepherd on the shores of Lake Tekapo

the area had been aroused during the trial of the sheep-stealer James Mackenzie (see Mackenzie Country), when he heard of the great plains in this highland region where the stolen sheep had been hidden.

Lake Te Anau   B 11/12

Region: Southland (Fiordland National Park)

Situation and ★topography

Lake Te Anau, the largest lake on the South Island (area 344sq.km/133sq. miles) lies in the north-east of Fiordland National Park. With three arms branching off to the west (South, Middle and North Fiords), it reaches deep into the mountain country of the National Park with its dense rain forests. The shores of the lake vary considerably in character; the east side is flat, with less rain, and is almost treeless.

Name

The name of the lake is probably derived from the Maori name for the cave system, which was well known to the Maoris in earlier times, Te Ana Au ("Cave of the Rushing Waters": see below). The caves are difficult of access and were forgotten for many years.

Water level; hydro-electric scheme

The surface of Lake Te Anau is around 200m/650ft above sea level, but the bottom of the lake, which is 417m/1368ft deep, reaches well below sea level.

Lake Te Anau is linked with Lake Manapouri (see entry), and is thus an important element in the Manapouri hydro-electric scheme.

Te Anau (town)

At the south-east end of the lake is the tourist resort of Te Anau (pop. 3000), which has increased enormously in size in recent years (though still not large). It offers a wide range of accommodation for visitors. It is a good base for excursions in Fiordland National Park and the Southern Alps.

Murchison Range

In 1948 a few specimens of the takahe, a flightless bird which was thought to be extinct, were rediscovered in the remote Murchison Range, on the west side of Lake Te Anau.

★★Te Ana Au Caves

In the same area and about the same time the unique glowworm caves were rediscovered after long searching. The Te Ana Au Caves, which are accessible only from the lake, are, in geological terms, very young and have little in the way of stalactitic formations. To a visitor entering the caves through the low entrance passage after the half-hour crossing of the lake, however, they are still extraordinarily impressive. The boat sails into the cave as far as an underground waterfall, from which visitors are taken in another boat to the marvellous Glowworm Cave. Glowworms, the larvae of insects which can live only in conditions of fairly high humidity, produce long sticky threads like a spider's web to which other small insects are attracted by the faint light generated by the glowworms during the digestive process. It is dark and quiet in the Glowworm Cave, with the glowworms twinkling like stars in the night sky. The trip to the caves, which is run by Fiordland Travel, starts and finishes at the Te Anau landing-stage.

★★Milford Road

From Te Anau there is a fascinating drive through the mountain world of Fiordland National Park to Milford Sound (see entry). The Milford Road runs along the east side of the lake and through the Homer Tunnel to reach the world-famed fjord. Fiordland Travel run coach excursions, which can be combined with a cruise on Milford Sound.

★★Milford Track

For keen walkers with a day or two to spare there is the strenuous Milford Track, which runs through scenery of breathtaking beauty. The starting-point is at Glade House, in the valley of the Clinton River, at the northern tip of Lake Te Anau.

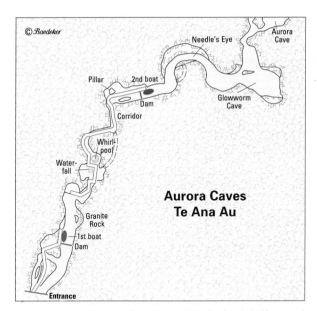

© Baedeker

Needle's Eye

Aurora Cave

Pillar   2nd boat

Dam

Glowworm Cave

Corridor

Whirl-pool

Water-fall

Aurora Caves
Te Ana Au

Granite Rock

1st boat

Dam

Entrance

Another very attractive excursion, taking a whole day, is to Lake Manapouri (see entry) and the underground hydro-electric station on its western arm; then over the Wilmot Pass and down the steep road to Deep Cove, on Doubtful Sound. From there visitors can cruise in a catamaran to the mouth of the sound on the Tasman Sea. This trip is possible only as an organised tour.

★Excursion to Doubtful Sound and Lake Manapouri

From Te Anau a sightseeing flight in a helicopter or seaplane offers an easy way to see the grand mountain scenery of Fiordland National Park and the South Island's world-famed fjords.

★Sightseeing flights

Lake Wanaka   C/D 11

Region: Otago

Drivers of hired cars are usually prohibited from using the 70km/44 mile long rough road (not recommended) from Queenstown (see entry) through the Crown Range and Cardrona; they must take instead the 50km/30 mile longer route on Highway 6 via Cromwell. On its way up to the Haast Pass Highway 6 runs along the north-eastern shore of Lake Wanaka.

Note for car drivers

70km/44 miles north-west of Queenstown is the quietly beautiful Lake Wanaka, set in a mountain world of gently rounded contours. It is 45km/28 miles long, with an area of 193sq.km/75sq. miles. The Clutha River, the mightiest river on the South Island, flows out of the south-east corner of the lake.

Situation and ★topography

From Lake Wanaka, in good weather, there are magnificent panoramic views of the mountains, with the peaks in Mount Aspiring National Park (see entry) visible in the distance. The country round the lake is particularly

★★Mountain panorama

245

beautiful in autumn, when the many deciduous trees brought here from Europe take on their russet colouring. The finest view of the lake is from Glendhu Bay, 14km/8½ miles west of Wanaka village.

History

In earlier times there were Maoris living round the lake and trading in greenstone (jade), which they found in the rivers on the west coast; but raids by tribes from the north around 1836 almost depopulated the area. When the first white men looking for new grazing grounds came here – Dr Chalmers in 1853, John T. Thomson in 1857 and John McLean, who established the first large sheep farms – the land was almost uninhabited.

Gold

Gold was found on the Cardrona River in the 19th century, and within a short time the beds of the Cardona and the Clutha, almost as far up as Lake Wanaka, had been thoroughly dug over by prospectors.

Wanaka
(village)

At the south-east end of the lake is the little township of Wanaka (pop. 2000), the largest settlement for many miles round. It was known as Pembroke until 1940.

Skiing areas

There are good skiing areas at Cardrona (south-west of Wanaka) and on the Treble Cone (west of Lake Wanaka).

Lake Hawea

15km/9 miles north of Wanaka village is Lake Hawea, the smallest of the three alpine lakes in the Otago region (30km/19 miles long, with an area of 140sq.km/54sq. miles). Highway 6 runs along the west side of the lake on its way to the Haast Pass. The village of Lake Hawea, at the south end of the lake, occupies the site of a Maori village which was attacked and destroyed in 1836.

The damming of the lake under the Clutha River hydro-electric scheme in 1958 raised the water level by around 20m/65ft. The water stored in the

Lake Wanaka, against a majestic backdrop of mountains

lake serves as a reserve supply in winter, when the catchment area of the Clutha River is blocked by ice.

The lake, which offers good trout and salmon fishing, is 410m/1345ft deep, so that its bed is 64m/210ft below sea level.

Lawrence   D 12

Region: Otago
Population: 600

90km/56 miles south-west of Dunedin is the little settlement of Lawrence, founded in 1862 and named after General Sir Henry Lawrence, a hero of the Indian Mutiny. It became the first gold-digging town in Otago after a Tasmanian prospector named Thomas Gabriel found rich deposits of alluvial gold nearby, in Gabriel's Gully, and announced his find in a newspaper. Within a short time the little settlement grew to a population of well over 10,000 – twice the size of Dunedin. Gold ceased to be worked in the area in the late 1930s, and Lawrence has now become the commercial centre of a huge farming area.
Situation and history

Lawrence has preserved a number of Victorian buildings dating from its Victorian heyday, including the Courthouse and the Post Office. Anthem House was for many years the home of John J. Woods, a local government official who composed the music of "God defend New Zealand", the country's national anthem. There is an interesting local museum in Ross Place.
Sights

Near the village is the Golden Gully (Gabriel's Gully), where the first gold in the region was discovered. Adjoining it is the Weatherston goldfield, with the ruins of a brewery.
★Golden Gully

11km/7 miles south-east of Lawrence is the little village of Waitahuna, which in the 19th century was also a flourishing gold-diggers' town.
Waitahuna

Lewis Pass   G 9

Region: Canterbury

100km/62 miles west of Hanmer Springs (see entry) Highway 7 goes over the Lewis Pass (864m/2835ft). The pass road, which links the Canterbury region with the north-west coast of the South Island, was completed in 1937. This route through the mountains was well known to the Maori tribes of the region, who used it on their way to the deposits of greenstone in the rivers on the west coast. Cannibal Gorge, near the summit of the pass, recalls the days when the Maori caravans making for the west coast took slaves with them as carriers; then on the way back, it is said, the slaves were killed and eaten.
★Pass road

There are a number of short trails starting from the summit of the pass (e.g. Tarn Nature Walk, Lewis Pass Lookout Walk). The St James Track (70km/44 miles) over the Ada Pass and Anne Saddle takes five days.
Walks from summit of pass

One place of interest on the road, which runs through scenery of great beauty, is the old Hurunui Hotel of 1869, which has been well restored. Farther on is the little spa of Maruia Springs. with hot springs.
Hurunui Hotel, Maruia Springs

At Springs Junction, 20km/12½ miles west of the pass, a road goes off on the south to the very beautiful Lake Sumner Forest Park. There are various attractive walking trails in this dense forest of southern beeches round Lake Sumner, the Robinson River and Lake Christabel.
★Lake Sumner Forest Park

Mackenzie Country   D/E 10/11

Region: Canterbury

Situation and topography

The Mackenzie Country is a highland region of some 5000sq.km/ 1930sq. miles lying below the mountains of the Southern Alps within which are the three large glacier lakes Tekapo, Pukaki and Ohau. It can be reached from the east either by way of the Burke Pass (Highway 8) or by the little known Mackenzie Pass (unmetalled track), to the south of the Burke Pass. This bare plateau covered with tussock grass, cold and snow-bound in winter, was settled mainly by Scottish sheep farmers with experience of hill farming.

Name

The region takes its name from a Scottish shepherd and sheep-stealer called James (Jock) Mackenzie, who is said to have stolen whole flocks of sheep in 1855 and driven his booty over a pass which he had discovered into this still unexplored highland region. He was assisted in his thefts by a marvellously skilled sheepdog named Friday. He was finally arrested – an event commemorated by a memorial stone on the Mackenzie Pass – and imprisoned in Lyttelton jail. He and his dog soon became legendary figures throughout the country, the subject of innumerable stories.

Farming

Sheep-farming, once practised on a large scale here, is now in decline. Some sheep farms have been turned into game farms surrounded by high wire fences.

Upper Waikati Power Development Scheme

In recent decades the Mackenzie Country has been much changed by the huge hydro-electric projects of the Upper Waikati Power Development Scheme. The large glacier lakes have been dammed, land on their shores has been drowned by rises in water level and new artificial lakes such as Lake Benmore have been created.

Twizel

The centre of all this activity is Twizel (pop. 1800), the largest place in this sparsely populated highland region.

Tourism

The Mackenzie Country has been opened up for tourism by the asphalted Highway 8. Large numbers of visitors now come here, attracted mainly by the glacier lakes but also, increasingly, by the recently established skiing areas; many others pass through the region on their way to Mount Cook National Park.

Fairlie

On Highway 8, an hour's drive north-west of Timaru, is the little township of Fairlie (Canterbury region; pop. 800), the commercial and administrative centre of the Mackenzie Country. It is named after Fairlie in Ayrshire, the home town of the owner of the town's first hotel. Until 1968 it was the terminus of a railway line from Timaru. The Transport Museum of the Mackenzie Carnival Society displays old carnival floats, coaches and agricultural equipment. The old railway station is incorporated in the museum. Nearby is an old smithy, grandly named the Mabel Binney Cottage Museum.

Two Thumb Ranges

Near Fairlie are the Two Thumb Ranges. Mount Dobson (50km/31 miles north-west of Fairlie) and Fox Peak (40km/25 miles north of Fairlie by way of Clinton) are popular winter sports areas.

★ Lindis Pass

Lindis Pass (970m/3183ft) links the alpine landscapes of the Mackenzie Country with the bare and arid hills of central Otago. The old Maori track through the hills was rediscovered by John T. Thomson while surveying this region in 1857 and was soon travelled by large numbers of gold prospectors. In the valley of the Lindis River a number of old farmsteads dating from the time of the early settlers can still be seen; particularly notable is Morven Hills farm.

Marlborough Sounds Maritime Park   H/I 7/8

Region: Nelson-Marlborough

The Marlborough Sounds, at the north-east corner of the South Island, are one of the most popular holiday areas in New Zealand – a system of drowned river valleys with an intricate pattern of waterways, islands, beaches and wooded hills forming a landscape of marvellous beauty. This much indented coast with its myriad of islets and inlets offers endless scope for boating enthusiasts, anglers and campers. On land, too, this is a quiet and peaceful area, for the roads running along the drowned valleys are narrow, winding, steep and usually not asphalted.

Situation and
★★ topography

The Marlborough Sounds are named after the Duke of Marlborough, a war hero like those other heroes who have given their names to places in New Zealand, Nelson and Wellington.

Name

Maori tradition has it that the two legendary figures Kupe and Ngahue, while fishing in Hawaiki, found a giant octopus eating their prey and pursued it across the Pacific. Kupe almost caught it in a cave on the Wairarapa coast of the North Island (near present-day Castlepoint) but it got away and was finally caught and killed in the labyrinthine waters of the Marlborough Sounds.

Maori mythology

Captain Cook, like many after him, liked this sunny region of water and hills. On his first visit in January 1770 he climbed a hill on Arapawa Island and, seeing the open sea to the east, realised – as Abel Tasman had done before him – that the North and South Islands of New Zealand were separate. Cook took possession of the South Island in the name of King George III and named Charlotte Sound after his queen. On his second voyage Cook put in at Ship Cove several times.

History

Later explorers like the French navigator Dumont d'Urville were taken by the beauty and the mild climate of the region. D'Urville discovered that the large island to the north which now bears his name was indeed an island and not part of the mainland.

From 1827 onwards whalers began to settle in the Sounds, including John Blenkinsopp, whose dubious land deal with Chief Te Rauparaha led to the Wairau affray, the only serious clash between Maoris and Pakehas (whites) on the South Island.

Some years later the first sheep-farmers arrived. Huge sheep farms were established inland from the Marlborough Sounds and steadily expanded. By 1870 there were more than a million sheep in the region.

In the 20th century sheep-farming in the area declined and there was a switch to fruit-growing and wine-production, for which the local climate was particularly suitable.

The Marlborough Sounds made headline news in 1986 when a Soviet cruise ship, the "Mikhail Lermontov", sank in Port Gore.

At the north-east corner of the South Island, 40km/25 miles north-west of Blenheim (see entry), is the little township of Havelock (pop. 500), in a setting of great beauty in the Marlborough Sounds. The settlement, named after General Sir Henry Havelock, who distinguished himself in the Indian Mutiny, was established on the site of an old Maori village to supply the needs of gold-diggers working at Wakamarina, 10km/6 miles west. The inhabitants now live mainly by fish-farming (mostly shellfish) in the inlets of the Marlborough Sounds.

Havelock

Havelock's other claim to fame is that the atomic physicist Ernest Rutherford and the missile scientist William Pickering went to school here. The old schoolhouse is now a youth hostel. In the former Methodist church is a memorial room commemorating Rutherford and Pickering.

249

The Marlborough Sounds: a paradise for nature-lovers and sailing enthusiasts

Pelorus Bridge	At Pelorus Bridge, 20km/12½ miles farther west, on the river, is a Scenic Reserve with a number of attractive walking trails. From Pelorus Bridge a road runs into the romantic Maungatapu Valley, through which the old road from Blenheim to Nelson (see entries) pursues a winding course.
Walks ★★ Endeavour Track	This path follows the footsteps of Captain Cook from Camp Bay over the Kenepuru Saddle to Ship Cove. The walk takes about 10 hours; on the way there are a modest inn and a number of possible camping sites.
★ Nydia Track	The very attractive Nydia Track starts from Mahau Sound, goes over the Kaiuma Saddle into Nydia Bay and continues to Tennyson Inlet. It is also a 10-hour walk; camping facilities in Nydia Bay.
Boat trips	A variety of boat trips in the Marlborough Sounds, either regular services or charters, are on offer from Picton and Havelock. A trip in a sailing boat has a particular appeal. At some places dinghies, luxurious yachts and large catamarans can be hired. Information from the Marlborough Sounds Maritime Park office in Auckland Street, Picton.

Milford Sound   B 11

Region: Southland (Fiordland National Park)

Getting there	By car or bus: from Te Anau (see Lake Te Anau) on Highway 94 to Milford (120km/75 miles). By air: from Queenstown and Te Anau.

Fiordland National Park Headquarters, Te Anau.

On the south-west coast of the South Island is one of New Zealand's scenic jewels, Milford Sound. Its very characteristic landscape is familiar from many photographs: in the foreground lush green vegetation, beyond this the still blue waters of the fjord and as a backdrop the massive pyramidal bulk of Mitre Peak.

Among the first white men to see this magnificent scenery was Captain Stokes, who put into the sound in the survey ship HMS "Acheron" in 1851. He anchored near the Bowen Falls and named the peak towering above the bay to a height of 1692m/5551ft Mitre Peak, from its resemblance to a bishop's mitre.

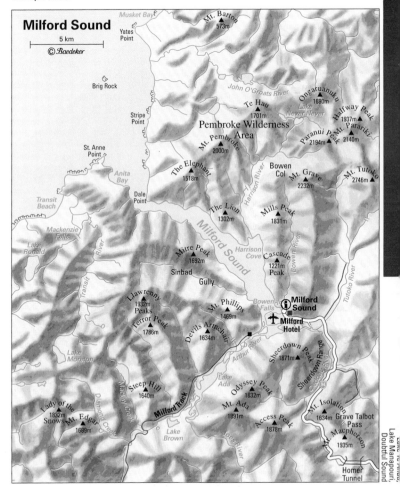

Milford Sound

5 km

© Baedeker

Musket Bay

Yates Point

Mt. Barton
573m

Brig Rock

John O'Groats River

Ongaruanuku
1690m

Te Hau
1701m

Lake Never Never

Halfway Peak
1937m

Stripe Point

Pembroke Wilderness Area

Mt. Pembroke
2000m

Paranui Pk
2194m

Mt. Parariki
2140m

St. Anne Point

The Elephant
1518m

Bowen Col

Mt. Grave
2232m

Mt. Tutoko
2746m

Anita Bay

Dale Point

The Lion
1302m

Harrison River

Mills Peak
1831m

Transit Beach

Mackenzie Falls

Lake Ronald

Milford Sound

Harrison Cove

Cascade Peak
1221m

Bowen River

Tutoko River

Transit River

Mitre Peak
1692m

Sinbad Gully

Llawrenny Peaks
1932m

Mt. Phillips
1469m

Bowen Falls

ⓘ Milford Sound

✝ Milford Hotel

Terror Peak
1786m

Devils Armchair
1634m

Arthur River

Sheerdown Peak
1871m

Lake Moreton

Steep Hill
1640m

Lake Ada

Odyssey Peak
1832m

Sheerdown Range

Lady of the Snows
1832m

Mt. Edgar
1699m

Milford Track

Mackay Creek

Diamond Creek

Mt. Ada
1891m

Access Peak
1878m

Mt. Isolation
1634m

Grave Talbot Pass

Mt. Macpherson
1935m

Lake Brown

Joes River

Homer Tunnel

Milford Sound extends inland for 15km/9 miles from its narrow mouth on the Tasman Sea. The high hills which enclose it rise steeply above the water. Rainfall is high at an annual 6000mm/240in.

In pre-European days the Maoris came here in the quest for greenstone. Then in the early 19th century seal-hunters found their way into the area. Among them was a Welshman called John Crano, who named the sound after Milford Haven in South Wales. The fjord became more widely known after Captain Stokes's visit. Then in 1878 a Scotsman named John Sutherland, a former soldier and seaman, came here to live the life of a hermit. He discovered the 580m/1900ft high Sutherland Falls, some distance inland, which can be seen only from the Milford Track. Quintin Mackinnon, another Scot, surveyed the land route to Milford Sound and discovered the Mackinnon Pass. Later, when increasing numbers of people began to come here, John Sutherland built an inn on Milford Sound which in 1923 was acquired by the State and enlarged.

History

The beautiful mountain road (120km/75 miles) from Te Anau (see Lake Te Anau) through the Eglinton Valley and the Homer Tunnel (named after a surveyor named Henry Homer) has made Milford Sound an easily accessible and very popular tourist attraction. (Note that in winter the road may be temporarily blocked by avalanches.)

★From Te Anau to Milford Sound

A variety of boat trips are on offer from Milford (book in high season). The sailing ship "Milford Wanderer" goes on cruises lasting several days to the many fjords along the coast (including Doubtful Sound), also ½ day trips. The finest views of the landscape are to be had from the water.

★Boat trips

The Milford Track, New Zealand's best known walking trail, is 54km/34 miles long and can be walked in four to five days. It begins at Glade House, near the north end of Lake Te Anau (see entry), and at first follows the Clinton River. It then continues through rain forest and a landscape of alpine aspect, going over the Mackinnon Pass, passing the wild and romantic Sutherland Falls and finally running down into the valley of the Arthur River.

★★Milford Track

The track, which is usually only passable from November to March, may be walked only in one direction, from Glade House to Milford Sound; walking in the opposite direction is not allowed. Walkers going on their own must put their names down at the Fiordland National Park office. Guided walks can be booked through travel agencies. The return from Milford Sound to Te Anau, after the usual boat trip, is by bus. In view of the high probability of rain suitable protective clothing should be taken. Insect repellents are also essential equipment, for the tiny black sandflies are a perpetual plague. The Maori tradition is that the goddess of death created sandflies in order to sour men's enjoyment of the perfect beauty of the landscape.

It is a short walk from Milford to the 160m/525ft high Bowen Falls, which plunge down from a hanging valley. They are named after a former governor.

★Bowen Falls

The wild Sutherland Falls can be seen only by walking the Milford Track. They are too far away to be seen on a day trip.

★Sutherland Falls

Mount Aspiring National Park

C/D 10/11

Regions: Otago and West Coast
Area: 3555sq.km/1373sq. miles

◀ *Mountain and meadow in the Milford Sound*

Mount Aspiring National Park

Information	Mount Aspiring National Park Headquarters and Visitor Centre, Wanaka; ranger stations at Glenorchy on Lake Wakatipu and Makarora on the Haast Pass road (Highway 6).
Situation and ★★topography	New Zealand's second largest National Park, a region of alpine landscape bordering on Fiordland National Park (see entry) to the south, centres on "New Zealand's Matterhorn", the 3027m/9932ft high Mount Aspiring, a massive rock pyramid which was given its name by the surveyor John T. Thomson, who saw it from a distance in 1857. It was first climbed in 1909. Round this giant cluster are other high peaks, forming a mighty mountain rampart when seen from a distance. Lake Wanaka and Lake Wakatipu are fed by rivers flowing down from the Mount Aspiring massif. The National Park displays almost the complete range of glacial land-forms, including glacier lakes, ground, lateral and terminal moraines, *roches moutonnées,* hanging valleys and glacial striations. The main access route is the Haast Pass road (Highway 6), an impressive mountain road which runs along the east side of Lake Wanaka and bounds the National Park on the north.
View of Mount Aspiring	The road from Wanaka through the Matukituki valley runs close to Mount Aspiring. It can often be first seen from Glendhu Bay, south-west of Wanaka.

Walks on Mount Aspiring

★★Routeburn Track	This magnificent mountain track begins in Fiordland National Park, on the road to Milford Sound (see entry) and continues through Mount Aspiring National Park to the north end of Lake Wakatipu (see Queenstown). The walk takes four days. There are guided walks along the track and on sections of it.

Mount Aspiring, which soars to over 3000 metres (10,000 feet)

This four-day walk – almost a round trip – begins at Paradise, near the north end of Lake Wakatipu, and ends at the Invincible Mine in the valley of the Rees River.

Rees-Dart Track

This track follows the course of the Wilkin River and then runs close to the eastern boundary of the National Park to the junction of the Wilkin with the Makarora River, to the south of the Makarora ranger station (Highway 6).

Wilkin Valley Track

Mount Cook National Park   D/E 10

Region: Canterbury
Area: 700.13sq.km/270sq. miles

Mount Cook National Park, which marches on the west with Westland National Park (containing the Fox and Franz Josef Glaciers), is readily accessible in spite of the relatively high altitude at which it lies.
   From Twizel and Lake Pukaki (see entry) an asphalted road (Highway 80) runs through magnificent mountain scenery to the little township of Mount Cook.
   From Christchurch and Queenstown there are flights by light aircraft to the Mount Cook airstrip.

Getting there

Mount Cook National Park Headquarters and Visitor Centre, Mount Cook.
   The Mount Cook visitor centre offers full information on the geology, flora and fauna and vulnerable ecology of this mountain region. Here too can be obtained information about the condition of tracks, rock-climbing and glacier routes and skiing facilities.

Information

The high-altitude skiing areas on Mount Cook offer skiing practically all year round. There are no ski-lifts, but light aircraft and helicopters fitted with runners take skiers up to the ski fields.

Skiing

Mount Cook National Park takes in the heart of the Southern Alps and their highest peaks. Round the highest peaks of all, Mount Cook (3754m/12,314ft) and Mount Tasman (3496m/11,470ft) cluster 15 other peaks over 3000m/9840ft and some 200 others over 2500m/8200ft. Through the National Park extends the Tasman Glacier, the largest in the Southern Alps, 29km/18 miles long and up to 3km/2 miles wide. Like most of the world's glaciers, it is steadily retreating.
   In December 1991 Mount Cook lost 11m/36ft in height when a massive avalanche of snow, ice and rock detritus plunged off the summit.
   The game introduced into the park in the early 20th century, mostly from Europe, have multiplied to such an extent as to become a real plague. Large numbers of animals have had to be culled, captured or kept in game farms.

Situation and
★★ topography

Probably Abel Tasman and Captain Cook did not see the mountains named after them when they sailed along the west coast of the South Island, since the country's highest peaks are likely to have been shrouded in clouds as they so often are today. The highest peak was named after Cook by Captain Stokes, who made a careful survey of the coasts of New Zealand in HMS "Acheron" in 1851. Mount Tasman was given its name eleven years later by the German geologist Julius von Haast. Mount Cook was first climbed on Christmas Day in 1894.

History

The little tourist resort of Mount Cook (alt. 762m/2500ft; pop. 600) lies at the foot of Mount Sefton, with a grandiose backdrop of mountains. It has a luxury hotel, the Hermitage, a number of chalets and, 2km/1¼ miles away at White Horse Flat, a large camping site. There is another large camping site at the tourist village of Glentanner Park, 20km/12½ miles south.

Mount Cook
(village)

The Copland Track, the finest but also most strenuous mountain trail in Mount Cook National Park, runs right across the park and into Westland National Park (see entry). It goes over the Copland Pass (2149m/7051ft) and

Walks
★★ Copland Track

255

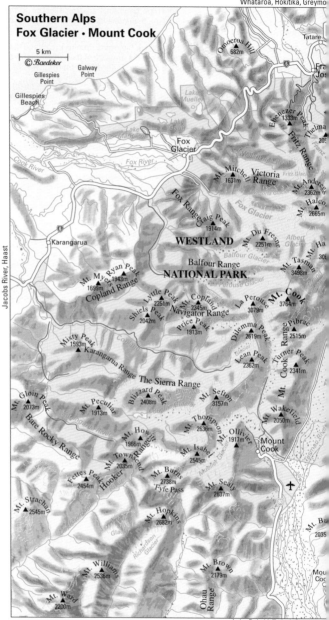

Southern Alps
Fox Glacier · Mount Cook

5 km

© Baedeker

Gillespies
Point

Galway
Point

Gillespies
Beach

Omoeroa Hill
682m

Tatare

Fra
Jos

Lake
Mueller

Lake
Saun

Ebenezer Peak
1333m

Thelma
205

Fritz Range

Fox
Glacier

Fox River

Cook River

Lake
Matheson

Mt. Mitchell
1631m

Victoria
Range

Waikukupa River

Fritz Glacier

Mt. Anderson
2362m

Mt. Halco
2665m

Fox Range

Craig Peak
1914m

WESTLAND

Mt. Du Fresne
2251m

Albert
Glacie

Mt. Ha
30(

Karangarua

Balfour Range

NATIONAL PARK

Balfour Glacier

Mt. Tasman
3498m

Jacobs River, Haast

Mt. Myross
1699m

Ryan Peak
1943m

Copland Range

La Perouse
3079m

Mt. Cook
3764m

Little Peak
2251m

Mt. Copland
2345m

Navigator Range

Shiels Peak
2042m

Price Peak
1913m

Pibrac
2515m

Dilemma Peak
2619m

Mt. Cook Range

Misty Peak
1593m

Karangarua Range

Lean Peak
2362m

Turner Peak
2341m

The Sierra Range

Mt. Gloin Peak
2073m

Mt. Peculiar
1913m

Blizzard Peak
2408m

Mt. Sefton
3157m

Mt. Wakefield
2050m

Bare Rocky Range

Mt. Thompson
2636m

Mt. Ollivier
1917m

Mount
Cook

Mt. Howitt
1966m

Mt. Townsend
2035m

Hooker Range

Mt. Isabel
2545m

Fettes Peak
2454m

Mt. Burns
2738m

Tyfe Pass

Mt. Sealy
2637m

Mt. Strachan
2545m

Mt. Hopkins
2682m

Mt. Bu
2035

Richardson
Glacier

Mou
Coc

Mt. Williams
2536m

Mt. Brown
2179m

Ohau
Range

Mt. Ward
2200m

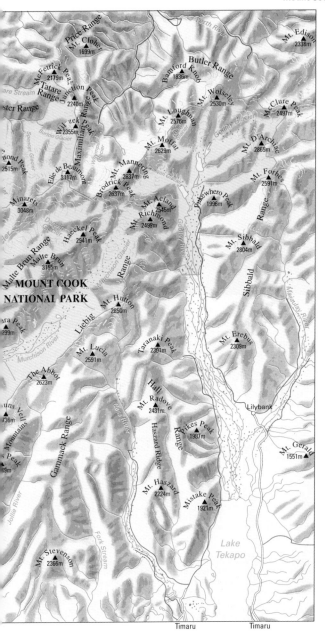

Mt. Edison
2338m

Price Range
Mt. Cloher
1699m

Butler Range
Bamford Knob
1836m

McFetrick Peak
2179m

Mt. Wolseley
2530m

Tatare Range
Junction Peak
2240m

McClure Peak
2497m

are Stream

ster Range

Mt. Loughnan
2576m

Wilczek Peak
2355m

Maximilian Range

Mt. D'Archiac
2865m

mond Peak
2515m

Mt. Moffat
2629m

Elie de Beaumont
3117m

Mt. Mannering
2637m

Mt. Forbes
2591m

Minarets
3048m

Brodrick Peak
2637m

Pukewhero Peak
1996m

Mt. Acland
2545m

Mt. Richmond
2499m

Range

Haeckel Peak
2941m

Mt. Sibbald
2804m

Malte Brun Range
Malte Brun
3155m

Range

Sibbald

MOUNT COOK
NATIONAL PARK

Mt. Hutton
2850m

Liebig

ara Peak
299m

Mt. Erebus
2309m

Murchison River

Mt. Lucia
2591m

Taranaki Peak
2391m

The Abbot
2623m

Hall

uns Veil
736m

Mt. Radove
2431m

Gammack Range

Mt. Gerald
1551m

Range

Pikes Peak
1997m

Peak
9m

Haszard Ridge

Lilybank

Jollie River

Mt. Haszard
2224m

Mistake Peak
1921m

Fork Stream

Mt. Stevenson
2366m

Lake
Tekapo

Timaru   Timaru

257

Mount Cook – king of the Southern Alps

climbs into the fields of névé on the majestic summits. This walk, for which three to four days must be allowed, is for thoroughly experienced walks and climbers only and should only be done with a local guide.

There are many other waymarked walks and trails of varying length in Mount Cook National Park, for example the Bowen Track, the Governor's Bush Walk, the Kea Point Walk, the Hooker Valley Walk, the Red Tarns Track and the Wakefield Track, all of them offering breathtaking views. Detailed descriptions of the routes can be obtained in the visitor centre in Mount Cook village.

★★ **Sightseeing flights**

Scenic flights from Mount Cook village offer tremendous bird's eye views of the summits and glaciers of Mount Cook National Park and Westland National Park. A landing on the Tasman Glacier or a snowfield is usually included.

Nelson

H 8

Region: Nelson-Marlborough
Population: 48,000

Situation and importance

The port town of Nelson lies on the south-east side of Tasman Bay, in an area famed for its mild climate. In its fertile hinterland various kinds of fruit aimed at the export market (particularly apples and pears) are grown, as well as wine grapes, hops and tobacco. In the surrounding hills there is a lucrative forestry industry, producing timber which is processed in the Nelson area and shipped from the port. The population of the area is increasing dynamically, growing within a decade by over 5%.

The town's harbour, Nelson Haven, is sheltered by a long breakwater. The town itself has many old wooden houses, both mansions and cottages. Its modern amenities include seafront promenades and many parks and gardens.

The ★ town

In recent years Nelson's beautiful situation has attracted many artists and craftsmen. South of the town on the road to Richmond is the Craft Habitat, an arts and crafts centre.

Artists' colony

Abel Tasman was the first European to anchor in the bay which now bears his name, in 1642. He did not land because the Maoris had attacked his ship's boat. In pre-European times Maori tribes from the North Island frequently crossed to the Nelson area, attracted by the rich fishing grounds and the deposits of greenstone. In the late 1820s Te Rauparaha and his allies several times attacked the villages and fortified settlements in Tasman Bay, and when William Wakefield came here in 1839 in search of new land he found only a few Maoris living in the Nelson area. The first settlers arrived in 1842, and the population soon grew to over 2000. A year later they were joined by large parties of German immigrants, led by a well-to-do businessman and wine-grower named Johann Beit. Many of them settled in a valley at the south end of Tasman Bay and established a thriving farming community. In 1858 Nelson, which then had a population of just under 3000, became the first settlement in New Zealand to be granted the status of a borough. It was then enjoying something of a boom, thanks mainly to the finding of gold to the north-west and east of the town. In 1862 the first horse-drawn railway was established to transport copper from the Dun Mountains, 20km/12½ miles away, to the port. The great physicist Lord Rutherford (see Famous People) was born in Nelson in 1871.

History

The town was named after the great naval hero. Its main street is called Trafalgar Street.

Name

Sights of Nelson and Surroundings

A brochure describing a 30km/19 mile long "scenic drive" round the town can be obtained from the Visitor and Information Centre at the corner of Trafalgar and Halifax Streets.

City tour

Every Saturday morning there is a flea market on the Montgomery car park (reached by way of Trafalgar Street, Hardy Street and Bridge Street).

Flea market

Prominently situated in Trafalgar Square is Christ Church Cathedral, on the site of a Maori *pa* destroyed by Te Rauparaha. In 1842 the New Zealand Company established a settlement here. After the Wairau affray the settlers, fearful of attack, fortified the settlement, calling it Fort Arthur in honour of their leader Arthur Wakefield, who had been killed in the affray. The first church was built on this site in 1850. Work on the Cathedral was begun in 1925, and after various changes to the plan, partly to make the building earthquake-proof, it was finally completed in 1967.

Christ Church Cathedral

The town's busy main artery is Trafalgar Street, lined with many shops. A notable building in the street is Melrose House, an Italian-style mansion built about 1875 which is now used by the municipality for ceremonial occasions. At the south end of the street is another handsome mansion, Fairfield House (1883).

Trafalgar Street

In Milton Street are two grand houses, Fellworth House and Grove House, built for wealthy local businessmen in the second half of the 19th century.

Milton Street

Botanical Hill (250m/820ft), covered with gardens, is regarded as the geographical centre of New Zealand. From the top of the hill there is a fine view of the town.

Botanical Hill

Nelson Lakes National Park

★Suter
Art Gallery

The Suter Art Gallery (open: daily 10.30am–4.30pm), between Bridge Street and Hardy Street, was founded by Bishop Suter in 1889. It has an excellent collection of pictures, with works by Woollaston, Gully, Lindauer, Van der Velden, Hodgkins and Richmond. Close by, in Nile Street, is an exhibition of works by native artists (open: daily 10am–5pm).

Near here are a number of cottages built in the 1860s for military personnel.

Bishop's School

The Bishop's School in Nile Street was built in 1844 on the initiative of Bishop Selwyn. It is furnished in the style of its period and is open to the public as a museum.

Nelson Haven

Nelson's harbour is a scene of busy activity. From here every conceivable type of New Zealand produce is shipped, particularly fruit, wine, timber and timber products. A cruise round the harbour gives a good impression of what is going on.

★Nelson
Provincial
Museum

In Isel Park, in the south-western district of Stoke, is Nelson Provincial Museum, which is devoted to the history of the town and the region. In addition to an excellent collection of Maori objects it has much interesting material on the Wairau affray, the only serious clash between Maoris and whites on the South Island. Open: Tues.–Fri. 10am–4pm, Sat. and Sun. 2–5pm.

Isel House

This 19th century mansion beside the Museum is furnished in the style of its period and is open to the public at weekends from October to Easter.

Broadgreen House

Broadgreen House, in Nayland Road, is another 19th century mansion with beautifully decorated windows, gable and porch. It is open to the public in summer, usually in the afternoon.

★Founders Park

2km/1¼ miles north of the town centre, in Atwhawai Drive, is the Founders Park, an open-air museum in which various buildings of the Victorian period (some of them reconstructions) are displayed. Of particular interest are an old windmill and an exhibition on the history of Nelson Haven.

★Princess Drive

From Princess Drive, the road to the Davis Lookout, there are a series of fine views.

Beaches

At the end of Rocks Road is Tahunanui Beach, the most popular of the town's beaches. Also popular are the beaches of Rabbit Island (25km/15 miles west) and Cable Bay (23km/14 miles north-east).

★Mount
Richmond
Forest Park

The densely wooded and very beautiful Mount Richmond Forest Park extends to the south and east of Nelson, over the hills of the Richmond Range and down into the valley of the Wairau River. A very popular walking trail is the Wakamarina–Onamalutu Track, which follows in the footsteps of the gold prospectors. The walk, which begins 20km/12½ miles south of Canvastown, takes two days.

★North-West
Nelson
Forest Park

The North-West Nelson Forest Park covers 3760sq.km/1452sq. miles of densely wooded mountain country extending from Tasman Bay (Motueka valley) over the Tasman Mountains to the west coast (Karamea Bay). A number of walking trails run through this primeval landscape with its expanses of lush vegetation. The best known are the Heaphy Track (see Abel Tasman National Park) and the Wangapeka Track (a four-day walk).

Nelson Lakes National Park   G 8/9

Region: Nelson-Marlborough
Area: 960sq.km/370sq. miles

Nelson Lakes National Park lies 120km/75 miles south of Nelson (see entry) and 100km/62 miles south-west of Blenheim (see entry). The gateway to the park is the township of St Arnaud on Highway 63.

Situation

Nelson Lakes National Park Headquarters and Visitor Centre, St Arnaud; ranger station on Lake Rotoroa.

Information

The National Park covers a wide expanse of wild mountain country traversed by the very visible Alpine Fault. This fault explains the difference in height between the hills to the north-east, which rise to over 2000m/6560ft, and those to the north-west, which are only around 1000m/3280ft high. The National Park is bounded on the east by the high St Arnaud Range. The highest peaks are snow-capped until well into summer. At a number of points in the park, particularly on the shores of lakes, there are expanses of dense beech and rain forest.

★Topography

Two long narrow lakes, Lake Rotoiti (alt. 610m/2000ft) and Lake Rotoroa, which lies around 100m lower, occupy valleys once gouged out by glaciers and closed off by terminal moraines. A minor road leads to Lake Rotoiti, which attracts water sports enthusiasts and others seeking a relaxing holiday. Lake Rotoroa is difficult to get to and therefore quieter; it attracts mainly anglers.

Lake Rotoiti, Lake Rotoroa

This rugged mountain country was first explored from Nelson. The first white man to reach Lake Rotoiti, in 1842, was a young surveyor called John S. Cotterell, who was killed in the Wairau affray in the following year. Lake Rotoroa was discovered in 1846 by William Fox, later prime minister of New Zealand, the surveyor Thomas Brunner and a Maori named Kehu. Soon afterwards Brunner and Kehu set out on a strenuous journey of exploration, lasting two years, in the north-west of the South Island. In 1859 the geologist Julius von Haast was commissioned by the provincial government to survey the wild mountain country and in the course of his travels gave names to some of the mountains and rivers in the National Park.

History

There are a number of trails of varying length in the National Park. There are longer walks in the Travers, Sabine and D'Urville valleys.
   Descriptions of the various routes can be obtained in the visitor centre in St Arnaud and the ranger station on Lake Rotoroa.

Walks

There are skiing areas on Mount Robert (south-west of Lake Rotoiti) and at Rainbow (25km/15 miles south of St Arnaud).

Winter sports

Oamaru

E 12

Region: Otago
Population: 14,000

Oamaru, situated 120km/75 miles north of Dunedin on Cape Wanbrow, is the commercial centre of northern Otago. The town rose to great prosperity in the 19th century. The climate is dry and warm. Inland from the town are extensive market gardens; beyond these, farther inland, is a region of intensive sheep-farming.
   Oamaru is also a busy port, thanks to the construction of a breakwater. An important contribution to the town's economy is made by the production of frozen meat, which is exported by sea.

Situation and importance

The white Oamaru limestone worked in many quarries in the surrounding area was used in the construction of many public buildings in New Zealand

Oamaru limestone

and even in Australia. The stone is easy to work when freshly quarried but hardens when exposed to dry air.

Sights

The town's principal sights can be seen on a signposted Historic Walk which starts from the Boer War memorial in Thames Street. The most notable monuments are the Court House (by Forrester and Lemon, 1883), the Athenaeum (1882), which houses the North Otago Museum (open: Mon.–Fri. 10am–4.30pm), the simple Old Post Office of 1864 and the imposing New Post Office of 1884 with its striking clock-towers. Opposite the post offices are two imposing banks designed by R. A. Lawson, the National Bank (1871) and the Bank of New South Wales (1883), which is now occupied by the Forrester Art Gallery (open: Mon.–Fri. 10am–4.30pm, Sun. 1–4.30pm). Notable churches are St Luke's (Anglican; 1865), at the corner of Itchen Street and Thames Street, St Paul's (Presbyterian; 1876), in Coquet Street, and St Patrick's (R.C.; 1893), in Usk Street.

Surroundings

★Totara Estate

8km/5 miles south of Oamaru on Highway 1 is the Totara Estate, where frozen meat was first produced in this area. Visitors can see round the old slaughterhouses and production plant. The trim farmhouse (1868) stands in the shade of tall trees. On the nearby hill is a monument to Thomas Brydone, who established frozen meat production in this area.

★Clark's Mill

4km/2½ miles farther south is Clark's Mill (1865), the only surviving water-mill in the Oamaru area, now preserved as an industrial monument.

★★Moeraki Boulders

35km/22 miles south of Oamaru, scattered about on the beach, are the Moeraki Boulders – massive spherical rocks up to 3m/10ft in diameter and weighing several tons. In Maori tradition they are calabashes and food

The Moeraki Boulders

baskets thrown ashore from the ancestral canoe many ages ago and now turned to stone.

The scientific explanation is that the boulders were formed on the sea-bed millions of years ago by the deposit of chemical concretions on hard cores. When the sea-bed was thrust upwards they were washed out of the softer rock by the surf and left on the beach. Some of them are still embedded in the rock. The net patterns on the surface of the boulders were produced by the extrusion of calcites.

Although the boulders are strictly protected as natural monuments, the smaller ones, regrettably, are steadily disappearing.

The pretty fishing village of Moeraki has a mainly Maori population. In the past there was a whaling station here.

Moeraki

Otago (region)

C–E 11–13

The Otago region, which is bounded on the north by the wide Waitaki River and on the south by Catlins Forest Park, takes in the green and often mist-shrouded coastal area in which the chief towns are Balclutha in the north, Dunedin in the middle and Oamaru in the north. The interior of the region is very sparsely populated; here the climate is of continental type, with dry, hot summers and very cold winters.

Central Otago consists of a plateau broken up by the folding movements in the Southern Alps, falling down sharply on the west but with a gentler gradient to the east. The Clutha, one of New Zealand's wildest and most abundantly flowing rivers, has carved out deep gorges in its westward course from the alpine Lakes Wanaka and Hawea. During the ice ages the landscape was refashioned. The hills, worn smooth by the ice, have rounded contours and are covered with tussock grass. The long fjord-like lakes were gouged out by glaciers and closed off by moraines.

Topography

In the west the Otago region reaches into the Southern Alps. Its highest peaks are Mount Aspiring (3027m/9932ft), Mount Earnslaw (1816m/5958ft) and the Remarkables, near Queenstown, which rise to almost 2500m/8200ft.

The region takes it name from the former Maori settlement of Otakau on the Otago Peninsula, north-east of Dunedin. The name of the village was applied to the peninsula and later to the whole region.

Name

Archaeological evidence has shown that the region was originally inhabited by moa-hunters, who moved north after the moas died out. In this southern latitude it was too cold to grow kumara (sweet potatoes), and the small groups which remained in the region moved to the coastal areas, where they lived on fern roots, fish and seals.

History

When Captain Cook passed this way he saw no Maoris on the Otago coast. In the early 19th century seal-hunters and whalers, mostly coming from Sydney, established themselves in the bays on the east coast. Following the murderous raids by Te Rauparaha and his allies the local Maoris were ready to sell land to the white settlers, though they were to be decimated by the diseases the settlers brought with them.

In the early 1860s the first gold was found at Lawrence in Central Otago, and thereafter prospectors flocked into the interior of the region. In 1860 the population of the whole region was no more than 12,000: eleven years later it had risen to 70,000.

The gold rush

The prospectors were deterred neither by the heat of summer nor the snowstorms of winter, and gold-diggers' camps sprang up like mushrooms all over the place – at Lawrence, but also at Clyde, Cromwell, Arrowtown, Macetown, Queenstown, Naseby, Ophir and St Bathans. These tented towns had large numbers of bars and hotels, casinos, saloons and music halls. When the alluvial goldfields were exhausted the gold had

An arid landscape in Otago

to be won by mining for gold-bearing seams of quartz and dredging the beds of the rivers.

After the gold rush

Some of the short-lived gold-diggers' settlements managed to develop their infrastructure and live on as market and commercial centres for the surrounding farming country. Irrigation converted barren valleys into flourish fruit-growing and market gardening areas. The export of frozen meat brought increased prosperity, since the sheep's meat as well as their wool brought in money. But as a result of erosion and a plague of rabbits many of the large sheep runs became uneconomic and were broken up by the government into smaller units which could be more intensively worked.

Hydro-electric potential

In course of time the high economic potential of the great masses of water flowing down from the mountains was realised, and great dams were built to store water for the production of hydro-electric power and irrigation and provide protection against flooding. In parallel with this development new roads were built. As a result the landscape of central Otago has been transformed.

Tourism

The infrastructure provided primarily for the hydro-electric schemes also opened up the region for modern (car-borne) tourism. Some of the old gold-digging settlements, like Queenstown, which had subsided into rural slumber were given a fresh lease of life; and Otago now attracts large numbers of visitors – walkers, climbers, winter sports enthusiasts and ordinary holidaymakers.

Picton   H/I 8

Region: Nelson-Marlborough
Population: 3300

Picton, where the ferries sailing between the South and the North Island (Wellington) put in, lies at the north-eastern tip of the South Island, at the head of one branch of picturesque Queen Charlotte Sound, 30km/19 miles north of Blenheim (see entry).

This little port town, where Katherine Mansfield (see Famous People) often stayed, is hemmed in on the landward side by steep hills. In spite of the busy ferry traffic it has preserved its original character. As the many yachts in its marina indicate, it is a popular holiday resort.

Picton was founded in 1848 on the site of an abandoned Maori fortified settlement. The name commemorates one of Wellington's generals who was killed in the battle of Waterloo. For many years Picton was in fierce competition with the neighbouring town of Blenheim (see entry) to become the seat of the provincial government of Marlborough province.

As early as 1862 there were calls in the press for a steamer service to link the railway systems on the North and South Islands. More than thirty years later, in 1898, Prime Minister Richard Seddon proposed the establishment of a train ferry service, and the proposal was very soon put into effect. In 1962 the ferry "Aramoana", which carries both railway rolling stock and motor vehicles, was brought into service.

The Smith Memorial Museum on London Quay commemorates the almost 140-year whaling traditions in this area. Whaling ceased only in the 1960s.

On the way to Waikawa Bay (north-east of the town) is the Victoria Domain Lookout, from which there are superb views of the town and Queen Charlotte Sound.

8km/5 miles away, to the north of Waikawa Bay, is the Karaka Point Reserve, in which are the remains of a Maori *pa*.

In Picton Harbour

★Queen Charlotte Sound

To the north of Picton is Queen Charlotte Sound, a very beautiful arm of the sea with many picturesque inlets. The best way of seeing the marvellous coastal scenery is by boat. The finest places are Mistletoe Bay, the Bay of Many Coves, Endeavour Inlet, Resolution Bay and Ship Cove. The Queen Charlotte Walkway, a beautiful trail offering no great difficulties, runs from Anakiwa to Ship Cove. There is also a motor road, Queen Charlotte Drive, through this picture book landscape. From Picton there are various organised boat excursions and fishing trips which take visitors, among other places, to Ship Cove, where Captain Cook called in several times, Queen Charlotte Sound and farther out into the Marlborough Sounds (see entry). For divers there is a trip to the wreck of the Soviet cruise ship "Mikhail Lermontov", which sank in Port Gore in 1986.

Cook Strait

At its narrowest point Cook Strait, the storm-swept channel between the North and South Islands of New Zealand, is only 23km/14 miles wide. The ferry crossing takes just under 3½ hours. The first hour (from Picton) is spent sailing through the beautiful Marlborough Sounds; then follows an hour and a half in the open sea, and finally three-quarters of an hour in Wellington's huge natural harbour.

Paparoa National Park · Pancake Rocks   F 9

Region: West Coast
Area: 306sq.km/118sq. miles

Situation

The Paparoa National Park (established 1987) lies on the west coast of the South Island, roughly half way between Greymouth and Westport (see entries).

Information

Paparoa National Park Visitor Centre, Punakaiki.
    The visitor centre has an interesting exhibition on the flora and fauna of the park, with a display explaining the origin of the Pancake Rocks. Information about walking in the park can also be obtained here.

★★Pancake Rocks

The principal feature of interest in the National Park is the Pancake Rocks, a curious limestone formation in which the strata look like a pile of pancakes. In the rocks are blowholes, through which, when there is a heavy surf, water spurts high into the air.
    The warm marine current which passes this way and the shelter afforded by the rocks produce a microclimate in which a rich subtropical vegetation (including many nikau palms) flourishes.

★Walk round the rocks

The best way of seeing the Pancake Rocks is to follow a footpath which starts at Dolomite Point. On the way there are safe platforms looking straight down into the seething blowholes. There are also beautiful views looking inland, extending in good weather as far as the Southern Alps.

Other walks

There are a number of short trails leading to interesting places on the wild coast – the Punakaiki Cavern Track, the Truman Track to Perpendicular Point, the Te Miko Track. There are also a number of longer walks into the hills and the valley of the Pororari River, notably the Punakaiki–Pororari Loop Track and the Upper Pororari Track.

★Inland Pack Track (Razorback Road)

A very strenuous but well worth while route is the Inland Pack Track, following an old route used in the 1870s which runs through the hills between the valleys of the Punakaiki River to the south and the Fox River to the north. This is a tough walk taking at least three days. (Note that there are no bridges over the rivers and streams.)

The Pancake Rocks

Queenstown   C 11/12

Region: Otago
Population: 4000

By road: from the west coast and Invercargill on Highway 6, from Dunedin on Highway 8. There are buses to and from all the major centres on the South Island.
　By air: There is an airstrip, used both by scheduled services and charter flights, at Frankton, 6km/4 miles north-east of Queenstown.

Getting there

Clocktower Information Centre, at the corner of Shotover Street and Camp Street.

Information

This old gold-diggers' settlement on the east side of Lake Wakatipu is now unchallenged as the leading tourist centre on the South Island. It is well supplied with hotels and other types of accommodation for visitors and offers a varied programme of entertainments and leisure activities throughout the year. For the more energetic holidaymakers there is a wide choice of activities, including bungy jumping, jetboat trips, white-water rafting, paragliding and rock-climbing.

Situation and importance

The Queenstown area was first explored in 1857 and 1859, and soon afterwards a sheep-farmer named William Rees staked out huge areas of grazing land. It was not long, however, before he had to leave his Camp Farm, when a prospector called William Fox found gold in the Arrow River. Rees's farm rapidly developed into a gold-diggers' settlement. The considerable quantities of gold found in the Shotover River and its tributaries Skipper's Canyon and Stoney Creek attracted large numbers of hopeful prospectors and adventurers. After the gold rush petered out and

History

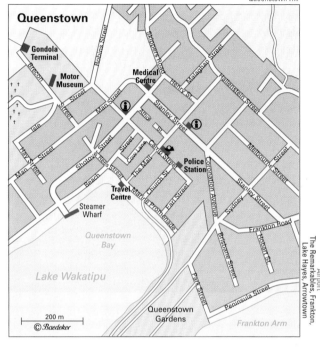

most of the prospectors left, Queenstown fell into a kind of twilight sleep, from which it awoke only when the great tourist potential of the area (mountain walks and climbs, white-water rafting, winter sports) was recognised.

★ Town centre

The town centre is charmingly situated beside a promontory reaching far out into Lake Wakatipu, now beautifully laid out as Queenstown Gardens. The best starting-point for a tour of the principal sights is the Old Stone Library (1877), which is built on to the Courthouse. From here the route runs under magnificent old trees into Camp Street. St Peter's Church (Anglican; 1932) looks much older than it really is. Church Street leads down to the shores of the lake. Passing the Lake Lodge of St Ophir (1873), we come to the place where William Rees established his sheep farm.

Then into the Queenstown Gardens. On the way back, at the end of the Mall (pedestrian zone), we come to Eichardt's Tavern, which has been on this site since 1871. On the pier at the end of the Mall is Underwater World, in which trout and eels can be seen in the clear waters of the lake; they are fed here, but otherwise live in freedom in the lake. Beside the pier are marks showing the level to which the lake rose in the floods of 1878 and 1983.

At the Steamer Wharf is moored the old-time steamer "Earnslaw". Then along the Esplanade on the seafront to St Omer Park, from which there are fine views of the lake and the town centre.

In the north-west of the town, near the lower station of the Skyline Gondola, is the Motor Museum (open: daily 9am–5.30pm), with a collection of vintage and veteran cars.

Queenstown and Lake Wakatipu, seen from Bob's Peak ▶

Queensstown

★Bob's Peak, Skyline Gondola

From Brecon Street an aerial cableway, the Skyline Gondola, runs up to the summit of Bob's Peak (446m/1463ft), from which there is an overwhelming view. Immediately below is Queenstown; beyond this is Lake Wakatipu; and beyond this again, forming a striking backdrop, are the peaks of the Remarkables.

★Cruise in SS "Earnslaw"

Cruises on the steamer "Earnslaw", which first went into service in 1912, are very popular. Some of the cruises include visits to sheep farms which are accessible only by boat. (The ship is taken out of service in June for its annual overhaul.)

★Skipper's Canyon

A trip through the 20km/12½ mile long Skipper's Canyon in a specially equipped bus is an exciting experience. Drivers who do the trip in a hired car are not covered by insurance.
The return trip can be by jetboat for part of the way.

★Shotover River

The Shotover River offers challenges to the adventurous visitor, with trips by jetboat in which the steersman has to battle against strong currents and white-water rafting in kayaks or rubber dinghies. There are organised rafting trips lasting several days, with overnight accommodation in tents.

★Kawarau River; bungy jumping

There are jetboat and rafting trips on the Kawarau River. The supreme experience for the daring, however, is a bungy jump from the Kawarau Bridge (see Baedeker Special, pp. 272–73).

Winter sports

Queenstown is the most popular winter sports centre in New Zealand, with a season lasting from June to September or October. Coronet Peak (1650m/5414ft), 15km/9 miles north of the town, has excellent facilities (ski-lifts, etc.) for skiers, as have the skiing areas high up in the Remarkable Mountains. They are reached by way of Highway 6 (signposted to Kingston) and the Tollgate (10km/6 miles east of Queenstown), from which it is a 14km/9 mile climb to the ski fields. There is a shuttle bus service.

Winter Festival

Queenstown's Winter Festival is held annually in July.

Pony trekking

There is plenty of scope for pony trekking in the hills round Queenstown and for rides to some of the large sheep farms or abandoned goldfields in the area.

Parachute jumping, paragliding, ballooning

Other activities for adventurous visitors are tandem parachute jumps, paragliding and ballooning. A trip in a balloon is a marvellous way of seeing the beautiful country round Queenstown.

Scenic flights

There are sightseeing flights from the Queenstown airstrip to the Southern Alps, Fiordland National Park and Milford Sound.

Steam train

An old-time steam train, the "Kingston Flyer", runs between Kingston, at the south-east end of Lake Wakatipu, and the little township of Fairlight.

Walks

Information

Information about walks in the Queenstown area can be obtained from the Department of Conservation's visitor centre at 37 Shotover Street.

Short walks

There are many attractive walks in the beautiful highland country round Queenstown, for example to One Mile Creek, Queenstown Hill, Sunshine Bay, the Frankton Arm, Lake Sylvan, Ben Lomond or the Big Hill.

★★Routeburn Track

This route runs from the valley of the Dart River over the Harris Saddle and down to the Te Anau–Milford Road, through the grand mountain world of Fiordland. The track is closed in winter. The walk, which takes three or four days, can be combined with the Milford Track (see Fiordland National Park).

This walk, a circuit which takes about four days, runs through the valleys of the Greenstone and Caples Rivers, which both flow into Lake Wakatipu. The best starting-point is Elfin Bay, on the west side of Lake Wakatipu.

Greenstone–Caples Track

This walk (four days) runs through the valleys of the Rees and Dart Rivers, going over the Mount Cunningham Saddle (1447m/4748ft). The best starting-points are Paradise, at the north end of Lake Wakatipu, or the Invincible Mine.

Rees–Dart Track

There are a number of tracks, in varying grades of difficulty, through the beautiful mountain world of the Remarkables, which rise to 2300m/7550ft.

★ Remarkables

This Z-shaped lake, hemmed in by high hills, has an area of 293sq.km/113sq. miles. It is some 80km/50 miles long, barely 5km/3 miles across at its widest point, and up to 378m/1240ft deep.

★ Lake Wakatipu

According to a Maori legend the lake came into being when a sleeping giant was burned to death. His heart still beats, however, at the bottom of the lake, causing variations in the level of the lake, which can rise or fall by several centimetres within five minutes.

The first Europeans reached Lake Wakatipu in 1853, and some years later the whole lake was surveyed. The Otago gold rush of the 1860s brought thousands of prospectors into the area. In those days there were thirty or forty passenger ships, including four steamers, plying on the lake. One old steamer, the "Earnshaw", is now one of the lake's tourist attractions.

Reefton   F 9

Region: West Coast
Population: 1200

Reefton lies in the valley of the Inangahua River, 80km/50 miles north-east of Greymouth (see entry) and about the same distance south-east of Westport (see entry). Once a flourishing gold-mining town, it is now merely a supply centre for farmers, forestry workers and workers in the coal-mining industry. Its former importance as a gold-mining centre is reflected in its name (the "reef town"); it was also known as Quartzopolis.

Situation and history

Large quantities of gold were found in the area in 1866, and the gold-bearing seams of quartz were mined from 1870 until well into the 20th century. In those days Reefton had its own stock exchange. Shares in the local gold-mines rose to unprecedented heights and then collapsed. After the gold-mines closed down coal-mining activity was intensified, but this too is now in decline.

Notable buildings which bear witness to the town's gold-mining heyday are the Church of the Sacred Heart (1878), St Stephen's Church (1878), the Courthouse (1872) and the School of Mines (1886), which has a rich collection of minerals. 2km/1¼ miles east of the town is Black's Point Museum (open: Aug.–May Tues.–Sun. 1–4pm), which vividly illustrates the history of gold-mining in the Reefton area. At Crushington, 2km/1¼ miles farther east, are two monster machines, the Wealth of Nations and the Globe Battery, in which the gold-bearing quartz was crushed.

Sights

North and east of Reefton extends Victoria Forest Park (area 2090sq.km/807sq. miles), in which are a number of old gold- and coal-mines. Also within the park, 40km/25 miles south of Reefton, is the ghost town of Waiuta, where gold was worked until 1951.

★Victoria Forest Park

Information about walks in the gold- and coal-mining area can be obtained from the Department of Conservation office in Reefton (Crampton Road).

No Fear of Falling?

What is it that makes people – some young, some not so young – jump from a great height into the void with only an elastic rope to save them from destruction? Is it that they have no idea of fear, is it purely for a thrill, is it as "the quickest way to a new self-awareness", as some have claimed? No one knows for sure. But there is no doubt that the extraordinary sport of bungy jumping, invented in New Zealand and introduced to Europe some years ago by a New Zealander who jumped from the Eiffel Tower, has caught on in no uncertain way.

The origins of bungy jumping are traced by some ethnographers to the island of Vanuatu in the New Hebrides – not so far from New Zealand. Until recently adolescent boys on Vanuatu used to throw themselves from a high bamboo tower with only lianas to save them. A boy who summoned up the courage to jump had taken an important step towards becoming a man. Bungy jumping was thus seen as an essential element in the rites of passage to manhood.

Others believe that it was Tarzan and Jane who invented bungy jumping. Any cinemagoer will remember how they got about the forest by swinging on lianas.

Modern bungy jumping originated in New Zealand – to be more precise, in the Queenstown area. Round Queenstown there are a number of gorges into which it is possible to jump with reasonable safety. In the mid eighties, however, a New Zealander went one stage farther. Attached to a high-tech rope made of strands of rubber, he jumped from the old bridge over the Kawarau River into the gorge 43 metres (140 feet) below. Since then there has been a steady stream of intrepid jumpers to the bridge, as well as those who go only to watch – seeking to get, one way or the other, a shot of adrenalin.

The elastic rope tied to the jumper's ankle brakes his fall relatively gently and safely. Then the rope springs back and pulls him up, then lets him down again. After bobbing up and down several times like a yo-yo he finally comes to rest and dangles helplessly at the end of the rope until he is picked up by a rubber dinghy.

There are now a variety of facilities for bungy jumping throughout New Zealand. Some practitioners jump from a platform on the jib of a crane, others from the roof of a sports stadium.

In Queenstown the "hot spots" for bungy jumpers are the Kawarau Bridge and, more recently, the 70m/230ft high Skipper's Bridge. The supreme challenge, however, is a jump from the 102m/335ft high Pipeline on the upper Shotover River.

A bungy jump costs between NZ$70 and $160, depending on the degree of difficulty and the arrangements for picking up the jumper after his jump.

The *dernier cri* among the adventure sports practised in New Zealand is "parapenting", a combination of parachute jumping and hang-gliding. Instruction in this sport can be obtained in the Queenstown area on Crown Terrace and in the skiing area on the Remarkables. Experienced parapenters seek out areas in the mountains of Central Otago with good thermals.

A bungy jumper in the Kawarau Gorge ▶

Southland A–D 12/13

Region | The Southland region, an area of rolling uplands and formerly swampy lowlands traversed by rivers, occupies the south-western tip of the South Island.

Topography | The Fiordland area of Southland is one of the most inaccessible and most sparsely populated parts of New Zealand. Here the deep valleys gouged out by glaciers on the west side of the mountains were filled with water when the sea level rose and became fjords. On the east side of the mountains the valleys were dammed by terminal moraines and became long narrow lakes, such as Lake Te Anau (the largest lake on the South Island), Lake Manapouri, Lake Monowai and Lake Hauroko.

History | Long before the coming of Europeans this area was occupied by moa-hunters and the early Maoris, who caught fish and hunted waterfowl and rats. These early inhabitants were driven out or decimated by Maori tribes from the north with a more advanced culture. The shy Maoris whom Cook encountered in Dusky Sound on his second voyage in 1773 had probably been driven out of their original territory by these invading tribes.

The first seal-hunters came here from Sydney in 1792 and established temporary settlements in Dusky Sound and elsewhere. From the 1830s whalers established permanent settlements like Jacob's River (now Riverton, west of Invercargill) and Bluff.

In 1854 the colonial government acquired large territories in Southland, expropriating many of the large landowners. Scottish settlers then moved in from Dunedin and founded Invercargill, laying it out on a regular plan. The forests were cleared and the swamps drained, producing rich grazing land for Romney sheep and dairy cows.

The lush green landscape of Southland

To improve the employment prospects of this sparsely populated region an aluminium smelter was built some twenty years ago at Bluff, using power supplied by the controversial Manapouri hydro-electric station. In spite of massive economic incentives and the increasing development of tourism in the beautiful Fiordland region the population has in recent years been declining.

Gore (pop. 11,000), Southland's second largest town, lies at an important road junction north-east of Invercargill (see entry) in an area of fertile pastureland, with some arable farming (grain) and horticulture. The areas of swamp and tussock grass which formerly made up the landscape were brought into cultivation by the early settlers.

Gore

Gore is known beyond the bounds of New Zealand for its Country Music Festival, held annually in June.

★ Country Music Festival

The South Island's sheep-shearing championship is held annually in Gore.

Sheep-shearing championship

At Mandeville, 30km/19 miles north-west of Gore, is a homestead of pioneering days, now protected as a national monument.

Mandeville

Stewart Island

B/C 13/14

Region: Southland
Population: 700

Stewart Island lies 30km/19 miles off the south coast of the South Island, separated from it by the Foveaux Strait. Triangular in shape and frayed by many inlets, it has an area of 1700sq.km/656sq. miles and a total coastline of over 1600km/1000 miles.

Situation

A small ferry takes two hours to make the crossing from Bluff to Halfmoon Bay, the only place of any size on the island. During the main holiday season (December and January) there is a daily service.
There are also days trips in light aircraft from Invercargill.

Getting there

The island's only commercial and tourist centre is the village of Halfmoon Bay (Oban). Here too is the only accommodation for visitors (a hotel, a lodge, a motel and a camping park with caravans for hire), which in the main holiday season are rapidly booked up. Advance reservation is therefore essential.

Accommodation

The island has a much indented coastline and is surrounded by a host of small islands. It is hilly and densely wooded, its principal peaks being Mount Anglem (980m/3215ft) in the north and Mounts Rakeahua (676m/2218ft) and Allen (749m/2457ft) in the centre. Much of the island is a nature reserve.
A warm marine current off the west coast warms the island, and the hills provide shelter from the stormy winds that prevail here. In consequence the climate is surprisingly mild for this latitude (47° south). In addition to peace and quiet and its almost intact natural flora and fauna the island's attractions include sunsets of great beauty.

★ Topography

Stewart Island, which in pre-European times was very sparsely populated, was discovered by Cook in 1770 – though he took the island for part of the mainland of New Zealand.
The Foveaux Strait was named after the deputy governor of Norfolk Island. One of the earliest white visitors to the island was William Stewart, first officer of the sealing ship "Pegasus", who landed in 1803 with a party of seal-hunters and gave the island its name. His ship is commemorated by

History

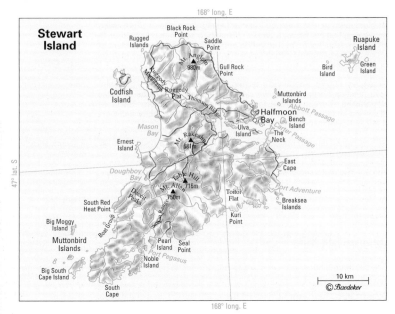

Port Pegasus, an inlet on the south-east coast. The seal-hunters were followed by whalers, as happened everywhere when the seals had been almost exterminated by over-hunting. The whaling season was in winter; in summer the whalers grew potatoes and kept sheep and cattle.

In 1864 the colonial government acquired almost the whole of Stewart Island from the Maoris, who retained the right to catch waterfowl (particularly muttonbirds) on the little offshore islands.

Economy

The main sources of income are fishing (particularly cod and crayfish), fish-farming (salmon, Foveaux oysters, etc.) and tourism.

Sights

Rakiura Museum

The Rakiura Museum, on the beach at Halfmoon Bay (Oban), illustrates the island's flora and fauna and the history of seal-hunting and whaling.

Acker House

Acker House, at the south end of Halfmoon Bay, was built of stone, clay and shells by an American whaler named Lewis Acker.

Walks,
boat trips

There is plenty of good walking on Stewart Island, with mountain huts for overnight accommodation. In summer there are guided walks.
There are attractive boat trips to Port Adventure Bay on the east coast and to the beaches in Paterson Inlet.

Timaru   F 11

Region: Canterbury
Population: 28,000

The port of Timaru, the second largest town in Canterbury region, lies on the east coast, on the southern edge of the great Canterbury Plain, half way between Christchurch and Dunedin. Along the coast extend the Tertiary basalts known as Timaru bluestone, forming a sheltered natural harbour. The Maori place-name Te Maru means "sheltered place". Timaru is now an important port for the export of New Zealand products (particularly frozen meat) and the commercial and administrative centre of an extensive hinterland.

Situation and importance

There was an old Maori settlement on this site, within which whalers established a base in the 18th century. In 1859 British immigrants landed here and founded a town of European type.

History

Timaru has produced some world-famous sportsmen, among them Robert Fitzsimmons, a world boxing champion in the late 19th century, and the runner John E. Lovelock, world record-holder for the mile, who won a gold medal for the 1500 metres at the 1936 Olympics in Berlin. Timaru also produced one of the most famous racehorses in the history of racing, Phar Lap, which in the 1920s and 30s won major races all over the world.

Sights

The place to go to in Timaru is Caroline Bay, with its carefully groomed parks and wide range of entertainments and leisure facilities. It is particularly lively and busy in summer. At Christmas it is the venue of the Timaru Christmas Carnival, a great annual occasion.

★ Caroline Bay

At the north end of Caroline Bay is Maori Park, in which is an eye-catching old wooden lighthouse of 1877.

Maori Park

In a modern octagonal building in Perth Street is the South Canterbury Museum (open: Tues.–Fri. and Sun. 1.30–4.30pm), which developed out of the old Pioneer Hall Museum. It offers an interesting survey of the history and natural history of the Timaru area. One fascinating item is a replica of the plane flown by the aviation pioneer Richard Pearse in 1903. Opposite the Museum is an obelisk commemorating the victims of two shipwrecks in 1882.

★ South Canterbury Museum

Beside the Museum is St Mary's Church (Anglican; 1886), built in the local bluestone in Early English style.

St Mary's Church

In Craigie Avenue is the Roman Catholic Basilica of the Sacred Heart (by W. F. Petre, 1911), with twin towers and a copper dome.

Basilica of the Sacred Heart

The Aigantighe Art Gallery, housed in an elegant building of 1905 in Wai-iti Road, has an interesting collection, including fine works by New Zealand artists. Attached to the gallery is a sculpture garden. Open: Tues.–Fri. 11am–4.30pm, Sat. and Sun. 2–4pm.

Aigantighe Art Gallery

To the north of the town is the Washdyke industrial zone. The name refers to an old installation in which sheep were washed before shearing which once existed in this area. Here visitors can see round a brewery, textile factories and milling works (by appointment, made through the Visitor Centre in George Street).

Washdyke

Surroundings

The popular City Walkway runs through Centennial Park and continues along the coast.

City Walkway

On the Opihi River (10km/6 miles north), on the north bank of the Pareora River (13km/8 miles south-west) and on Otaio Beach (20km/12½ miles south) there are attractive paths running through beautiful scenery.

Other walks

Cave

35km/22 miles west of Timaru on Highway 8 is the hamlet of Cave (pop. 130), a small farming settlement which grew up round an outpost of the huge Levels sheep station, which once belonged to the Rhodes brothers. It was from this farm that the notorious Scottish sheep-stealer James Mackenzie (see Mackenzie Country) allegedly stole the sheep which he then drove into the still unexplored highland country.

On a hill 2km/1¼ miles from Cave is St David's Memorial Church (Presbyterian), which commemorates the pioneers of the Mackenzie highlands. This beautiful little Norman-style church with a battlemented tower is built of natural ice-smoothed stone. It is open daily.

★Maori rock paintings

In a wide area round Timaru, in caves and rock overhangs, are rock paintings which show that this area was settled by the Maoris or their predecessors at a very early period. The finest of these paintings are at Dog Rock, 1km/¾ mile east of Cave, and Craigmore, 30km/19 miles south-west. Information from the Visitor Centre in George Street, Timaru.

Geraldine

Region: Canterbury
Population: 2000

Situation and importance

The little agricultural market town of Geraldine lies 35km/22 miles north of Timaru, between the plain and the highlands. Early white settlers planted European species of trees here.

Sights in surrounding area

In Pleasant Valley, 17km/10½ miles west of Geraldine, is St Anne's Church (Anglican; 1862), the oldest church in South Canterbury.

16km/10 miles north-west of Geraldine is Orari Gorge Farm, established in the mid 19th century. The farm buildings, including a cottage of 1859, are protected as national monuments and have been restored by the Historic Places Trust. The farm is still occupied and there is only restricted public access.

Two local beauty spots are the Waihi Gorge (13km/8 miles north-west) and the Te Moana Gorge (19km/12 miles west).

★Peel Forest Park

23km/14 miles north of Geraldine is Peel Forest Park, 600 hectares/1500 acres of almost entirely unspoiled woodland with romantic waterfalls and attractive picnic areas.

Nearby are the old buildings of Mount Peel Station, a sheep farm established in the 1860s.

Mesopotamia. Erewhon

The track ends at Mesopotamia (70km/43 miles north-west of Geraldine), which, like the neighbouring Erewhon Station, belonged to the English writer Samuel Butler. (Erewhon can be reached only on a roundabout route by way of Mount Somers.)

Waikouaiti   E 12

Region: Otago
Population: 1000

Situation and history

An hour's drive north of Dunedin on Highway 1 is Waikouaiti, the oldest European settlement in Otago. In the 1830s a whaler named Johnny Jones (1809–69), a sharp businessman, settled here and established a whole chain of whaling stations all the way down the west coast as far as the Foveaux Strait. When the whaling industry declined he switched to farming and property dealing; he organised the settlement of immigrants; and as a supplier of foodstuffs he was virtually indispensable to the newly founded town of Dunedin in its first difficult years. In Waikouaiti itself he showed himself a generous benefactor and patron.

Two handsome old wooden buildings dating from pioneering days are the Presbyterian Church (1863) and St John's Church (Anglican; 1858). St John's Church (R.C.) was built in 1871. The old farmstead of Matanaka at the north end of the bay also dates from pioneering days.

The Early Settlers Museum, housed in a former bank dating from the turn of the century, contains interesting mementoes of the early days of the settlement.

Sights

Waikouaiti's safe bathing beach attracts many day visitors. The dunes were consolidated around the turn of the century by the sowing of grass and later by the planting of pines.

★Bathing beach

Waimate   F 11

Region: Canterbury
Population: 3000

50km/31 miles south of Timaru (see entry) is Waimate, the commercial centre of a large surrounding agricultural area. On land which in the 19th century was covered with huge totara forests grain is now grown, as well as flower bulbs and berry fruits.

Situation and importance

The first settlers in this area in the 19th century were loggers and sawmill workers engaged in clearing the ancient totara forests. In 1854 the Studholme brothers came here from Christchurch looking for new grazing land, and, with the agreement of the old Maori chief Huruhuru, established a huge sheep farm, the Te Waimate Station, which also reared cattle and horses. The horses bred here found markets as far afield as Australia.

History

Sights in Waimate and Surroundings

The first farmhouse, the Cuddy, was built by the Studholme brothers in 1854 of wood from a single totara tree. A sheep-shearing shed and a wool-shed were built at the same time. The buildings, still in private ownership, are protected as national monuments.

★Studholme Farm

St Augustine's Church (Anglican) was built in 1872 of rough-sawn wood, with a striking little tower over the crossing. The interior bears witness to the prominent position of the Studholme family in the local community.

St Augustine's Church

This museum of local history (open: Mon.–Fri. 1–5pm, Sun. 2–4pm) is housed in the old Courthouse of 1879.

Historical Museum

In Seddon Square, the old village square, there are monuments to Michael Studholme, the Maori chief Huruhuru and Dr Margaret Cruickshank, New Zealand's first woman doctor, who cared for the population of the town until 1916.

Seddon Square

From the summit of Mount John (446m/1463ft), in the nearby Hunter's Hills, you can get some idea of the vastness of the Canterbury Plain.

Mount John

Waitaki River   E/F 11

Regions: Otago and Canterbury

The broad Waitaki River is fed by the snowfields and glaciers of the Southern Alps, and its principal tributaries come from the alpine Lakes Tekapo, Pukaki and Ohau (see entries). With these and numerous other tributaries it has a catchment area of almost 12,000sq.km/4600sq. miles. It forms the boundary between the Canterbury and Otago regions.

Two gigantic hydro-electric schemes have transformed the course of the river and the face of the landscape. On the upper course of the river, near Twizel, there is the Upper Waitaki Hydro Power Scheme, and on its middle course are the Benmore, Aviemore and Waitaki hydro-electric stations, each supplied by an artificial lake created by damming the river. Much of the river's course is now a chain of lakes. The water stored in the lakes is also used in a variety of agricultural and horticultural irrigation schemes in the arid plains on the lower course of the river.

There are fish ladders at the dam for the benefit of trout and salmon fishers – and of the fish.

★ Maori rock paintings

At Takiroa, near Duntroon (on the south bank of the river), are very fine rock paintings by nomadic Maori tribes. They are easily accessible from Highway 83.

Twizel

A few kilometres south of Lake Pukaki, on the Twizel River in the Mackenzie highlands, is Twizel (pop. 1800), originally a camp for construction workers on the Upper Waitaki hydro-electric scheme. Under this project the water level of Lakes Tekapo, Pukaki and Ohau was raised by the construction of dams, the lakes were linked by canals and lower down, in the middle Waitaki valley, other dams were built, creating artificial lakes like Lake Benmore. In the course of these developments, which radically changed the landscape and were highly controversial, a holiday and leisure complex, named the Mackenzie Hydro Lakes, came into being round Twizel. This offers excellent facilities for fishing, boating and cruising on the lakes. In recent years a number of skiing centres have also been established.

West Coast · Westland   B–F 8–11

The West Coast or Westland region extends for more than 500km/310 miles along the west coast of the South Island, from Jackson Bay and the Haast River in the south to Karamea in the north, in a narrow coastal belt of dense rain forest backed inland by high mountains which is nowhere more than 50km/30 miles wide. The region has a population of only 35,000, which has been steadily declining for many years.

The principal towns in the region are Greymouth, Westport and Hokitika (see entries). It has many relics of the pioneering days of loggers and gold-diggers – although the infrastructure has been much improved since then by the building of roads.

Discovery

Tasman and Cook sailed along this inhospitable coast, and the hinterland was later explored by Thomas Brunner and Julius von Haast, who discovered the region's extensive coalfields.

Greenstone and gold

In pre-European times the Maoris on the west coast greatly prized the hard *pounamu* (greenstone, nephrite, jade) found here, from which they made weapons and jewellery. In the mid 19th century, when Brunner and von Haast travelled through the dense rain forests, iron had long replaced greenstone for making weapons; but in 1864 two Maoris were still looking for greenstone when they found gold in the Greystone area. When news of this got round whole boatloads of prospectors began arriving in Hokitika, and many found their way through the Southern Alps over little known passes to the rainy west coast with its promise of wealth. Within a year there were no fewer than 40,000 of them in Westland, digging up swampland, impenetrable forests and river-beds in quest of gold. The recently established settlement of Hokitika grew within a short time into a town of 10,000 inhabitants, New Zealand's most important port after Auckland. By the end of the 1870s the goldfields were practically worked out, and only a few gold-diggers were left laboriously scratching at gold-bearing veins of quartz at Reefton and in the interior.

An unspoiled primeval landscape in the west of the South Island

Something of the atmosphere of the west coast in the 19th century can still be felt in the reconstructed gold-diggers' settlement of Shantytown to the south of Greymouth (see entry).

After the end of the gold rush the economy of the region increasingly depended on timber and coal. Coal-mining began to flourish, particularly to the north of Westport and on the Grey River. In spite of the large deposits still available, however, mining has declined sharply in recent years, and many abandoned mines have already been overgrown by the lush vegetation of the rain forest.

Coal

The high rainfall on the west coast has produced a type of rain forest which is unique in the world. This lowland rain forest shows a variety of species rarely found anywhere else. Recent proposals to exploit its economic potential by extensive felling have met fierce resistance from friends of nature all over the world.

★★ Lowland rain forest

Fishing and pastoral farming have now become major contributors to the economy of the region. Fishing and fish-farming (particularly salmon and trout) are widely practised, and large cattle and sheep farms have been established in many places. A recent development is game farming, with large enclosures containing game whose meat brings the highest prices in export markets (e.g. roe-deer and fallow deer).

Fishing and farming

The long isolation of the southern West Coast was ended by the opening of the road over the Haast Pass in 1965, which gave a great boost to tourism on the west coast. It now became possible to make a circuit of the whole South Island. The imposing Fox and Franz Josef Glaciers (see entry) are major tourist attractions. The Westland National Park (see entry) was opened in 1960 and much extended in 1982.

Tourism

Westland National Park   D/E 10

Region: West Coast
Area: 1176sq.km/454sq. miles

Information

Westland National Park Headquarters and Visitor Centre, Franz Josef village; information bureau in Fox Glacier village.

Te Wahipounamu
Nature Reserve

Westland National Park and Mount Cook National Park together form the large Te Wahipounamu Nature Reserve, which is included in UNESCO's list of world heritage sites, mainly because of its unique expanses of rain forest.

★★Topography

Westland National Park, established in 1960 and considerably enlarged in 1982, extends from the west coast at Gillespie's Point and Okarito (white heron reserve) to Mount Tasman (3498m/11,477ft), one of the highest peaks in the Southern Alps. The National Park's principal attractions are the Fox and Franz Josef Glaciers (see entry), which flow down from the permanent ice-caps of the 3000m/10,000ft peaks of the Southern Alps to an altitude of 300m/1000ft above sea level, where evergreen rain forest and tall tree ferns flourish.

Climate

Directly on the coast it is relatively warm and less wet, with an annual rainfall of around 2500mm/100in. In the western foothills of the Southern Alps it is around 5000mm/200in., and in the high alpine and summit regions it is over 7600mm/300in. In Westland National Park visitors must expect to encounter violent and long-continuing falls of rain and snow – without which there would of course be no snowfields, glaciers or rain forests.

Highway 6

The main road through the National Park is Highway 6, which gives access to all the major natural attractions and many lesser ones.

The Fox Glacier in Westland National Park, reaching down into the rain forest

There are a number of waymarked trails in the National Park. Before setting out on a walk it is essential to enquire about the condition of the trail at the visitor centre in Franz Josef or the Fox Glacier tourist village, which also supply detailed descriptions of the routes.

Walks

Westport   F 8

Region: West Coast
Population: 4500

The little port town of Westport, the second largest place in the West Coast region, lies on the north side of the estuary of the Buller River. In spite of its isolated situation it is an important commercial centre serving a large surrounding area.

Situation and importance

Its economic resources are the abundant supplies of timber in the surrounding area, the huge coalfields in the hinterland of the Paparoa Range and the limestone quarries on Cape Foulwind, which have promoted the development of a large cement-producing industry.

Westport grew out of a 19th century gold-diggers' camp, but it survived after the end of the gold rush thanks to the large deposits of coal in the area. This "black gold" is shipped abroad from Westport and transported to Christchurch by rail.

History

The town centre is laid out on a regular plan. The Coaltown Museum (open: daily 8.30am–4.30pm), housed in an old brewery in Queen Street, displays the history of coal-mining in fascinating detail. Two other features of interest are the venerable St John's Church (Anglican) and the imposing Bank of New South Wales.

Sights

Two popular beaches are Carter's Beach (5km/3 miles from the town in the direction of Cape Foulwind; surfing) and North Beach (suitable for families).

Bathing beaches

20km/12½ miles west of Westport is Cape Foulwind, with a handsome lighthouse. It was given its name by Captain Cook, who had to battle with contrary winds here.

★ Cape Foulwind

Tauranga Bay, with its friendly colony of seals, attracts many day visitors.

★ Tauranga Bay

There are attractive trails round Cape Foulwind and in the old gold- and coal-mining areas. Information, particularly on the Britannia Track and the Denniston Walkway, from the Visitor Information Centre, 1 Brougham Street, Westport.

Walks

Gold was, and to some extent still is, mined north of Westport at Waimangaroa (16km/10 miles), Denniston (25km/15 miles), Granity (29km/18 miles), Stockton (35km/22 miles) and Ngakawau (32km/20 miles). In the past the transport of the coal, mined high up on steep hills, was difficult. At Denniston the coal was brought down in a funicular.

★ Coal-mining areas

283

Cook Islands

After the exertions of sightseeing, or to get away from the stresses of modern life, where better to relax than the idyllic beaches of the Cook Islands?

Cook Islands

The Cook Islands realise everyone's dream of an island in the South Seas.
Scattered like pearls in the vast expanses of the South Pacific, they lie
between longitude 156° and 170° west and between latitude 8° and 23°
south, some 3500km/2175 miles north-east of New Zealand. Their charms –
unspoiled natural beauty and idyllic palm-shaded beaches – have not been
spoiled by mass tourism.

★★Topography
The Cook Islands consist of a northern group of seven and a southern
group of eight, lying 1000km/620 miles apart. Their national territory
extends over a total area of 2,201,490sq.km/850,000sq. miles, but their land
area is no more than 240sq.km/93sq. miles. Lagoons within the islands
have a total area of 566sq.km/219sq. miles. The total area of the islands
with their lagoons is thus only 0.366% of the national territory.

The islands in the northern group, with a total area of only 28sq.km/
11sq. miles, are Penrhyn, Rakahanga, Manihiki, Pukapuka, Suwarrow,
Palmerston and Nassau. The southern group consists of Rarotonga (the
chief island in the archipelago), Mangaia, Atiu, Mauke and Mitiaro, Aitutaki,
Manuae and Takutea, with a total area of 212sq.km/82sq. miles. The most
visited of the islands, and the best equipped to cater for visitors, are
Rarotonga and Aitutaki. On the other islands there are only modest hotels
and accommodation in private houses; but it is a marvellous experience to
pay a flying visit to one or other of these almost entirely unspoiled islands.
A 40- or 50-minute flight from Rarotonga will take you deep into the past.

Getting there
Air New Zealand flies twice weekly from London via Los Angeles to Rarotonga. It is also possible to combine a visit to New Zealand with a trip to the
Cook Islands. Air New Zealand flies from Auckland to the islands, and
reasonably priced package deals are available. Cook Islandair and Air
Rarotonga fly regular services to almost all the islands in both the northern
and the southern group.

On arrival in the islands visitors will be required to produce a return ticket
and evidence that they have booked hotel accommodation.

Geology
Like most of the Pacific islands the Cook Islands are either purely volcanic
or coral atolls on a basalt base. Five types of island can be distinguished:
the high volcanic island of Rarotonga; the raised coral islands of Mangaia,
Mauke, Atiu and Mitiaro, with a volcanic core and a surrounding plain of
coralline limestone; Aitutaki, consisting of a central volcanic island and a
surrounding barrier reef; the atolls of Manuae, Palmerston, Penrhyn, Manihiki, Rakahanga, Pukapuka and Suwarrow; Takutea and Nassau, islands of
sand on a coralline limestone base.

Mangaia, Atiu, Mauke and Mitiaro are islands of a type which is very rare
in the Pacific. In a term borrowed from the Maori language they are
described as makatea islands: i.e. islands consisting of a central volcanic
hill surrounded by a broad, gently sloping plain of coralline limestone.
They originated soon after the ending of volcanic activity, when the volcanic islands were gradually sinking into the sea. As they sank their fringing
coral reefs rose. Later, forces from the earth's interior thrust the extinct
volcanoes with their fringing reefs up again, and these were then levelled
off by the surf and later by atmospheric weathering. The makatea was born.

Both in origin and in age the atolls in the northern group share common
characteristics. With the exception of Penrhyn, which lies on top of its own
volcano, all of them came into being at about the same time on the highest
points of a massive submarine volcanic ridge.

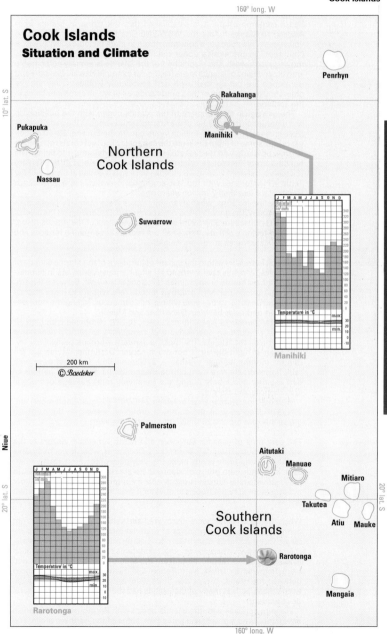

Cook Islands
Situation and Climate

160° long. W

10° lat. S

Penrhyn

Rakahanga

Pukapuka

Manihiki

Nassau

Northern
Cook Islands

Suwarrow

Rainfall
in mm

| J | F | M | A | M | J | J | A | S | O | N | D |

Temperature in °C

max.

min.

Manihiki

200 km
© Baedeker

Niue

Palmerston

Aitutaki

Manuae

Mitiaro

Takutea

Atiu   Mauke

Southern
Cook Islands

Rainfall
in mm

| J | F | M | A | M | J | J | A | S | O | N | D |

Temperature in °C

max.

min.

Rarotonga

Rarotonga

Mangaia

20° lat. S

20° lat. S

160° long. W

287

The islands in the southern group, however, cannot be shown to have had a common origin. It is established that the string of islands from Aitutaki to Mauke follow the WSW/ENE line of a series of submarine volcanoes. This points to a common origin in plate tectonic activity, with a "hot spot" in the earth's upper mantle over which the Pacific plate is moving north-west. The disposition of the islands is entirely comparable with other chains of islands in the Pacific, for example Hawaii. Mangaia and Rarotonga are out on their own and completely isolated. They are the oldest and the youngest of the Cook Islands, all of which came into being in the Tertiary.

The geological development of the islands began with the building up and emergence from the sea of the first volcanic islands in the early Tertiary (Palaeocene), some 60–65 million years ago. In the Eocene, 38–60 million years ago, some of them sank into the sea again. The reef corals then began to grow upwards, and the first atolls and reef islands came into being. The building up of Rarotonga occurred only towards the end of the Tertiary (Pliocene), between 2.3 and 2.8 million years ago. It ended at the turn of the Tertiary/Pleistocene, with the last eruptions for which there is evidence taking place less than 2 million years ago.

During the ice ages, when even the tropics were markedly cooler than they are today, the growth of the reefs continued. Depending on the level of the sea ($\div$100–120m/330–390ft) and the movements of the islands resulting from tectonic activity, almost all the islands have marine terraces and cliff and beach lines at varying heights.

Climate

The Cook Islands lie within the sphere of influence of the marine climate of the tropics, which is characterised by slight annual variations in temperature, high air humidity and rainfall throughout the year. Between December and April the northern group of islands falls within the inner tropical convergence zone. In this area whirlwinds can occur, hitting the northern islands in particular between December and March.

High temperatures (see climatic tables, p. 287) combined with high air humidity produce an oppressive and sometimes extremely oppressive climate on all the islands. The months January–April are particularly trying: even at night the air is not much cooler. December–March are the rainiest months (annual average c. 2200mm/85in.). Overcast days with rain, however, are rare even during these months. Prolonged periods of bad weather occur only during the (relatively rare) passage of tropical disturbances and storms.

Water temperatures range between 24°C/75°F (August/September) and 27°C/81°F (February) in the southern group of islands; in the northern group they are around 28°C/82°F throughout the year.

When to go

The best time of year for European and North American visitors to the southern group of islands is from May to December, when fewer rainy days and the cooling trade winds make the sultriness of the air perfectly tolerable. In the northern group of islands there are no seasonal differences. In these latitudes the climate is oppressive throughout the year, and visitors not accustomed to the tropics should limit their stay to not more than two weeks.

History

When the Cook Islands were discovered and settled by Polynesians is not certainly known, though datings of material recovered by excavation indicate that the islands have been occupied by man for at least 1100 years.

Nor is it known where the original inhabitants came from. There is much evidence that the Maoris came from the area of the Society Islands and were followed by tribes from Tonga and Samoa. The great distances between the islands meant that there were only occasional contacts between them, so that many of the islands had their own distinctive cultural development.

Western contacts with the islands began with Portuguese and Spanish navigators, who sighted, and landed on, some of the northern atolls. The

A young Maori couple in the costume of the South Seas

first more detailed description of the archipelago was given by Captain Cook, who reached Manuae on September 23rd 1773 during his second voyage. He named the southern group the Hervey Islands, after Augustus Hervey, a Lord of the Treasury. After him came others, mostly seafarers or missionaries; among them were the "Bounty" mutineers.

From 1823 onwards the influence of the English missionaries on Rarotonga extended to all the islands in the group. They brought the Christian message of brotherly love, which put an end to tribal wars and the tradition of human sacrifices, but they also brought in diseases which in the next few years were to carry off half the native population. Since the widely scattered islands were never united under a single ruler the British mission centre on Rarotonga, with its schools and its Takamoa College (founded 1837), became the unifying factor in the islands. For many years the islanders' fears about possible European claims on their territory were groundless: at first neither Britain nor France showed any territorial interest in the remote islands west of Tahiti. This situation changed with the French intervention in Tahiti and the first Maori rebellions in New Zealand. It was the chiefs of Rarotonga who, fearful of French intentions, first sought British protection in 1844. A formal application followed in 1865; but it was another 23 years before a British protectorate over Rarotonga was proclaimed in 1888. In subsequent years this was extended to all the islands.

The establishment of a Parliament on the British model in Rarotonga and the adoption of British law which followed strengthened the bonds between Britain and the islands. Soon practical and geographical considerations pointed to the advisability of putting the islands under the protection of New Zealand; and in 1901 they were annexed by New Zealand and given their present name of Cook Islands.

These eventful years were followed by a long period of peace and stability, until in the early 1960s, under pressure from the United Nations, who suspected New Zealand of colonial ambitions in the South Pacific, government responsibilities were gradually transferred to the Parliament on Rarotonga, and in 1965 the Cook Islands became independent. Since then they have remained in close association with New Zealand, which retains responsibility only for defence and foreign policy.

Population
and religion

The islands have a population of some 19,000, producing a population density of 78 inhabitants to the sq.kilometre (202 to the sq. mile). The overwhelming majority are Maoris of Polynesian descent. More than 31,000 "Cook Maoris" live and work in New Zealand. Rarotonga, with almost 11,000 inhabitants, is by a considerable margin the most densely populated island, followed by Aitutaki (pop. 2400) and Mangaia (pop. 1100). Three of the islands are uninhabited. The national languages are English and Maori. Some 70% of the population are Protestants, around 10% Catholics.

Economy and
society

The economic base of most Pacific island states is agriculture. Their small-ness and remoteness are usually obstacles to economic development, the scope for which is dependent on the size of the island and its natural conditions. The economic production of most island states is directed in varying degree to meeting the needs of the domestic market.

This is true in full measure of the Cook Islands, which are handicapped by the small size of the individual islands and to a large extent also by the poor fertility of the soil. This is particularly the case with the islands in the northern group and with Takutea and Manuae in the southern group, where the coralline limestone has only a thin covering of humus. In these islands the only economic resource is the undemanding and salt-tolerant coconut palm. The volcanic islands are more favoured by nature, with soils which in many places are highly fertile. These islands, inheriting the colonial planta-tion economy, grow tropical fruits and tuberous plants in monoculture. On Rarotonga, Atiu and Mauke the main crops are pawpaws, bananas and, on a smaller scale, coffee, while Mangaia specialises in pineapples and Aitutaki in bananas.

The islands export tropical fruits (mainly pawpaws, bananas, pineapples and copra), as well as processed products such as orange juice and tinned pineapples. The production of cultured black pearls also makes a contribu-tion to the economy. Fishing and fish-processing play only a subordinate role. A canning plant, two small clothing factories and a number of craft workshops provide some industrial employment. The largest employer, however, is the government, which has over 900 employees. The opening of Rarotonga's international airport in 1974 gave a boost to tourism, which has become increasingly important to the islands' economy. Some 30% of the working population are now employed in the tourist trade, compared with 20% in industry. Only 6% of the population work in agriculture, which accounts for 17% of the gross domestic product. Even with the increasing revenue from tourism – the annual number of visitors, mainly from New Zealand and Australia, is now over 40,000 – the prospects for further economic development are limited. And this in spite of the fact that the islands' political and economic relationship with the former protecting power, New Zealand, brings great economic and financial advantages which have given the people of the Cook Islands a relatively high standard of living. The islanders' unrestricted access to the New Zealand labour market, however, has a down side. Continuing emigration, particularly of skilled workers, has had negative effects on the population structure, on the national sense of identity and on social life, which have created a feeling of national disorientation and hopelessness among those who remain behind.

Islands of the Southern Group

★Rarotonga

With an area of 67.2sq.km/25.9sq. miles, Rarotonga is the largest of the Cook Islands, with almost 60% of the total population of the archipelago. Its bizarre landscape and lush tropical vegetation make it, in the opinion of many visitors, one of the most beautiful of the Polynesian islands. The chief place, Avarua, is the administrative, economic and cultural centre of the Cook Islands.

Rarotonga is the visible tip of a mighty volcanic cone which reaches down to 4500m/15,000ft below sea level. The hilly interior consists of a number of much weathered overlapping volcanoes. Thanks to rapid weathering in the moist tropical climate the slopes of the hills have been deeply indented by rivers. Round the rugged interior is a coastal plain some 1000m/1100yd wide, covered with fertile alluvial sands and dunes in which grow various ornamental and useful plants, coconut palms, pawpaws, bananas, coffee. Between the belt of dunes and the volcanic hills is s swampy depression which, as on other islands, is used for growing taro.

The island is surrounded by a fringing reef which encloses a narrow lagoon, linked with the open sea by a number of gaps in the reef. Only on the south and south-east is the reef farther from the coast, separated from it by the Muri Lagoon, with two sand islands and an island formed of a volcanic rock known to the inhabitants as taakoka.

Rarotonga can be explored on the regular buses, in a hired car or on a moped or bicycle. All the places on the island can be reached on a 30km/19 mile long asphalted ring road, and most of the hotels and other accommodation are on this road within sight of the sea. A second road, negotiable almost all the way, serves the agricultural areas at the foot of the hills, and from this road minor roads and a number of tracks lead into the interior. A good way of getting to know the island is to join a guided walk. The cross-island walk from the north coast up to the pinnacle rock Te Rua Manga (413m/1355ft) and then via Wigmore's Falls to the south coast takes about four hours. Only those with a good head for heights should attempt the ascent of Te Kon (588m/1929ft), from which there are breathtaking views. Another possible excursion is to the Marae Trai-te-tonga, the most sacred cult site on the island, with old Polynesian buildings.

Mangaia (area 51.09sq.km/19.7sq. miles; up to 169m/554ft), the most southerly and the second largest island in the archipelago, is in the shape of an irregular circle. The lower slopes of the central volcanic ridge are deeply indented by rivers. Round the central core are numerous irregularly shaped swampy depressions up to 366m/400yd across, bounded at the lower end   Mangaia

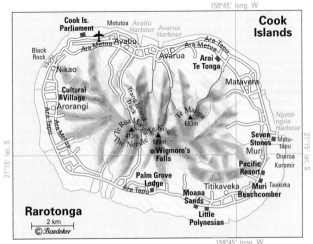

by limestone cliffs up to 60m/200ft high, sometimes falling almost vertically down. The cliffs are part of the 1200–1600m/1300–1750yd wide plain of coralline limestone (makatea), much affected by karstic action, which surrounds the island's volcanic core. The water flowing down from the hills seeps away into dolines and extensive cave systems, to re-emerge on the shore or in karstic springs near the coast.

The island is well provided with roads and tracks, and its fertile volcanic soil yields good crops of pineapples, coffee and other tropical produce for export.

Atiu

Atiu (area 27sq.km/17sq. miles; up to 72m/236ft), almost square in shape, lies north-east of Rarotonga. It is the third largest of the Cook Islands. It consists of a much weathered central volcanic massif in the form of a shallow dome, the slopes of which are slashed by radially oriented gorges. Round the foot are swampy depressions completely surrounding the island's volcanic core. These in turn are succeeded by a 1000m/1100yd wide raised platform of coralline limestone (makatea), which falls down to the sea, at some points edged by cliffs between 6 and 9m (20 and 30ft) high. The surface of the makatea is much affected by karstic action, with underground cave systems. Surface water drains down to the coast through dolines and caves. The island is surrounded at a distance of 45 to 90m (50 to 100yd) by a surf-lashed reef some 90m/100yd wide, with gaps at intervals which allow small ships to reach the landing-stages.

From the Taunganui Landing a road cuts through the interior of the island, with narrow roads or tracks leading to individual houses or to the taro swamps. Another road runs along the north and west coasts to the Tarapaku and Vai Piaka Landings. Almost all the inhabitants live in the five small villages on the volcanic plateau, in which are the island's shops and administrative buildings, as well as a small coffee-roasting plant. There are a number of walking trails through the island's tropical jungle and pineapple plantations. Characteristic features of Atiu are the large limestone caves, which can be explored with the help of guides. There are many sandy beaches, but the coral reefs near the coast tend to make bathing unattractive.

Mitiaro

The island of Mitiaro (area 22.25sq.km/8.6sq. miles), north-east of Rarotonga, is in the form of an irregular oval. Like Atiu and Mauke, it has a raised reef surrounding the volcanic core and is enclosed by a continuous fringing reef; but, unlike these islands, it consists not of a single volcano but of four low volcanic hills no more than 12m/40ft high surrounded by a belt of swampy land.

The only settlement on the island is at the Omutu Landing, with all the houses clustering round the post office, radio station, copra drying building, etc. From here gravel roads, each 2km/1¼ miles long, run along the coast; the way over the swamps into the interior is on causeways of piled-up stones. Two features of interest are a doline 8m/26ft deep and a stalactitic cave containing a lake of cold milky water which smells strongly of sulphur and has a slightly bitter taste.

There are practically no sandy beaches, but visitors can cool off in a number of pools on the fringing reef.

Mauke

Mauke (area 18.4sq.km/7.1sq. miles) is the most easterly of the Cook Islands. The interior of the island is occupied by a much weathered basalt plateau with fertile soils, rising to a height of 30m/100ft, which is surrounded by a plain of coralline limestone up to 1.6km/1 mile wide. In between the two there are occasional swampy depressions which are used for growing taro. The island is enclosed by a narrow fringing reef with a surf platform on the inner side. There are six gaps in the reef which allow small boats to reach the landing-stages.

There are two villages on Mauke, one near the Taunganui Landing, with the post office, school and administrative offices, the other on the central plateau, with the church and a number of shops. The villages are linked by a good road, and another road runs round the island. There are a number of large limestone caves. Like Atiu, Mauke has beautiful beaches, but here too the nearby reef with its broad surf platform interferes with bathers' pleasure.

Aitutaki (area 18.02sq.km/7sq. miles) – which is almost an atoll – is a popular holiday island, particularly for day or longer excursions from Rarotonga. It consists of a main island of deeply weathered basalt, with an area of 16.8sq.km/6½sq. miles, which is surrounded by a wide lagoon. Its highest hill is Maungapu (124m/407ft). The lagoon, which at many points is shallow, is surrounded by a triangular barrier reef marking the outline of the volcano which rises from a depth of 4000m/13,000ft below sea level. On the eastern reef are twelve small coral islands (motus) with a total area of 2.2sq.km/0.85sq. mile. The only sand island is on the south-western reef. Two little basalt islets, Rapota and Moturakau, lie off the reef in the south-west of the lagoon. All 15 motus are fringed with coconut palms. The coastal areas of the main island also have coconut and pandanus palms. The scanty vegetation of the higher islands reflects the fact that they have a lower rainfall than Rarotonga.

⋆Aitutaki

On the west side of the reef there is a gap which gives boats and motor lighters access to the little harbour of the chief place on the island, Arutanga, in which are the island's post office, administrative offices, hospital and shops. There are other small settlements in the north and east of the island, easily reached on good roads. Most of the accommodation for visitors is on the west side of the island, in sight of the lagoon. Aitutaki's main source of income apart from tourism is its banana plantations.

The atoll is formed by two horseshoe-shaped islands, Manuae and Auoto (or Te-Au-O-Tu), separated from one another by the lagoon. The two islands, which have a total area of only 6sq.km/2.3sq. miles, consist of coral sand. The islands and the lagoon are surrounded by a continuous coral reef.

Manuae

Of the two islands only Manuae – an island of coconut plantations – has a permanent, if fluctuating, population. In addition to houses and administrative offices the little settlement has a health centre and a number of copra drying plants. The additional workers required seasonally come from the neighbouring islands. Outside the lagoon there is an anchorage for seagoing ships. A gap in the reef allows smaller vessels through. The other island, Auoto, can be reached only by boat over the lagoon. Within the lagoon and in the scrub near the shore white and blue herons and some other birds make their home. The turtles which are still numerous here bring up their young in the lagoon.

Visitors can reach Manuae only by boat at irregular intervals.

Takutea is an oval sand island with an area of 2.2sq.km/0.8sq. miles surrounded by a coral reef. It is planted with coconut palms which, since Takutea is uninhabited, are looked after from Atiu.

Takutea

Islands of the Northern Group

The atolls in the northern group consist of narrow elongated reef islands (motus), reaching a maximum height of between 3 and 6m (10 and 20ft) above sea level, set round a central lagoon. Some of the motus were once larger, as old beach defences and cliff lines show, but have been partly destroyed by tidal waves resulting from hurricanes (as, for example, in 1942). On the seaward side the beaches have been raised by the pebbles and boulders thrown up by the surf and by beach defences; on the lagoon side they fall away gently. The concave coastline of many atolls is the result of displacements of the reef and submarine faults. The gaps in the atoll are mostly narrow and very shallow. There are anchorages for larger vessels within the lagoon only on Penrhyn and Suwarrow. The islands receive necessary supplies from Rarotonga in small vessels which call several

General

times a year and on their return voyage carry the islands' produce, mainly coconuts and copra.

The larger buildings on the islands (churches, administrative offices, schools, etc.) are built of coralline limestone, which offers protection against the storm tides which can sweep over these low-lying islands. Other buildings are mainly of wood and roofed with corrugated iron or palm leaves. The Polynesians still prefer the traditional method of construction, adapted to the climate, using pandanus wood and leaves. Rainwater is collected in large tanks and cisterns to meet local needs. Apart from rats and mice there are no wild animals on the islands. Pigs and poultry are kept for domestic consumption. Large numbers of seabirds nest on most of the islands, particularly on Suwarrow. Outside the reefs there are good fishing grounds.

Penrhyn

Penrhyn is the largest atoll in the Cook Islands, with an area of 9.8sq.km/3.8sq. miles. There are three passages through the reef, which has two motus of some size on the south-west side and numerous smaller ones to the north, east and south. Near the western passage through the reef is Omoka village, the chief place on the islands, with various public buildings and administrative offices. Tautua village, the second largest settlement, lies 14km/8½ miles from Omoka on the opposite side of the lagoon.

Manihiki

Manihiki (area 5.3sq.km/2sq. miles) is one of the most beautiful atolls in the Cook Islands. It resembles Aitutaki in its triangular conformation. The lagoon is surrounded by a continuous reef, with no navigable passages through it. The two motus, which are among the longest in the group, rise no higher than 5m/16ft above sea level. The water between individual motus is rarely more than 1m/40in. deep. The chief place on the island is Tauhunu village, which has the necessary public buildings and a shed for storing coconut products. There is a smaller village, which can be reached only by boat over the lagoon, at the northern tip of the atoll. Visitors can see round the pearl farm in the lagoon.

Rakahanga

Rakahanga (area 4.04sq.km/1.6sq. miles) is square in form. There are only shallow passages through the surrounding reef. The long and relatively broad reef islands have been broken up into smaller motus only near the gaps in the reef. There are broad sandy beaches on the north-eastern shore of the atoll; elsewhere the beaches are of shingle, sometimes very coarse. The only village with shops is to the south-west.

Palmerston

Palmerston (area 2sq.km/0.9sq. miles) is an irregularly shaped atoll with 35 motus. The shallow lagoon is surrounded by a continuous reef with no passages of any depth. Only one of the motus is permanently inhabited. Many buildings in the trim little village were built with timber from shipwrecks. In addition to public buildings such as churches and the radio station there are rainwater tanks for collecting the community's water supply. The lagoon is shallow and suitable only for small outboard motorboats and canoes.

Pukapuka

Pukapuka (area 1.2sq.km/½sq. mile), also known as Danger Island, is a triangular atoll consisting of three motus and a sandbank. Motu Kotawa and Motu Ko are uninhabited but are under cultivation. On Motu Pukapuka are three small villages (Roto, Yato and Ngake) of low houses and huts. Roto is the main centre, with the post office, administrative offices, church and shops. Here too are substantial houses built of wood and coralline limestone. The only vehicles on the island are bicycles. The shallow lagoon is suitable only for motorboats or outrigger boats.

25km/15 miles south-east of Pukapuka is Tima Reef, a small flat coral island only 450m/490yd across. It is believed to be a fragment of the Pukapuka atoll, which was formerly much larger.

Nassau

The oval sand island of Nassau (area 1.2sq.km/½sq. mile) is covered by chains of dunes up to 9m/30ft high and surrounded by a broad reef platform ranging in width between 90 and 130m (100 and 140yd) which makes landing on the island extremely dangerous. The island has large coconut plantations, and in the swampy depressions between the dunes taro is grown. There are a number of springs of fresh water. The land on Nassau is worked from the neighbouring island of Pukapuka.

This atoll has the form of an irregular circle. Its small size (0.4sq.km/0.15sq. mile) and few motus are the result of the destruction caused by violent whirlwinds within the last hundred years. The atoll was uninhabited until the mid 1960s, when an Englishman named T. Neal settled here and lived as a hermit for more than ten years. The population has now risen to ten.

Suwarrow

**Practical
Information
from A to Z**

Accommodation

See Hotels, Private accommodation, Camping and caravanning, Youth accommodation

Air Services

Major international airports

Auckland
Auckland International Airport
Location: 21km/13 miles south of city centre.
To and from airport: half-hourly shuttle bus service (tel. (09) 275 7685/307 5210) between airport and Downtown Air Terminal (tel. (09) 379 6056) (journey time ¾ hour, fare NZ$9); taxis (fare about NZ$30).
Airport tax: NZ$20.
Information: Air New Zealand, Air N2 Travel Centre, corner of Queen Street and Custom Street tel. (09) 357 3000
British Airways: The Delworth Building, Queen and Custom Street, CP Box 3160; tel. (09) 356 8690

Christchurch
Christchurch International Airport
Location: at Harewood, 10km/6 miles north-west.
To and from airport: shuttle bus service; taxis.
Airport tax: NZ$20.
Information: Air New Zealand, tel. (03) 379 5200 or 379 0690

Wellington
Wellington International Airport
Location: 9km/5½ miles south-east, near Lyall Bay.
To and from airport: shuttle bus service; taxis.
Airport tax: NZ$20.
Information: Air New Zealand, tel. (04) 495 2910/388 9737

Cook Islands
(Rarotonga)
Rarotonga International Airport
Airport tax: NZ$20.
Information: Air New Zealand, tel. (02) 26302
N.B.: Passengers flying with Air New Zealand have the option of a stopover in Rarotonga. Air New Zealand flies Los Angeles–Honolulu–Rarotonga–Auckland.

Airports for domestic services

In addition to New Zealand's three international airports there are a number of important regional airports for domestic flights: on the North Island Rotorua, Hamilton and Palmerston North, on the South Island Nelson, Queenstown and Dunedin.

Other New Zealand airports are: on the North Island Kaitaia, Kerikeri, Whangarei, Tauranga, Whakatane, Gisborne, New Plymouth, Wanganui, Napier/Hastings and Paraparaumu; on the South Island Takaka, Motueka, Blenheim, Westport, Hokitika, Mount Cook, Timaru, Wanaka, Milford Sound, Te Anau and Invercargill.

Cook Islands,
Niue
Rarotonga, the principal island in the Cook Islands group, is included in Air New Zealand's network of services. From Rarotonga Polynesian Airlines fly to the other islands in the archipelago and to Niue, using smaller aircraft.

◀ For the adventurous holidaymaker: a jetboat trip through the Shotover Canyon

An Air New Zealand Jumbo

Airlines

The leading New Zealand airline **Air New Zealand**, flies both international
and domestic services. Its international services include one-stop flights to
and from London Heathrow via Los Angeles. It occupies a dominant position in domestic services, flying to and from 31 domestic airports as well as
the Cook Islands.

New Zealand
airlines

Ansett New Zealand flies to a number of airports in New Zealand and in
Australia and other neighbouring countries.

The **Mount Cook Airline** flies to major New Zealand airports, particularly
tourist centres, and also to many smaller places. It also operates air tours
and charter flights.

A number of smaller regional airlines provide connecting services with
the major airlines and operate charter flights.

Air New Zealand, Head Office,
Private Bag, Auckland,
tel. (09) 379 7515,
fax (09) 388 0575
In Britain: tel. (0181) 741 2299
Toll-free reservation in the USA:
(800) 262 1234
Toll-free reservation in Canada:
(800) 663 5494

Information and
reservations

Ansett New Zealand, Head Office,
PO Box 4168, Auckland,
tel. (09) 309 6235,
fax (09) 309 6434

Air Services

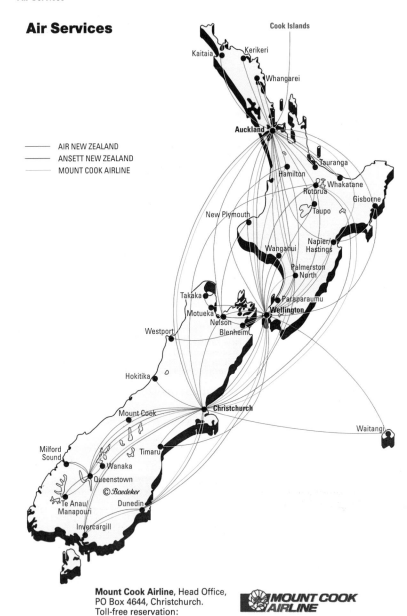

AIR NEW ZEALAND
ANSETT NEW ZEALAND
MOUNT COOK AIRLINE

Cook Islands

Kaitaia
Kerikeri
Whangarei

Auckland

Tauranga
Hamilton
Whakatane
Rotorua
Taupo
Gisborne

New Plymouth
Napier/
Hastings
Wanganui
Palmerston
North

Takaka
Paraparaumu
Motueka
Wellington
Nelson
Blenheim

Westport

Hokitika

Mount Cook
Christchurch

Waitangi

Milford
Sound
Timaru
Wanaka
Queenstown
© Baedeker
Te Anau/
Manapouri
Dunedin

Invercargill

Mount Cook Airline, Head Office,
PO Box 4644, Christchurch.
Toll-free reservation:
tel. (0800) 800737 in New Zealand only.

MOUNT COOK AIRLINE

Polynesian Airlines serve the Cook Islands and the island of Niue, and also provide connections with major New Zealand and foreign airlines.

Polynesian Airlines

The main foreign airlines flying to Auckland and/or Wellington and/or Christchurch (for routes, see Getting there) are Air Pacific, British Airways, Cathay Pacific, Garuda Indonesia, Malaysia Airlines, Royal Tongan Airlines, Singapore Airlines, Thai International, Qantas and United Airlines.

Foreign airlines

British Airways have one-stop flights between London and Auckland, with fast airside transfer at Los Angeles.
 Information and reservations: BA, Qantas House, 154 Queen Street, Auckland; tel. (09) 356 8690

British Airways

The three New Zealand airlines offer various special rates for visitors. The **Explore New Zealand Air Pass**, is valid on all domestic flights on Air New Zealand, the Mount Cook Airline, Eagle Air and Air Nelson, and consists of from three to eight flight coupons offering a considerable reduction on standard fares. The pass must be bought before leaving home along with a ticket to New Zealand.
 The Mount Cook Airline has the **Kiwi Pass**, which covers an unlimited number of flights on its complete network, though each route may be flown only once.
 Ansett New Zealand has a variety of special rates, including the **Discover New Zealand Tariff**, which gives a reduction of 20%.

Air passes and discounts

A departure tax (airport tax), at present NZ$20, is payable by all passengers leaving airports in New Zealand (and the Cook Islands) for foreign destinations.

Departure tax

Light aircraft can be hired by visitors holding a pilot's licence and an English radio-telephony certificate after a check on their competence. For information enquire locally.

Private flying

Alcohol

Alcoholic drinks can normally only be obtained in licensed restaurants and hotels and in special shops known as "bottle stores". Bottle stores are open Monday to Saturday, frequently until 10pm. The opening hours for bars are normally Mon.–Sat. 11am–10pm; no alcohol may be supplied on Sunday.

Sale of alcohol

Restaurants showing the sign "BYO" ("bring your own") have no licence to serve alcohol, but guests may bring their own wine or beer. There may be a small corkage charge.

BYO

Automobile Association

The New Zealand Automobile Association (AA) has offices in all major towns. Members of the UK Automobile Association and other motoring organisations are entitled to the services of the AA free of charge, and on presentation of their membership card can obtain certain AA publications free of charge and others at much reduced prices. In addition to various road maps the AA publishes the following brochures of interest to visitors: the "North Island Accommodation Guide", the "South Island Accommodation and Camping Guide" and the "Outdoor Guide" (addresses and prices of camping, walking, rafting, etc., facilities).

Main AA offices

99 Albert Street, Auckland
Tel. (09) 377 4660, fax (09) 309 4564

North Island
Auckland

Bathing Beaches

Wellington	342 Lambton Quay, PO Box 1053, Wellington Tel. (04) 473 8738
South Island Christchurch	702 Colombo Street. PO Box 994, Christchurch

Bathing Beaches

Lonely beaches	Seafronts lined with concrete hotels, massed ranks of beach umbrellas and sunbathers: these you will not find – so far at any rate – in New Zealand. Most of the beaches are lonely and uncrowded, and usually enclosed by lush green vegetation. There are still many little bays and inlets where you will scarcely see another human being all day.
Sandy beaches	New Zealand's sandy beaches show a wide spectrum of colour – black volcanic sand on the west coast, white calcareous sand in subtropical Northland, pinkish-red sand on the Coromandel Peninsula, golden sand at the northern tip of the South Island.
Popular beaches	It is an almost impossible task to list all New Zealand's bathing beaches. Listed here are a few places where bathing is a particular delight:
North Island	Bay of Islands, Bay of Plenty, Hawke's Bay near Napier, Hot Water Beach and Hahei on the Coromandel Peninsula, Ninety Mile Beach at the northern tip of the North Island, Orewa Beach near Auckland.
South Island	Banks Peninsula, beaches at the northern tip of the island in the Abel Tasman National Park, round Nelson and in the Marlborough Sounds, at the Moeraki Boulders, round Dunedin (particularly Tunnel Beach), Papatowai and Purakanui Bay in the Catlins, on Stewart Island and round Christchurch (particularly Sumner Beach and Taylor's Mistake).
Season; water temperatures	The bathing season is from the end of October to the beginning of March. On beaches in the north and east of the North Island water temperatures reach 20°C/68°F or more. On the most popular beaches in the South Island, for example in Golden Bay, Tasman Bay and the Marlborough Sounds and around Christchurch, water temperatures are usually around 18° to 20°C (64° to 68°F).
Nude bathing	Nude bathing is, in general, frowned on in New Zealand. Even topless bathing or sunbathing is not generally acceptable.
Dangers	Some of the most popular beaches have lifeguards, but in many places bathers are left on their own. Great caution is required on long beaches exposed to the open sea, since there can be very dangerous currents. Sandflies, which can give very painful bites, can be troublesome, particularly in the late afternoon and evening. They are especially bad on the west coast of the South Island.

Bed and Breakfast

See Hotels

Bungy Jumping

The challenging sport of bungy jumping (see Baedeker Special, p. 272–73) originated in New Zealand and is now popular throughout the world. The early bungy jumpers threw themselves off the old bridge over the Kawarau River into the gorge 43m/140ft below, saved from destruction only by a rubber rope attached to one ankle. The rope brakes the jumper's fall, then pulls him/her up and lets him/her down again several times, after which they are picked up by a rubber dinghy. One of the ultimate challenges is a jump from the 102m/335ft high Pipeline on the upper Shotover River.

A bungy jump costs between NZ$70 and $160 or more, depending on the degree of difficulty and the arrangements for collecting the jumper after his jump.

Costs

Business Hours

Department stores and other shops are usually open Mon.–Thur. 9am–5.30pm, on Friday or another weekday until 9pm (late-night shopping). In the larger towns shops are also open Sat. 9.30am–2pm (sometimes to 4.30pm); some of them also open Sun. 9am–4.30pm.

Shops

Dairies in New Zealand are the equivalent of the British corner shop. They are usually open daily 7am–10pm. In cities and tourist centres some stay open until midnight.

Dairies
(corner shops)

Alcoholic drinks can be bought only in licensed bottle stores, which are open Mon.–Sat. 9am–6pm, often until 10pm. Wine, however, is now also sold in supermarkets and grocery stores.

Bottle stores

Mon.–Fri. 10am–4pm.

Banks

Mon.–Fri. 9am–5pm. Some travel agencies and airline offices have longer opening hours.

Public and
other offices

Camping and Caravanning

New Zealand is an ideal country for holidaymakers who like to get about on their own with a tent or caravan. The roads are good and there is little traffic. There are well over 500 official camping sites, but there is also plenty of scope for camping without using the official sites. "Wild" camping is permitted provided that permission is asked from the owner of the land and the regulations about the disposal of waste are observed. Special conditions apply in many national parks. Information about current regulations can be obtained from offices of the New Zealand Tourism Board or from car rental firms (see Car Rental). The hire charge for a camper van (motor caravan) for four people is between NZ$200 and $300 a day.

There is no lack of camping sites in New Zealand. Even quite small places have sites for tents and caravans, ranging from sites with basic facilities to motor camps provided with every amenity. The sites – usually well situated – are clean and tidy and well equipped with facilities (communal kitchens, refrigerators, washing machines, driers). Motor camps have power sockets for camper vans and arrangements for the disposal of waste. There may also be accommodation for people travelling without either a tent or camper van, ranging from a modest cabin to a comfortable (and relatively expensive) tourist flat.

Camping sites

The 200 or so DoC camping sites usually have only the most basic facilities but compensate for this by the beauty of their settings. They are also fairly inexpensive.

Department of
Conservation sites

Car Rental

Charges	Since most camping sites are run by local authorities the charges are relatively low. On the best sites the charge for two people with a camper van is at present around NZ$30 per night. Average rates per person per night are around NZ$10 (tent), $10–20 (camper van), $15–40 (cabin) and $40–80 (tourist flat).
Lists of sites	The Camp and Cabin Association and the New Zealand Automobile Association publish complete lists of all camping sites in New Zealand, which are updated annually. The DoC also produces an annual list of its sites available from most DoC offices.
Information	Camp and Cabin Association of New Zealand, 4A Kanawa Street, Waikanae Department of Conservation, PO Box 10420, Wellington (site list also obtainable from New Zealand Tourism Board offices).
"Wild" camping	Tents may be pitched and camper vans parked almost anywhere in New Zealand except where there is a "No camping" sign. No more than seven days may be spent in the same place. As a matter of politeness the farmer or owner of the land should be asked for permission, and the site must be left clean and tidy.
Spirit stoves	Methylated spirits may be used in spirit stoves but not white spirit.

Car Rental

Car rental firms	The leading international car rental firms such as Avis, Hertz and Budget operate in New Zealand and have offices at the international airports and elsewhere. They offer advantageous deals, which can be booked before leaving home. There are also many local rental firms, among the largest of which are Maui and NZ Rent-a-Car. A list of recommended car rental firms can be obtained from New Zealand Tourism Board offices (see Information).
Booking	The minimum age for renting a vehicle is 21. A valid driving licence must be produced (British, United States, Canadian and Australian licences, among many others, are accepted in New Zealand).
	It is cheaper to book through one of the international car rental firms before leaving home, and it is vital, particularly during the main holiday season, to book well in advance.
	Rental charges vary according to the time of year, the type of vehicle and the period of hire. Currently the minimum charge per week (including unlimited mileage, tax and insurance) is about NZ$400. There is also the additional cost of GST (goods and sales tax) as well as any supplementary insurance which maybe required. (It is advisable to take out insurance against damage to windscreens, which is usually not covered and is liable to occur on New Zealand's many gravel roads.)
Deposit	When hiring a car or camper van a deposit of around NZ$500 must be paid. This requirement can be met by production of a credit card.
One-way rental	There is no difficulty, at any rate with the large rental firms, in arranging one-way hire without additional charge, for example between Auckland and Christchurch. The vehicle can be returned to the firm's depot at Wellington (North Island) or Picton (South Island) and a new one picked up on arrival.
Insurance	Before signing the rental agreement you should check which roads may be used. On some roads there is no insurance cover.
Fly/drive	Travel operators and airlines offer attractive fly/drive packages which include flights, hire of car or camper van and accommodation, if required, in hotels or motels. Visitors are then free to choose their own route.

Practically all types of vehicle are available for hire, from small cars to limousines (with or without driver) and cross-country vehicles with four-wheel drive.

Types of vehicle

A camper van is an ideal vehicle for a touring holiday in New Zealand. You are relatively independent and can spend the night almost wherever you like, either in open country or on one of the numerous camping sites. The Maui, Newmans and Mount Cook rental firms offer a wide choice of camper vans (from NZ$150 upwards per day) and rather larger "motor homes". The condition of these vehicles, however, sometimes leaves a good deal to be desired: poor insulation, defective heating, inadequate water containers, no waste-water tank and no mosquito screens on the windows to provide protection against the bloodthirsty sandflies are not uncommon problems. And the hard suspension may give anyone travelling in the living compartment an uncomfortable ride.

Camper vans (motor caravans)

Motorcycles are also available for hire and are much in demand during the New Zealand summer. A helmet can be hired at an extra charge of around NZ$20.

Motorcycles

For a stay of more than two months it may be worth while to buy rather than hire a car or motorcycle. You may find attractive offers in the Car Fair held in Auckland (Newmarket district) every Saturday morning. Before buying it is essential to check that the car has a new "WoF" (warrant of fitness). Selling the car at the end of your stay can be a time-consuming business. Some second-hand car dealers, however, are prepared to agree on a price at which they will buy the car back.

Buying a car

Casinos

Gaming houses similar to those in Las Vegas are a recent development in New Zealand, and there are now casinos in Auckland and Christchurch, open only to adults of 20 or over. A reasonable standard of dress is required (no jeans!).

Harrah's Sky City Casino
A casino designed by well-known contemporary artists, with a large gaming hall, a theatre seating 700, several restaurants and various other gambling and sports facilities.

Auckland

Christchurch Casino
30 Victoria Street; tel. (03) 365 9999
Open: Thur. 11am to Mon. 3am.

Christchurch

Chemists

Chemists' shops are open during normal business hours. Emergency service outside these hours is provided on a rota system, details of which are published in the local press.

Children

Leaving aside the long and tiring flight, a holiday in New Zealand has a great deal to offer families with children, in particular plenty of open space where children can play and romp about without danger from traffic or wild animals. Even small places have children's playgrounds, and in restaurants there are children's menus and high chairs as a matter of course.

The beaches of the Coromandel Peninsula, the Hauraki Gulf, Great Barrier Island, the Marlborough Sounds and the northern tip of the South Island are particularly suitable for children.

Attractions for Children

Albatross colony, Dunedin
Here albatrosses can be watched nesting, sitting on their eggs and flying. Information: tel. (03) 477 4176 or 478 0499. Admission charge. Closed Sept.–Nov.

Kelly Tarlton's Underwater World, Auckland
Information: tel. (09) 528 0603
Open daily 9am–9pm. Admission charge.

Paradise Valley, Rotorua
A park with live animals from many parts of the world. Visitors are allowed into the lion cubs' enclosure when they are being fed. Children should be carefully supervised. Information: tel. (07) 348 9667. Admission free, but a voluntary contribution is requested.

Penguin Place, Dunedin
Here yellow-eyed penguins and seals can be seen in their natural surroundings. Admission free.

Coach Services

The most important form of passenger transport in New Zealand is the coach. A dense network of coach services links all the major cities and towns and the main tourist centres. Most services, however, operate only on weekdays; on Sundays there are very few coaches, and in some areas none at all. It is essential to book in advance, particularly during the main tourist season (December to March).

Coach companies
The largest private coach companies in New Zealand are Newmans on the North Island and Mount Cook Landline on the South Island. In addition there are InterCity Coachlines and an evergrowing number of smaller companies such as the Kiwi Experience and Magic Bus Company.

InterCity Travel Pass
Visitors to New Zealand can obtain various types of travel pass which allow unlimited coach travel within a given area and are very good value for money.

The InterCity Travel Pass (information: tel. (09) 357 8400) covers travel on trains, ferries and coaches run by the InterCity transport corporation. On the South Island it also includes certain services run by Newmans.

There are the standard *3 in 1 Travelpass New Zealand* and the more comprehensive *Complete New Zealand Travelpass* or *4 in 1 Travelpass*. The 4 in 1 pass includes one flight on Ansett New Zealand between the North and South Islands or within either island.

InterCity Travelpasses can be bought only outside New Zealand or on arrival in New Zealand. The current price for a 3 in 1 pass ranges from NZ$350 for 5 days' travel over 10 days to $690 for 22 days' travel over 8 weeks; for a 4 in 1 pass the corresponding figures are $580 and $920. Children pay two-thirds of the adult price.

Kiwi Coach Pass
Mount Cook Landline's Kiwi Coach Pass covers travel on all InterCity and Newmans routes, as well as those of Great Sights Gray Line, Northliner and Kiwi Experience. Also included is one flight with Air Nelson over the Cook Strait from Wellington to Nelson or Blenheim. Holders of this pass also enjoy a reduction of up to 20% on sightseeing flights with the Mount Cook Airline and boat trips with Fuller's Cruises.

The Kiwi Coach Pass at present costs around NZ$400 for 11 days and NZ$800 for 45 days. It is obtainable outside New Zealand, but can also be bought in New Zealand on production of the visitor's passport and air ticket.

The Newmans Flexi Pass is also accepted by the Northliner, Mount Cook and Kiwi Experience companies. A One Island Pass covers either the North or the South Island; a Two Island Pass covers both. Passes are issued for a specified number of days within a three-month period. A seven-day pass costs NZ$295 for one island, NZ$395 for both. Ten-day and 15-day passes are also available.

Newmans
Flexi Pass

Other coach companies offer a variety of inducements for backpackers, such as Kiwi Experience's *Backpacker's Pass*.

Backpacker's
Pass

InterCity Coachlines, Beach Road, PO Box 3625, Parnell, Auckland; tel. (09) 357 8400. Wellington; tel. (04) 472 5111. Christchurch; tel. (03) 379 9020.
Mount Cook Line, PO Box 4644, Christchurch; toll-free reservations tel. (0800) 800737.
Newmans Coachlines, PO Box 90–821, Auckland; toll-free reservations tel. (0800) 733500.
Kiwi Experience, 36 Customs Street East, PO Box 1553, Auckland; tel. (09) 366 1665. Wellington; tel. (04) 385 2153. Christchurch; tel. (03) 311 0550.

Information

Crime

New Zealand's crime rate is relatively high. Tourists have so far been little troubled, but it is advisable for visitors, particularly those travelling by car or camper van, to take sensible precautions. Break-ins to cars have considerably increased in recent years. In hotels, motels and other holiday accommodation the built-in safes should be used for keeping valuable documents and other items. Jewellery is best left at home. Parts of Auckland are increasingly unsafe.

Cruises

See Shipping Services

Currency

New Zealand's unit of currency is the New Zealand dollar (NZ$1 = 100 cents). There are notes for 5, 10, 20, 50 and 100 dollars and coins in denominations of 1, 2, 4, 10, 20 and 50 cents and 1 and 2 dollars.

Banks are open Mon.–Fri. 9am–4pm. There are bank branches at airports and almost every large shopping centre.

Banks

There are no restrictions on the import or export of either New Zealand or foreign currency in the form of banknotes, coins, travellers' cheques or other means of payment.

Currency
regulations

Customs Regulations

Changing money	There are exchange offices as airports and seaports. It is better to change most of your money in New Zealand rather than at home, since you will get a better exchange rate in New Zealand; but some money should be changed before leaving home in order to avoid the long queues at the airport.
	Any surplus New Zealand money left at the end of your stay should be changed in plenty of time, particularly if your departure is at night. You are unlikely to get a good rate for New Zealand money outside New Zealand.
Credit cards	Credit cards – particularly American Express, Diners Club, MasterCard (Eurocard) and Visa – are a very common form of payment in New Zealand. A credit card is also useful when you are hiring a car, since it can be used in place of a deposit.
Travellers' cheques	Travellers' cheques denominated in New Zealand dollars can be cashed in banks, hotels, restaurants and many shops. Some banks and large hotels will also accept travellers' cheques denominated in British pounds and US dollars.
Eurocheques	Eurocheques are not accepted in New Zealand.
Cash	Cash in any currency can be exchanged in New Zealand.
Currency for a long stay	If you are spending some time in New Zealand it is worth while opening a giro account with the Bank of New Zealand. You can then draw cash at any branch of the bank in New Zealand, and in the meantime your money will be earning interest.
Loss of money	If you lose travellers' cheques or a credit card you should inform the police and the appropriate bank as soon as possible. If you are left without money your embassy or consulate (see Diplomatic and Consular Offices) will help; any money they lend you must be repaid as soon as you get home.
Prices	See entry
Goods and services tax	See entry

Customs Regulations

In addition to personal effects, visitors over the age of 17 are allowed the following concessions, free of duty and tax: 200 cigarettes or 30 cigars or 250 grams of tobacco, or a mixture of all three not weighing more than 250 grams; 4.5 litres of wine and 1.125 litres of spirits or liqueur; and goods up to a total combined value of NZ$700.

To prevent the importation of animal and plant diseases (from which New Zealand is relatively free) it is unlawful to bring most untreated or un-processed animal and plant materials into New Zealand.

New Zealand's customs controls are thorough and there are heavy penalties for evasion of duty.

To prevent the spread of epidemics and disease the cabins of aircraft are disinfected before the passengers leave, as is their luggage. Shoes and other items of equipment may be imported only if they are clean.

Information	Full information about New Zealand's customs and entry regulations is given in the "Customs Guide for Travellers", obtainable from New Zealand Tourism Board offices.

Visitors to New Zealand may purchase duty-free goods, which are not liable to local taxes, from airport duty-free shops on arrival and departure. Duty-free shops in downtown Auckland, Wellington and Christchurch will deliver purchases to airport departure lounges.

Duty-free shopping

Cycling

A cycling tour of New Zealand is an experience of a very special kind. From north to south of each of the two main islands it is a two-week trip at an average of 70km/44 miles a day. The best time of the year for cycle touring, now becoming increasingly popular, is between October and April, when numbers of biking enthusiasts, including many from overseas, take to the roads.

Visitors contemplating a cycle tour in New Zealand should be fit and in good training, for the roads are often winding, sometimes narrow and not infrequently very hilly; and cyclists must be prepared to contend with almost permanent wind and showers of rain which, though usually brief, can be very heavy. The main roads are mostly asphalted, but minor roads – for example New Zealand's highest road, from Arrow Junction to Wanaka, east of Queenstown – are often merely gravel tracks. Cities and busy main roads are best avoided, both because of the exhaust fumes and because bus and lorry drivers tend to overtake cyclists by very narrow margins. The best plan is load your bicycle on to some form of public transport and head for quieter roads.

It has been compulsory since 1994 for cyclists to wear helmets.

Helmets

Bicycles can be hired in almost every New Zealand town. Service facilities and spare parts are readily available in larger towns.

Bicycle hire

Your bicycle should be a sturdy machine with good gears. The hire charge for a bicycle is usually between NZ$15 and $30 a day.

In addition to a good bicycle you should have proper equipment: watertight cycle bags, rainproof clothing, helmet, a light tent for emergencies, and a sun cream with a high protection factor.

If you like to use your own machine you can bring it with you. Most airlines carry bicycles free or at a very reasonable charge.

Your bicycle

Some specialised travel operators offer cycle tours lasting one or more weeks, with an accompanying vehicle to carry luggage. Information: Pedaltours, PO Box 37–575, Parnell, Auckland;
   tel. (09) 302 0968, fax (09) 302 0967

Organised cycle tours

Dangers

See Crime; Health (sunburn, sandflies, parasites)

Diplomatic and Consular Offices

New Zealand's Diplomatic and Consular Offices

High Commission
New Zealand House
Haymarket, London SW1Y 4TQ
Tel. (0171) 973 0366/63, fax (0171) 973 0370

United Kingdom

USA	Embassy
	37 Observatory Circle NW
	Washington DC 20008
	Tel. (202) 328 4848, fax (202) 667 5227

Consulates in Chicago, Houston, Los Angeles, New York, Salt Lake City, San Diego, San Francisco and Seattle

Canada	High Commission
	Suite 727, Metropolitan House
	99 Bank Street
	Ottawa, Ontario K1P 6G3
	Tel. (613) 238 5991, fax (613) 238 5707

Consulate in Vancouver

Australia	High Commission
	Commonwealth Avenue
	Canberra ACT 2600
	Tel. (6) 270 4211, fax (6) 273 3194

Consulates in Brisbane, Melbourne and Sydney

Diplomatic and Consular Offices in New Zealand

United Kingdom	High Commission
	44 Hill Street, Thorndon
	Wellington
	Tel. (04) 472 6049

Consulates in Auckland and Christchurch

USA	Embassy
	29 Fitzherbert Terrace, Thorndon
	Wellington
	Tel. (04) 472 2068

Consulates in Auckland and Christchurch

Canada	High Commission
	61 Molesworth Street
	Wellington
	Tel. (04) 473 9577

Consulate in Auckland

Australia	High Commission
	72–78 Hobson Street
	Wellington
	Tel. (04) 473 6411

Consulate in Auckland

Diving and Snorkelling

New Zealand's 10,000-km/6200-mile long coastline offers endless opportunities for scuba divers and snorkellers. The best diving grounds on the North Island are the Poor Knights Islands (a particularly colourful underwater world, with visibility up to 70m/230ft) and the Bay of Islands (also good visibility), and on the South Island are Fiordland and Stewart Island (huge forests of seaweed and paua shells). The waters of the Cook Islands, with their numerous reefs of coralline limestone and atolls, are a mecca for scuba divers. The reefs formed by the calcareous deposits left by tiny marine creatures and the lagoons they enclose are a biotope inhabited by a great variety of vividly coloured marine life.

Hazards to watch out for, however, are dangerous and poisonous denizens of the sea such as moray eels and sea snakes.

Exploring wrecks is also popular with divers. Around the islands something like 50 wrecked ships lie on the sea-bed, including the Greenpeace ship "Rainbow Warrior" and the Russian cruise ship "Mikhail Lermontov", which sank in the Marlborough Sounds in 1986.

Some areas around the coasts are now statutorily protected, and scuba diving and snorkelling in these areas is strictly controlled. The hunting and killing of marine animals is prohibited in some areas. Certain biotopes which are particularly endangered may not be entered, or may be entered only with special permission.

Protection of nature

In New Zealand and in the Cook Islands there are well equipped diving centres which are of particular service to visitors who have come by air. If you have brought your own equipment you may need an adaptor for different types of air cylinders. When hiring scuba equipment you will usually be asked for a certificate of competence.

Scuba diving

The wreck of the Greenpeace ship "Rainbow Warrior", which was sunk in Auckland harbour by French secret agents in 1985, was towed to the Bay of Islands and sunk in Matauri Bay at a depth of 26m/85ft. The wreck is now overgrown with marine flora and provides a home for a great variety of sea creatures. There are organised diving trips from Paihia (day trips, with two dives). Information from Paihia Dive Hire and Charter Ltd, PO Box 210, Bay of Islands, tel. (09) 402 7551.

Wreck of "Rainbow Warrior"

This marine reserve at Leigh, north of Auckland, is popular with scuba divers and snorkellers. At quite a shallow depth and with excellent visibility a great variety of underwater life (particularly fish) can be observed at close quarters.

Goat Island Marine Reserve

New Zealand Underwater Association, PO Box 875, Auckland; tel. (09) 849 5896.

Information

Dress

New Zealanders prefer light casual clothing: typical dress for a man is shorts and knee-length white stockings. Ties are obligatory only in some top-class restaurants, and evening dress is rarely worn.

In late spring, summer and autumn (October to May) summer clothing can be worn, with something warm for the evening. In the winter months and early spring (June to September) warm clothing is required.

Essential items of clothing, at any time of year, are windproof and rainproof clothing, a hat or cap, sunglasses and sun cream, a pullover and stout and comfortable footwear.

Drinking Water

Tap-water is safe throughout New Zealand; table and mineral waters of excellent quality are available all over the country.

Water from springs, rivers, streams and lakes should always be boiled before drinking. In recent years parasites have been a danger in many parts of the country (see Health).

Warning

Electricity

Electricity is supplied throughout New Zealand at 230/240 volts, 50 hertz, although most hotels and motels have 110 volt sockets for electric razors. For all other items an adaptor will be required, as power sockets take only Australian-type plugs with three flat prongs.

Emergencies

Dial 111

In the larger towns dial 111 for police, fire or ambulance services. When being told of the emergency the operator will call out the appropriate service.

Other emergency numbers can be found at the beginning of the local telephone directory. In country areas the emergency numbers are shown on the telephone dial.

Entry Regulations

See Customs Regulations, Travel Documents

Events

A and P Shows

Visitors will enjoy a visit to one of the A and P Shows (Agricultural and Pastoral Shows) – more than a hundred in all – which are held at many places in New Zealand throughout the year. In the early days of settlement these shows were important occasions for farmers enabling them to learn about the latest farming methods and equipment. Some of them have taken on the aspect of a popular festival with special events such as sheepdog trials and sheep-shearing competitions.

Information

Events are listed in two booklets, "New Zealand Festivals and Calendar of Events" and "What's On in New Zealand", available from New Zealand Tourism Board offices.

Calendar of Events

January

Highland Games and New Zealand Championship Heavy Field Events, held on New Year's Day at Waipu (Northland).

Horse racing and rodeo (beginning of January) at Glenorchy (north of Lake Wakatipu).

Horowhenua A and P Show (January 24th/25th) at Levin on Lake Horowhenua (between Wellington and Palmerston North).

Cup Day in Auckland.

Far North Rodeo and A and P Show at Kaitaia.

Fiordland Summer Festival at Te Anau.

Summertime Festival in Christchurch and Napier.

Annual Yachting Regatta (end Jan./beginning Feb.) in Auckland. The regatta celebrates the anniversary of the foundation of the town on January 29th 1840: the sporting event of the year, in which over 1000 boats take part.

Kiwi Dragon Boat Festival in Auckland.

National tennis championships in Wellington.

Waitangi Day (New Zealand Day; February 6th) in the Bay of Islands, commemorating the treaty of Waitangi in 1840.
Marlborough Wine and Food Festival (beginning of February) on Brancott Estate (between Nelson and Blenheim).
Speight's Coast to Coast Triathlon (mid February), from Kumara Beach on the west coast to Sumner Beach, near Christchurch, on the east coast: a running, cycling and kayaking race of over 200km/125 miles.
New Zealand National Deep Sea Fishing Competition in the Bay of Islands.
Art Deco Weekend in Napier: a jazz and art festival.

February

Golden Shears sheep-shearing competition (beginning of March) in Masterton.
International Festival of the Arts (in even-numbered years) in Wellington: classical and modern music, ballet, poetry readings, arts and crafts.
Maori Canoe Regatta at Ngaruawahia (between Hamilton and Auckland).
Round the Bays Run, Auckland: one of the largest mass runs in the world, with 70,000 runners.
Wild Food Festival at Hokitika: food and drink of the early settlers.
Highland Games (Easter) at Hastings.

March

Arrowtown Autumn Festival (mid April).
Gumboot Day at Taihape.
Kumara Festival in Dargaville

April

Fletcher Challenge Marathon (beginning of May), on Lake Rotorua.
Kiwi Festival (mid May) at Te Puke ("kiwi capital of the world").

May

National Agricultural Field Days (mid June) in Hamilton: New Zealand's most important agricultural show.
DB Draught Marathon in Christchurch.
International Film Festival in Wellington.

June

Winter Festival (mid July) in Queenstown.

July

Solo Highland Piping Championship at Invercargill.
Festival of Fashion and Art in Nelson.
Boat Show in Wellington.

August

International Trout-Fishing Competition (mid September) at Rotorua.
New Zealand Luge Championships, at changing venues.
Snow Festival at Wanaka.
Spring Festival at Alexandra.

September

Whitebait Festival at Greymouth (on west coast of South Island).
Freshup Alpine Ironman Triathlon at Queenstown.
Auckland International Marathon (end October).
Taranaki Rhododendron Festival (end Oct./beginning Nov.) in New Plymouth.
AMP New Zealand Open Golf Championship (Oct./Nov.).
International Orchid Show in Palmerston North.

October

Canterbury Show (first week in November) in Christchurch: a three-day agricultural show with horse racing.
Otago Goldfields Heritage Celebrations (mid November).
International Trout-Fishing Tournament, Rotorua.

November

International Air New Zealand/Shell Golf Open, Auckland.
Pre-Christmas parades by children in the larger towns.

December

Fishing

Angling is a very popular recreation in New Zealand, whose coastal waters, rivers and lakes are well stocked with fish. Fishing in the sea is free, but fishing inland waters is permitted only with a licence obtainable for a day, week, month or season in fishing tackle and sports shops. However, it is not easy to hire fishing tackle in New Zealand.

Freshwater fishing
The main fishing season on inland waters is from October to March. The species preferred by anglers are trout and salmon.

Surfcasting, deep-sea angling
Surfcasting and deep-sea angling are also very popular. There is a world-famed big game angling area off the north-east coast of the North Island. The season is from January to May.

Information
New Zealand Professional Fishing Guides Association, PO Box 16, Motu, Gisborne.

Flying

Parapenting
Parapenting, a cross between hang-gliding and parachuting, is initially easier to learn than either. There are courses of instruction at Queenstown; the 620m/2035ft high Crown Terrace is the jumping-off point. In the skiing area on the Remarkables parapenters take off and land on skis.

Hang-gliding, paragliding
There are a number of areas in New Zealand which offer excellent conditions for hang-gliding and paragliding. Among the best places are Coronet Peak and the mountains on Lake Wanaka.

Gliding
New Zealand is also a good place for gliding enthusiasts, as was demonstrated by the world championships of 1995.

Flying light aircraft
Conditions for flying are particularly good in the Queenstown area. There are a number of airfields where aircraft can be hired by holders of the appropriate pilot's licence. Some pilots also take passengers.

Food and Drink

New Zealand cuisine
Breakfast in New Zealand is the traditional British breakfast, consisting of eggs and bacon, sausages, etc., or fish with "hashed browns" (fried potatoes). Typically British, too, is the national dish of many New Zealanders – roast lamb with mint sauce and greens. For many years these were the main specialities of New Zealand cuisine. Not surprisingly, therefore, New Zealand cooking, until well into the 1980s, was looked down on by gourmets as a mere variant of the unimaginative cuisine of the home country. Things are now very different. For some time now New Zealand chefs have been training in Europe and immigrants from many countries have brought in their national culinary skills and recipes. New Zealand now has a number of gastronomic high spots, and not only foreign speciality restaurants – and there is now a distinctive New Zealand cuisine which gourmets and gastronomic critics can appreciate. The basis for it is the wide range of high quality foodstuffs produced in New Zealand.

Food

Lamb
Among the specialities of New Zealand cuisine are various lamb dishes. (How could it be otherwise, with 70 million sheep?). Unlike Europeans,

New Zealanders prefer a rather older lamb (a yearling or hogget), with an equally delicate but rather stronger taste. Visitors should seek out restaurants which have won the "Lamb Award" and offer a wide range of lamb dishes. Particular favourites are lamb chops, lamb's kidney and lamb's liver, as well as sushi-style lamb balls.

Beef and pork feature on the menu in the form of delicate and succulent steaks. So far New Zealanders have no worries about mad cow disease (BSE) or swine fever.

Beef and pork

New Zealanders are particularly fond of chicken which is a favourite lunch-time dish.

Poultry

Game, particularly venison, is becoming increasingly popular; but it lacks the typical gamey taste, since it comes from roe and red deer which have been reared on game farms and are almost tame. Some restaurants also serve wild pig, rabbit and wild duck.

Game

Several dozen species of fish, many of them virtually unknown in Europe (for example hapuka, tarakihi and snapper), feature on the New Zealand menu, as do various crustaceans – lobsters, crayfish, shellfish and oysters – and dory. Two particular delicacies are whitebait and toheroa, a rare species of shellfish.

Fish and seafood

Fish and seafood are usually served fresh, since no part of New Zealand is more than 130km/80 miles from the sea. Oysters are usually not fresh, being sold without their shells.

New Zealand has the largest trout in the world, but the sale of trout is prohibited by law, so that if you want to eat a trout you must either catch it yourself or go to a restaurant.

Thanks to its good climate and fine soils New Zealand produces an enormous range of fruit and vegetables. Succulent accompaniments to the main meat dish are tamarillos (tree tomatoes), which are little known in Europe, and the kumara, the world's softest and juiciest sweet potato. The New Zealanders are health fanatics, and many of them have only fruit and vegetables for lunch. Apples, pears, nashis (a cross between apple and pear), strawberries and all kinds of citrus fruits are only a few of the varieties of fruit that are exported world-wide. And of course there is the kiwi fruit, developed in New Zealand from the humble Chinese gooseberry, which is now known all over the world.

Fruit and vegetables

A sweet which has become a national dish is the pavlova (named in honour of the Russian ballerina Anna Pavlova, who was popular in New Zealand in the 1920s). This consists of a meringue base topped with whipped cream and fruit (particularly kiwi fruit). Another passion of New Zealanders is ice-cream, of which they are said to be the largest consumers in the world.

Desserts

A sudden pang of hunger between meals can be eased in one of the countless branches of American hamburger and pizza chains. There are also numerous Chinese takeaways and fish and chip shops (the fish usually being hoki). Also very popular are meat pies, served piping hot from the microwave.

Fast food

A gastronomic experience of a very special kind is a meal cooked in a hangi, a Maori open-air earth oven. Various kinds of meat (pork, beef, poultry, etc.), fish and vegetables (particularly sweet potatoes) are wrapped up in large leaves and laid on a red-hot lava stone in a hole in the ground. The food is then covered with damp cloths and the hole is filled up with earth. After one or two hours' cooking the dish is served on the leaves.

Hangi

Some hotels, particularly in the Rotorua area, offer hangi meals, often combined with a Maori show. Hangi meals are also organised by churches and other organisations as a means of raising funds.

It should be added that a hangi meal does not agree with everyone.

315

Getting There

Cheese	Cheese-lovers will find plenty to interest them in New Zealand. In recent years creameries and cheese factories have steadily increased the range of New Zealand cheeses, creating new varieties such as Aihette and Kapiti.
Bread	New Zealand's bread is not its strongest point. Most of it is flabby and lacking in nutritious value but suitable for toasting. But here too there are signs of improvement due to increased health-consciousness. Well-made bread incorporating a few unmilled grains is now available, and "health stores" sell nourishing and satisfying bread. In the larger towns French bakeries sell French white bread (baguettes) and croissants.

Drinks

Table and mineral waters	Still or slightly carbonated table and mineral waters are widely available.
Tea	As is to be expected in a country with so many people of British descent, tea is one of New Zealand's most popular drinks.
Coffee	Coffee does not play a great part in New Zealand life, and much of it is instant. There are increasing numbers of cafés, however, offering Italian-style espresso and cappuccino (though with a dash of cinnamon rather than cocoa on the frothed-up milk).
Fruit juices	New Zealand offers a great range of high quality fruit juices – apples, pears, cherries, kiwi fruits, etc.
Beer	New Zealand has one of the highest rates of consumption of beer per head in the world. It is drunk cold, full to the brim, with no head. Almost every pub serves both lager and ale. The best known New Zealand brands are Steinlager, Lion Brown, Lion Red, Rheineck, Speight's and Dominion Brown.
Wine	See entry
Restaurants	See entry

Getting There

The overwhelming majority of visitors to New Zealand travel by air. Some cruise ships call in at New Zealand ports, but there are no longer any regular passenger services by sea from either Europe or North America.

From North America the most frequent services are from Los Angeles; there are also some flights from San Francisco and other US airports. From Europe there is a choice of routes – either westward via the United States (Los Angeles and Honolulu) or eastward via Hong Kong, Singapore or other intermediate points. The most convenient route from Britain, by British Airways and Air New Zealand, is from London Heathrow via Los Angeles to Auckland.

International airports	New Zealand's leading international airport is Auckland. Some airlines also fly to Wellington (North Island) or Christchurch (South Island).
Stopovers	A flight to New Zealand from Europe or North America is long and tiring. Most airlines allow one or more stopovers on the way. Stopovers on the western route from Europe are possible, for example, at Los Angeles, Honolulu, Tahiti, Fiji, West Samoa, Tonga and the Cook Islands, and on the eastern route at Singapore, Bangkok, Denpasar (Indonesia), Kuala Lumpur (Malaysia), Hong Kong, Seoul (South Korea) and Tokyo. Since a flight from Europe to New Zealand involves travelling halfway around the world, it is possible, with a round-the-world ticket offered by Air

New Zealand and other airlines, to make a complete circuit of the globe by taking the eastward route on the outward journey and the westward route when flying home, or vice versa.

The principal foreign airlines flying to Auckland and/or Wellington and/or Christchurch are:

Foreign airlines

Air Pacific (Los Angeles–Fiji–Auckland/Christchurch)
British Airways (London–Los Angeles–Auckland)
Cathay Pacific (Frankfurt/Zurich–Hong Kong–Auckland)
Garuda Indonesia (Berlin/Frankfurt/Munich/Zurich–Denpasar–Auckland)
Malaysia Airlines (Frankfurt/Munich/Zurich–Kuala Lumpur–Auckland)
Royal Tongan Airlines (Los Angeles–Honolulu–Tongatapu–Auckland–Sydney)
Singapore Airlines (Frankfurt/Berlin/Zurich–Singapore–Auckland/Christchurch)
Qantas (Frankfurt/Zurich–Hong Kong/Bangkok/Singapore/Bali–Sydney–Auckland/Christchurch)
Thai International (Frankfurt/Zurich–Bangkok–Sydney–Auckland)

To combat jet lag it is advisable to avoid high-protein food on the flight and drink plenty of liquid (but not too much alcohol). Set watch to new time and adjust body routines to new time before flying if possible. To get into the new daily rhythm it is best, on arrival in New Zealand, not to go to bed until the evening, after an easily digestible meal. Take exercise before and after flying.

Jet lag

Before leaving home it is advisable to check on the free baggage allowance. Some airlines have a fairly low limit; Air New Zealand is more generous, with an allowance on International flights on the westward route of two items, each weighing no more than 32 kilograms (70 pounds).

Baggage

Service buses, taxis and shuttle buses (usually large taxis) operate transfers between the airport and hotels. Charges are fixed and reasonable.

Airport transfer

You should confirm your return flight at least 72 hours in advance; otherwise the booking is cancelled. It is advisable to check in two hours before departure, as some airlines tend to overbook. A departure tax, at present NZ$20, is payable on leaving New Zealand.

Return flight

Golf

Golf is a popular sport in New Zealand, not an elite recreation as it is in some countries. There are around 410 golf courses in New Zealand. Many of them are set in beautiful surroundings: among the most attractive are the courses at Waitangi and Titirangi (near Auckland), Wairakei (near Taupo), Queenstown (one of the most beautiful courses in the world) and Rotorua (Arikikapakapa, possibly the only golf course in the world where pools of boiling mud are among the hazards).

Foreign visitors are welcome in most clubs, though on certain days or at certain times the course may be reserved for club members. There are few countries in the world where golf can be played at less expense, on courses which are almost always relatively empty, than in New Zealand.

Green fees for visitors are usually between NZ$20 and $30 and upwards of $50 for the most exclusive courses. Clubs and trolleys can be hired, and professionals are available for coaching.

Green fees

The main golfing season is from October to May.

Season

Information New Zealand Golf Association, PO Box 11842, Victoria Street, Wellington; tel. (04) 472 2967.

Goods and Services Tax

GST (goods and services tax) is charged on all goods and services. The current rate is 12½%.

Health

Inoculations Inoculations are not required for visitors from Europe, North America and many other countries unless they have travelled by way of a problem area identified by the World Health Organisation. Consult your doctor if you have any doubts about current requirements.

Sandflies and parasites New Zealand has no poisonous snakes or other dangerous animals, but it is plagued by sandflies. They seem to have troubled Captain Cook, who mentions them in his account of his voyages. According to Maori legend they were created by the goddess Hine Nui Te Po when she saw Fiordland for the first time, fearing that without them men would want to stay for ever in that beautiful region. In areas with high air humidity, along the banks of rivers and on beaches, there are something like ten species of these tiny (2 millimetre long) midges, whose bite is painful and gives rise to an annoying itch. An effective repellent is Dimp; but it should be borne in mind that while it does no harm to the skin it does dissolve plastic. The best plan is to cover up as much as possible, with long trousers and long sleeves.

Recently wasps have also become a problem, particularly in the riparian forests in the north and centre of the South Island. Visitors who are allergic to wasp stings should carry suitable sprays, creams or antihistamines.

Since 1990 many of the rivers and lakes of the National Parks have become infested with the parasite Giardia lamblia, which is spread in human and animal excreta. The parasite finds its way from the mouth into the intestinal tract and within three weeks gives rise to severe diarrhoea. This clears up quickly with suitable drugs. Water from rivers or lakes should always be boiled or chemically purified before drinking.

Medical care See entry

Chemists See entry

The Hole in the Ozone Layer; Sunbathing

In recent decades activities on our planet, particularly human activities, have had the result that carbon dioxide and fluorocarbons, among many other substances, rise into the upper atmosphere (the stratosphere, between 11km/7 miles and 50km/30 miles above the earth) and cause the protective layer of ozone at that height to become steadily thinner. The destruction of the ozone layer is particularly dramatic above the southern hemisphere. Over the South Pole there is now a huge hole in the ozone layer, the size of which varies with the seasons. From time to time patches of thinner ozone layer extend over New Zealand and may last for a considerable time.

Dangers of sunbathing The ozone layer normally shields the earth against the short-wave ultraviolet radiation which is harmful to many organisms. When the ozone layer becomes thinner these ultraviolet rays are able to get through and affect life on earth. The result is an increase in the ultraviolet B rays which are dangerous for the human skin. In this situation visitors who spend hours tanning themselves in the sun are exposing themselves to the probability of sunburn, premature ageing of the skin and a much increased risk of skin cancer.

The New Zealand meteorological service is actively concerned with the problem of the ozone layer. It publishes regular forecasts of the condition of the layer and of cloud cover which may block the ultraviolet B rays. An ultraviolet index has been evolved which acts as a measure of the intensity of radiation and thus of the danger of sunburn and the risk of skin cancer.

Warning system

A low index figure means that ultraviolet radiation is low and no particular protective measures are required. At the first warning level, indicating moderate radiation, long periods of sunbathing should be avoided and the skin (particularly of small children) should be protected against the sun. At the second level, indicating high radiation, sunbathing should be avoided altogether and protection against the sun by suitable clothing, sunglasses and sun cream is essential. At the third level, indicating extremely high radiation, sunbathing is dangerous and outdoor activities should be undertaken only with complete protection against the sun for all parts of the body, including the face, the back of the neck, arms and legs.

The radiation forecasts and warnings of the New Zealand meteorological service are broadcast daily on New Zealand radio and are available by telephone (dial 0900).

Ultraviolet forecasts

Your skin should be gradually accustomed to the rays of the sun. Around midday, when radiation is particularly strong, you should keep in the shade. The use of sun creams with a high protection factor is strongly recommended, and sunglasses with maximum ultraviolet protection should be worn. When out in the sun you should avoid the use of perfume and decorative cosmetics, which make the skin more sensitive to light. When using certain drugs sunbathing is inadvisable: you should seek medical advice on this point if necessary.

Advice for sunbathers

Help for the people with Disabilities

In New Zealand many hotels, restaurants, tourist sights and even the railways have facilities for people with disabilities, and Air New Zealand has special seats and wheel chairs for their use. People with disabilities, however, may still have problems with buses. In some National Parks, for example in the Paparoa and Tongariro National Parks, there are special paths for wheel-chair users. Wheel-chairs can be hired free of charge at certain points in the town of Rotorua, e.g. at the Mike Hale, John Cubbon and David Meek pharmacies.

The New Zealand Tourism Board produces a free brochure, "Access – a Guide for the Less Mobile Traveller", which lists all hotels, restaurants and tourist sights with facilities for the disabled.

Brochure

Telephone information service (toll-free): dial (0800) 801981
New Zealand Disabilities Resource Centre, 60 Bennett Street, PO Box 4547, Palmerston North; tel. (06) 353 5320, fax (06) 353 5340
Disabled Persons Advice Bureau, Disabled Resource Trust, John F. Kennedy Goods Centre, Woburn Road; tel. (04) 569 3091
Disabilities Information Service, 314 Worcester Street, Christchurch; tel. (03) 366 6189

Information

Hongi

The Maoris do not greet one another by shaking hands or kissing but by rubbing noses with one another: a form of greeting known in the Maori language as *hongi*.

Hotels, Motels, Lodges, Bed and Breakfast

Hotel chains

Luxury hotels belonging to the big international hotel chains – Hyatt, Regent, Sheraton, etc. – are found only in large cities and tourist centres, for example in Auckland, Rotorua and Christchurch. They are all in the highest price category.

Hotels in the upper and middle price ranges, motels and motor inns can be found in all the main tourist areas and beauty spots. Most of them offer international standards of comfort and amenities; they include hotels in various chains such as Parkroyal and Travelodge run by the Southern Pacific Hotel Corporation. The State-run THC (Tourist Hotel Corporation) Hotels are found in areas of great natural beauty, for example in some of the National Parks. Many hotels belong to international chains, and it is possible to arrange bookings or purchase hotel vouchers before leaving home

Small hotels, pubs

In many provincial towns visitors will find small and very reasonably priced hotels. Many pubs also have a few rooms to let, usually rather noisy. More than three dozen such establishments have formed the Pub Beds group.

Motels

Visitors who prefer to cater for themselves can stay in motels which are equipped with cooking facilities, crockery and cutlery, television, etc.

Lodges

A lodge in New Zealand offers luxurious living in a setting of almost completely unspoiled natural beauty, combined with various sporting activities, good cooking and exemplary service. The cost of full board ranges between NZ$250 and $800 per day.

Bed and breakfast

New Zealand's Federation of Bed & Breakfast Hotels

The fastest growing sector of the hotel industry is bed and breakfast, a type of accommodation following the British model. Large numbers of houses throughout New Zealand which offer bed and breakfast accommodation, have formed a Federation of Bed and Breakfast Hotels. In many of these houses, with standards of comfort and amenity ranging between modest and luxurious, guests are treated as members of the family.

★ Heritage Inns of New Zealand

Bed and breakfast accommodation of a special kind is provided in carefully restored houses of the colonial period. More than two dozen such houses have formed an association, the Heritage Inns of New Zealand. A night in one of these houses, some of which are of great elegance, costs between NZ$50 and $200. It is essential to book in advance.

Qualmark

The New Zealand Tourism Board and the New Zealand Automobile Association have developed the Qualmark classification system. It applies in the first place to the various types of tourist accommodation such as hotels, motels and camping sites, which are awarded from one to five stars. It is planned to extend the system to other providers of services to tourists, including buses and taxis.

Tariffs

The price of a double room in modest hotels and motels ranges between NZ$20 and $70 a night; in hotels with high standards of comfort and amenity prices range up to 200 dollars a night; and in luxury hotels and some lodges a charge of several hundred dollars is by no means unusual.

Price categories

In the following list hotels are classified in three categories of price (for a double room):

A = over NZ$150   B = NZ$70–150   C = below NZ$70

Hotels on the North Island (a Selection)

Ascott Parnell (B), 36 St Stephen's Avenue; tel. (09) 350 9012, fax (09)   Auckland
309 3729, 9 rooms
   Comfortable accommodation in a historic building situated in a side street. The centre of Parnell Village is within easy reach. Smoking is not permitted.

Auckland Central Backpackers (C), 9 Fort Street; tel. (09) 358 4877, fax (09) 358 4872, 144 r. (300 beds)
   Centrally situated, this is Auckland's biggest information exchange for backpackers. Restaurant with view of harbour. The rooms are adequate, but the place is sometimes noisy.

Bavaria Guest House (B), 83 Valley Road; tel. (09) 638 9641, fax (09) 638 9665, 11 r.
   As the name indicates, this comfortable bed and breakfast hotel is German-run.

Berlin Lodge (C), 5A Oaklands Road, Mount Eden; tel. (09) 638 6545, 14 r.
   Under German-Swiss management. French and German spoken as well as English.

★ Hyatt Auckland (A), corner of Princes Street and Waterloo Quadrant; tel. (09) 366 1234, fax (09) 303 2932, 275 r.
   A luxury hotel with an excellent restaurant on the top floor.

★ Regent (A), Albert Street; tel. (09) 309 8888, fax (09) 379 6445, 332 rooms and suites
   Centrally situated. Large and elegantly furnished rooms; best rooms on harbour side. Heated pool on roof.

★ Kimberley Lodge (A), Pitt Street, Russell; tel. (09) 403 7090, fax (09)   Bay of Islands
401 7239, 4 rooms and suites
   The most luxurious hotel on the Bay of Islands, with magnificent views of Russell and Kororareka Bay.

★ Faintail Lodge (A); tel. (07) 549 1581, fax (07) 549 1417, 12 suites   Katikati
   A well cared for country house, 4km/2½ miles south of Katikati (north of Tauranga). Famed for its cuisine.

Hôtel du Vin (A), Mangatawhiri Valley; tel. (09) 233 6314, fax (09) 233 6215,   Mangatawhiri
46 r.   Valley
   A five-star hotel 60km/37 miles south of Auckland in a beautiful setting of forests and vineyards. An excellent place for sporting activities or merely for relaxation. The restaurant is one of the best in New Zealand.

Victoria Guest House (C), 15 Victoria Street; tel. (06) 377 0186, 5 r.   Masterton
   A bed and breakfast hotel near the town centre, in a lovingly restored building of 1886.

Old Oak Inn (C), Beach Road, Waterfront; tel. (09) 406 0665, 8 r.   Mangonui
   A small and very comfortable hotel in a handsome and historic old building. Round the corner is the bus stop of the overland coaches.

Edgewater Motor Lodge (B), 359 Marine Parade, Beachfront; tel. (06)   Napier
835 1148, fax (06) 835 6000, 20 r.
   A centrally situated motel with facilities for the disabled. Well furnished rooms, some of which have a magnificent view of the sea.

Hotels, Motels, Lodges, Bed and Breakfast

Pinehaven Travel Hotel (C), 259 Marine Parade; tel. and fax (06) 835 5575, 6 r.

A bed and breakfast hotel with a fine view of the sea. Just round the corner are the railway station and bus station.

Ngaruawahia

Brooklands Country Estate (A), RD 1; tel. (07) 824 4756, fax (07) 825 4873, 8 r.

A small luxury hotel in the beautiful Waikato region, an hour's drive from Auckland. The main building dates from the turn of the century. Golf course.

Paihia

Austria Motel (B), 36 Selwyn Road; tel. and fax (09) 402 7480, 7 r.

Clean and attractive rooms. A few minutes' walk from the shops and the seafront.

Waitangi Resort Hotel (B), Waitangi National Trust Grounds; tel. (09) 402 7411, fax (09) 402 8000, 138 r.

The largest hotel north of Auckland; much patronised by coach parties. Some of the rooms, refurbished in 1991, are more comfortable and more tastefully appointed than the others.

Pauanui

Puka Park Lodge (A), Mount Avenue; tel. (07) 864 8088. fax (07) 864 8112, 50 chalets

This luxury hotel on the Coromandel Peninsula, one of the finest in New Zealand, is under German management. The chalets are scattered about in the bush: not a single tree was felled to make room for them. Service is good, and the restaurant in the main building has an excellent reputation. Nearby is a beautiful beach.

Rotorua

Cedar Lodge Motel (B), 296 Fenton Street; tel. (07) 349 0300, 15 apartments.

This functional modern motel is particularly for families with children. Each apartment has its own pool.

★ Sheraton Rotorua (A), Fenton Street; tel. (07) 347 7139, fax. (07) 348 8378, 130 r. and 8 suites

The best rooms are on the top two floors, with magnificent views. The hotel is famed for its hangi meals.

Russell

Okiato Lodge (A), James Clendon Place, Okiato Point; tel. (09) 403 7948, fax (09) 403 7515, 4 suites

A few minutes' drive from Russell. The suites are furnished in modern/rustic style. Facilities for all kinds of water sports in the bay.

Te Maiki Villas (B), Flagstaff Road; tel. (09) 403 7046, fax (09) 403 1706, 9 r.

Comfortably furnished rooms with fine views of the bay below Flagstaff Hill.

Taupo

★ Huka Lodge (A), Huka Falls Road; tel. (07) 378 5791. fax (07) 378 0427, 17 suites

This stylish lodge, run by a Dutch manager, sets the standard by which all other sport lodges in New Zealand are measured. Radio, television and telephone in all suites.

Thames

Brian Boru Hotel (B), Pollen Street; tel. (07) 868 6523, fax (07) 868 9760, 23 r. and 8 apartments.

This little hotel occupies a venerable 19th century building. The owners run tours to little-known spots on the Coromandel Peninsula, and on alternate weeks organise Murder Mystery Weekends.

Wanaka

Wanaka Motor Park (C), 212 Brownston Street; tel. and fax (03) 443 7883, 2 flats and 21 cabins.

A few minutes' drive from the town. Open throughout the year. The cabins are well equipped, and some have a high standard of amenity. It is less than an hour's drive to the Treble Cone skiing area.

Museum Hotel (B), 51–61 Cable Street; tel. (04) 385 2809, fax (04) 385 2483, 36 r.

Wellington

This hotel is in a busy commercial street and is much favoured by businessmen. It is possible to get reduced rates at weekends. The rooms looking out on the harbour are very attractive; the others are less so.

★Parkroyal Wellington (A), corner of Featherston Street and Grey Street; tel. (04) 472 2722, fax (04) 472 4724, 232 r. and 7 suites

The new "first house in the square" was opened in 1990 and is said to be one of the best hotels in New Zealand. Its reputation is due mainly to its excellent service. When booking in here you should ask for a room with a sea view.

★Plaza International (A), Wakefield Street; tel. (04) 473 3900, fax (04) 473 3929, 186 r. and 17 suites

An elegant and luxurious hotel.

Tinakori Lodge (B), 183 Tinakori Road, Thorndon; tel. (04) 473 3478, fax (04) 472 5554, 10 r.

This bed and breakfast hotel is situated in a quiet street in a historic quarter of the town. The rooms are plain but well appointed, and the owners are friendly and helpful. Prices are moderate.

Hotels on the South Island (a Selection)

See Queenstown

Arrowtown

The Chalet (B), Main Road, Arthur's Pass, Canterbury; tel. and fax (03) 318 9236, 8 r.

Arthur's Pass

This bed and breakfast hotel is in the style of a Swiss chalet. There is an attractive restaurant. Smoking is not permitted.

Antrim Glen Motor Inn (B), 22 Riccarton Road; tel. (03) 348 0909, fax (03) 348 9876, 34 r.

Christchurch

Pleasant and well-appointed rooms.

Kingsgate Christchurch Hotel (A), 766 Colombo Street; tel. (03) 379 5880, fax (03) 365 4806, 90 r.

A centrally situated and well-run hotel. Shopping mall and parks within easy reach.

Pacific Park (B), 263 Bealey Avenue; tel. (03) 377 3374, fax (03) 366 9973, 66 r.

This motel is 2km/1¼ mile north of the city centre. The rooms, recently renovated, are neat and attractive.

Parkroyal Christchurch (A), corner of Durham Street and Kilmore Street; tel. (03) 365 7799, fax (03) 365 0082, 297 r.

In this "first house in the square" you should ask for a room with a view of Victoria Square and the river. There are four restaurants, including the exclusive Canterbury Tales Restaurant and the Yamagen (excellent Japanese cuisine).

Oliver's Lodge, Main Street; tel. (03) 449 2860, fax (03) 449 2862, 12 r.

Clyde

This comfortable lodge, which will appeal especially to nature-lovers, is set in a particularly beautiful part of Central Otago. It offers excellent facilities for fishing, riding, shooting, boating and, in winter, skiing.

Cargill's Motor Inn (B), 678 George Street; tel. (03) 477 7983, fax (03) 477 8098, 51 r.

Dunedin

Near the city centre. Tastefully appointed rooms.

Hotels, Motels, Lodges, Bed and Breakfast

Southern Cross Hotel (A), 118 High Street; tel. (03) 477 0752, fax (03) 477 5776, 110 r.

Externally this hotel has a nostalgic air of the past, but the interior is modern and equipped with every amenity. There are three restaurants and two bars.

Greymouth

Golden Coast Bed and Breakfast (C), 10 Smith Street; tel. (03) 768 7839, 4 r.

This family guest house, set in a beautiful garden, is only a few minutes' walk from the town centre.

Invercargill

Ascot Park Motor Hotel (B), corner of Tay Street and Racecourse Road; tel. (03) 217 6195, fax (03) 217 7001, 54 r.

The best hotel in the town, beside a beautiful park.

Lake Brunner

Lake Brunner Lodge (A), Mitchell's Road, Kumara, Westland; tel. and fax (03) 738 0163, 9 suites

A comfortable lodge on the south side of Lake Brunner, just under an hour's drive from Hokitika. It offers a range of outdoor activities, particularly fishing.

Lake Moeraki

Lake Moeraki Wilderness Lodge (B), Hokitika; tel. (03) 750 0881, fax (03) 750 0882, 20 r.

Set in beautiful scenery on the west coast, to the north of Haast, this lodge does not offer the same degree of luxury as other hotels in the same price category, but the beauty of its unspoiled natural surroundings compensates for this. Guests can fish for trout and observe the rare dwarf penguins.

Mount Cook Village

★Hermitage Hotel (A); tel. (03) 435 1809, fax (03) 435 1879, 104 r.

This mountain hotel is one of the best of its kind in New Zealand.

Mount Cook Travelodge (B); tel. (03) 627 1809, fax (03) 435 1879, 55 r.

This lodge is primarily designed for mountain walkers and climbers who do not want a high degree of luxury. There are magnificent views of some of the highest peaks in the Southern Alps. Open: Sept.–Apr. only.

Nelson

California House (B), 29 Collingwood Street; tel. (03) 548 4173, 4 r.

This bed and breakfast hotel, in an old house restored in colonial style, lies just outside the town. No smoking.

Cambria House (B), 7 Cambria Street, Nelson; tel. (03) 548 4681, fax (03) 546 6649, 5 r.

A bed and breakfast hotel, in a house dating from 1860, which offers very comfortable accommodation and a quiet and peaceful situation.

Picton

Admiral's Lodge (B), 22 Waikawa Road; tel. (03) 573 6590, fax (03) 573 8318, 8 r.

This comfortable bed and breakfast establishment is near the beach and within a few minutes' walk of restaurants and shops.

Queenstown

Millbrook Resort (A), Malaghans Road, Arrowtown; tel. (03) 442 1563, fax (03) 442 1145, 20 suites

This luxurious hotel complex, designed in rustic style, lies 20km/12½ miles from Queenstown. There is a very popular golf course.

★ Nugget Point Resort (A), Arthur's Point Road; tel. (03) 442 7630, fax (03) 442 7308, 35 r.

Situated high above the Shotover River, this is by far the best hotel in the Queenstown area. In winter it attracts winter sports enthusiasts who come to ski on nearby Coronet Peak.

Te Anau Motor Park (C), Manapouri Road; tel. (03) 249 7457, fax (03)   Te Anau
249 7536
  Situated on the shores of Lake Te Anau, this motor camp has well-kept
and very reasonably priced cabins and tourist flats.

Hotels on Stewart Island (a Selection)

Rakiura Hotel (C), Horseshoe Bay Road; tel. (03) 219 1096, 5 r.   Halfmoon Bay
  A simple motel in a quiet situation 2km/1¼ miles from the town. The
rooms can accommodate up to six people.

Stewart Island Lodge (A), Nichol Road; tel. and fax (03) 219 1085, 4 r.
  The most luxurious hotel on Stewart Island, with superb views of the bay
and the surrounding mountains. The island, a paradise for bird-watchers, is
the only place where the brown kiwi can still be seen in its natural surroundings. The hotel is famed for its cuisine (fish is a speciality).

Hotels on the Cook Islands and Niue (a Selection)

Edgewater Resort (A), 7km/4½ miles from Avarua; tel. (02) 25435, 182 r.   Rarotonga
  Situated on the north-west coast of Rarotonga, this is the largest and
liveliest hotel in the Cook Islands. It has its own swimming pool and several
tennis courts, and guests can use snorkelling equipment free of charge.
Bicycles, mopeds and cars can be hired.

★Manuia Beach Hotel (A), near Arorangi, on the west coast; tel. (02) 22461,
20 bungalows
  A luxurious hotel on an idyllic beach, with marvellous sunsets. It has an
excellent restaurant and a bar; the service is top class. Golf, tennis, squash,
sailing, snorkelling; swimming pool.

Muri Beachcomber (A), Muri Beach; tel. (02) 21022, 10 bungalows
  This small holiday complex, with its own swimming pool, lies in a
tropical garden on picturesque Muri Lagoon (east side of Rarotonga).
Sailing boats, surfboards, snorkelling equipment and bicycles can be hired
nearby.

★Pacific Resort and Villas (A), Muri Beach; tel. (02) 20427, 49 apartments
(some of them in bungalows)
  One of the finest hotels in the Cook Islands, on the east side of Rarotonga.
The bungalows are situated in a tropical park and are ideal for a relaxing
holiday. There are two restaurants and a bar on the beach. Sailing, wind-
surfing, snorkelling, scuba diving, tennis and squash.

Rarotongan Resort (A); tel. (02) 25800, 150 r.
  This was the first large hotel to be built on Rarotonga and is still the
island's favourite rendezvous; it particularly welcomes families with children. The "Polynesian nights", with a generous buffet supper and music
and dancing, attract large numbers of people. It has its own floodlit tennis
courts and a large swimming pool. Canoeing, wind-surfing, sailing, snorkelling, scuba diving.

Aitutaki Lagoon Resort (A); tel. (02) 31201, 25 apartments   Aitutaki
  This Polynesian-style hotel, simply furnished, lies on the dazzlingly white
sandy shores of the Aitutaki Lagoon. It offers ample scope for water sports
enthusiasts – sailing, snorkelling, scuba diving, deep-sea angling.

Information

Niue

Niue Hotel (B), 3km/2 miles south of Alofi; tel. (02) 4092, 30 r.
   The hotel has an excellent restaurant and two bars. It is widely famed for its Polynesian dance shows, mainly during the main holiday season. Tennis and golf can be played nearby. There are organised snorkelling and diving trips and walks (fairly strenuous) round the island.

Other types of accommodation

See Camping and Caravanning, Private Accommodation, Youth Accommodation

Information

New Zealand Tourism Board

The New Zealand Tourism Board produces a very useful "Holiday Planner"
and a variety of other information about
New Zealand's tourist attractions and
faciliities. Its head office is in Wellington:

New Zealand Tourism Board
Civic Centre
Wakefield and Victoria Streets
PO Box 2199
Wellingtom
Tel. (04) 801 4000, fax (04) 801 3030

Branches of the New Zealand Tourism Board in the United Kingdom, the United States, Canada and Australia:

United Kingdom

New Zealand House
Haymarket
London SW1Y 4TQ
Tel. (0171) 930 1662
Fax (0171) 839 8929

USA

1111 North Dearborn Street, Suite 2705
Chicago IL 60610
Tel. (312) 440 1345
Fax (312) 440 3808

501 Santa Monica Boulevard, No 300
Los Angeles CA 90401
Tel. (310) 395 7480 or (800) 388 5494
Fax (310) 395 54 53

780 Third Avenue, Suite 1904
New York NY 10017–2024
Tel. (212) 832 8482
Fax (212) 832 7602

Canada

888 Dunsmuir Street, Suite 1200
Vancouver BC V6C 3K4
Tel. (604) 684 2117 or (800) 888 5494
Fax (604) 684 1265

Australia

145 Eagle Street
Brisbane QLD 4000
Tel. (07) 3831 8315
Fax (07) 3831 5337

Como Office Tower, Level 19
644 Chapel Street
South Yarra, Melbourne, VIC 3141
Tel. (03) 9823 6283. Fax (03) 9823 6276

35 Pitt Street, Level 8
Sydney NSW 2000
Tel. (02) 9247 5222. Fax (02) 9241 1136

Information Offices on the North Island

Tourist information offices throughout New Zealand are
marked by a green "i".

Auckland Downtown, 299 Queen Street, Aotea Square; tel.
(09) 366 6888. Open: Mon.–Fri. 8.30am–5.30pm, Sat.–Sun.
8.30am–5pm.
Auckland Airport, International Terminal (ground floor), tel.
(09) 275 6467. Open: daily 5am–2am or until last flight
clears customs
Auckland Airport, Air New Zealand Domestic Terminal
(ground floor), open: daily 8am–9pm
Auckland, Manukau, George Bolt Memorial Drive, tel. (09) 275 5321, open:
daily 7.30am–8.30pm
Auckland West, Scenic Drive, Centennial Memorial Park, Titirangi; tel. (09)
817 7134

Auckland

Maritime Building, Marsden Road, Paihia; tel. (09) 402 7426	Bay of Islands
Normandy Street, Dargaville; tel. (09) 439 8360	Dargaville
209 Grey Street, Gisborne; tel. (06) 868 6139	Gisborne
c/o Stonewall Store, Pah Beach, Tryphena; tel. (09) 429 0448	Great Barrier Island
Municipal Building, Anglesea Street, Hamilton; tel. (07) 839 3360 or 839 3580	Hamilton
Russell Street North, Hastings; tel. (06) 876 0205 or 878 0510	Hastings
55 High Street, Hawera; tel. (06) 278 8599	Hawera
Jaycee Park, South Road, Kaitaia; tel. (09) 408 0879	Kaitaia
Pavilion Building, 25 Laings Road, Lower Hutt; tel. (04) 570 6699 or 569 7428	Lower Hutt
5 Dixon Street, Masterton; tel. (06) 378 7373	Masterton
Broadway, Matamata; tel. (07) 888 7260	Matamata
Salisbury Avenue, Mount Maunganui; tel. (07) 575 5099	Mount Maunganui
Marine Parade, Napier; tel. (06) 835 7579 or 835 4161	Napier
81 Liardet and Leach Streets, New Plymouth; tel. (06) 758 6086	New Plymouth
54 Clyde Street, Ohakune; tel. (06) 385 8427	Ohakune
St John and Elliott Streets, Opotiki; tel. (07) 315 8484	Opotiki
80 Maniapoto Street, Otorohanga; tel. (07) 873 8951	Otorohanga
Civic Centre, The Square, Palmerston North; tel. (06) 358 5003	Palmerston North

Information

Rotorua	67 Fenton Street, Rotorua; tel. (07) 348 5179
Stratford	Broadway and Miranda Streets, Stratford; tel. (06) 765 6708
Taumarunui	Railway Station, Hakiaha Street, Taumurunui; tel. (07) 896 7494
Taupo	13 Tongariro Street, Taupo; tel. (07) 378 9000
Tauranga	The Strand, Tauranga; tel. (07) 578 8103
Te Aroha	102 Whitaker Street, Te Aroha; tel. (07) 884 8052
Te Kuiti	Rora Street, Te Kuiti; tel. (07) 878 8077
Thames	405 Queen Street, Thames; tel. (07) 868 7284
Tokoroa	Leith Place, Tokoroa; tel. (07) 886 6149
Turangi	Ngawaka Place, Turangi; tel. (07) 386 8999
Waitomo Caves	Main Street, Waitomo Caves; tel. (07) 878 7640
Waiuku	2 Queen Street, Waiuku; tel. (09) 235 8924
Wanganui	101 Guyton Street, Wanganui; tel. (06) 345 3286
Wellington	Civic Centre, Wakefield and Victoria Streets, Wellington; tel. (04) 801 4000
Whakatane	Boon Street, Whakatane; tel. (07) 308 6058
Whangarei	Tarewa Park, 92 Otaika Road, Whangarei; tel. (09) 438 1079
Whitianga	Albert Street, Whitianga; tel. (07) 866 5555

Information Offices on the South Island

Alexandra	22 Centennial Avenue, Alexandra; tel. (03) 448 9515
Arthur's Pass	Main Road, Arthur's Pass; tel. (03) 318 9211
Balclutha	63 Clyde Street, Balclutha; tel. (03) 418 0388
Blenheim	1C Main Street, Blenheim; tel. (03) 578 9904
Christchurch	Christchurch City, 75 Worcester Street and Oxford Terrace; tel. (03) 379 9629 Christchurch Airport, International Terminal and Domestic Terminal, open: daily 6.30am–9.30pm. Tel. (03) 353 7774
Cromwell	47 The Mall, Cromwell; tel. (03) 445 0212
Dunedin	48 The Octagon, Dunedin; tel. (03) 474 3300
Fox Glacier	Main Road, Fox Glacier; tel. (03) 751 0807
Franz Josef Glacier	Main Road, Franz Josef Glacier; tel. (03) 752 0796
Gore	Medway and Ordsal Streets, Gore; tel. (03) 208 9908
Greymouth	Regent Theatre, Mackay and Herbert Streets, Greymouth; tel. (03) 768 5101
Haast	Main Road at Jackson Bay Road, Haast; tel. (03) 750 0809

Amuri Avenue and Jacks Pass Road, Hanmer Springs; tel. (03) 315 7128	Hanmer Springs
Sewell Street at the corner of Weld Street, Hokitika; tel. (03) 755 8322	Hokitika
The Esplanade, Kaikoura; tel. (03) 319 5641	Kaikoura
Waverley Street, Karamea; tel. (03) 782 6820 or 782 6652	Karamea
Value Tours Building, Highway 77, Methven; tel. (03) 302 8955	Methven
236 High Street, Motueka; tel. (03) 528 6543	Motueka
Bowen Drive, Mount Cook; tel. (03) 435 1818	Mount Cook
Trafalgar and Halifax Streets, Nelson; tel. (03) 548 2304	Nelson
Ferry Terminal Building, Picton; tel. (03) 573 6855 Railway Station, Auckland Street, Picton; tel. (03) 573 8838 or 573 7477	Picton
Main Road, Punakaiki; tel. (03) 731 1895	Punakaiki
Shotover and Camp Streets, Queenstown; tel. (03) 442 8238	Queenstown
Main Street, Halfmoon Bay; tel. (03) 219 1218	Stewart Island
Commercial Street, Takaka; tel. (03) 525 9136	Takaka
Fiordland Travel, Te Anau Terrace; tel. (03) 249 7419	Te Anau
14 George Street, Timaru; tel. (03) 688 6163	Timaru
Wairepo Road, Twizel; tel. (03) 435 0802	Twizel
99 Ardmore Street, Wanaka; tel. (03) 442 1233 or 443 7414	Wanaka
1 Brougham Street, Westport; tel. (03) 789 6658	Westport

Inoculations

See Health

Jetboats

The commercial development and operation of jetboats originated in New Zealand, and a high-speed trip on a jetboat through beautiful river scenery and narrow gorges or in a Hamilton jet (named after the inventor: see Famous People) over a great expanse of shallow water is one of the special holiday experiences that New Zealand can offer. Passengers in a jetboat need no particular qualities of fitness or training – only strong nerves as the boat jets at hair-raising speed towards rocks and cliff faces. Life-jackets are provided.

Jetboat trips as a tourist attraction began in Queenstown, where passengers were taken on a breath-taking journey through the Shotover Canyon. They are now on offer on other rivers as well, for example on the South Island the Waimakariri at Christchurch, the Buller and the Makarora, on the North Island the Rangitikei, at the east end of the Bay of Plenty, and the Whanganui.

Maori Contacts

Information	Department of Maori Affairs Auckland; tel. (09) 789 169
Interesting Maori villages	Piki Rangi Maori Centre, Christchurch Maori Arts and Crafts Centre, Rotorua/Whakarewarewa Maori Village, Rotorua/Ohinemutu Rewa Village, Kerikeri (Bay of Islands) Maori Marae, Waitangi (Bay of Islands) Turangawaewae Marae, Ngaruawahia (near Hamilton)
Important museums with Maori art	War Memorial Museum, Auckland Waikato Museum, Hamilton National Museum, Wellington

Maps

The map of New Zealand supplied with this guide can usefully be supplemented by maps on a larger scale for particular areas. Up-to-date maps can be obtained in New Zealand at filling stations, in bookshops and from the New Zealand Automobile Association.

The following is merely a selection of the maps available.

1:1,250,000 — Touring Map – Info Map (official publication; 2 sheets; with roads, shading, National Parks, leisure and recreational facilities, table of distances, town plans and information on climate and traffic regulations).

1:1,000,000 — New Zealand (official publication; 2 sheets; with contours, roads, National Parks and index of places).

ITMB Traveller's Reference Map of New Zealand.

1:500,000 — New Zealand Coast to Coast (official publication; 4 sheets; with contours, shading and roads).

1:250,000 — Heinemann's New Zealand Atlas (prepared in collaboration with Department of Survey and Land Information; with roads, shading and index of places).

Special maps — A variety of maps for special purposes can be obtained in New Zealand, including walkers', cyclists' and climbers' maps, geological maps, etc.

Medical Care

Hygienic conditions and medical services in New Zealand are well up to European and North American standards. Even in country areas every place of any size will have a doctor and/or a pharmacist. All hospitals have an accident and emergency service. The larger hotels and motels usually have a doctor on call to deal with emergencies.

Insurance — Medical care in New Zealand can be expensive (see below), and visitors are strongly advised to take out short-term health insurance for the period of their visit. Cover should include transport home by air if required.

Sample charges for medical care:
general practitioner, surgery consultation: about NZ$35–50

Road Signs

Parking

© *Baedeker*

No parking
(Mon.–Sat. 8am–6pm)

No parking
(bus stop)

Warnings

Falling rock

Road works

Diversion

Slippery road

General
danger warning

Right-hand
lane closed

Unsurfaced
road ahead

School
bus

Bends ahead

Level crossing

Road narrows

Bumpy road ahead

Pedestrian
crossing

Side winds

Roundabout

Bend

Directions

Give way

Narrow road:
give way

Limited Speed Zone
(50kmph if road is in
poor condition,
otherwise 100kmph)

Distances
in kilometres

SOUTH
ISLAND

Nelson Picton

Greymouth

Franz Josef

Mount Cook

Lake
Pukaki

Christchurch

Timaru

Milford
Sound

Queenstown
Cromwell

Te
Anau

Dunedin

© Baedeker

Invercargill

Journey times
in hours
and minutes

general practitioner, domiciliary visit: about NZ$45–60
specialist, consultation: from NZ$80
dentist: from NZ$60
hospital stay, per day (public hospital, including doctors' fees): about
NZ$650
private nursing home, per day (accommodation only): about NZ$300

Drugs

Visitors bringing in a quantity of drugs are advised to have a doctor's certificate to avoid possible problems with the New Zealand customs.

Protection against sun

As is well known, the ozone layer which blocks harmful ultraviolet radiation has been severely damaged over the South Pole and the southern hemisphere. It is essential, therefore, to avoid excessive exposure to the sun.
The use of sun creams with a high protection factor is an essential precaution.

Insect bites

Although New Zealand has no poisonous snakes or dangerous wild animals it does have sandflies, which can be a pest in wetter areas. Walkers in particular should cover up as much as possible, wearing long trousers and long sleeves.

Emergencies

Dial 111

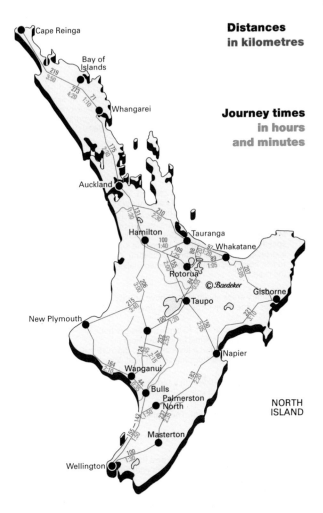

**Distances
in kilometres**

**Journey times
in hours
and minutes**

Cape Reinga

Bay of
Islands

219
3:50

275
4:20

71
1:10

Whangarei

175
2:00

Auckland

131
1:30

210
2:30

Hamilton

100
1:40

Tauranga

109
1:25

88
1:20

97
1:20

Whakatane

89
1:05

Rotorua

© *Baedeker*

207
3:05

Gisborne

206
3:00

215
3:10

84
0:50

Taupo

241
3:10

New Plymouth

124
1:45

125
2:15

232
2:15

100
1:20

150
2:05

Wanganui

164
2:10

Napier

44
0:40

183
2:20

Bulls

Palmerston
North

142
1:30

**NORTH
ISLAND**

Masterton

55
0:50

100
1:30

Wellington

Motoring

As in Britain, drive on the left, and overtake on the right. On a roundabout
traffic coming from the right has priority.

    Take particular care when turning right. Pedestrians crossing a road
should look first to the right and then to the left.

Rules of the road

There are multi-lane motorways only round the three cities of Auckland,
Wellington and Christchurch. Main roads (State Highways, numbered in
single figures) and country roads (Highways, numbered in double figures)

Roads

are well engineered and well built, asphalted and well signposted, though in some areas with many bends.

Some roads are not asphalted, drive with care on such roads, because of the dust and the loose chips.

Narrow bridges

Drivers will frequently encounter narrow bridges which carry only one line of traffic and must be crossed alternately in each direction. In some areas, particularly on the South Island, the density of traffic is so low that it would not be worth while building two-lane bridges over rivers and valleys.

Some bridges carry both the road and the railway. In such a case a "Give way" sign will indicate that traffic coming in the other direction has priority. The railway, however, always has priority.

Density
of traffic

Motoring is a pleasure in New Zealand, for outside the larger towns there is relatively little traffic. In New Zealand eyes a rush hour is when there is a queue of three cars at traffic lights.

Driving style

Most New Zealand drivers drive carefully and defensively, but for some speed has a particular charm. Watch out for the car in front of you pulling up sharply or turning off without indicating. The real danger on New Zealand roads, however, comes from the animals which can suddenly stray on to the road.

Priority
for sheep

In country areas sheep always have priority. Woe betide the motorist who injures a sheep by inconsiderate driving!

Speed limits

Outside built-up areas: 100km/62 miles per hour
In built-up areas: 50km/31 miles per hour
Within 100m/110yd of a level crossing: 30km/19 miles per hour
When overtaking a stopping school bus: 20km/12½ miles per hour

Traffic signs are in line with international standards. Distances are given in kilometres (km) and speeds in kilometres per hour (km/h).

Seat belts

Seat belts must be worn. There are heavy fines for not wearing a belt.

Alcohol

The blood alcohol limit is 0.5 per 1000.

Police

Police vehicles in action switch on a flashing red light and sound their siren. To stop a driver they sit on his tail with light flashing and siren sounding.

Parking ban

No-parking areas in towns are marked by road signs and yellow lines. Drivers parking in these areas make themselves liable to heavy fines and may have to pay a high recovery charge if their car is towed away.

Driving licence

British, American, Canadian, Australian and many other national driving licences are accepted in New Zealand.

Fuel

Much the same brands of petrol and diesel fuel as in Europe are available in New Zealand, and at similar price levels.

Filling stations

In well populated areas and on main trunk roads there are plenty of filling stations, but there may be problems in remoter areas. In country areas, too, many filling stations close from midday on Saturday to 6am on Monday. It is advisable, therefore, to fill up regularly.

Museums

Most towns and many smaller places have museums – some of them with very large collections of material – devoted to the history and natural environment of New Zealand and the Pacific region.

The country's most important museums are the Auckland Museum, the National Museum in Wellington, the Canterbury Museum in Christchurch and the Otago Museum in Dunedin.

The principal museums are mentioned in the Sights from A to Z section of this guide. As regards opening times and admission charges it is advisable to enquire at local information offices. Many museums are closed at least once a week, most common is Monday. In some cases admission charges are quite high; some museums have concession rates for children, students and senior citizens.

The increasing interest in the arts since the Second World War has been reflected in the opening of many new art galleries. There are now something like two dozen public art galleries in New Zealand.

Art galleries

National Parks

New Zealand's 13 National Parks (four on the North Island and nine on the South Island), with a total area of more than 2.3 million hectares/5.7 million acres, occupy around 10% of the country's land area. In addition there are three Maritime Parks on the coast and 19 Forest Parks. Thus just under a fifth of New Zealand's total area is protected in this way. All the National Parks and nature reserves are open to the public. The Department of Conservation (DoC) is responsible for the maintenance of these reserves.

The Forest Parks offer scope for pleasant short walks and are much frequented by town-dwellers. For longer hikes, sometimes lasting several days, there are the National Parks, which are traversed by a network of trails and have huts provided by the DoC for overnight accommodation. The trails maintained by the DoC are planned to allow walkers to choose which way to go and which sights to see en route.

During the main holiday season the National Parks attract large numbers of hikers, and some of them find it necessary to limit the numbers admitted. Some of the National Parks are open throughout the year, others are closed in winter. Before setting out on a walk, therefore, you should check with the local DoC office that the trail will be open.

Department of Conservation, Head Office, PO Box 10420, 59 Boulcott Street, Wellington; tel. (04) 472 5821
Department of Conservation, Private Bag 68–908, Newton, Auckland; tel. (09) 307 9279

Information

All plants and animals are protected.

Conduct in National Parks and other reserves

NEW ZEALAND
ENVIRONMENTAL
CARE CODE

Toilet waste must be buried well away from water points and paths. Other rubbish must be taken with you and properly disposed of.

Rivers, streams and lakes must be kept clean. Do not wash in them with soap or shampoo.

Take great care in lighting fires.

Do not leave the waymarked trails.

Be particularly careful in your behaviour in Maori settlements and respect their sacred places.

National Parks

North Island Urewera National Park (opened 1954, area 212,672 hectares/525,300 acres). The largest continuous area of primeval forest on the North Island, with lonely Lake Waikaremoana; innumerable small Maori settlements; unsurfaced roads.

Tongariro National Park (opened 1887, area 78,651 hectares/194,268 acres). New Zealand's oldest National Park, in a mountainous region marked by volcanic activity, with several Maori cult sites. It is included in UNESCO's list of world heritage sites.

Egmont National Park (opened 1900, area 33,534 hectares/82,829 acres). Named after the extinct volcano of Taranaki (Mount Egmont, 2518m/8262ft), one of New Zealand's most photographed mountains. Popular skiing area.

Whanganui National Park (opened 1968, area 74,231 hectares/183,351 acres). Named after the Whanganui River, which follows a winding course through a picturesque valley and is navigable by boat or canoe.

South Island Abel Tasman National Park (opened 1942, area 22,530 hectares/55,650 acres). The smallest National Park but one of the most beautiful. Idyllic coastal scenery.

Kahurangi National Park (opened 1995, 400,000 hectares/1,000,000 acres). At the north-eastern tip of the South Island. Striking geological formations, caves, lowland forest; many endemic plants and animals.

Nelson Lakes National Park (opened 1956, area 96,121 hectares/237,419 acres). Beautifully situated lakes with facilities for water sports and fishing.

Paparoa National Park (opened 1987, area 30,327 hectares/74,908 acres). Its particular attractions are the Pancake Rocks and the blowholes which shoot up jets of water when the tide is high.

Arthur's Pass National Park (opened 1929, area 99,270 hectares/245 acres). Valleys, gorges, cliffs, rock walls, mountains, dense forests, waterfalls and keas.

Te Wahipounamu, an area taking in the Westland, Fiordland and Mount Cook National Parks which is on UNESCO's list of world heritage sites.

Westland National Park (opened 1960, area 117,547 hectares/290,341 acres). Glaciers (Franz Josef, Fox, Tasman) and subtropical rain forest. Trout-fishing.

Mount Cook National Park (opened 1953, area 70,013 hectares/172,932 acres), with New Zealand's highest peak (3754m/12,317ft). Alpine vegetation. Glacier walks, climbing, nature walks.

Mount Aspiring National Park (opened 1964, area 355,518 hectares/878,129 acres). Named after Mount Aspiring (3035m/9958ft). Alpine landscape. Climbing and hill walking.

Fiordland National Park (opened 1952, area 1.2 million hectares/3 million acres). New Zealand's largest National Park, with imposing mountains, lakes, fjords and almost impenetrable forests. The last retreat of two almost extinct species of flightless birds, the takahe and the kakapo.

Maritime Parks

North Island Bay of Islands. At the subtropical north-eastern tip of the North Island, with quiet inlets and lonely islands. Water sports. Of historical interest as the

National Parks and Walking Trails in New Zealand

NATIONAL PARKS
1 Bay of Islands Maritime and Historic Park
2 Northland Forest Park
3 Hauraki Gulf Maritime Park
4 Coromandel Forest Park
5 Kaimai-Mamaku Forest Park
6 Pirongia Forest Park
7 Raukumara Forest Park
8 Pureora Forest Park
9 Whirinaki Forest Park
10 Te Urewera National Park
11 Egmont National Park
12 Whanganui National Park
13 Tongariro National Park
14 Kaweka Forest Park
15 Kaimanawa Forest Park
16 Ruahine Forest Park
17 Rimutaka Forest Park
18 Haurangi Forest Park
19 Tararua Forest Park

20 Abel Tasman National Park
21 Marlborough Sounds Maritime Park
22 Kahurangi National Park
23 Mount Richmond Forest Park
24 Nelson Lakes National Park
25 Victoria Forest Park
26 Lewis Pass National Reserve
27 Paparoa National Park
28 Hanmer Forest Park
29 Lake Sumner Forest Park
30 Arthur's Pass National Park
31 Craigieburn Forest Park
32 Westland National Park
33 Mount Cook National Park
34 Mount Aspiring National Park
35 Otago Goldfields Park
36 Fiordland National Park
37 Catlins Forest Park
38 Stewart Island

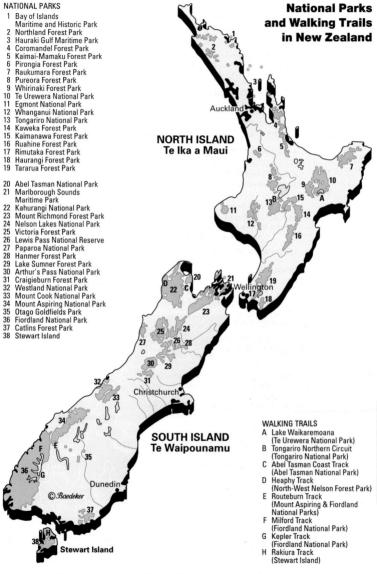

WALKING TRAILS
A Lake Waikaremoana (Te Urewera National Park)
B Tongariro Northern Circuit (Tongariro National Park)
C Abel Tasman Coast Track (Abel Tasman National Park)
D Heaphy Track (North-West Nelson Forest Park)
E Routeburn Track (Mount Aspiring & Fiordland National Parks)
F Milford Track (Fiordland National Park)
G Kepler Track (Fiordland National Park)
H Rakiura Track (Stewart Island)

place where the Maoris first landed in New Zealand a thousand years ago and the treaty of Waitangi was signed in 1840.

Hauraki Gulf, to the east of Auckland. Some 50 islands. Rare species of animals and plants.

South Island   Marlborough Sounds, at the northern tip of the South Island. Rias (drowned valley systems).

Observation of Wild Life

With its great expanses of almost natural landscape New Zealand offers wide scope for the observation of wild life. Sunbathing seals, yellow-eyed penguins and albatrosses will become as familiar to the nature-lover as the playful mountain parrots (keas: see Introduction, p. 22) and nocturnally active kiwis (see Baedeker Special, p. 24). Various travel firms and local tourist organisations offer specially organised trips for the observation of wild life.

Royal albatrosses   On the Otago Peninsula, near Dunedin, you can, if you are very lucky, see the royal albatross (*Diomedea epomophora*), whose nesting-places are normally near the Antarctic. These albatrosses, with a wing-span of up to 3 metres (10 feet), are among the largest birds in the world.

Muttonbirds   Muttonbirds nest mainly on Stewart Island and the small neighbouring islands. From time immemorial the young birds have been prized by the Maoris for their down. Tens of thousands of them are caught every year.

Gannets   Gannets nest on the east coast of the North Island. Excellent divers, they are easily recognised by their pointed wings, their powerful beaks and their heads with black-rimmed eyes.

Seals   Seals can be observed on the remote west coast of the South Island. They also find their way up Milford Sound and the Otago Peninsula.

A seal family basking in the sun

Whales are no longer hunted off the coasts of New Zealand with harpoons, as they were until 1964, but with cameras and camcorders. On the Kaikoura coast, some 130km/80 miles south of Blenheim on the east side of the South Island, they can – with luck – be seen close up from a rubber dinghy with an experienced guide. In the course of their travels over the oceans of the world they regularly appear in the coastal waters off the north-east of the South Island, where they find an abundance of food. Under the Mammals Protection Act of 1978 they are now protected within the 322km (200 mile) fishing zone round New Zealand. From April to June sperm whales can be seen, in summer killer whales, in June and July the "singing" humpbacked whales.

Whales and dolphins

The season for dolphins is from October to May. At some points they are particularly friendly, and many a tourist has had the experience of swimming with a dolphin. Occasionally Hector's dolphin, a species so far found only in New Zealand waters, can be seen.

Whale Watch Kaikoura Ltd, Railway Station, PO Box 89, Whaleway Station Road, Kaikoura; tel. (03) 319 5045

Information

Dolphin Encounter, 58 West End, Kaikoura; tel. (03) 319 6777

NZ Sea Adventures, The Dolphin Experience, PO Box 85, Kaikoura; tel. (03) 319 6622

Opening Times

See Business Hours

Outdoor Life

New Zealand is a Promised Land for all those – particularly young people – who enjoy an adventurous outdoor holiday. Its great tracts of almost totally unspoiled and sparsely populated natural landscape offer endless scope for all kinds of open-air activities – trekking and camping, fishing, shooting, riding, flying, climbing, walking, mountain biking, motorcycle scrambling, swimming, scuba diving and snorkelling, golf and cricket, skiing and heli-skiing, sailing, white-water canoeing, jetboating, bungy jumping, survival training and many more. Those looking for risk, those who want the feeling of butterflies in the stomach, those who want to see what they are made of, will find what they want in New Zealand.

But all this has not been without cost to the natural environment. Thoughtless holidaymakers have left scars on the landscape with their cross-country vehicles and mountain bikes. The National Park authorities are attempting to control the problem by imposing admission charges and strict regulations, but the problem still exists and all users of the countryside must bear it in mind as they pursue their various activities.

Photography

Films of all kinds can be bought in chemists' shops, photographic shops and supermarkets. They tend to be dearer than in Europe and North America, so photographers should take a sufficient supply of films from home.

Films

Films are developed in many specialist shops within a day. Prints, slides and enlargements are also produced very rapidly.

Development

Postal Services

Filters	In view of New Zealand's very clear air (no haze, little in the way of industrial waste gases) it is advisable to have skylight and ultra-violet filters.
Protection from rain	Cameras and lenses should be protected from the heavy rain that can occur in New Zealand by keeping them in a stout plastic bag (e.g. a cool bag). Some camera bags are not completely rainproof.
Photographing people	Before photographing people you should ask their permission. This is particularly important in the case of Maoris.

Postal Services

Normally postal services are provided by post offices, but in some country areas the post office may be combined with a shop.

In addition to the usual postal services post offices are also responsible for telecommunications (telephone, telegrams, fax, teleprinter).

Opening times — Post offices are open: Mon.–Thur. 8.30 or 9am–5pm, Fri. 8.30 or 9am–8pm.

Postage; other services — An airmail letter (up to 20 grams; with "Fast post" sticker) to Europe costs NZ$1.80. It takes between 7 and 12 days for the letter to reach its destination.

An airmail postcard (up to 10g) or aerogram to Europe costs NZ$1.

Mail sent by sea takes at least eight weeks to reach Europe.

Poste restante mail is kept by the post office for a month and then returned to the sender by sea. Visitors can also arrange in New Zealand for mail to be forwarded to their next address. Hotels will keep mail for delivery on arrival.

Special issues and complete sets of stamps can be obtained from the philatelic departments of the larger post offices.

Post-boxes — In New Zealand there are separate post-boxes for ordinary mail (red) and airmail or "fast post" (blue).

Postcards — New Zealand post offices also sell very attractive postcards.

Prices

Prices in New Zealand are broadly comparable with prices in Europe, though imported goods are distinctly dear. Two people with average standards of expenditure will spend perhaps NZ$250 to $350 per day for food, car hire and accommodation in a motel.

Goods and services tax — Goods and services tax (GST) is payable on all goods and services; the current rate is $12\frac{1}{2}\%$.

Private Accommodation

Farmstay (country holidays) — The best way to see something of rural life in New Zealand is to take a farm holiday. Many farmhouses have rooms or holiday flats for letting to visitors. On some farms there are opportunities for riding.

Homestay (accommodation in private houses) — Visitors can experience everyday life in New Zealand by taking a room in a private house (private home, city home). Many house-owners are glad to meet visitors from abroad and make very good hosts. Dinner, bed and breakfast in a private house cost between NZ$60 and NZ$185. Advance booking is essential.

Many local tourist information offices will arrange short farmstays and homestays. Addresses are given in a brochure, "Where to Stay", obtainable from New Zealand Tourism Board offices. Accommodation can also be arranged by the following agencies:

Rural Tours, The Country Experience, 92 Victoria Street, PO Box 228, Cambridge; tel. (07) 827 8055, fax (07) 827 7154
Farmhouse and Country Home Holidays, Auckland; tel. (09) 410 8280, fax (09) 410 8380

Public Holidays

National holidays:

Statutory holidays

New Year's Day (January 1st)
Waitangi Day or New Zealand Day (February 6th): commemorating the foundation of New Zealand
Good Friday (March/April)
Easter Monday (March/April)
Anzac Day (April 25th): commemorating the New Zealand and Australian troops who fell at Gallipoli in 1915
Queen's Birthday (first Monday in June)
Labour Day (fourth Monday in October)
Christmas Day (December 25th)
Boxing Day (December 26th)

Each province has its own anniversary day:

Regional holidays

Wellington: January 22nd
Auckland: January 29th
Northland: January 29th
Nelson: February 1st
Otago: March 23rd
Southland: March 23rd
Taranaki: March 31st
Hawke's Bay: November 1st
Marlborough: November 1st
Canterbury: November 9th
Westland: December 1st

Since New Zealanders like their long weekend, public holidays are usually moved to the Monday before or after the actual date.

Long weekends

The long school holidays, and thus the main holiday season, are from the middle of December to the end of January. There are shorter holidays in the second and third weeks of May and a week in July. The winter holidays begin at the end of August and end in mid-September.

School holidays

Public Transport

Public transport is reasonably adequate in and around the larger towns. For longer distances air services (see Air Travel) are used. There are frequent flights between the cities of Auckland, Wellington and Christchurch. Rail travel (see Railways) is comfortable, but there is usually only one train a day between towns. Seats must therefore be booked in plenty of time. There are relatively frequent coach services (see Coach Services) between major towns and tourist centres. Here too, it pays to book seats in advance wherever possible. There are special bus services for backpackers and cyclists.

Quarantine

Thanks to the country's remoteness many kinds of organisms and diseases are unknown in New Zealand, and accordingly the authorities maintain strict control on the importation of plants and animals. On arrival in New Zealand visitors must complete a declaration listing any food or articles of plant or animal origin they have brought with them. Even dirty shoes, clothing, bicycles, etc., are regarded with extreme suspicion. Any suspicious items are quarantined or refused admission.

Radio and Television

Radio

The two state-run stations, Radio New Zealand and National Radio, broadcast programmes on medium wave and VHF throughout New Zealand. Away from the larger towns listeners can sometimes receive only a few medium-wave transmitters. There are also a number of private radio stations which broadcast news for tourists.

Tourist Information FM Radio

The Tourist Information FM Radio station broadcasts round the clock. In addition to programmes on the history and culture of New Zealand it carries advertisements by hotels, restaurants and other matters of interest to tourists.

Television

Television services are provided mainly by Television New Zealand Ltd, with two channels. The programmes consist largely of American soap operas and films, though there are also some programmes on New Zealand themes.

A privately run channel, TV3, came on the air in 1989. Sky TV is available on payment with the help of a decoder. In some tourist centres, notably Rotorua and Queenstown there are local television stations with non-stop programmes on the sights of the region.

Rafting

White-river rafting

White-river or white-water rafting is one of the special attractions of an adventure holiday in New Zealand. It can be practised on both the North and South islands. The rivers suitable for the sport are not long, but they are certainly wild. Several dozen specialist travel operators in New Zealand offer rafting holidays in varying grades of difficulty, and some offer guided kayak and canoe trips. Participants must be at least 13 years old; equipment and accommodation are part of the package.

Rafting areas

The best rafting rivers on the North Island are the Wairoa, the Rangitikei and the Mohaka. On the South Island there are the Buller, the Shotover, the Kawarau, the upper course of the Rangitata (all in the Queenstown area) and the 64-km/40-mile long Landsborough River, which has the steepest gradient of any New Zealand river and flows through country of great scenic beauty. The best months for rafting are October and April/May, when the climate is at its pleasantest, but it is perfectly possible to enjoy rafting at other times of year, provided that the rivers have a sufficient flow of water.

Information

New Zealand Professional River Rafting Association, PO Box 77, Tauranga
Go West Rafting, PO Box 99, Buller River; tel. (03) 523 9315
Pororari Canoe Hire, PO Box 2, Punakaiki; tel. (03) 731 1870

Black-river rafting is the name given to rafting on underground rivers, for example on the Ruakuri, one of the underground rivers in the Waitomo Caves (North Island). To reach the river it is necessary to abseil down into these deep caves with their fossils and their glowworms.

Black-river rafting

A trip by canoe or kayak on the rivers, lakes and the quieter coastal waters of New Zealand is a delightful way of enjoying the country's beautiful scenery. Particularly good areas are the Abel Tasman National Park at the northern tip of the South Island, on the east coast off Great Barrier Island and in the Marlborough Sounds. A variety of organised trips are available. You can canoe alone, but it is safer and more interesting to have a knowledgeable local guide. The necessary equipment is provided by local travel operators.

Kayaking

Abel Tasman Kayaks, Marahau, Motueka; tel. (03) 527 8022
Ocean and River Adventure Company, Main Road, Marahau Beach, Motueka; tel. (03) 527 8266

Information

Railways

Rail travel in New Zealand is a relaxed and comfortable means of getting about the country, though only on the main lines. The branch lines – more and more of which are being closed down – are generally less known for their comfort.
   At present New Zealand has a total rail network of 4300km/2670 miles. The track is narrow-gauge (3ft 6in.). Trains usually take longer than overland coaches to cover the same distance. Passengers usually travel in comfortable coaches with panoramic windows, and there are often modern and well equipped restaurant cars. Many of the lines run through magnificent scenery, with an occasional commentary on points of particular interest.

Express trains

The following are the principal trains run by Tranz Scenic:

Auckland–Wellington–Auckland (685km/426 miles)
Journey time: 10 hours 30 minutes

Overlander (day train)

Auckland–Wellington–Auckland (685km/426 miles)
Journey time: 10 hours 55 minutes

Northerner (night train)

Auckland–Tauranga–Auckland
Journey time: 3 hours 25 minutes

Kaimai Express

Auckland–Rotorua–Auckland
Journey time: 4 hours 5 minutes

Geyserland Express

Wellington–Napier–Wellington (334km/208 miles)
Journey time: 5 hours 20 minutes

Bay Express

Christchurch–Invercargill–Christchurch (594km/369 miles)
Journey time: 8 hours 50 minutes

Southerner (day train)

Christchurch–Picton–Christchurch (350km/217 miles); connection to Picton–Wellington ferry
Journey time: 5 hours 20 minutes

Coastal Pacific

Christchurch–Greymouth–Christchurch
Journey time: 4 hours 25 minutes

TraNZAlpine

EXPRESS TRAINS

——————— The Overlander
——————— The Northener
——————— The Kaimai Express
——————— The Geyserland
——————— The Bay Express
——————— The Coastal Pacific
——————— The TranzAlpine
——————— The Southerner

– – – Ferry

Auckland

Tauranga
Hamilton
Rotorua

Napier

Palmerston
North
Wellington

Picton
© Baedeker

Greymouth
Arthur's
Pass
Christchurch

Dunedin
Invercargill

Railways
(Passenger Services)

Booking	Since there is often only one train a day, it is quickly booked up. It is essential, therefore, to make your booking well in advance.
Information, Reservations and booking	Correspondence to: Tranz Scenic, Tranz Rail Ltd, Private Bag, Railway Station, Wellington. Within New Zealand tel. 0800 802 802 7am–9pm daily, free fax. 0800 101 525. From other countries: tel. 64–4–498 3301, fax. 64–4–498 3089.
InterCity Travel Pass (see also under Coach Services)	The InterCity Travel Pass (for visitors to New Zealand only) offers unlimited travel for a specified period on the trains, ferries and coaches of the InterCity system at a very reasonable price; on the South Island certain services run by Newmans coaches are also included. There is the standard "3 in 1" pass and the extended "4 in 1" pass, which also includes a flight on Ansett New Zealand, either between the North and the South Island or within either of the islands.

The InterCity Travel Pass can be bought outside or on arrival in New Zealand. A pass for 22 days at present costs for "3 in 1" NZ$690, for "4 in 1" NZ$920. Children under 4 travel free; between the ages of 4 and 15 they pay half the adult rate.

Restaurants

In all the larger towns and in holiday resorts there is a wide range of restaurants, and in addition there are numerous pubs, bistros, cafés, American-style fast food establishments and take-aways offering meals at very moderate prices. Thanks to the great influx of immigrants in recent years there are now numerous speciality restaurants offering a variety of national cuisines, particularly Chinese, Indian, Italian and even Mexican.

In New Zealand it is usual to book a table in advance by telephone. On entering a restaurant guests should wait to be taken to a table. They may be reminded of this by a notice at the entrance "Wait to be seated".

In good restaurants the price of the main dish is likely to range between NZ$20 and $50. In some establishments the prices can be much higher.

Prices

In most restaurants there is only one bill per table. It is then for the guests to decide who should pay.

The bill

As a rule New Zealanders tend to eat out early. Many restaurants serve meals only until 9.30pm.

Times of meals

Alcoholic drinks may be served only in licensed restaurants. The usual licensing hours are Mon.–Sat. 11am–10pm. No alcohol may be served on Sunday.

Alcohol

Restaurants showing the sign "BYO" ("Bring your own") are unlicensed, but guests may bring their own wine or beer, paying only a small corkage charge.

Restaurants on the North Island (a selection)

★Antoine's, 333 Parnell Road; tel. (09) 379 8756

Auckland

Auckland's best and most expensive restaurant, which has for many years been a Mecca for gourmets from far and wide.

★Chinatown, 8 Lorne Street; tel. (09) 366 1642

Perhaps Auckland's best Chinese restaurant, with prices in the middle range.

Cin Cin on Quay Brasserie and Bar, Ferry Building (Ground Floor), 99 Quay Street; tel. (09) 307 6966

Freshly caught fish and pizzas cooked in a charcoal oven are specialities. The wine list offers a choice of over 100 wines, mostly from New Zealand. From the restaurant there is a fine view of the harbour. Some guests may be disturbed by the music, which is often very loud.

Harbourside Seafood Bar and Grill, Ferry Building (Ground Floor), 99 Quay Street; tel. (09) 307 0556

On warm evenings guests can enjoy a lobster (a speciality of the restaurant) and also a magnificent view of Waitemata Harbour and Hauraki Gulf. Unusually for a fish restaurant, it also has excellent game and lamb dishes.

Hard to Find Mexican Café, 47 High Street; tel. (09) 373 4681

Mexican specialities (tortillas, enchilada, etc.). Patronised mainly by the younger set.

★The French Café, 210 Symonds Street; tel. (09) 377 1911

An elegant restaurant whose chefs have won many awards. Its specialities are lamb, game and salmon. Opening off the street is its associated Brasserie, with excellent food at lower prices.

Restaurants

Hamilton

Death by Chocolate, 42 Jervois Road; tel. (07) 360 2828
This is the place for people, young or old, with a sweet tooth.

Left Bank Café, Marlborough Place, off Victoria Street; tel. (07) 839 3354
A very popular restaurant famed for its cuisine.

Hastings

Vidal Winery Brasserie, 913 St Aubyn Street; tel. (06) 876 8105
Situated amid the vineyards to the south of the town, this restaurant is renowned for its steaks and above all for its wine. In summer you can eat on the terrace in the garden, in winter round an open fire.

Masterton

Sweet Inspirations Dessert Restaurant, 434 Queen Street, Kuripuni; tel. (06) 378 2641
Even those who don't care for sweet things can enjoy a meal here. The menu offers a wide range, particularly soups and poultry and fish dishes.

Napier

Bayswater Restaurant, Hardinge Road, close to Bridge Street, Ahuiri; tel. (06) 835 8517
The cuisine is creative, with new menus every few weeks. The restaurant offers an excellent selection of New Zealand wines. Prices are moderate. On fine days there is a beautiful view from the terrace over Hawke's Bay.

Beaches Restaurant, War Memorial Building, Marine Parade; tel. (06) 835 8180
Excellent fish dishes. Magnificent view over Hawke's Bay.

Ju Ju's, 80B Emerson Street; tel. (06) 835 3976
Those who like Thai cuisine – now increasingly popular – will find what they want here.

New Plymouth

The Devon Seafood Smørgåsbord, 390 Devon Street East; tel. (06) 759 9099
The restaurant's fish and meat dishes and very appetising vegetarian food appeal to many guests, but its speciality is Swedish-style smørgåsbord, a cold and hot buffet with a variety of meat and fish, egg dishes, vegetables, salads and cheese.

Paihia

Esmae's, 41 Williams Road; tel. (09) 402 8400
Typical New Zealand cuisine (lamb, fish, game, pork, poultry). Vegetarian dishes are also on the menu.

Pauanui

Keith's, Pauanui Boulevard, Pauanui Beach, Coromandel Peninsula; tel. (07) 864 8825
The best restaurant on the Coromandel Peninsula, ideal for gourmets. Snacks served at the bar.

★ Puka Park Lodge, Pauanui Beach; tel. (07) 864 8088
The restaurant of this exclusive lodge (see Hotels), with an elegant exterior, is noted for its fine cuisine. Booking is essential.

Rotorua

★ Poppy's Villa Restaurant, 4 Marguerita Street; tel. (07) 347 1700
This elegant restaurant, in an Edwardian villa, offers its exquisite cuisine.

Rendezvous Restaurant, 116 Hinemoa Street; tel. (07) 348 9273
A friendly restaurant, popular for its fish dishes and grills, occupying a building of the colonial period in the commercial district of Rotorua.

You and Me, 31 Pukuatua Street; tel. (07) 347 6178
This restaurant offers interesting combinations of New Zealand and French cuisine. The chef is Japanese!

★The Gables, The Strand; tel. (09) 403 7618   Russell
   One of the best restaurants on the Bay of Islands, offering high-class New Zealand cuisine (fish, seafood, lamb, game).

Mountain House, Pembroke Road; tel. (06) 765 6100   Stratford
   This restaurant, owned by a Swiss lady, offers the best of New Zealand cuisine.

Truffles Restaurant, 116 Lake Terrace; tel. (07) 378 7856   Taupo
   Mainly New Zealand dishes (lamb, game, poultry). Marvellous view of Lake Taupo and the mountains.

Old Thames Restaurant, 705 Pollen Street, Grahamstown; tel. (07) 868 7207   Thames
   Specialities are fish and lamb dishes.

Brasserie Flip, RSA Building, 103 Ghuznee Street; tel. (04) 385 9493   Wellington
   A French-style restaurant offering international dishes and excellent New Zealand wines. Booking is essential in the evening.

Petit Lion, 8 Courtney Place; tel. (04) 384 9402
   Everything here is top class: the food, the service – and the prices.

★Pierre's, 342 Tinakori Road, Thorndon (out of city centre); tel. (04) 472 6238
   The chef, Pierre Meyer, is Swiss. His preference for Mediterranean cuisine is unmistakable.

★The Grain of Salt, 232 Oriental Parade (first floor); tel. (04) 384 8642
   This restaurant, from which there is a view of the town and the harbour, is not cheap, but the chef has won awards for his New Zealand-cum-French cuisine.

Tinakori Bistro, 328 Tinakori Road, Thorndon (out of city centre); tel. (04) 499 0567
   New Zealand dishes presented with French refinement. In good weather you can eat out of doors.

Restaurants on the South Island (a selection)

Rocco's Restaurant, 5 Dodson Street; tel. (03) 578 6940   Blenheim
   The best Italian restaurant within a wide area. In winter guests are kept warm by an open fire.

Mykonos, 112A Lichfield Street; tel. (03) 379 7452   Christchurch
   The excellent Greek cuisine attracts a large clientele. Booking is essential.

Pegasus Arms, 14 Oxford Terrace; tel. (03) 366 0600

Pedro's Restaurant, 143 Worcester Street; tel. (03) 379 7668
   Excellent New Zealand cuisine and Spanish specialities.

★Scarborough Fare, corner of Scarborough Road and Sumner Esplanade; tel. (03) 326 6987
   Rated one of the best restaurants in the country.

Sign of the Takahe, Dyers Pass Road, Cashmere Hills; tel. (03) 332 4052
   The restaurant, housed in a building like a castle transported from Europe to the Cashmere Hills, has marvellous views of the Southern Alps and the city. Its specialities are game and lobsters. Booking is essential. Male guests must wear jacket and tie.

Restaurants

Clyde — Oliver's Restaurant, 34 Sunderland Street; tel. (03) 449 2860
This restaurant, in a house of 1863 which has recently been restored, is widely famed for its cuisine and for its fine wines from Central Otago.

Dunedin — Palm's Café, Lower High Street, between Rattray and Dowling Streets; tel. (03) 477 6534

Fairlie — Rimuwhare, 53 Mount Cook Road; tel. (03) 585 8058
An excellent vegetarian restaurant with a view of the Queen's Gardens.

Invercargill — Aino's Steak House and Restaurant, Waikiwi Shopping Centre, Dee Street; tel. (03) 215 9568
The oldest restaurant in Invercargill. Its specialities are steaks and fresh fish.

★Donovan, 220 Bainfield Road; tel. (03) 215 8156
Housed in a turn-of-the-century building on the outskirts of the town. Its chefs have won a number of awards.

Nelson — Chez Eelco, 296 Trafalgar Street; tel. (03) 548 7595
The oldest street café in New Zealand, offering a choice of imaginative snacks. Patronised by locals and younger visitors.

Picton — Marlborough Terranean, 31 High Street; tel. (03) 573 7122
New Zealand cuisine with a French touch appeals both to locals and visitors.

Queenstown — Hillary's, Quality Hotel Terraces, Frankton Road; tel. (03) 442 7950
Specialities are game and lamb, but the restaurant's fish and seafood are also excellent. Fine views of Lake Wakatipu and the Remarkable Mountains.

Roaring Meg's, 57 Shotover Street; tel. (03) 442 9676
A pleasant restaurant in a late 18th-century gold-digger's house, one of the oldest buildings in the town.

The Cow, off Beach Street; tel. (03) 442 8588
Famed throughout the town for its pizzas and pasta dishes. You will usually have to wait for a table.

Te Anau — Bluestone Restaurant, Quality Hotel, 20 Lakefront Drive; tel. (03) 249 7421
Specialities are crayfish, lamb, game, etc. – that is, typical New Zealand dishes. From the restaurant there is a fine view of the snow-capped peaks of the Southern Alps.

Wanaka — Capriccio Restaurant, 123 Ardmore Street; tel. (03) 443 8578
Italian and New Zealand specialities. Fine views of Lake Wanaka and the mountains.

Stewart Island — Annie Hansen's Dining Room, South Sea Hotel, Elgin Terrace; tel. (03) 219 1120
Good New Zealand cooking; prices are high. Dinner is served only from 6pm to 8pm.

Stewart Island Lodge, Nichol Bay, Halfmoon Road; tel. (03) 219 1085
A gourmet restaurant widely famed for its fish dishes.

Restaurants on the Cook Islands and Niue

★Flame Tree, Muri Beach   Rarotonga
   This is the best and most expensive restaurant on the island, situated on
the idyllically beautiful Muri Lagoon. It is open only in the evening. Fish
dishes and various Asian specialities.

Sails, Muri Beach
   A well-run restaurant in the Muri Lagoon Sailing Club. Fish dishes of
outstanding quality.

Trader Jack's, Avarua
   This quayside restaurant, with something of the atmosphere of a cosy
pub, serves interesting Polynesian dishes (particularly fish and seafood) at
reasonable prices.

Restaurant in Rapae Hotel, near Arutanga   Aitutaki
   Every Friday evening there is an "Island Night", with a tasty Polynesian
buffet.

Niue Hotel Restaurant, south of Alofi   Niue
   This restaurant, recently restored after storm damage, offers both Polynesian and international specialities.

Sails, at Coral Garden Motel (4km/2½ miles from Alofi)
   You can eat well in this little restaurant, which also has a bar.

Sailing

Sailing is a very popular sport in New Zealand. Sometimes in the Hauraki
Gulf it seems as if every single inhabitant is in a boat on the water. New
Zealand yachtsmen have been successful in many of the world's great
sailing races most notably the Admiral's Cup.
   Among the finest sailing waters in the world are the Hauraki Gulf and the
Bay of Islands on the North Island and the Marlborough Sounds at the
north-eastern tip of the South Island.
   Boats can be hired with or without a skipper and crew, and in many
regattas – for example in the classic race from Auckland to Nouméa in New
Caledonia – it is possible to join the crew of one of the competing boats or
find a place on an escort boat.

New Zealand Yachting Federation, PO Box 4173, Auckland   Information

Shipping Services

Modern ferries ply between Wellington on the North Island and Picton on   **Ferries**
the South Island; in winter there are at least two crossings daily, in summer   Wellington–Picton
up to four. Boats have comfortable seats on deck and cabins for those who
require them as well as a restaurant and bar, cinemas, rooms with video
games and a children's playroom.
   The crossing of the Cook Strait, one of the windiest and most turbulent
waterways in the world, takes about 3½ hours. The fare (one-way) is around
NZ$35 for an adult and for a vehicle, depending on length, from $110. You
must arrive at the ferry terminal an hour before departure. Between
November and March and on public holidays it is usually essential to make
an advance booking.

Shooting

Bluff–Stewart Island	There is a regular ferry service between Bluff, at the southern tip of the South Island, and Halfmoon Bay (Oban) on Stewart Island. On this service booking is usually essential in the main holiday season.
Information and booking	Interislander, New Zealand Rail, Private Bag, Wellington. In New Zealand tel. (0800) 802 802 (toll-free booking) from abroad 64–4–498 3301 or in New Zealand fax 0800 101 525, from abroad 64–4–498 3089.
Boat charter	In virtually all coastal towns boats can be chartered for deep-sea angling expeditions or sailing trips. In many of the larger ports there are passenger ferries which will take visitors to places such as Fiordland or some of the sub-Antarctic island groups.
Cruises	Many of New Zealand's coastal towns, particularly Auckland, Wellington, Christchurch and Dunedin, as well as the Cook Islands (Atiu, Takutea, Aitutaki, Rarotonga, Palmerston, etc.) are ports of call for cruise ships operating in the Pacific. Also New Zealand ports are frequently staging-points in cruises in the South Seas. There are also short cruises from the Australian ports of Sydney and Cairns to New Zealand and/or the Cook Islands.

Shooting

New Zealand offers a variety of sport for shooting enthusiasts, including red deer, chamois, ducks, geese and other small game. There are no close seasons and no limits on bags. Visitors are generally not allowed to bring in their own guns, but professional guides, whose help should always be sought, are able to supply guns and ammunition.

Further information can be obtained from New Zealand Tourism Board offices.

Shopping

Markets	The largest markets in New Zealand are the Victoria Market in Auckland, the Wakefield Market in Wellington and the Art Centre Market in Christchurch. Some markets are open daily, but the busiest times are at the weekend.
Shopping malls	The principal shopping malls in Auckland are Queen Street, Karangahape Road and the Downtown complex at the harbour; in Wellington Willis Street and Customhouse Quay and in Christchurch the shops round Cathedral Square.
Souvenirs	The most popular – and the best – souvenirs to bring back from a holiday in New Zealand are articles made from natural materials such as wool, leather, wood and jade.
Sheepskins, wool and wool products	With more than 60 million sheep, New Zealand is one of the world's largest producers of wool. Wool products are on offer in every conceivable form and colour: hand-knitted pullovers, scarves, blankets, carpets, bedside rugs, etc. New Zealanders themselves are fond of the "swanny", a check-patterned woollen jacket which provides protection against rain as well as cold. If you go in for knitting or weaving you will be able to stock up with wool. Particularly popular in New Zealand is wool from Perendale sheep, which is good for knitting and dyeing.
Furs	Furs are popular buys, particularly Persian lamb and fur from the opossum.

Popular items are jackets, coats, waistcoats, boots and shoes, handbags and gloves of leather or lambskin. Articles made of polished lambskin are particularly light and soft. There are bargains to be had, too, in articles made of leather from game animals (particularly roe deer).

Leather

Typical souvenirs from New Zealand are examples of Maori woodcarving, which can be both beautiful and decorative. The best places to look for them are the Maori Arts and Crafts Centre in Rotorua and the East Cape area. Work by trained Maori woodcarvers, however, is difficult to find. The export of works of art of the classic Maori culture – i.e. of antiques – is prohibited.

Warning: The numerous wooden articles with the Maori "look" offered to tourists are almost always industrially produced reproductions of traditional objects.

Woodcarving

Greenstone (a stone similar to jade) is used in the making of jewellery, particularly on the west coast of the South Island (Hokitika). The Maoris formerly used greenstone in the manufacture of weapons and hard-wearing tools. Many items of greenstone jewellery such as the *hei-tiki,* a kind of necklace, are still made in traditional Maori style. Jewellery is also made from other semi-precious stones such as agate and amethyst. In the old gold-digging areas tourists are offered nuggets of gold and pieces of gold jewellery in the form of small earrings.

Jewellery

A very popular souvenir is an ash-tray made from the shimmering bluish-green shell of the paua, a type of abalone. The shells are also used to make jewellery. If you are very lucky you may find an undamaged paua shell on more remote beaches.

Paua shells

New Zealand pottery is much sought after by visitors, and New Zealand glass is also beginning to make a name for itself. Fine examples of pottery and glass are to be seen in the increasingly numerous craft shops.

Pottery, glass

Natural products such as honey, jam, smoked meat and kiwi fruit wine also make good souvenirs.

Foodstuffs

New Zealand wines are excellent. Particularly to be recommended are Chardonnay, Sauvignon Blanc and Semillon.

Wine

Some items of sporting equipment can be bought in New Zealand at lower prices than in Europe or North America.

Sports articles

New Zealand claims to read more books and periodicals per head of population than any other country in the world. There are, therefore, plenty of bookshops in which visitors can buy – among much else – guide books and illustrated books on New Zealand.

Books

Post offices in the larger towns often have special counters for philatelists.

Postage stamps

Second-hand objects can be bought cheaply in privately run garage sales ("boot sales") and in "demolition yards", a kind of flea market usually run by professional dealers.

Garage sales, demolition yards

See entry

Prices

See entry

Goods and services tax

Sport

New Zealanders are great sports enthusiasts. At every opportunity, particularly at weekends, they get away from their workaday life and head for the great outdoors to follow their sporting interests, whether as active participants or as spectators. All the elements are called into play – land (walking, tennis, rugby, etc.), water (fishing, swimming, surfing) and air (gliding, parachute jumping, etc.).

Bowls	The British and New Zealand form of bowls is rather more sedate than its French and Italian equivalents, boules and boccia. It is played on an immaculately manicured bowling green and the players are dressed in white.
Cricket	Cricket has a large and enthusiastic following in New Zealand. Important matches attract large and sometimes unruly crowds in the same way as rugby matches.
Football	Since New Zealand first played in the World Cup in 1982 football has become increasingly popular. Matches are played throughout New Zealand on Sundays.
Hockey	Hockey has long been popular in New Zealand, and it was given a great boost when the New Zealand team won a gold medal in the Montreal Olympics in 1976.
Light athletics; the marathon	All types of light athletics are popular in New Zealand. Championships are held at many places in summer and early autumn. There is particular interest in long-distance running. New Zealand runners won gold medals in the marathon at the Olympic Games in Rome (1960) and Montreal (1976). Tens of thousands of runners take part in the Round the Bays Run which takes place annually in March in the Auckland area.
Netball	Netball is the most popular women's sport in New Zealand. The netball championships in May and June attract large numbers of spectators.
Riding, horse-racing	In few parts of the world are there so many horses per head of population as in New Zealand, and riding is, not surprisingly, a very popular sport. Pony trekking is an attraction offered by many farms and lodges, for example in the Urewera National Park, where visitors can explore the old ancestral lands of the Maoris on horseback. Flat races and steeplechases draw large numbers of spectators. Every town of any size has its own racecourse, and there are around 450 race meetings (usually on Sundays and Wednesdays) every year. The two big events of the year are the Auckland Cup (during the Christmas holidays) and the Great Northern meeting at the beginning of June.
Rugby	Rugby is by far the most popular spectator sport in New Zealand, and at weekends between April and September tens of thousands of fans flock to rugby grounds throughout the country to support their team. The All Blacks, New Zealand's national team, have a formidable international reputation. Before a match they are famed for performing the intimidating Maori war chant, the haka. Enthusiasm rises to fever pitch at international matches, usually played in Auckland's Eden Park, which can accommodate 47,000 spectators.
Tennis	New Zealand towns are well supplied with tennis courts (some of them grass courts), and most hotels in the top price category have their own courts. Information: New Zealand Tennis Inc., PO Box 11541, Wellington.
Other sports	See also Cycling; Diving and Snorkelling; Flying; Golf; Rafting; Sailing; Surfing and Wind-Surfing; Walking; Water Sports; Winter Sports

Surfing and Wind-Surfing

Surfing and wind-surfing are popular sports, particularly in the warmer part of the year, at many points on the New Zealand coast. Instruction is available at the main centres and surfboards and surfing suits can be hired from many sports shops. New Zealand's surfing beaches offer plenty of scope for both beginners and experts. Winds are often strong, most notably on the north coast of the North Island or on the Tasman Sea, where the waves are sometimes several metres high.

A good place for beginners is Takapuna Beach, near Auckland, which usually has a light east wind. Wind-surfing is also possible on some inland waters, for example on Lake Taupo in the centre of the North Island.

New Zealand Surfriders Association, PO Box 1026, Gisborne.   Information

Taxis

There are plenty of taxis at airports and in towns and tourist centres. They can be picked up at a taxi rank or called by telephone (24-hour service in most places). They are relatively expensive, and in addition the driver expects a tip of around 10%. More reasonably priced are the communal taxis and minibuses (shuttle buses) which often ply between airports and their town terminals.

Telephone Services

Modern public telephones are operated either by coins (payphones) or telephone cards (cardphones). Subscriber trunk dialling (STD) is available in all new telephone kiosks.   Public telephones

Increasing numbers of public telephones are now card-operated. Telephone cards (NZ$5, $10, $20 and $50) can be bought in post offices, the Telecom Centre, hotels, motels and motor camps, and also in all dairies (corner shops).   Card-operated telephones

Trunk and international calls can be made from all private telephones and from the telephones installed in most hotel and motel rooms.   Private and hotel telephones

Local calls from a public telephone cost 40 cents. An STD call to Europe costs at present around $3 a minute during the day and $2 a minute between midnight and 8am.   Charges

For directory enquiries dial 0155 for New Zealand and 0172 for other countries.   Toll-free information

From New Zealand to the United Kingdom: 0044
From New Zealand to the United States or Canada: 001
From the United Kingdom to New Zealand: 0064
From the United States or Canada to New Zealand:01164   International dialling codes

Time

New Zealand lies near the International Dateline, and is thus one of the first places in the world to see the new day. It is 12 hours ahead of Greenwich Mean Time.

In summer New Zealand has Daylight Saving, when the clocks are put forward an hour. Daylight Saving begins on the first Sunday in October and ends on the last Sunday of the following March.

Tipping

In principle tips are given in New Zealand only in appreciation of extra-special service, consideration or kindness. They should be at the discretion of the visitor, particularly in restaurants, for waiter service in bars or for room service. Service charges are not usually added to hotel or restaurant bills. Nevertheless the practice of tipping is creeping in, particularly in the larger towns and tourist centres. If you have been well served in a restaurant you may feel like leaving a tip of perhaps 5–10% of the bill. Taxi-drivers and porters will usually expect a suitable tip.

Travel Documents

Entry

All visitors to New Zealand must have a passport. British citizens do not need a visa, and on arrival in New Zealand will be issued with a permit for a stay of up to six months. United States and Canadian citizens do not require a visa, and on arrival in New Zealand will be issued with a permit for a three-month stay. Australian citizens do not need a visa and can stay as long as they like.

On arrival in New Zealand visitors will be asked to produce their passport, a ticket for return or onward travel, the arrival card giving their personal details which they will have filled in on the plane and, more rarely, evidence that they have sufficient means, in the form of cash, traveller's cheques or credit cards, for the duration of their stay (with a guide figure for sufficiency of means of NZ$1000 a month).

If you want to stay longer than your entry permit allows you must apply to the Immigration Office for a visa. But if you know from the start that you are likely to stay longer it is advisable – and cheaper – to seek a suitable visa before leaving home.

Driving licence

British, United States, Canadian and Australian driving licences are accepted in New Zealand. To hire a car in New Zealand you must produce your driving licence and must be at least 21.

Other documents

Other documents it is advisable to have with you are your inoculation record, your AA (or other motoring organisation) membership card and details of your insurance cover.

It is a good idea to carry photocopies of important documents. This makes it easier to replace them. If you lose your passport you should inform the police and your local embassy or consulate.

Walking and Climbing

Some 30% of the area of New Zealand is now protected by the nature or landscape reserves of one kind or another.

Not surprisingly, therefore, walking and climbing – trekking, tramping, bushwalking, backpacking – are among the New Zealanders' most popular leisure activities.

There is plenty of scope everywhere in New Zealand, even in the outskirts of the cities, for short walks taking no more than a day. Some of these are waymarked with the letter "W". Longer routes are often described as tracks.

Walks and tracks

The two finest routes in New Zealand – some would say the finest in the world – run through the magnificent scenery of Fiordland National Park on the South Island. They are the Milford Track (over 50km/30 miles long) and the Routeburn Track (40km/25 miles). A fit walker can do each of them in four days, with overnight accommodation in simple huts.

★★Milford Track, ★★Routeburn Track

There are numerous other tracks (for example the Hollyford Valley Walk) which are maintained by wardens or the Department of Conservation's rangers.

Many walks can be done at any time of year, but others, particularly in the mountains, should not be attempted in winter. On many tracks walkers are required to let the local Department of Conservation office know that they propose to do the walk. Some walks should be attempted only with a local guide.

Most walks do not call for the very highest standard of fitness, since there are more than 1000 huts only 4 or 5 hours' walking apart. These huts do not offer any great luxury, but they do provide a place to sleep, water, toilets and sometimes cooking facilities. Since they tend to be overcrowded during the main holiday season, it is a sensible precaution to take along a small, light tent. The charge for a night in a hut ranges between NZ\$5 and \$20; more than 350 of them are free. Note, however, that some parks and trails have restrictions on "free" camping.

Huts

Many agencies run guided walks, normally for quite small parties. Accommodation is usually in comfortable huts (with hot showers), and the participants need take only a light pack and weatherproof clothing. Everything else (sleeping bags, etc.) is provided by the organisers.

Guided walks

The best time for walking is during February and March after the main holiday season. During this period there are fewer walkers on the tracks and there is less difficulty in finding accommodation in huts. Moreover the weather tends to be more settled and it is not so hot.

Walking season

Essential items of equipment for walkers are stout footwear, a not-too-heavy rucksack, a light sleeping bag and perhaps a light tent, cooking utensils, provisions, rainwear, a warm pullover, a hat or cap, protection against the sun and against sandflies, and good maps. Up-to-date maps and brochures can be obtained from Department of Conservation offices.

Equipment

Before setting out on a long walk (i.e. one lasting several days) you should inform the local Department of Conservation office, sign the register in each hut and inform the DoC office when you have completed the walk. There are risks when walking alone. It is highly dangerous to cross rivers when they are in spate. Never wash your hands in a river. Excreta should not be disposed of in rivers or streams but should be buried well away from the path. Leave no litter: take your litter with you and dispose of it in a suitable place. In dry weather be very careful about lighting fires.

Rules of conduct for walkers

Sir Edmund Hillary (see Famous People) trained for his ascent of Everest on Mount Cook, the country's highest peak. New Zealand's climbing schools are world class. Favourite climbing areas in the Southern Alps are Mount Cook, Mount Tasman and the mountains in Mount Aspiring National Park; and on the North Island there are Taranaki (Mount Egmont) and Mount Ruapehu. In all these areas visitors can join climbing trips led by experienced guides.

The climbers' mecca

Department of Conservation, PO Box 10420, Wellington.

Information

355

Water Sports

As is to be expected in an island state, New Zealanders are strongly drawn to the water. Round the coasts are bathing beaches of enchanting beauty; the seas off the North Island and round the Cook Islands are popular with scuba divers and snorkellers; and in many parts of the country there are superb sailing waters. The wild rivers of the interior offer trips in jetboats, canoes and rubber dinghies, and the lakes offer endless scope for boating and water sports of all kinds.

Rowing

New Zealand is one of the great rowing nations of the world. In recent years its oarsmen have won world championships and gold and silver Olympic medals. The national rowing championships are held annually in February.

Other
water sports

See Bathing Beaches; Diving and Snorkelling; Rafting; Sailing; Surfing and Wind-Surfing

Weather

Weather forecasts

Telephone forecasts: dial 0900
Weather bulletins every hour on New Zealand Radio

See also Climate; Practical Information from A to Z, When to Go

Weights and Measures

New Zealand has been on the metric system since 1967, though the old Imperial measures are still occasionally used. Some equivalents:

Length

1 mile = 1.61 kilometres
1 foot = 30.48 centimetres
1 inch = 2.54 centimetres

Fluid measure

1 pint = 0.568 litre
1 gallon = 4.546 litres

Weight

1 ounce = 28.35 grams
1 pound = 0.454 kilogram
1 stone = 6.35 kilograms

Temperatures

Temperatures are normally given in °C (Celsius). To convert Celsius to Fahrenheit, multiply by 9, divide by 5 and add 32.

When to Go

Climate

Broadly speaking, the North Island lies in the subtropical climatic zone, the South Island in the temperate zone, with sub-Arctic conditions in the mountains. For a fuller discussion of New Zealand's climate see p. 17.

"Reversed"
seasons

New Zealand's seasons are the reverse of those of the northern hemisphere. Spring lasts from September to November, summer from December to February, autumn from March to May and winter from June to August.

The North Island, lying nearer the Equator, has a subtropical climate, while   Weather
on the South Island the climate is temperate, comparable with the climate
of Europe but rather warmer. There is no marked rainy season, though
there is rather more rain in winter. The west coast of the South Island can be
especially wet. Showers of rain do not usually last long, though they can be
very heavy. Temperature variations are relatively small, with a range of
around 10°C/18°F. Winter temperatures seldom fall below freezing point.
Snow usually falls only on land above 1000m/3300ft. Winds are predominantly westerly.

Thanks to its mild climate, with few extremes of heat or cold, New Zealand   **When to go**
can be visited at any time of year.

Spring in New Zealand (September–November) is a season of agreeable   Spring
temperatures, a good time for walking and cycle touring. In the mountain
regions of the South Island spring comes rather later: most walking trails
are opened around mid-October. But everywhere in New Zealand it is
necessary to have warm clothing for the evening and protection against
rain.

The summer months (December–February) are undoubtedly the best time   Summer
to visit New Zealand. Relatively high temperatures (averaging around
25°C/77°F) and between 6 and 8 daily hours of sunshine enhance the
country's scenic attractions, and on the North Island summer is the season
with the lowest rainfall. In many parts of the country, for example in the
Nelson area, it can be quite hot. This is New Zealand's main tourist season;
the schools are on holiday, and many factories also have their annual
break. There is great activity on bathing beaches, at mountain huts, on the
roads and on walking trails. Early booking (of a flight to New Zealand,
hotels, ferries, the hire of a motor camper, etc.) is therefore essential. In
addition to summer clothing visitors should bring something warm for the
evening, which can sometimes be quite cool.

Autumn (March–May) is a good time for walking and cycling. In the moun-   Autumn
tains there are the first falls of snow. Most mountain trails are closed from
mid-April or sometimes earlier. As in spring, it is advisable to have warm
clothing for the evening and protection against rain.

At high altitudes the New Zealand winter (June–August) brings surpris-   Winter
ingly low temperatures and heavy falls of snow; at lower levels it is generally milder than in Europe. But even at lower altitudes warm clothing is
necessary.

Wine

As recently as 1975 a German visitor and wine-lover, when asked what he
thought of New Zealand wines, replied "You can't call *that* wine!". Much
has changed since then, and New Zealand wines now enjoy a very different
reputation often winning medals in international competitions. Wine critics
agree that the best New Zealand wines can challenge the great wines of
Europe and the world.
    The first vines were brought to New Zealand by immigrants in 1850; but
until the early 1980s New Zealanders – traditionally beer-drinkers – showed
only a passing interest in wine. Until then mixtures of grapes produced
sticky sweet wines of port and sherry style and mediocre table wines sold in
3-litre plastic packs. In order to moderate the acidity of such mass products
they were, quite legally, diluted with tap-water. Practically none of this
wine could be marketed abroad. New Zealand wine-growers brought in
new types of grape and the necessary know-how from France, Germany
and California. Many European wine-makers, mainly from Austria and

Germany, immigrated to New Zealand, bringing their experience and their skills with them.

With its good soil and excellent climate, New Zealand offers ideal conditions for wine-growing. Its temperate summers and mild winters make it a cool climate wine country. To some extent conditions in New Zealand are comparable with those on the Rhine and Moselle and in Burgundy and Bordeaux. Its wine-growing areas have expanded rapidly: whereas New Zealand had around 4000 hectares/10,000 acres of vineyards in the mid eighties, it now has some 6100 hectares/15,250 acres. The main wine-growing areas are north of Auckland (around 4% of the total area under vines), the east side of the North Island (Gisborne and Hawke's Bay, each 25%) and round Blenheim on the South Island (33%). The remainder consists of wine estates in the Bay of Plenty, Northland and the Wairarapa area on the North Island, and round Canterbury, Nelson and Central Otago on the South Island, the most southerly wine-growing area in the world. The Blenheim area alone produces around 15,000 tons of grapes a year.

The wineries have no difficulty in selling their products on the domestic market; New Zealanders, have acquired a taste for wine. Annual consumption per head in New Zealand is now around 21 litres (37 pints) per head, and in certain social circles it has become obligatory to know about wine, or at least to be able to talk about it.

"Buyer's Guide"   There is now an extensive literature about New Zealand wines. The front runner among works of reference, picture books and periodicals is the "Buyer's Guide to New Zealand Wines" by Michael Cooper, a New Zealander who also knows his way around the wine-growing areas of France, Germany, California and Australia. His book ranges from the first vines planted in New Zealand to the wineries of the present day.

Sale of wine   Until a few years ago the sale of wine was strictly regulated, but controls have since been relaxed. Since 1990 wine can be bought not only direct from a wine-dealer or in a bottle store, as previously, but also in supermarkets and grocery stores. The pricing of wine has also adjusted to international standards, and for a bottle of top-class New Zealand wine you may have to pay anything up to NZ$50.

White wines   The most popular varieties of grapes used in making white wine are Chardonnay, Müller-Thurgau, Sauvignon Blanc and Riesling; Chardonnay now accounts for 21% of the total area under vines, particularly in the Marlborough, Hawke's Bay and Gisborne areas. Chardonnay is used in the making of a great variety of wines – young, fruity, heavy and dry. Since it is almost invariably dry it has been called the red wine drinker's white wine. In the spring of 1993 the leading British wine magazine "Decanter" tested 130 wines to discover where the best Sauvignon Blanc was grown. Marlborough in New Zealand was adjudged to be the winner.

Another popular grape, Riesling, grown mainly on the South Island, particularly in the Marlborough, Nelson, Canterbury and Central Otago areas. New Zealand Riesling is more like the drier Alsatian and Australian version than the lighter German one.

Other types of white wine are Breidecker, Chenin Blanc, Ehrenfelser (a cross between Riesling and Sylvaner, Gewürztraminer (which is declining because of its poor resistance to bad weather), Morio-Muskat, Osteiner, Pinot Blanc, Pinot Gris, Scheurebe (very rare in New Zealand) and Sémillon, which is added to Sauvignon in the proportion of 15% to reduce its high acidity.

New Zealand also produces sparkling wines, including some made by the *méthode champenoise*.

First place among red wines is Cabernet Sauvignon. Originally brought to New Zealand from Bordeaux in the 1890s, it is grown mainly in the Hawke's Bay area. In second place is Pinot Noir, which is grown mainly in the Wairarapa area, at the south end of the North Island. Merlot, the principal grape of the Bordeaux region, is frequently mixed with Cabernet Sauvignon to give it a soft, fruity taste. More than half New Zealand's Merlot is grown in the Hawke's Bay region. Other grapes used are Cabernet Franc (over 75% on the North Island) – a grape which is added in small quantities to many top-class New Zealand red wines – Durif (very rare), Pinotage, Refosco and Syrah (Australian Shiraz).

Red wines

Almost all wineries welcome visitors, and offer conducted tours and wine-tastings.

Visits to wineries

Winter Sports

The best months for skiing – that is, the months with the best prospects of good snow – are July, August and September, when the snowline comes down to 1000m/3280ft. Skiing equipment can be hired in ski resorts, which also have chair lifts, ski-tows, etc., and skiing instructors. During the winter months package holidays offer accommodation, skiing instruction and lift passes. Information about the various skiing areas can be obtained from New Zealand Tourism Board offices (see Information). The New Zealand skiing areas are all above the tree-line and thus offer plenty of space.

Season

An increasingly popular form of skiing is heli-skiing, in which skiers are taken up to the skiing area in helicopters or light aircraft fitted with skids. Facilities for heli-skiing are available on Mount Hutt and in other areas. More than 400 pistes can now be reached in this way. The longest descent in New Zealand (24km/15 miles) is on the Tasman Glacier.
  Heli-skiing is an expensive sport, costing up to NZ$600 for between three and five descents per day.

Heli-skiing

Some skiing clubs have their own skiing areas ("club fields"), which can be in very remote areas. They lack the facilities of the popular skiing resorts, but do offer the pleasure of skiing on pistes which (so far) are usually not too busy.

Club fields

Popular skiing areas

On the North Island there are only two skiing areas of any size, Whakapapa and Turoa, both on the slopes of Mount Ruapehu (2797m/9177ft) in the Tongariro National Park. Since there is still some activity within this volcano, skiers are liable to encounter steaming mud springs and cavities in the ground in the course of their descent.

North Island
Ruapehu

There is a smaller skiing area on the extinct volcano Taranaki (Mount Egmont, 2512m/8242ft), on the west side of the North Island.

Taranaki
(Mount Egmont)

The more important skiing areas are distributed across the South Island. The highest peaks, with the longest and steepest pistes, are in the Southern Alps.

South Island

The Southern Lakes region between Queenstown and Wanaka contains four extensive skiing areas: Coronet Peak, the Remarkables, Cardrona and Treble Cone. Here the pistes offer magnificent views of evergreen valleys with deep blue lakes. Langlauf skiing is available in the Pisa Range near Wanaka.

Southern Lakes

Mount Hutt	There is another extensive skiing area on Mount Hutt, 100km/60 miles west of Christchurch in the centre of the South Island. It has a very long season, from the end of May to the beginning of November. Mount Hutt is the only place in New Zealand where World Cup races are held.
Other skiing areas	Other popular skiing areas on the South Island are Temple Basin, in Arthur's Pass National Park; Amuri, in Hanmer Forest Park; Mount Lyford, south-west of Kaikoura; Mount Dobson; Tekapo, on Lake Tekapo; and the area west of Lake Ohau.

Youth Accommodation

| Youth hostels | There are some 55 youth hostels in New Zealand. There are no age limits on admission. A night in a youth hostel (dormitory accommodation) costs between NZ$20 and $30. Meals are not provided, but there is a kitchen in which hostellers can cook for themselves and usually a small food shop.

If you don't have an international youth hostel card you can become a member of the Youth Hostel Association of New Zealand for NZ$34: you can join at any youth hostel. The overnight charge is then only between NZ$11 and about $20.

Members of Hostelling International (HI) may be able to obtain concessions, for example on InterCity trains and coaches, Air New Zealand and Ansett New Zealand (standby flights only). |
|---|---|
| Information | Youth Hostel Association of New Zealand, National Office, PO Box 436, Christchurch; tel. (03) 379 9970, fax (03) 365 4476. |
| Backpacker hostels | Backpackers' hostels – the private sector's answer to youth hostels – are steadily increasing in number and offer an alternative to youth hostels. The backpackers' hostels differ from youth hostels in often having – except in the larger towns – something of a family atmosphere. The accommodation and facilities are much the same as in youth hostels, with dormitories, double and single rooms, showers and toilets on each floor, communal kitchens and day rooms. Charges are broadly similar to those in youth hostels.

Originally the backpackers' hostels were used only by young people, but they are now also patronised by older age groups. In these hostels you can often obtain information on, and sign up for, organised backpacking trips. |
| Information | Budget Backpacker Hostels New Zealand Ltd, 99 Titiraupenga Street, Taupo; tel. and fax (07) 377 1568 |

Index

Principal Sights of Tourist Interest

Note: The places listed above are merely a selection of the principal sights – places of interest in themselves or for attractions in the surrounding area. There are of course innumerable other sights in New Zealand, to which attention is drawn by one or more stars.

Tourist sights in New Zealand

* **major sights**

** **outstanding sights**

* Cape Reinga
* Ninety Mile Beach
** Bay of Islands
* Kerikeri
* Waimate North
** Waitangi
** Russell
* Hokianga Harbour
** Paihia
** Whangarei **
* Waipoua Kauri Forest
** Puhoi
** Hauraki Gulf
* Great Barrier Island
* Kaipara Harbour
** Coromandel Peninsula
* Waiwera
** Auckland
** Mayor Island
** Waikato River
** Pukekohe
** Bay of Plenty
East Cape
North Island
** Hamilton
* Te Aroha
** Tauranga
* Kawhia
** Waitomo Caves
** Rotorua
** Urewera Nat. Park
** Wairakei
** Gisborne
* New Plymouth
** Tongariro Nat. Park
** Egmont Nat. Park
Lake Waikaremoana
** Wanganui River
Lake Taupo
* Stratford
** Napier
* Hawke Bay
* Wanganui
* Cape Kidnappers
** Marlborough Sounds
* Palmerston North
* Cape Farewell
** Foxton
** Kapiti Island
** Otaki
** Abel Tasman Nat. Park
** Nelson
** Masterton
** Picton
Castle-point
* Westport
** Nelson Lakes Nat. Park
Lake Grassmere
** Wellington
** Greytown
** Pancake Rocks
** Buller River
** Hanmer Springs
Tasman Sea
* Shantytown
* Arthur's Pass Nat. Park
** Kaikoura
** Franz Josef Glacier
** Mt. Cook Nat. Park
** Christchurch
** Fox Glacier
** Westland Nat. Park
* Haast Pass Road
Lake Ohau
Banks Peninsula
L. Tekapo
L. Pukaki
* Ashburton
** Mt Aspiring Nat. Park
* Timaru
* Peel Forest Park
* Milford Sound
* Wanaka
* Lindis Pass
* Waitaki Valley
South Island
Fiordland Nat. Park
** Queens-town
** Arrowtown
* Clyde
** Moeraki Boulders
Lake Te Anau
* Alexandra
** Port Chalmers
L. Manapouri
* Lawrence
** Dunedin
L. Hauroko
* Gore
South Pacific Ocean
** Invercargill
** Nugget Point
* Stewart Island
** Bluff

© Baedeker

For an alphabetical list of the principal sights, with page references, see opposite page

Imprint

109 illustrations
5 town plans, 7 ground-plans, 28 general maps, 1 profile, 10 diagrams, 37 drawings, 1 large map of New Zealand

Original German text: Dr Gerlinda Lamping, Professor Heinrich Lamping and Reinhard Zakrzewski, with contributions by Georg Bareth, Achim Bourmer, Rainer Eisenschmid, Carmen Galenschovski, Dr Cornelia Hermanns, Gabriele and Helmut Linde, Beate Szerelmy and Andrea Wurth

Editorial work: Baedeker-Redaktion (Rainer Eisenschmid, Helmut Linde)

Cartography: Christoph Gallus, Hohberg; Haupka-Verlag, Bad Soden (large map of New Zealand)

General direction: Rainer Eisenschmid, Baedeker Stuttgart

Source of illustrations: Air New Zealand (2); Ansett New Zealand (1); Auckland Public Library (1); Alexander Turnbull Library (4); Bareth/Prokop (9); Camp and Cabin Association of New Zealand (1); Canterbury Museum (1); Falter (4); Historia (1); IFA (2); Insel-Verlag (1); Janicke (28); Krebsbach (6); Lade (4); Legner (5); Mainbild (7); Mauritius (2); Mount Cook Airline (1); National Maritime Museum, Greenwich (1); New Zealand Department of Conservation (2); New Zealand Tourism Board (2); New Zealand Federation of Bed and Breakfast Hotels (1); Ott (5); Schapowalow (1); Schrama (1); Schweiger/OKAPIA (2); Schuster (1); Steffens/Bauer (9); Stetter (2); Süddeutscher Verlag (1); Tlusty (2); Tom McHugh/NAS/OKAPIA (1); Ullstein Bilderdienst (1)

English translation: James Hogarth

1st English edition 1997

© Baedeker Stuttgart
Original German edition 1995

© 1997 Jarrold and Sons Limited
English language edition worldwide

© 1997 The Automobile Association
United Kingdom and Ireland

Published in the United States by:
Macmillan Travel
A Simon & Schuster Macmillan Company
1633 Broadway
New York, NY 10019–6785

Macmillan is a registered trademark of Macmillan, Inc.

Distributed in the United Kingdom by the Publishing Division of the Automobile Association, Fanum House, Basingstoke, Hampshire RG21 2EA

A CIP catalogue record of this book is available from the British Library

Licensed user:
Mairs Geographischer Verlag GmbH & Co.,
Ostfildern-Kemnat bei Stuttgart

Printed in Italy by G. Canale & C.S.p.A – Borgaro T.se –Turin

ISBN 0–02–861911–0 USA and Canada
       0 7495 1593 7 UK